BORN TO BATTLE

ALSO BY JACK HURST

Men of Fire: Grant, Forrest,
and the Campaign that Decided the Civil War

Nathan Bedford Forrest: A Biography

BORN TO BATTLE

GRANT AND FORREST: SHILOH, VICKSBURG, AND CHATTANOOGA

The Campaigns That Doomed the Confederacy

JACK HURST

BASIC BOOKS

A Member of the Perseus Books Group
New York

Copyright © 2012 by Jack Hurst
Published by Basic Books,
A Member of the Perseus Books Group

Books published by Basic Books are available at special discounts for bulk purchases in the United States by corporations, institutions, and other organizations. For more information, please contact the Special Markets Department at the Perseus Books Group, 2300 Chestnut Street, Suite 200, Philadelphia, PA 19103, or call (800) 810-4145, ext. 5000, or e-mail special.markets@perseusbooks.com.

Book design by Linda Mark

Library of Congress Cataloging-in-Publication Data
Hurst, Jack.
  Born to battle : Grant and Forrest : Shiloh, Vicksburg, and Chattanooga : the campaigns that doomed the Confederacy / Jack Hurst.
    p. cm.
  Includes bibliographical references and index.
  ISBN 978-0-465-02018-8 (hardcover : alk. paper)
  ISBN 978-0-465-02926-6 (e-book)   1. Shiloh, Battle of, Tenn., 1862.
2. Vicksburg (Miss.)—History—Siege, 1863. 3. Chattanooga, Battle of, Chattanooga, Tenn., 1863. 4. Grant, Ulysses S. (Ulysses Simpson), 1822–1885. 5. Forrest, Nathan Bedford, 1821–1877. 6. United States—History—Civil War, 1861–1865—Campaigns.   I. Title.
  E473.54.H87 2012
  973.7'31—dc23
                                                                2011050156
10 9 8 7 6 5 4 3 2 1

To the memory of my mom,
Shirley Jackson Hurst,
Proud descendant of four Mayflower passengers,
Commoners all

"The richest ore is oftenest found deep down, and it is in the low stratum of human life that we will find the jewels that will glisten for ages."

—Immigrant industrialist
Andrew Carnegie

CONTENTS

GLOSSARY
OF PARTICIPANTS

Beauregard, Pierre Gustave Toutant—One of the Confederacy's five top-ranking full generals; West Point–trained member of the Louisiana Creole elite; brilliant planner of too-complicated battles; dramatic, fiery, and dashing; unloved by President Jefferson Davis for a tendency to preen in the press and argue with his commander in chief.

Bragg, Braxton—West Pointer and nationally known Mexican War hero who resigned from the army as a lieutenant colonel in 1856 to become proprietor of a Louisiana sugar plantation after marrying into great wealth. He was a highly opinionated and caustic observer of people and events, a favorite of Jefferson Davis, and a great driller and disciplinarian. He commanded at Mobile during the war's early stages.

Breckinridge, John C.—Confederate brigadier general; Kentucky-born and Kentucky-based lawyer and politician. US vice president in the administration of James Buchanan, Breckinridge was a sitting US senator and unsuccessful Democratic presidential candidate in 1860 before resigning to join the Confederacy.

Buckner, Simon Bolivar—Confederate major general; West Pointer; prewar friend and benefactor of Grant; model of rectitude or, put another way, a balky and mulish stickler for the rules. Captured at Fort Donelson, Buckner was eventually paroled to command the Department of East Tennessee. An excellent writer of caustic prose, he briefly founded and edited a Chicago newspaper in the 1850s.

Buell, Don Carlos—Union major general; West Pointer; Ohio native; commander of the Department of the Ohio and its Army of the

Cumberland; distinguished prewar career soldier; Grant's contemptuous self-styled rescuer at Shiloh; strict disciplinarian but very slow to commit to a fight.

Chalmers, James R.—Confederate colonel; Virginia native; educated in South Carolina. His wealthy family owned property in northern Mississippi, which his father represented as a senator. The elder Chalmers had approved Forrest's appointment as constable of DeSoto County; thus, Chalmers and Forrest knew each other—sort of. Early on, Chalmers was colonel of a Mississippi regiment at Mobile under Bragg, whom Chalmers admired.

Dana, Charles A.—Federal assistant secretary of war; former New York newspaper editor charged with observing and reporting on efficiency and the like to Secretary of War Edwin Stanton. Dana was sharply opinionated with pronounced likes and dislikes; the former included, most notably and profoundly, Ulysses S. Grant; the latter, John McClernand. He was seen at different times and by different officers as an indispensable observer and a waspish busybody.

Forrest, Nathan Bedford—Confederate colonel promoted to brigadier general after Shiloh. Forrest had risen from tending leased fields to wealth as a slave-trader across the western South; he also had a brief but notable political career on the Memphis city council. Although he was a fearless and dangerous military wizard, superiors looked down on him for his lack of education and polish.

Gould, A. Wills—Confederate artillery lieutenant in Forrest's cavalry; quieter friend and schoolmate of Forrest artillery notable John W. Morton; brave and knowledgeable but sensitive and ready to resent a slight.

Grant, Ulysses S.—Federal major general; captor of Forts Henry and Donelson. An Ohio tanner's son who had reluctantly gone to and graduated from West Point, Grant had resigned from the army with a reputation for drunkenness to fall into poverty as a farmer; he barely got back into the army in 1861 as second choice for colonel of the Twenty-first Illinois Infantry. A reputation for thirst still dogged him.

Hooker, Joseph "Fighting Joe"—Federal major general; West Point class of 1837; born in Massachusetts of New England elite; glittering Mexican War record; intensely ambitious. Hooker spent most of 1861 to

1863 on the eastern front, where he took a lackluster turn commanding the Army of the Potomac.

Johnson, Bushrod Rust—West Point–educated Confederate brigadier general from Ohio. Johnson's self-obscured past included helping his Quaker brothers deliver fugitive slaves up the Underground Railroad and getting cashiered from the army for a smuggling scheme in Mexico. A college professor who kept his own counsel after returning to military life, he escaped surrender at Fort Donelson after two days of hiding out among other prisoners.

Johnston, Albert Sidney—Confederate western commander; Jefferson Davis's favorite soldier. A Kentucky native, Johnston had headed the army of the Texas Republic; when Texas joined the Union, he became colonel of the celebrated Second US Cavalry on the frontier. While commanding the Confederacy's huge Department No. 2, he became reviled after retreating from Kentucky to Alabama following the Union victories at Forts Henry and Donelson.

Johnston, Joseph E.—Confederate full general; non-Tidewater Virginian. Johnston enjoyed wide popularity that obscured his intense ambition for high rank. He protested to Jefferson Davis that he deserved supremacy among the generals of the Confederacy, instead of the fifth slot Davis had given him. A brilliant executor of West Point dogma, he was excellent at defense but hesitant to attack.

Kountz, William J.—Union river transportation official; whisky-hating Pittsburgh steamboat magnate with connections to Secretary of War Edwin Stanton and Union general in chief George B. McClellan. Kountz became Grant's director of river transport in late 1861. He filed charges of drunkenness against Grant on the eve of the Henry-Donelson campaign. Grant, before leaving on the campaign, ordered him fired and arrested.

Lee, Stephen D.—Young, rising Confederate artillery officer; born in secession's cradle, Charleston, South Carolina; 1854 graduate of West Point. An artillerist in the prewar army, Lee began his Confederate career on the eastern front on the staff of General Beauregard.

Logan, John A. "Black Jack"—One of Grant's favorite brigadiers; prewar southern Illinois congressman instrumental in persuading his Southern-leaning district to back the Union. Logan became a hard-fighting colonel and, after Shiloh, a brigadier general. He acquired his nickname from the color of his hair and eyes.

Longstreet, James—Confederate major general; born in South Carolina; West Pointer. An in-law of Grant who served in Grant's wedding, Longstreet spent most of his service on the eastern front, where Robert E. Lee called him his "Old War Horse."

McArthur, John—Union brigadier general; native Scot. The son of a blacksmith, McArthur founded Excelsior Iron Works in Chicago. His brigade fought with more gallantry than success at Fort Donelson, where it was the rightmost unit on a Federal right wing that was crushed and rolled up by the Confederate assault on the battle's final day.

McClellan, George B.—Federal general in chief; Philadelphia native; scion of an elite family; West Pointer. McClellan had been outraged to see Grant drunk on duty in the antebellum army. He left the prewar army to become a railroad entrepreneur. After Fort Sumter, he reentered the service and succeeded aging Winfield Scott as general in chief. He was a wonderful organizer, outfitter, and driller of armies but a timid fighter of them.

McClernand, John A.—Union brigadier general; prewar southern Illinois congressman; sometime courtroom associate of prairie lawyer Abraham Lincoln. Very friendly and encouraging to Kountz, the filer of drunkenness charges against Grant, McClernand seemed incessantly to seek Grant's job, often by duplicitous means.

McPherson, James B.—Union colonel; brilliant young engineer; graduated first in the West Point class of 1853. Henry Halleck sent McPherson to Grant (who already had an engineer) during the Henry-Donelson campaign to clandestinely monitor Grant's drinking. The two Ohioans immediately took a liking to each other. Grant asked for McPherson's permanent transfer to his army, where he became, with Sherman, one of Grant's two foremost favorites.

Morgan, John Hunt—Confederate cavalry colonel; independent raider par excellence. Alabama-born and Kentucky-educated, Morgan was a Lexington, Kentucky, businessman when the war opened. Utterly fearless, he preferred independent command to working in subordinate positions with higher-ranking commanders.

Morton, John W., Jr.—Boyish twenty-one-year-old Confederate artillerist; cultivated son of a Nashville physician. Morton performed with heroism at Fort Donelson, where he was captured; after his exchange, he sought service with Forrest, who had refused to participate in the Donelson surrender.

Pemberton, John C.—Confederate major general. Philadelphia-born but Southern-leaning even during his cadetship at West Point, Pemberton graduated twenty-seventh of fifty in 1837. He was a warm friend of Jefferson Davis, who first gave him command of the Department of South Carolina, Georgia, and Florida. His friendship with Davis, more than talent, influenced his rise.

Polk, Leonidas—Confederate major general. Although a West Pointer, Polk had no army experience prior to 1861. On graduation he had become an Episcopal cleric, and he was bishop of the Southwest when the war opened. He owed his high Confederate commands to closeness with Jefferson Davis since their West Point days together. Whatever his ministerial qualities, his soldierly performance was at best plodding.

Rawlins, John A.—Union captain; Grant chief of staff; prewar attorney and fellow townsman of Grant in Galena, Illinois; impassioned partisan in behalf of Grant and equally impassioned foe of the bottle; generally considered the only person besides Grant's wife, Julia, from whom the general would tolerate discussion of his drinking.

Rosecrans, William S.—Union major general; West Pointer, graduating fifth in the class of 1838. Commissioned a brigadier general in May 1861, Rosecrans fought well in West Virginia under George McClellan before coming west. He was an excellent planner of strategy but high-strung, nervous, and erratic in battle.

Sherman, William Tecumseh "Cump"—Union major general; son of an Ohio Supreme Court justice; foster son of Ohio US senator Thomas Ewing; member of the elite. Sherman fought with valor at the First Battle of Bull Run or Manassas. He suffered a condition resembling a nervous breakdown while commanding in Kentucky in 1861 and, described as "crazy" by newspapers, was reassigned at his own request. After being gently returned to duty in early 1862 by Henry Halleck, he started to become Grant's best friend by waiving his higher rank and subordinating himself to push supplies forward to Grant at Fort Donelson.

Smith, Charles Ferguson—Federal brigadier general; one of the US Army's most eminent antebellum officers; Philadelphia-born career soldier; one of Grant's instructors at West Point and his most valued—and valuable—confidant in 1861 and early 1862. At Fort Donelson, Smith's assault breached the Confederate lines and brought on the surrender. His advice to offer no terms except unconditional surrender made Grant a popular sensation.

Smith, William F. "Baldy"—Union colonel; member of the staff of General Irvin McDowell at the First Battle of Bull Run; Vermont-born West Pointer, graduating fourth in the class of 1845; exceptional engineer officer who spent the war's first half on the eastern front and was a close friend of General in Chief McClellan.

Streight, Abel—Federal colonel; Indiana transplant from a rural New York farm via a ten-year sojourn in Cincinnati; daring. With little education, Streight became a miller, then a lumberman and a carpenter. On the eve of war, he wrote a pamphlet strongly espousing unionism and was appointed colonel of the Fifty-first Indiana Infantry.

Thomas, George H.—Federal major general; born to Virginia slaveholders; stolid and intensely honorable, but somewhat stiff-necked and quietly aloof. Sherman's roommate at West Point, Thomas graduated twelfth in their class, six places behind Sherman. He was first-ranked below Sherman in Kentucky in 1861. He won the obscure but highly important Battle of Mill Springs or Logan's Crossroads in Kentucky in January 1862.

Van Dorn, Earl—Mississippi plantation scion; West Pointer, graduating fifty-second in a class of fifty-six; antebellum career soldier; brave and dashing, but more attentive to other men's wives than to his own or to such vital military duties as reconnaissance; another Jefferson Davis friend and favorite.

Wallace, Lewis "Lew"—Union major general; antebellum attorney; son of an Indiana governor. Along with John McClernand, Wallace was one of the two Grant subordinates who appeared most thirsty for glory and whose political connections seemed to make Grant most wary. As commander he took it upon himself to go to the aid of McClernand's collapsing division, thereby saving what was left of Grant's right wing on the climactic day at Fort Donelson.

Wharton, John A.—Nashville-born Confederate colonel leading the hard-fighting Eighth Texas Cavalry; hot-headed but polished; educated at South Carolina College; member of the Texas Secession Convention.

Wheeler, Joseph—Twenty-six-year-old Confederate infantry colonel in early 1862; Georgia-born son of a Connecticut-rooted Augusta banker. Wheeler spent portions of his early life in Connecticut and New York City and graduated near the bottom of his West Point class. Dashing and fearless but officious and humorless, he would become an erratic cavalry leader.

INTRODUCTION

SCOUTING THE GROUND

Bloody autumn, 1863. After a disastrous summer, the Confederate States of America's prospects were fading fast.

Defeat had dogged its armies. Starved-out Vicksburg, the Confederacy's last hold on the Mississippi River, fell to Ulysses S. Grant in July, a day after George Pickett's annihilated charge crowned Robert E. Lee's crushing defeat at Gettysburg. Down a vital railroad connecting Lee's Virginia base to its Deep Dixie breadbasket, the valiant but ill-led Army of Tennessee won a September victory at Chickamauga in Georgia, sending its Union foe fleeing to Chattanooga. But the Confederate commander, General Braxton Bragg, had pursued laxly, and the Federals had entrenched. And Nathan Bedford Forrest neared the end of his patience.

Forrest was a violent, unschooled, but brilliant brigadier general of cavalry. He had a lengthening record of battlefield wizardry and an obsessive will to win, and he had urged Bragg to stay on the Federals' heels after Chickamauga. When Bragg did not, Forrest rode to headquarters to find out why—and returned still puzzled. "What does he fight his battles for?" aides overheard him mutter.[1]

Having risen from a leased Mississippi hill farm to self-proclaimed millionaire status before the war, Forrest had seen his fierce intelligence and much Confederate blood squandered by Bragg and other high-toned Southern aristocrats and West Pointers. For most of the seventeen months that Bragg had commanded the Confederacy's primary western army, he had demeaned and slighted Forrest. Influenced by the wife whose immense family wealth he had married into, Bragg disliked Tennesseans, regarding those in his ranks as unreliable, and Forrest had been born and raised in the Tennessee backwoods before becoming a Memphis businessman. He also was a volunteer, a soldier class that Bragg the professional held in sour contempt.[2]

BRIGADIER GENERAL NATHAN BEDFORD FORREST

Soon after Forrest's unproductive canter to headquarters, Bragg issued him another slap. He took Forrest's command and gave it—temporarily, he said—to Major General Joe Wheeler, a West Pointer of flawed judgment under whom Forrest had vowed never to serve again. Forrest took a rare and much-needed leave, which he had hardly begun when Bragg sent him orders to report to Wheeler. It was the last straw. Forrest rode to headquarters again, this time taking along an in-law. The relative said Forrest barged into Bragg's tent, ignored a proffered handshake, and poked the index finger of his left hand into Bragg's face. He began reciting a litany of the abuses that Bragg had subjected him to. Then his rising temper topped out with a threat he was manifestly able to fulfill.

"If you ever again try to interfere with me—or cross my path," he promised, "it will be at the peril of your life."[3]

As the steaming Confederate stalked from Bragg's tent, Union major general Ulysses S. Grant lay in agony in Vicksburg, Mississippi.

His horse, spooked by a train whistle after a troop review near New Orleans, had reared and fallen on him. He was almost certainly drunk. The accident knocked him unconscious, badly wrenched his right leg, and injured that whole side of his body. The leg was "swollen from the knee to the thigh," he later wrote, adding that "swelling, almost to the point of bursting," ballooned his torso to his armpit. The pain was agonizing. "I lay in the hotel something over a week without being able to turn myself in bed."[4]

It was bad timing. In July, in one of military history's hardest-won campaigns, Grant had taken Vicksburg and split the Confederacy in two. But that was July. Union major general William Starke Rosecrans's September defeat at Chickamauga, which threatened the entire Federal Army of the Cumberland with capture or annihilation, appeared to revive the South's foundering fortunes. Outnumbered Federals at Chattanooga were besieged, starving, and about to abandon their recent conquest of East Tennessee and their invaluable capture of the Confederacy's Virginia-to-Georgia railroad. Grant's Washington superiors ordered him to rush 20,000 more men to Chattanooga to forestall calamity.

He did so—and more. Putting the 20,000 on the march from Memphis, he wired the Chattanooga commander, Major General George H. Thomas, to hold on, no matter what. He himself would be there as soon as possible, he said, and he did not exaggerate. On crutches, he took a steamboat to Louisville, then a train to northern Alabama. There aides lifted him onto a horse for the trek's final leg, a sixty-mile ordeal on rain-drowned roads. At Chattanooga, they took him from the saddle and helped him into headquarters. Without even changing his muddy pants, he demanded a detailed briefing and asked myriad questions. That the army was outnumbered and ringed by foes on higher ground did not faze him. He wanted to attack.

For two days he plotted nonstop, then okayed an already-planned night strike. The plan sent men and pontoons floating down the Tennessee River to surprise Confederate guards. His Federals bridged the river, opened the supply line into Chattanooga, and allowed Union reinforcements from northern Alabama to flood in. Three weeks later, the

MAJOR GENERAL ULYSSES S. GRANT

troops he had ordered from Memphis began arriving. And he launched his attack.[5]

The Federals took the tops of the mountains in two assaults on separate days. Grant and his officers tried to direct them from below. When the outcomes were known, only riflemen could take bows. On November 24 three divisions under Major General Joe Hooker captured Lookout Mountain in the murk of a heavy fog. The following day, in full view, the 19,000 troops of General George Thomas, the stolid "Rock of Chickamauga," had hit the Confederate center and overwhelmed its first line of rifle pits. Their assignment had been to take and hold that position while other forces hit and turned the Confederate flanks. But once there, under murderous fire, they disobeyed Grant's orders and swarmed on up Missionary Ridge. The mass insubordination could have been fatal; if their charge had failed, a Confederate counterattack pursuing their fallback down the mountain might have knocked out the Union center. It could have crushed the whole Federal army. But Thomas's men made sure that could not happen. They went over the two upper trench lines on the heels of the fleeing defenders. It was a rout.[6]

Abraham Lincoln was grateful. He sent a message thanking and praising Grant and his army for "the courage and perseverance with which you, and they," had plunged the Federal sword into Dixie's bowels. Soon afterward, Lincoln would promote Grant to lieutenant general, the nation's first permanent holder of that rank since George Washington. And he would order him east to face Robert E. Lee.[7]

+—◦—+

The twin events—Grant's defeat of the Confederates at Chattanooga and Forrest's post-Chickamauga tongue-lashing of his commander—were pivotal. Grant's triumph, following his isolation of trans-Mississippi Dixie with the victory at Vicksburg, set the stage for General William T. Sherman's fiery slicing of the eastern South into two more halves. And Forrest's berating of Bragg marked the final alienation of the South's most feared western warrior from its aristocratic councils—and any chance of Forrest's contributing his mental powers to its strategic plans. Such a chance, in truth, had never existed.

Contrasting Grant and Forrest, two opposing giants of the western theater, brings a rich new perspective to the study of the Civil War. The two events at Chattanooga in late 1863—one public, the other private—portended the fates of secession and slavery, and the two men's separate progressions toward this dual climax shed new light on how and why the war was won and lost. Yet the tandem significance of the two events has gone unnoted—possibly because it is best understood by those who find it the least comfortable: admirers of the Old South. Forrest's treatment by his superiors suggests that a chief cause of the Confederacy's death was insistence on blue-blood leadership. Other nonaristocratic notables who might have played more major roles include John Brown Gordon, who finally rose to command a wing of Lee's Appomattox remnant, and Patrick R. Cleburne, a native Irishman who was likely the best unit commander of infantry west of the Appalachians. We can never know the number of others buried in obscurity, but Forrest's potential for higher command appears the most gravely wasted.

Grant and Forrest, opposites on the surface, were alike underneath. They also were night-and-day different from their commanders and peers. Each hailed from closer to his society's bottom than its top. Their lives had been steeped in the kind of daily desperation that is war's essence. Both had fought weather and fate in the fickle fields of agriculture. Each had struggled with his hands against long odds to feed and protect his family. Hard lives had forced them to capitalize to the fullest on scant resources and watch out for the main chance. Their resultant common credential for military generalship was humble, widely disdained, yet pivotal in the end. Call it calluses.

Besides Forrest, just twenty-four other Confederates would become full general or lieutenant general in this conflict. Only two would be, like Forrest, non–West Pointers, and these two were as unlike Forrest as possible. One, Richard Taylor, was the son of a president, Zachary Taylor. The other, Wade Hampton (to be precise, Wade Hampton III), was similarly a son of privilege, reputedly the largest landowner in the South. The third was Forrest, the onetime tiller of a leased hill farm.

At the top of the Federal army, Grant was in the company of men of the same pride, power, and wealth. His superior, Henry Halleck, was a lion of the West Point intelligentsia as well as a rich corporate attorney, and his peers included a grandson of a signer of the Declaration of Independence and a relative of Mary Todd Lincoln. His immediate subordinates included a longtime associate of President Lincoln, former congressmen, and the son of a governor. Grant's father had been a tanner.

Grant had a West Point education, but this only differentiated him from Forrest superficially. Both came from the same social level and were looked down on for it. Grant's drinking, for which he was widely scorned by other Union officers, was the subject of derision largely because of his background and resultant lack of polish. By contrast, "Fighting Joe" Hooker was known widely to drink—and apparently on battlefields, which Grant never did—yet alcohol was rarely, if ever, mentioned as one of his flaws. Like Grant, Hooker left the army in the mid-1850s and was late being invited back into it, but when he did return, it was as a brigadier general. Grant barely made it back in as a replacement colonel. And both men reentered an army in which whisky—especially among officers, who could best afford it—was a staple.

Vitally, though, Grant had the benefit of joining an army less class-conscious than Forrest's. The Union high command was led by a president born in a log cabin. Grant's was an army filling with new Americans who had emigrated north instead of south because Dixie's slavery-monopolized job market offered far less chance of earning a livelihood. The North's officer corps allowed—though hardly encouraged—working-class input; the South's did not. Dixie barred such elements from her councils of decision.[8]

The difference was crucial. Northern inclusiveness permitted the rise of Grant, the man universally regarded as most responsible for winning the war, while Southern insularity predestined the Confederacy to squander the brilliance of Forrest, whose fertile brain and vicious valor might have helped fashion an opposite outcome. But he got no chance. He served under a Southern ruling oligarchy comprised of civilian and military representatives of the 10,000 planter families that owned at least fifty slaves each. A tiny fraction of the region's 8 million white residents, this crème de la crème held title to one-quarter of the Confederacy's 4 million slaves. Its high-toned members rarely invited an uncultivated ex-farm-renter into their drawing rooms, let alone their war rooms.[9]

Members of this Southern aristocracy proclaimed brotherhood with their poorer white neighbors based on mutual superiority to enslaved blacks, but their contempt for anybody below their social level was blatant. As a US congressman, future Confederate president Jefferson Davis had made a bitter foe of a common-born colleague, former tailor Andrew Johnson, with a thoughtless remark that Johnson took as slighting people who worked with their hands. An 1858 speech by South Carolina senator James Hammond, intending to target the Northern working class, breathed disdain for every nonslaveholding laborer. "In all social systems," he intoned, "there must be a class to do the menial duties, to perform the drudgery of life. . . . It constitutes the very mudsill of society." Three-quarters of the South's white population performed that sort of drudgery.[10]

Hammond and his peers also made sure the mudsill stayed in its place. Formal education—and social mobility in general—was far less available in the South than the North. Another South Carolinian, William Harper, wrote that God "did not intend" that every human be "highly cultivated"; rather, "it is better that a part should be fully and highly educated and the rest utterly ignorant." The latter were suitable only for the

work of making the upper class comfortable. In the North, where education was more available, Grant could get enough of it to qualify for a
West Point appointment. Even had Forrest been able to get the education, he would hardly have gotten the appointment. In the South, such
plums rarely went to former lessee farmers.[11]

Grant and Forrest, unlike most of their peers, knew life at the bottom.
Grant had peddled firewood on St. Louis street corners to keep his family's bodies and souls together; he sold his pocket watch for $20 one year
to give them a Christmas. Forrest, like Abraham Lincoln, wielded an axe
with the skill of experience; he once split rails for fifty cents per hundred
to earn boat passage back to Mississippi from Texas. But where the book-
ish Lincoln ended in the White House, the less literate Forrest rose only
to the Memphis city council. He was elected for his fearless forthrightness
in an incident rife with overtones of the Old South's least savory elements.
Himself a trader in human chattel, he gave crucial testimony in the trial
of one slave merchant who had murdered another. The killer claimed the
dead man, a friend of Forrest who died in Forrest's house, had willfully
sold him a free African American, who afterward recovered his liberty in
court. Forrest testified unhesitatingly against his city's richest slave
trader—and supplanted him soon afterward.[12]

Such hands-on familiarity with life at the bottom, seamy or otherwise,
proved invaluable to both men as Civil War generals. Forrest and Grant
exemplified the yeomanry that did most of the war's bleeding and dying
and, unlike their superiors, identified more with their men than their peers.
Because this identification was so obvious, each had intra-army struggles
with famed West Pointers who viewed them with scorn. But their working-
class roots proved an incalculable asset. Each knew firsthand what was
possible, and impossible, for his men to accomplish. Both also used networks of spies to gather information, because each understood the need to
know all he could beforehand about a planned task; their previous lives had
depended on such things. Having lived where opportunity seldom
knocked, each knew the necessity of capitalizing on it when it did. Unlike
their superiors, who had rarely had to devote life-and-death attention to
anything, they obsessed about initiative, aggressiveness, persistence, and
speed. And their stressful lives had long since accustomed them to war's
continual anxiety.

Both Grant and Forrest showed unique mental agility in campaigning. In his daring gambles to reach and besiege Vicksburg, Grant rejected West Point wisdom in favor of his own ingenuity. Like Forrest, he used military theory against West Point–trained opponents, doing the opposite of what they expected him to. Vanquishing the treachery and contempt of peers and higher-ups, he triumphed in the epic campaigns of Fort Donelson, Shiloh, Vicksburg, and Chattanooga. No one knew it yet, but he had already beaten Lee when he came east to fight the vaunted Virginian in 1864. His western leadership had slashed the arteries of Lee's star-crossed nation.

Mainstream scholars rightly question the abilities of the Confederate high command. Yet, perhaps influenced by its cultivation and learning, they have largely accepted the Richmond coterie's contemporary minimizations of Forrest. Jefferson Davis and his minions saw the Tennessean as merely coarse and offensive to their genteel sensibility, as a cartoonish half-literate who would not follow orders and could never have become more than the peerless raider he unquestionably was.

But the Confederate high command was manifestly fallible. Scholars accepting its judgments of Forrest seem not to have noticed that he did not start out the way he ended—defiant, sullen, and imperious. At Fort Donelson, Shiloh, and many other battles, he followed every order, only to see aristocratic commanders squander all chance for victory. At least as much as his abrasiveness, their sneers and ineptitude drove him to rebellion and self-exile—and their Confederacy to its grave.

I

GLANCING BACK

1

LATE WINTER–
EARLY SPRING 1862—GRANT

Laurels Tarnished

In mid-March 1862, Major General Ulysses S. Grant reaccepted command of his army. The month preceding his reappointment had been bewildering.

Thirty-some days earlier at Fort Donelson in northern Tennessee, fighting myriad enemies in gray and blue, he had captured the largest force taken in any American war up to that time. His feat smashed the center of a Confederate line that had stretched westward from the Appalachian foothills to the Mississippi River. Grant's twin victories at Fort Henry and Fort Donelson threw the Confederates out of southern Kentucky all the way across Tennessee into Alabama and Mississippi. These triumphs transformed the war, exploding the stalemate that had followed the Federal defeat at Bull Run in Virginia in July 1861. His initiative had given the Union a juggernaut western momentum. Dubbed "Unconditional Surrender Grant" by victory-hungry Northern newspapers, he rose immediately from brigadier to major general.

Until Donelson, however, Grant had been a dead man walking. Charges of scandalous drunkenness had been filed against him just days before the battle. He had arrested his chief of river transportation, a meddlesome and politically connected civilian named William J. Kountz, for obstructing troop movements, and Kountz had retaliated by launching the charges in the chain of command. They alleged that a "beastly," drunken Grant had been incapable of conducting business on a flag-of-truce boat, had drunk with "rebels," had been repeatedly drunk since, and had indulged in "Conduct unbecoming an Officer and a Gentleman." Recipients of the document could not have known that its filer was a temperance fanatic who may not have even been in the vicinity when the reported excesses occurred.[1]

So Grant, on the eve of his Henry-Donelson coup, had been in a most vulnerable position. His superior (and the initial recipient of the Kountz document), Major General Henry W. Halleck, was working to promote—and replace him with—a prominent West Pointer, sixty-three-year-old Brigadier General Ethan Allen Hitchcock. Federal command of the trans-Appalachian front was split between Halleck in St. Louis and Brigadier General Don Carlos Buell in Kentucky, and Halleck worried that Grant's seedy, rumpled aggressiveness would embarrass him and hamper his chance to best Buell in army politics.

Grant had needed to achieve something big before Kountz's charges destroyed his career. He had pestered Halleck into letting him and naval flag officer Andrew Foote go after Forts Henry and Donelson on the Tennessee and Cumberland rivers. Reluctantly, Halleck had finally assented, hoping to achieve a victory before Buell did. It worked. The Henry-Donelson captures made Halleck preeminent in the West.

Yet, no sooner had he distinguished himself at Henry and Donelson than Grant staggered, stabbed in the back. Mysterious foes in his own ranks, armed with his reputation as a drunkard, toppled him. On March 5, Halleck relieved him of his duties, and Grant appeared headed back to the oblivion from which he had sprung. Then suddenly, on March 13, Halleck changed his mind.

Turning unaccountably kind, Halleck stepped forward to seem to save Donelson's disgraced victor. It was a sham. Halleck had manufactured the crisis himself. He let Grant believe that General in Chief George McClellan (who had been outraged at encountering an intoxicated Grant in the antebellum army) and President Abraham Lincoln had demanded his dismissal, but the actual foe had been Halleck himself. He wanted Grant gone and would use any pretense to accomplish that end. He had only wilted when Lincoln, grateful for the Donelson victory, began asking questions about what was happening to Grant. Had he left his command without proper authority? Had his reports not been timely? Had he been insubordinate? Halleck, knowing he had manufactured this controversy himself, quickly minimized it and kicked it under the rug.[2]

Grant knew none of this. Relieved at having dodged a political bullet, he resumed his duties. His new task was large: to organize the huge force gathering to harvest the fruits of the Henry-Donelson victories.

To Grant's way of thinking, those triumphs should have been followed up by quick strikes southward. "My opinion was . . . that immediately after the fall of Fort Donelson the way was opened to the National forces all over the South-west without much resistance," he later wrote. He thought Federal troops already in uniform could have fanned out to the rail centers of Chattanooga, Tennessee, and Corinth, Mississippi, as well as the Mississippi River cities of Memphis and Vicksburg. A quick Union advance into these areas, in his opinion, would have denied the Confederate armies "tens of thousands" of potential Southern recruits.[3]

Instead, many of these Southerners were being recruited now, while the Union army took its time readying its next blow. Thousands were reportedly gathering at Corinth to try to stop the southward Federal drive along the Tennessee River. Corinth was a major hub on the Memphis & Charleston Railroad, whose tracks were bringing in more troops. A Confederate victory in front of the Mississippi town would begin recouping the South's staggering Henry-Donelson losses.

Grant's return to command made him a target of Confederate desperation, but that did not worry him. Grateful for Halleck's inexplicable reversal, Grant could look back on his Henry-Donelson campaign with relief and pride. The Donelson triumph had whipped both his anonymous Union enemies and 20,000 Confederates. Three-fourths of the latter he had captured and sent to Northern prisons.

But the victory also obscured major errors. Flag Officer Foote's gunboats had battered Fort Henry into submission before Grant's army could arrive. Grant had then attacked Donelson without knowing how many Confederates were inside its fortifications—only to find that they contained more troops than he had outside. He had assumed the ironclad gunboats that had decimated Fort Henry would make similar rubble of Fort Donelson—but Donelson's apprentice cannoneers all but blew the ironclads out of the Cumberland River. On the battle's third and climactic day, Grant rode out four icy miles north of the left end of his lines to persuade Foote not to take the crippled but still-feared river monsters north for refitting. While he was gone, the Confederates burst from the far end of their entrenchments and rolled the south end of the Union line northward more than a mile. Grant had neglected to leave anyone in charge at headquarters; he returned from his conference with Foote to find a wrecked right wing and mounting dismay among his troops.

Yet Grant kept his head. The Confederate attack finally faltered, and he rightly guessed that to bring such force against the lower end of the line, the enemy had to have stripped most of his strength from the upper end. Grant's innate aggressiveness only increased under stress. He ordered the commander on his left—stalwart Brigadier General Charles Ferguson Smith, his tactics instructor at West Point—to ready a charge. Then he ordered an all-out counterattack, promising that the trenches on the left would be lightly defended. Sure enough, Smith's charge overran that end of the defenses.

Smith later gave Grant the words with which newspapers would transform the erstwhile pupil into an overnight hero. When a Confederate party arrived with a message requesting surrender terms, Grant looked to Smith. "No terms to the damned rebels," growled the oldster. Even though the appeal to negotiate came from Confederate brigadier Simon Bolivar Buckner, a Grant friend and antebellum benefactor, Grant took Smith's advice. "No terms except immediate and unconditional surrender can be accepted," Grant replied to Buckner's note. "I propose to move immediately upon your works."

With Smith occupying one end of his trenches and his Confederates in disarray, Buckner surrendered. Grant, with Smith's indispensable assistance, had saved himself. Despite the errors they concealed, the Henry-Donelson victories stymied Halleck's intention to fire this man whom history would come to regard as most responsible for winning the war.

Few men looked less likely to save the Union. Born and reared in the comparative wilds of southern Ohio, Grant had rarely impressed even his own family. He had gone to West Point reluctantly, at his thrifty father's insistence (a West Point education being free). Before that, he had spent most of his youth plying fields and roads with workhorses, thus avoiding the blood and stink of his father's tanning business. At West Point, he studied war indifferently, preferring to read adventure novels from the academy library and draw sketches that showed some talent. He stood out from classmates in just two respects: for serving as president of the Point's literary society and setting an academy horse-jumping record that would stand for a quarter century.

After graduation, he spent eleven years in the army. He participated, he later recalled, in about as many battles of the Mexican War as one person could. His behavior under fire was rock steady; his feats included intrepidly riding through house-to-house fighting in the streets of Monterrey, amid hails of bullets, to request more ammunition for a unit that was running out. He did this despite being an officer and an adjutant, then gave the credit to his horse, Nelly. Such exploits won him brevet promotions to first lieutenant and captain, but he reached the latter rank permanently only years later, just prior to his abrupt departure from the army.

Grant resigned in April 1854, apparently to escape allegations of drunkenness. He had endured a long, monotonous posting in the remote Pacific Northwest, half a continent away from his beloved wife, Julia, and their family. Soon after making captain, he reportedly showed up at a company pay table stupefied by drink, and his commander, an eastern-born martinet and nephew of President John Quincy Adams, reportedly threatened to file formal charges if Grant did not resign. A friend speculated that he chose the latter to avoid scandalizing his family. He went to farming in Missouri near the plantation of his father-in-law, working in the fields beside slaves. But bad weather and national financial panics ruined him. He had to peddle firewood in shabby clothes on the streets of St. Louis to survive. Only a job in a Galena, Illinois, leather-goods store owned by his father rescued him from want.

War pulled him out of obscurity at age thirty-nine. Politically he was middle-of-the-road, believing the Union should remain whole. He neither supported slavery nor espoused its abolition, but he seemed to empathize with slaves as fellow humans; he freed the only one he ever owned. Because of his West Point education, city fathers in Galena asked him to organize and train a company of volunteers, and he did. He turned down an offer to be its captain, however, because men with less—or no—army experience were becoming colonels. He held out for higher rank, though his reputation as a drunkard and lack of political influence hamstrung him for a time. The Illinois governor finally named him colonel of the Twenty-first Illinois Infantry only because the initial appointee could not handle its rowdy troops.

Then Grant's luck, so bad for so long, turned. Congressman Elihu Washburne of Illinois, seeking as many generals for his state as possible, got Grant commissioned as a brigadier. Before long, he was commanding the burgeoning Union base at Cairo, Illinois—from whence he and Foote attacked Fort Henry. Following his triumphs there and at Fort Donelson, Grant's grit earned him his promotion to major general; it also won him a personal triumph as consequential as those victories. The charges of drunkenness he had endured throughout the Henry-Donelson campaign and during his brief, puzzling suspension from command, were worse than those that had driven him from the army seven years earlier. These latest ones, amplified in another version sent directly to the War Department, had alleged that his inebriation was chronic and involved such sensational sins as drunkenly losing his sword and ascending a hotel's stairs on all fours. But this time he refused to allow the charges and the possibility of their publication, now that he had attained the stature of a general—to cow him. His determination had hardened. The smashing victory he had won at Fort Donelson sustained him. With Halleck's abrupt decision to reinstate him, the accusations seemed to have been buried on a desk somewhere up the chain of command.[4]

G rant's first task was to rejoin his men. During his post-Donelson removal, his erstwhile army had swelled from three to five divisions: 39,000 men. Halleck had put General Smith in command and ordered them seventy-five miles farther south on the Tennessee River.

Smith's orders were to do nothing to bring on a full-scale battle. He debarked most of his force just north of the Mississippi state line at two steamboat landings, Pittsburg and Crump's, and allowed his ground commander, Brigadier William Tecumseh Sherman, to arrange them willy-nilly. There was no order to entrench. West Point wisdom held that telling a soldier to dig for safety was tantamount to telling him he should fear.

The fifty-six-year-old Smith, like many of his soldiers, was still ill from Donelson. He had slept on the snow there after giving up his tent to the wounded. Now a trifling injury challenged his weakened constitution. Jumping into a rowboat on the swirling Tennessee, he barked a shin, and the oncoming springtime temperatures helped to infect it. Soon erysipelas had Smith bedridden in Savannah, Tennessee. Halleck, under scrutiny by Washington for his removal of Grant, returned the army to the Donelson victor.

Grant hurried south from Fort Henry and took up the reins. He had to provide for his troops' many wants while they—and he—awaited orders for the next shove southward. The coming pounce, he predicted in a letter to Julia, would result in "the greatest battle . . . of the War." Their target would be the railroad hub at Corinth, Mississippi. But he could not expect to command in the battle. Halleck had claimed that honor for himself. So Grant and his men sat on hold, awaiting the arrival of their chief from St. Louis and, from Nashville, more help. A second large Federal army under Major General Buell was marching overland from the Tennessee capital to join them. But Buell, who had dawdled in sending help to Grant at Fort Donelson and then in "taking" unoccupied Nashville, was again delaying. At Columbia, he insisted on rebuilding a bridge torched by the Confederates during their southward retreat rather than cross the Duck River by pontoon.

Between Grant and Buell lay a gulf of bad blood. Buell had resented Grant's promotion to major general following the victories Grant scored at Fort Henry and Fort Donelson while Buell was resisting Lincoln's calls to advance. Buell soon became a major general too—but after Grant. So the prewar captain who had resigned in an 1854 whisky stink was now senior to the distinguished antebellum career officer.

That was not all. Buell only "took" Nashville after Grant, trying to help, ordered one of Buell's divisions to return to their commander by boat from Fort Donelson and land in the Tennessee capital. They arrived there before he did himself. This embarrassed and angered Buell, who had feared to move his own 7,000 men into the city because Lieutenant Colonel Nathan Bedford Forrest and forty of his cavalrymen still lurked there.

A few days later, newly minted major general Grant came down to Nashville to meet still brigadier general Buell. There he disagreed with Buell's insistence that Confederates might attack him in Nashville at any moment. Grant correctly maintained that the Confederates were retreating as fast as they could march.[5]

Not everyone in Buell's command was as methodical or hesitant as the commander himself. Kentucky-born Brigadier William "Bull" Nelson, an ambitious twenty-year navy veteran who had become one of Buell's division commanders, was electrified by the danger to Grant's army and the opportunity it offered Nelson himself. Grant's force was on the west bank of the Tennessee, where the broad river would separate it from Buell's aid even after the Nashville column arrived. So on March 27 Nelson persuaded Buell to let his division ford the Duck, which it did, shivering, on March 29. The rest of Buell's army was left behind as Nelson marched hard toward Grant's headquarters at Savannah, Tennessee, nine miles north of Pittsburg Landing, but on the river's east bank.

Grant fidgeted and worked. Previous to 1861 he had commanded only a company of troops, and now he had to supervise tens of thousands. "I am very glad you are having a pleasant visit," he wrote Julia at the home of friends in Louisville, Kentucky. "I wish I could make a visit anywhere for a week or two. It would be a great relief not to have to think for a short time."[6]

His men's needs were not the only things on Grant's mind. He knew Confederates were gathering around Corinth, twenty-five miles southwest of Pittsburg Landing. Their numbers were reported to be anywhere from 20,000 to five times that, and Grant wanted to attack before they consolidated. He was certain they would not leave the Corinth fortifications in force. He knew, though, that a significant Confederate unit was "hovering," as he put it, to the west of his troops at Crump's Landing. He had a division's supplies stockpiled at Crump's, five miles north of Pittsburg on the same side of the Tennessee, and he worried that Confederates might raid there before he could send reinforcements.

Signs of mischief multiplied. On the afternoon of Friday, April 4, a handful of men from the Seventieth Ohio, posted five miles out the road toward Corinth from Pittsburg, ventured past their pickets in a nasty rainstorm and disappeared. The Seventy-second Ohio heard firing, and two of its companies went to investigate. Their probe turned into a firefight. When the two companies did not return, 150 cavalrymen of the Fifth Ohio went after them, and the troopers found the infantrymen skirmishing with a large force of Confederate cavalry. The Union horsemen charged and drove the Confederates, only to run into infantry and artillery.[7]

Grant was concerned, and not just that the enemy appeared to be "in considerable force." Halleck had ordered that no battle be opened until Buell arrived, and Buell was somewhere on the road from Columbia. Grant took a steamer to Pittsburg Landing from Savannah that evening and rode out for a look at the skirmish site. "The night," he afterward recalled, "was one of impenetrable darkness, with rain pouring down in torrents; nothing was visible . . . except as revealed by the frequent flashes of lightning." Two Federal officers and a few enlisted men had been captured; four others had been wounded. As far as Grant could tell, though, all was quiet.

His expedition was nevertheless eventful. His horse fell on the watery road and pinned its rider. He returned to Savannah with an ankle so swollen that the boot had to be cut off. Still, he had learned that out in front, much closer than Corinth, were Confederate cavalrymen accompanied by at least three pieces of artillery and some infantry. "How much," Grant wrote Halleck on Saturday, April 5, "cannot of course be estimated. I have scarcely the faintest idea of an attack (general one) being made upon us, but will be prepared should such a thing take place."[8]

He turned out to be anything but, as he learned all too well the next morning. The Confederates had beaten Halleck to his great battle. On April 6, 44,000 Southerners came yipping out of the Sabbath dawn and into Sherman's camps around a country church called Shiloh. Their mission was unholy: to destroy Grant's army before Buell's could arrive.

2

LATE WINTER–
EARLY SPRING 1862—FORREST

Hurry

For Confederate lieutenant colonel Nathan Bedford Forrest, the time between mid-February and mid-March 1862 had been even more appalling than it had been for Grant.

Four hundred square miles of Forrest's new homeland—the ambitious, year-old Confederate States of America—had dropped from Richmond's control in less than a fortnight. Near the northeast end of this lost vastness was Nashville, the first Confederate state capital to fall. With it went many of its crammed supply depots and all its vital industrial facilities. For Forrest, as for other Confederates, the losses were personal as well as military. On the new Confederacy, he had gambled 3,400 acres of prime Mississippi cotton land, other holdings, and a lot of cash amassed in two and a half decades of antebellum labor. At Forts Henry and Donelson, he had seen this wealth's future imperiled. At Donelson, four generals whose combined talents did not equal his own had ignored his recommendations and wasted his valor.

Forrest had ridden away from Donelson in disgust, leading hundreds of cavalry, infantry, and artillerymen. Refusing to participate in the generals' sorry surrender, he had vowed to cut his way out of the siege—one that they, over his repeated protests, maintained the Federals had reestablished around the fort. But Forrest and his men had had to cut nothing. He had been right: the Federal siege was incomplete. The escapees rode out without drawing a saber.

Forrest had fought like a demon at Donelson. Fifteen bullet marks tattered his overcoat. But he had sustained every nick for naught. He could only ride to Nashville and try to save as much of the Tennessee capital's stockpiled matériel as possible.

O nly a fool would not have tallied a personal cost. A single watchword had characterized Forrest's postboyhood life: hurry. The family he was born into in south-central Tennessee had owned a modest acreage, but only temporarily. Before his blacksmith father's early death, they were reduced to leasing northern Mississippi hill land. As a teenager Forrest had breakfasted by candle to enter the fields by dawn, wasting not a ray of daylight. He had spent evenings on the hearth, sewing clothes and shoes for younger siblings.

Manhood came early and became a frantic fight to escape the clutches of poverty. He chased and caught runaway slaves for the rich of his region, earning enough money to start buying and selling human chattel himself. Then, like the aggressive poker player he became, he threw the wealth earned from this early slave trading into buying and selling not only more slaves but also lots and buildings in Memphis, Tennessee, and ever-larger expanses of frontier cotton land. He strove for two decades, gathering a net worth he would come to claim, with a salesman's bent toward accentuation of the positive, equaled an improbable "million and a half of dollars." He then wagered it all on this new Confederacy, even spending sizable sums of his own wealth to arm and equip men he recruited. At Fort Donelson he had watched with dismayed outrage as his timid, blue-blooded Confederate commanders seemingly threw away their new nation and, with it, the fruit of his labors.[1]

Forrest had spent the prime of his adulthood advancing toward the ranks of the South's landed gentry. Amassing the wealth was the easier part of this upward climb. Aristocrats tended to look down on the humbler station he hailed from and its attendant lack of refinement. When they did so to his face, he responded in fury. As a young farmer, he had shot a neighbor's bull dead after the landowner had repeatedly let the animal break down fences and consume Forrest's crops. He then put a bullet in the man's clothes when he came, armed, to protest. On the town square of Hernando, Mississippi, a twenty-five-year-old Forrest had single-handedly fought and bested another area landowner—as well as the man's overseer and two kinsmen—with a two-shot pistol and a knife. And as a young husband scrambling to earn a living, Forrest had started a brickyard and constructed a building for an academy in Hernando, only to clash hotly with city fathers who took their sweet time paying.

Soon after, Forrest had left Hernando for a larger arena. He moved the few miles north to Memphis, a brawling river town second only to New Orleans in the western slave trade. In less than a decade, making incessant forays as far away as Texas, he became a titan in that seamy but lucrative business. He won election to the Memphis city council three times in the late 1850s, rising to chair its finance committee. He formed friendships with those among the powerful who accorded him respect—and collided with any who, consciously or otherwise, did not. In one council meeting, when a fellow alderman declaimed that the body had taken a "coward-like" action, Forrest rose in abrupt challenge. As described in the flat prose of the *Memphis Daily Appeal*, "Alderman Forrest said that Alderman Finnie meant him in his attack, for [Finnie] knew he was a fighting man."

In early 1859, Forrest left the slave business and returned to Mississippi. He identified his vocation to the 1860 census taker as "planter," a far more socially acceptable vocation than slave trading. He was entitled; he not only owned but also now occupied 3,345 Coahoma County acres of the best cotton land in Mississippi. The place boasted a six-room house that a neighbor later described as "not beautiful but comfortable . . . in a grove of magnificent oak trees and facing the public road." The house fronted two rows of cabins that the census said housed thirty-six slaves.

Owning three dozen human chattel put Forrest comfortably in the Southern planter class—entry level was considered ownership of twenty, a long stride above "farmer." He probably owned more slaves on other properties or in the slave jails of his late firm's offices from Memphis to Vicksburg, but at least here on this Coahoma County property, he remained well short of the aristocratic status to which he likely aspired. Aristocrats were understood to own at least fifty slaves. These barons of bondage comprised Dixie's elite, numbering just 10,000 families in a Southern white population of 1.5 million families. Yet, even these privileged 10,000 did not constitute the top rung of the Southern social ladder. Its wealthiest and most powerful planters, the South's de facto rulers, owned more than a hundred slaves each and numbered just 3,000 families.

Forrest doubtless had visions of reaching this lofty level, arithmetically if not socially. In 1861, his plantation harvested 1,000 bales of cotton, or $30,000 worth. That could have bought him thirty more slaves. By then, though, he had changed professions again, this time choosing the one that suited him best: soldier.

When history notices Nathan Bedford Forrest at all, it tends to view him as a military miracle. His feats are presented as special blessings of the gods of war, unheralded by previous experience. This is likely because historians tend to glorify the profession of arms and the graduates of its schools. Forrest would have laughed. While he appreciated attention, he plainly never saw himself as unprepared for the great conflict. He knew different. His wartime exploits were part and parcel of who he had always been.

His range of preparatory experience was panoramic. He knew how to plan ahead, as his antebellum rise to riches attests. He had personally driven enough slave gangs along the roads of the South to know logistics and develop the instinct of absolute command. His labor on subsistence farms had taught him to value every piece of equipment to the utmost and to jerry-rig substitutes for any he did not have. His slave jails had taught him the mechanics of keeping captives and accounting for every one, along with every meal they must be fed and every tool they might be required to use. Card playing and armed civilian encounters—in, but in no way restricted to, his capacity as a Hernando constable—had taught him aggressiveness, the value of the bluff, and the imperative of pressing every advantage to the kill. Finally, he was a past master of guns and horses. Near its end, he would sum up his life as a battle from the start. The Civil War was just another phase.

In June 1861, six days after Tennesseans voted to secede, he had enlisted in a Memphis cavalry company as a private. Influential friends thought this was a waste, and Forrest probably soon did too. The friends had prevailed on Tennessee governor Isham G. Harris and General Gideon Pillow, commander of Tennessee's provisional army, to vault him upward. Both Memphis lawyers, Harris and Pillow surely knew that Forrest's reputation as a man of action would draw recruits, whom Forrest was rich enough to outfit. He spent less than a month as a private before being commissioned a lieutenant colonel and instructed to raise a cavalry battalion. It was the week of his fortieth birthday.

Forrest likely entered the high officer corps of the Confederate army with eager respect, presuming he would join like-minded individuals of valor and action. At Fort Donelson, he learned otherwise. The elite cadre was peopled with too many men too similar to the blowhards of the Memphis city council.

Forrest's senior commander at Donelson, ex–US secretary of war Brigadier General John B. Floyd, had proved yellow as fool's gold; Floyd's three subordinate generals were little better. The second in command, rich Tennessee politico Gideon Pillow, was only semicompetent, if that. The third, courtly West Pointer Simon Buckner of Kentucky, was pompous and argumentative. The fourth, West Point graduate turned college professor Bushrod Johnson, was unassertive as a phantom. This quartet merely tried not to lose the battle—and thus lost.

On February 12, 1862, the first day of the fighting at Fort Donelson, Major General Ulysses S. Grant's 15,000 infantrymen advanced twelve miles overland from Fort Henry to encircle the part of Donelson not bounded by the Cumberland River. Forrest and his 1,000 or so troopers mounted the sole opposition outside the fort. In five hours of hard skirmishing, they brought half of Grant's army to a temporary standstill. But when Forrest warned that Grant was attempting to surround the fort and only more infantry could prevent it, Buckner ordered Forrest back inside the trenches.

On the struggle's icy fourth day, the Confederates charged out of the left end of their entrenchments. Forrest was in the vanguard as they began pushing the Union right back onto its center. After some three hours, he saw white flags here and there within the fierce clots of Federal resistance. Having learned the psychology of violence and fear in many prewar face-offs, he begged to lead a charge to try to turn the piecemeal Union withdrawals into a stampede. But Bushrod Johnson shrank from making pivotal decisions. No, he said, the Federals might be laying a trap.

So the Confederate push, slower and bloodier than Forrest thought necessary, lasted seven hours. Forrest's troopers, awash in gore, took or helped take clusters of Federal artillery and droves of prisoners. Around the last cannons anchoring the Union right, blood from men and horses pooled in the snow, splashing onto those still fighting.

The Confederates pushed Grant's stout and stubborn Federal volunteers back a mile or more. Then came a supreme act of military ineptitude in a day with more than its share. Pillow, the Confederates' operational commander, halted the attack and declared victory. He ordered the troops back to their trenches, abandoning the frozen ground they had bought with blood. Pillow intended for the men to collect their gear and escape to Nashville. But Grant refused to let them get away. He countercharged.

For all his overcoat's bullet marks—not to mention a second horse that perished beneath him when a cannonball passed through its flanks—Forrest's finest hour at Fort Donelson may actually have occurred off the battlefield. Later that night, when the generals gathered and decided to surrender, the lieutenant colonel harangued his superiors with an impertinent speech. He had not come to Fort Donelson to surrender, he said. He had promised the parents of his men he would take care of them, and he would not see them starve or freeze to death in a Northern prison. He would rather see their bones bleaching on the hills around Fort Donelson. He wanted to lead them in a breakout bid.

Buckner had succeeded to the fort's command to allow Floyd and Pillow to skedaddle shamefully. Before leaving, Pillow prevailed on Buckner to let Forrest try to take his men out. Forrest gathered most of his men and others who had horses or scrambled up to ride double with the cavalry. Then, because several scouts insisted that the Federals had reblocked the dry route, he led them out a flooded riverside road. The icy backwater was one hundred yards wide and, unbeknownst to them, four feet deep, a fact they wouldn't learn until somebody tried to cross it. Forrest was the first man in.

He took his fugitives to Nashville, which was still under Confederate control. A few days' hard labor there salvaged 600 boxes of military clothing, 250,000 pounds of bacon, and 40 wagonloads of ammunition for the

Confederate cause—an effort opposed by the poor, hungry, and desperate residents of the Tennessee capital. Their wealthier townsmen had fled in headlong panic. Railroad cars were jammed. Long lines of public and private vehicles trailed southward-streaming remnants of the western Confederate army.

Federal troops reached the Nashville suburbs on February 23, a week after Donelson's fall. Forrest and forty of his men, the last Confederates to leave the city, rode to Murfreesboro ahead of the Federal advance. There, western commander Albert Sidney Johnston ordered the cavalrymen farther south to Huntsville, Alabama.

By then, Forrest may have gotten wind of a mixed reaction to his escape. The Southern public saw it as heroic, but some aristocrats and West Pointers equated it with the cowardice shown by Floyd and Pillow. The generals had fled for their lives, Floyd with some of his Virginia troops on commandeered steamboats and Pillow with a couple of staff members in a skiff. Forrest, by contrast, had intended to fight his way out.

On February 25, after arriving at Huntsville, Forrest gave his men a two-week furlough. They returned on March 10 with newly enlisted friends. Two officers had recruited whole new companies. The proliferated units now totaled a full regiment whose troopers did not share the high command's low view of their commander. By acclamation, they elected him full colonel.[2]

II

SHILOH:
"THE DEVIL'S OWN DAY"

3

APRIL 6, FORENOON—FORREST

"Main Force and Ignorance"

Western Confederate defenses were collapsing in domino fashion. The fall of Forts Henry and Donelson had given federal gunboats control of the Tennessee River all the way to northern Alabama, outflanking installations on the Mississippi as far south as Memphis. A climax was coming fast.

Almost overnight, General Albert Sidney Johnston, the western Confederacy's chief commander, had become hotly unpopular. A raging Southern press denounced him for the fall of Henry and Donelson and the hundred-mile retreat that followed. By now, another top Confederate was on the scene, and Johnston turned to him for assistance. P. G. T. Beauregard, hero of Fort Sumter and Manassas (and like Johnston, ranked at full general), had been sent west in mid-February because his considerable vanity clashed with that of Jefferson Davis. Johnston asked Beauregard to supervise the withdrawal of the western wing of the Kentucky defense line, now halved by the Henry-Donelson disaster. Beauregard complied, bringing that half of Johnston's army to Corinth, Mississippi, from Columbus, Kentucky. Johnston meanwhile personally led the eastern half's retreat from Bowling Green through Nashville to Huntsville, Alabama. From there Johnston headed it west to link up with Beauregard.

Forrest led his newly expanded regiment out of Alabama in mid-March, bound for the northern Mississippi hamlet of Burnsville. There, a dozen miles east of Corinth on the Memphis & Charleston Railroad, he reported as ordered to Major General John C. Breckinridge of Kentucky, recent vice president of the United States and now commander of a Blue-grass brigade. Most of Forrest's troopers spent the next days drilling. Twenty, though, rode a few miles north to the banks of the Tennessee River, assigned to watch the progress and direction of the Federal army of Major General Don Carlos Buell. They soon confirmed that Buell was heading southwestward from Nashville, apparently to join the Federals pushing south along the Tennessee River. This information agreed with other intelligence from Confederate spies and sympathizers in Middle Tennessee, and Forrest duly reported it to General Johnston.[1]

Confederates knew the bridges they had destroyed in their retreat from Nashville could delay Buell for only so long. Soon after Johnston arrived at Corinth in late February, Beauregard told him that elements of the Henry-Donelson army were coming upriver. By mid-March they were debarking in large force at Pittsburg Landing, twenty-five miles from Corinth. Forrest's and other reports indicated that Buell's column would arrive in early April. Additional intelligence likewise called for quick Con-federate action. On April 2, General Frank Cheatham's division, twenty-four miles north of Corinth at the Bethel, Tennessee, railroad station, reported pressure from Federals. Cheatham believed—correctly—that the opposing troops were Major General Lew Wallace's division from Crump's Landing. This led Beauregard to think Grant was dividing his army, sending a large part westward fifteen miles to raid the Mobile & Ohio Railroad and perhaps farther, toward Memphis. That and Buell's imminent approach led Beauregard on April 2 to pen Johnston an abrupt memo in the margins of Cheatham's message.

"Now," it said, "is the moment to advance and strike the enemy at Pitts-burg Landing."[2]

Johnston was reluctant. He knew many of the troops gathering at Corinth were raw. Beauregard and Major General Braxton Bragg at length persuaded him. Because of his late infamy, however, Johnston gave Beau-regard operational control of the army for the coming battle, while retain-ing titular leadership. Beauregard quickly—perhaps too quickly—drafted a plan. It designated Breckinridge's corps as the reserve, and Forrest re-mained assigned to Breckinridge. This likely was no accident. Breckinridge, with no military training, had gotten his own assignment less than a week earlier. He replaced Major General George Crittenden, a West Pointer removed for flagrant drunkenness after investigation found discipline "wretched" in his command.

Most superiors doubtless thought Forrest's assignment to Breckinridge appropriate. One of Forrest's own aides later recalled that after the Donelson escape, the Tennessean was "much criticized" among other officers "for what he had already done": this, the aide wrote, made Forrest negatively "conspicuous in the cause." Some of this had to do with his avoidance of the Donelson surrender, but more seems to have stemmed from his lack of training and his headlong ferocity in combat. Federals attributed his early triumphs to nothing more than overpowering numbers—or "main force and ignorance"—the aide wrote, adding that most Southern officers thought he would not last long. His immediate subordinate at the time, Major David C. Kelley, later wrote that some of Forrest's own officers feared the potential consequences of their chief's "disregard . . . of the ordinary rules of tactics" and his recklessness "in personal exposure."[3]

The theater commander may have viewed him differently. Forrest's authorized biography claims that his Fort Donelson performance made him "a favorite" of General Johnston. Postwar, a prominent Kentucky Confederate recalled that Forrest's name "had become widely known" even before Donelson, after he routed Union cavalry at Sacramento, Kentucky. In that clash, he commanded 300 Confederates against 168 Federals and killed three Federal officers with his own hands. At Donelson, Brigadier General Simon Buckner had reported that Forrest acted "with his usual gallantry." Had deeds measured worth in the Confederacy, Forrest's feats at Sacramento and Donelson might already have made him its most accomplished—if not respected—cavalry leader thus far in the western war.[4]

But apart, perhaps, from Johnston, no one else in high command seemed to notice Forrest's effectiveness—thus his assignment to the reserve. He rode from Burnsville to Johnston's headquarters in Corinth to get his orders to join Breckinridge. Johnston surely had little to do with that. Operational commander Beauregard likely relied for such assignments on the new chief of staff, Braxton Bragg, who had scant appreciation for citizen soldiers.

Beauregard patterned his battle plan on Napoleon's at Waterloo. The Beauregard version, however, was convoluted, requiring 44,000 mostly ill-trained Confederates to travel two rough and tricky routes. Not only were the Ridge and Bark Roads to Pittsburg Landing miry from recent, continuing rain, but they also joined each other eight miles from the target. The two columns would have to take turns passing through the junction.

Furthermore, Beauregard arranged his attackers in a formation that jeopardized commanders' control of their units. Each of the four corps— under Major Generals William J. Hardee, Leonidas Polk, Bragg, and Breckinridge—was directed to spread out across the entire three-mile front. Bragg's would be 1,000 yards behind Hardee's, and Polk's 800 yards behind Bragg's, trailed by Breckinridge's reserves. Hardee's 13,228-man Army of Central Kentucky was divided roughly in half, with 6,439 of its personnel transferred to Breckinridge. Bragg's numbers were 13,589; Polk had 9,136.[5]

The Federals had arranged their Pittsburg Landing camps more for offense and comfort than defense. Some extended north to south, facing west, to facilitate formation into columns for the anticipated march toward Corinth. Some camped near the best water source. So they spread out willy-nilly, bounded on three sides by flooded streams—the wide Tennessee River to the east and northeast, Owl Creek to the northwest, and Lick Creek to the southeast. The Confederates, approaching from the only open side, hoped the Federals had essentially trapped themselves in a three-walled box.

The Confederates intended to drive Grant back onto Owl Creek. That would push him away from the protection of his Tennessee River gunboats, his sources of resupply, and all possibility of aid from an arriving Buell. Somehow, Beauregard's plan diverged from that intention. To shove the Federals back onto Owl Creek, the attack formation should have been overbalanced to the Confederate right, to separate Grant from the river and his base. Instead, arranging troops equally across the front, as Beauregard did, seemed designed to drive Grant backward into the river.[6]

The Confederate trek to Pittsburg Landing was a nightmare. The rain-soaked roads were bad enough, but Beauregard's precise, impractical orders as to logistics and which troops should proceed first through the intersection of the Ridge and Bark Roads made things worse. The army and its artillery and wagon trains ended up taking three days to traverse the nineteen miles to the battlefield. And the first line of attackers, Hardee's corps, got into position more than a half day before the rest of the army. Thousands of young, half-disciplined Confederates had to idle away hours within earshot of the Union picket lines.

Keeping thousands of volunteers quiet as time dragged on proved impossible. They engaged in rowdy outbursts and pulled triggers to see if their weapons would fire in the dampness. Through the night of April 5, Union bands serenaded their fitful slumbers. Federal discovery of their presence seemed certain. In fact, it appeared to happen time and again. Most notable, of course, was the prolonged skirmish that brought Grant out on the hellish night of April 4. As Hardee reported from near the infamous crossroads to Chief of Staff Bragg,

> GENERAL: The cavalry and infantry of the enemy attacked Colonel [James] Clanton's regiment, which was posted, as I before informed you, about 500 or 600 yards in advance of my lines. Colonel Clanton retired, and the enemy's cavalry followed until they came near our infantry and artillery, when they were gallantly repulsed with slight loss.[7]

Confederates captured some members of the Seventy-second Ohio detachment, and their disappearance brought more Union infantry and cavalry hurrying to the scene. Ohio major Leroy Crockett's eyes widened as Confederates conducted him to the crossroads where Hardee's camp was located.

"Why, you seem to have an army here," Crockett said wonderingly.[8]

⊹—●—⊹

Thanks to the unforeseen difficulties of the march to Pittsburg Landing, the Confederate attack, originally scheduled for Friday, April 4, was postponed to Saturday, then Sunday.

The excitable Beauregard became frantic. Surprise was essential to his plan; yet, the two armies were practically on top of each other. Hearing bands playing and bugles blowing, he sent orders to have the racket shushed. His courier returned with news that this could not be done; Federals were making the racket. Assuming that the delays had cost his Confederates the advantage, Beauregard demanded the attack be scrubbed. The likelihood that the Union army would be ready for them was not the only difficulty. Their three days' rations had been consumed on the march. Hunger loomed so darkly that, when General Hardee wrote his report, he remembered lack of rations as the sole problem.[9]

About 4 p.m. on April 5, Johnston finally reasserted his authority over Beauregard. The attack would not be cancelled, he said. He hardly needed to voice his reason. The Confederates could not back away again after seven weeks of retreating and consolidating for the announced purpose of striking an all-out blow. The psychological effect on their new nation would be devastating.[10]

A withdrawal now would be even more damaging to Johnston himself. He had breasted public rage for seven weeks. The abuse that would

GENERAL ALBERT SIDNEY JOHNSTON

follow another retreat without a fight would humiliate him beyond endurance. On April 3, he had issued a proclamation to the recently dubbed Army of the Mississippi that began, "I have put you in motion to offer battle to the invaders of your country. With the resolution and disciplined valor becoming men fighting, as you are, for all worth living or dying for, you can but march to a decisive victory over the agrarian mercenaries sent to subjugate you and despoil you of your liberties, property, and honor." He went on to note that soldiers of his army were "expected to show yourselves worthy of your race and lineage," as well as of "the women of the South." It closed with the promise that "your general will lead you confidently to the combat." Johnston had invested everything in the assault on Pittsburg Landing. There could be no going back.[11]

But the Confederate generals were still second-guessing the attack plan when predawn firing broke out in a field two miles west-southwest of Pittsburg. Johnston seemed relieved. "The battle has opened, gentlemen," he told the others. "It is too late to change our dispositions."[12]

One thing worried him, though. The Confederate delay might have allowed Buell to arrive in time to support Grant. And if Buell crossed the Tennessee River farther south at Hamburg Landing, he could come up the Hamburg-Savannah Road, ford shallow Lick Creek, and strike the Confederate attackers in their vulnerable right flank. To guard against that, Johnston sent five more infantry companies, led by Colonel George Maney of the First Tennessee, hurrying to Lick Creek to join the defenders already assigned there: a Tennessee rifle regiment and Forrest's cavalry.[13]

With the Confederate lookouts on the right reinforced, Johnston turned back toward the front. At the left-center of the intended battlefield, in Sherman's camps, stood Shiloh Church, an unimposing Methodist meetinghouse that an Ohio colonel wrongly judged to "belong to Baptists of the hard shell persuasion." Toward and to the right of this rough-hewn chapel, the wide waves of Johnston's Confederate tide—44,699 men, counting cavalry and artillery—finally began spilling forward en masse onto Grant's 41,330 Federals around Pittsburg Landing. It was 6:30 a.m.[14]

4

APRIL 6, FORENOON—GRANT

"I Think It's at Pittsburg"

Ever after, Grant and Sherman would insist it was no surprise. For the rest of their lives, they would point to the continual skirmishes with Confederate units for days beforehand as proof that they had seen the attack coming. They would add, with similar truth, that they made defensive adjustments almost up to the moment it began.[1]

But their Federals had not entrenched. To have done so would have bucked the judgment of General Charles Ferguson Smith, Grant's mentor-friend and one of the top officers of the prewar army. Gruff old Smith had scoffed at fortifying. Attack, indeed; he growled that he only wished the Confederates would. He may even have meant to invite them to. Before Grant arrived, Smith had planned to order Sherman's and Lew Wallace's divisions to that vulnerable west bank of the Tennessee, where the Corinth-congregating Confederates could get at them without having to cross the river. So Grant had gone ahead and ordered them there. "We can whip them to hell," Smith said.[2]

Sherman chose the Pittsburg Landing campsite for another credible reason that Smith doubtless considered. In this spring flood season, much of the ground along the Tennessee was inundated, but the road up from Pittsburg Landing rose onto a low, broad plateau that was comparatively dry and well drained.

Brigadier Bull Nelson's hard-marching division of Don Carlos Buell's army arrived at Grant's headquarters in Savannah, on the river's east side, on April 5. His mind on the offensive, Grant rebuffed Nelson's anxiety and directed him to bivouac on the east bank for a couple of days. Boats to ferry Nelson's men down to Hamburg Landing were scarce, he explained. No need to hurry.[3]

Despite Smith's cockiness, Grant had shown some intent to follow Major General Henry Halleck's cautionary directives. He ordered his chief engineer, Lieutenant Colonel James B. McPherson, to mark out a trench line at Pittsburg Landing. But when it turned out to run behind some bivouacs already established near water, Grant did not order the sites changed.

Other adjustments may have been in abeyance pending the arrival of Buell and Halleck. Halleck had ordered Grant to bring on no battle, so Grant and his division commanders ignored the increasing Confederate provocations. And more permanent fortifications were not thrown up, most likely, because doing so ran contrary to Grant's aggressive nature. He expected to move toward Corinth as soon as Halleck arrived.[4]

Thus, most of Grant's and Sherman's reasons for their professed lack of surprise were intellectually dishonest. They correctly maintained that the sight of Confederates at Pittsburg Landing on April 6 was not unexpected. The sight of so many, however, was.

Many Federal officers and men did not share the Smith-Grant confidence. Several subordinate Union colonels were as convinced that they were about to be attacked as Sherman claimed to doubt it.

Sherman scoffed at their concerns. The Confederates would never come out of their fortified base and attack the Federals in theirs, he asserted, echoing Grant and Smith. Getting angry, he went out of his way to humiliate the nervous colonels, telling one to "take your damn regiment back to Ohio" and court-martialing another. He insisted that the parties of Confederates were just reconnoitering.[5]

Union pickets sensed otherwise. Since April 3, they had seen growing numbers of enemy cavalry watching them from behind trees and bushes. Colonel Everett Peabody, brigade commander in the division to the left front of Sherman's, disobeyed an order from Brigadier General Benjamin M. Prentiss. Prentiss had told some Peabody pickets to pull back and not to be alarmed by the sound of widespread movements in the woods around them after dark on the night of April 5. Before dawn on April 6, Peabody

BATTLE OF SHILOH

sent out five companies to try to capture and interrogate some of the "prowling" Confederates.[6]

The party soon encountered the enemy. They traded volleys for an hour, but the Confederates were so numerous that the Federals pulled back, dragging dead and wounded, as day dawned. Prentiss meanwhile heard heavy firing growing louder and ordered his division into line, then hurried it a quarter mile forward. There, at about 6:30 a.m., just after meeting his retiring pickets, he ran head-on into the center of Albert Sidney Johnston's army.

Confederates and Federals began firing as fast as they could reload, but Prentiss was overmatched. Colonel Francis T. Quinn of the Twelfth Michigan Infantry saw an enemy line in his front stretching right and left, "and every hill-top" behind that line "was covered with them." The sight was more than daunting.[7]

Prentiss's men, new to combat, retreated to their camp, then through it. Dodging between tents, they lost formation, as well as many of their number, some falling to Confederate fire and more sprinting for the rear.

At about 7 a.m., Sherman, still skeptical, rode toward the increasing clamor. He was looking through his binoculars and deciding that this was indeed a sharp skirmish when Confederates burst from the undergrowth to his right and shot an aide dead beside him. Belatedly, he realized—and shouted—the truth: "We are attacked!" He threw up his right hand to shield himself and took a shot in it. Ordering Colonel Jesse Appler of the Fifty-third Ohio to stand his ground, Sherman galloped off for reinforcements.

Appler was the officer Sherman had told the day before to take his regiment back to Ohio. He now appeared eager to comply. Under assault by the Sixth Mississippi, Appler went to pieces. His troops were so decimating the Mississippians with cannon and musket fire that only a minority of the Sixth's 425 men remained unhurt, but Appler suddenly shouted, "Retreat and save yourselves." The Fifty-third Ohio broke and fled in disorder through the Fifty-seventh, which Sherman had just sent to Appler's aid. Some of the Fifty-third rallied and stayed on the field, along with—briefly—Appler. But soon, dismayed by his officers' refusal to obey his fearful commands, he fled.[8]

Despite Appler's personal skedaddle, the Ohioans drew a lot of blood. The Fifty-third and Fifty-seventh had managed to mangle two regiments commanded by Colonel Patrick R. Cleburne, the Irish immigrant and foster Arkansan destined to become perhaps the hardest-fighting infantry commander in the western Confederate armies. The bloodshed seems to have been overwhelmingly in the Ohioans' favor. Sherman later claimed Appler's line broke after losing but two enlisted men and no officers.[9]

—✦—

William T. Sherman had some excellent traits—high intelligence in particular—but a placid, steady nature was not one of them. This perhaps owed to his boyhood experience of his father's death, which shattered his world and thrust him into a foster family. That wrenching experience was reinforced in adulthood by a number of life's capricious twists of fate. He often seemed to lack self-confidence and, as if trying to shore it up, overcompensated with boisterous, often outrageous talk. His contemptuous dismissal of the threat of Confederate attack at Shiloh was typical.

In private, Sherman may not have been so sure there was no danger. His professed skepticism was perhaps a desperate attempt to quell his own growing apprehensions. Although he had spent thirteen years in the army, he had seen no antebellum combat. The Seminole War in Florida had been a simmering thing that afforded him no opportunity to bleed, shed blood, or experience battle, and during the Mexican War, he had served in California, even farther from the fighting.[10]

Once this new and much larger war began, though, Sherman showed that fear of losing his own life was not his problem. He had led men in combat at Bull Run, was grazed twice by bullets there, and had a horse killed under him. He trembled only for his country. He had long doubted the national will to reunite the states, as well as his—or anybody else's—capacity to do anything about the looming cataclysm. His problem was more one of ambivalence than fear. Although Southerners would come to hate his name, he felt affection for them. He despised abolitionists for tearing the nation apart, shared Dixie society's extreme racial animus, and thought Southerners and the South all but impossible to defeat.

Yet, he remained unionist to the bone. At the advent of secession, he had been in the second year of his prewar life's most fulfilling job as inaugural superintendent of the future Louisiana State University. But when Louisiana troops took over the Federal arsenal in Baton Rouge, he resigned. He felt beholden to the Union for his West Point education.[11]

Sherman had brought a division of "perfectly new" volunteers, as he called them, to these camps around Shiloh Church, and he had seen little in this war to assure him of their competence. He had watched mobs of volunteers flee the Confederate guns at Bull Run. Given command in the state of Kentucky, he had insisted he needed 200,000 such volunteers to prevent Confederates from overrunning the whole Midwest. The figure seemed huge so early in the war. When, as a result, newspaper headlines pronounced him insane, he requested to be relieved of the Kentucky assignment and was granted transfer. That bitter memory influenced him in the run-up to Shiloh. If he agreed with his fearful colonels, he told someone on April 5, "they'd say I was crazy again."

Nobody could call him that, though, when he agreed with the colonels the next morning.[12]

Around 7 a.m. the Confederates overran the Union camps "yipping and yelping," as one Federal remembered. Many of the erstwhile campers bolted. The hundreds of fugitives began a gradual exodus that would swell into the thousands as many fled as far as they could without drowning: to and under the overhanging banks of the Tennessee River.[13]

Grant's unreadiness for a wholesale assault did not stem from lassitude. For three weeks he had pushed to visit on the Confederates what they had come here to visit on him: destruction. While gathering intelligence about the Southerners massing at Corinth, he had dispatched an aide, Captain W. S. Hillyer, to St. Louis to beseech Halleck to let him assail Johnston's army before it was ready. Just that morning, April 6, Hillyer had returned. Grant's plea had been rejected out of hand. Bring on no battle, Halleck reiterated.[14]

Now, over an early breakfast at Savannah, Grant heard the fighting nine miles away. He had been awaiting Buell's arrival for a talk; otherwise, he would have left already for Pittsburg Landing, where he had planned to move his headquarters that day. On April 4, he had received word that the Senate had confirmed two of his subordinates, John McClernand and Lew Wallace, as major generals. That would make the grasping McClernand the ranking officer at Pittsburg Landing, surpassing Sherman, unless Grant went there himself. So Grant decided to do that. Buell, sulky as when he and Grant had met in Nashville in late February, had arrived in Savannah the previous evening, April 5. But he did not inform Grant, indicating continuing reluctance to coopperate.[15]

Buell had still not reported in when, a few minutes past 7:00, everybody at Grant's breakfast table lapsed into silence at the alarming sound coming from the southwest. Chief of Staff Joseph D. Webster stated the obvious. "That's firing." An orderly rushed in and said the sound was coming from upriver. Everybody went to the door. "Where is it?" Webster asked. "At Crump's or Pittsburg?"

"I think it's at Pittsburg," Grant said. He was on crutches; the ankle sprained in the horse fall in the thunderstorm thirty-six hours earlier was swollen and throbbing. He leaned against Webster to strap on his sword, and everybody headed for the steamboat *Tigress*. The craft's engines were already running in preparation for the staff's expected departure that morning.[16]

Before leaving, Grant wrote three messages, two to division chiefs of Buell's army. Bull Nelson, whom Grant had so casually told to stay on the Tennessee's east side, was now ordered to march down that bank to a point opposite Pittsburg Landing and ferry across from there. Brigadier General Thomas J. Wood should hurry his men to Savannah and march them onto Pittsburg-bound steamboats. The third dispatch informed Buell that Grant could not wait longer in Savannah for their meeting.[17]

Grant headed upriver probably between 7:15 and 7:30. Before 8:00, six miles north of Pittsburg, he ordered the *Tigress* to run in close to Crump's Landing. There Lew Wallace paced the deck of another boat. The two briefly conferred. Grant told Wallace to get his division ready; instructions would be coming.[18]

Likely between 8:00 and 8:30, *Tigress* nosed into Pittsburg Landing under a thundering din from the plain above. A handful of stragglers clustered nearby. The lame major general strapped his crutch rifle-like to his saddle and rode upward toward the roar of the battle. Finding two newly arrived regiments of Iowans, he ordered them into line above the bluff. They were to stop further stragglers from retreating and organize them into makeshift units to return to the fight.[19]

Grant next ordered wagons of ammunition collected to go to the front, then headed there himself. Arriving, he found his engineer, Lieutenant Colonel McPherson, holding the command together as well as possible. The situation was grim. The most advanced Union line—a brand-new, totally green division under Brigadier General Prentiss—had initially been located two miles southwest of Pittsburg Landing. Most of Prentiss's 5,400 men had fallen back nearly half that distance during the early morning, more than 1,000 of them becoming casualties. To the left, Brigadier General Stephen A. Hurlbut's division began pulling back and trying to slow the Confederate steamroller that thinned, then at around 9:00 stampeded, much of Prentiss's unit. To the right, Sherman and McClernand retreated too, but more deliberately.[20]

Then fate aided Prentiss's remaining 2,000 troops and the Hurlbut units they were falling back on. As they overran the Federal camps, the famished Confederates stopped to bolt food they found there. This gave the mingling Prentiss and Hurlbut units time to reform a remnant along a farm lane. Years of travel by animals and wagons had slightly depressed its bed, and it lay amid a thicket fronted and flanked by open fields. Later exaggeratingly dubbed the Sunken Road, this path linked McClernand on Prentiss's right and Sherman, even farther to the right, with Ohio, Illinois, Indiana, Iowa, and Missouri units to the left between Prentiss and the Tennessee River. The depression and its fierce defense would on this day earn another name honoring its flying bullets: the Hornet's Nest.[21]

People who saw Grant that morning detected no great concern. Having assured himself that the Pittsburg Landing attack was no feint preceding a knockout blow aimed at Crump's, he sent a message to Lew Wallace to bring his division from there. He also wrote another message to Bull Nelson: "You will hurry up your command as fast as possible. The boats will be in readiness to transport all troops of your command across the river. All looks well, but it is necessary for you to push forward as fast as possible." When aide William Rowley asked if things were not looking "squally," Grant demurred. "Well, not so very bad," he said. Wallace would surely be along soon.[22]

The Federal line was still receding at 10 a.m. as Grant rode to the right. There he found Sherman embattled, his right hand wrapped in bloody cloth. But Sherman was not his normal nervously excited self. Battle seemed to calm and focus him. With those of his men who had not run, he was trying to fight his way back to the church. He told Grant he needed more ammunition. Grant said wagonloads of it were coming and complimented the performance of Sherman's green troops.

Grant wheeled away to gallop to points more needful of personal direction. "I never deemed it important to stay long with Sherman," he would write afterward. He visited and revisited his other corps commanders and told them Lew Wallace's and Nelson's divisions were approaching. He ordered Prentiss in the center to hang on in the sunken lane "at all hazards" and personally helped somewhat to stabilize the still-retreating line. Parts of McClernand's, Sherman's, Prentiss's, Hurlbut's, and Brigadier General William H. L. Wallace's units—the Union's right and center—were taking a savage Confederate hammering but holding.[23]

The initial sight of a bloodied Sherman in the fray seems to have remained large in Grant's mind. His own efficiency and coolness under fire in the Mexican War had led one combat associate to describe him as a man of fire, so at home where bullets flew that he seemed to belong there. Now he perceived in Sherman, so radically unlike him in many other ways, another man of fire. His battle report would go out of its way to praise Sherman. This favorable impression on his commander could only have been deepened by messages like one Sherman gave to a courier that day: "Tell Grant if he has any men to spare I can use them; if not, I will do the best I can. We are holding them pretty well just now—pretty well—but it's hot as hell."[24]

5

APRIL 6, AFTERNOON—FORREST

"Under My Own Orders"

For hours Colonel Forrest fretted.

From behind the Confederate right along Lick Creek, he had heard the battle roaring to his left front all morning. But his assignment was only to help protect a ford where the road between Hamburg and Savannah crossed the creek; he was to warn headquarters of any sign of a flank attack by Buell. With Forrest's men rode three youths slightly younger than his youngest troopers: his fifteen-year-old son Willie and two comrades also in their mid-teens. A few days before the battle, Forrest had ridden for two days to the headquarters of General Leonidas Polk to find Willie congenial companionship: the sons of the Episcopal bishop of Tennessee and of Confederate general Daniel S. Donelson.[1]

At the sound of heavy firing, Colonel George Maney, the officer General Johnston had sent to the ford that morning, ordered Forrest to cross to the Lick's northwest bank. Maney gave similar orders to his five First Tennessee Infantry companies and to Colonel D. H. Cummings's Nineteenth Tennessee.

Forrest could only guess at what was happening farther northwest. During the morning, the Confederate left and right had driven forward more than a mile, pounding the Federal line into a horseshoe. The Union center—a ragtag collection of men from McClernand's, Sherman's, Prentiss's, Hurlbut's and William Wallace's commands who had not run for the river—hung on at the thicket-shrouded Sunken Road.

Confederate mistakes, hunger, and weariness aided the defenders. General Beauregard's plan, which spread Bragg's, Hardee's, Polk's, and Breckinridge's troops in successive waves across the whole front, guaranteed that the farther each line penetrated these woods, thickets, bogs, and areas of human resistance, the more it became mixed with the other lines. Control dissolved. The four corps commanders divided up portions of the front to regain their ability to supervise, but this took time. That was hardly the only problem. Their troops' haversacks had been emptied of rations the previous day, and many were sleep deprived from the nightmare march from Corinth and incessant picket duty. Famished and frazzled, they stopped to eat at the cook fires and tents of the overrun camps, giving the Federals time to regroup.[2]

More than a mile to the right rear, Forrest grew impatient. Time passed. Distant battle thunder increased. About 11 a.m., Maney sent him to recheck for evidence of Buell at cavalry stations southward on the Hamburg road. While he was gone, Maney decided Buell would not land at Hamburg, then exercised the discretion Johnston had given him. He marched to the fighting, taking his five companies of the First Tennessee and leaving the Nineteenth and Forrest's cavalry at the ford "to carry out their instructions existing before my presence with them." When Forrest returned, the Nineteenth, too, had vanished.[3]

Forrest became agitated. His mood could not have been helped by the arrival and quick departure of another unit. Beauregard had sent the Georgia Mountain Dragoons to the ford area for duty with Colonel Wirt Adams's cavalry regiment. A Major Brewster of General Breckinridge's staff had tried to guide the Dragoons across unfamiliar ground. The trek had taken them five miles. When they arrived and found that the Adams unit had left, Brewster seems to have wearied of guide duty. He suggested to the ranking Dragoon, Captain Isaac Avery, that the Georgians stay with Forrest. Avery refused; instead, he reported, he "proceeded at a hard gallop to the field" to overtake Adams. His brusque tone suggests he preferred the leadership of Adams—a distinguished Mississippi legislator, banker, and planter—to that of the comparatively unpolished Forrest.[4]

Avery's appearance at the ford was just one of many signs of concern about the Confederate right that morning. At 4 a.m., more than an hour before the Confederates began their attack, General Bragg had sent scouts to locate the Federal left. When they reported that it far overlapped the Confederate right, the high command sent more muscle in that direction, toward the Tennessee River. By around 10:00, Johnston and Beauregard had ordered several infantry brigades there.[5]

After the Georgia cavalry departed, Forrest again checked down the Hamburg Road. He also sent a courier after Maney to protest the unceremonious departure when it remained unknown whether Buell was coming from Hamburg. Maney was a Nashville attorney, a kind of man with whom Forrest had never felt very brotherly. He plainly had taken umbrage now at Maney's seeming disregard. As soon as Forrest returned from again finding no Federals, he ordered his horsemen formed for battle and made them an abrupt speech.

"Boys," he shouted, "do you hear that rattle of musketry and the roar of artillery?"

"Yes, yes," they yelled.

"Do you know what it means? It means that our friends and brothers are falling by hundreds at the hands of the enemy—and we are *here guarding a damn creek*! We did not enter the service for such work, and the reputation of this regiment does not justify our commanding officer in leaving us here while we are needed elsewhere. Let's go and help them. What do you say?"

"Yes, yes!" they roared again.

Shortly after receiving the nagging note from Forrest, Maney learned that Beauregard had ordered all units forward into the fight. Soon, another message arrived: the Nineteenth Tennessee and Forrest's cavalry were moving up behind him.[6]

Forrest pushed his troopers into a gallop up the Savannah road. They had gone a mile, maybe more, when they came to a fork. To the left, in the direction of the loudest firing, a road ran westward from Pittsburg Landing to the town of Purdy. Forrest turned onto it looking for Maney, wishing to report for further duty—likely coolly—to his most recent immediate superior.

But he could not. Maney had found his own immediate commander, Brigadier Frank Cheatham, who had rushed him into battle. Maney led a brigade charge against Federal batteries pounding the Confederate right-center from the left side of Benjamin M. Prentiss's retreating line. Maney's charge had just been bloodily repulsed when Forrest arrived a little past 2 p.m. He found himself and his men targeted by the Federal batteries Maney's charge had not dislodged.

Forrest apparently suggested to Cheatham a joint charge across the field. The general, a Tennessee planter and Mexican War veteran whose brother was mayor of Nashville, likely regarded this suggestion from an unbloodied colonel as presumptuous after the vain attempt just concluded. Cheatham said no. Forrest protested that his men could not stay where they were, under heavy fire. If Forrest charged, Cheatham replied, he would do it under his own orders.

"Then I'll do it," Forrest said. "I'll charge under my own orders."[7]

Forrest and his men galloped toward the eastern end of the Hornet's Nest, which the Federals already had stoutly defended against piecemeal Confederate assaults. His troopers passed unharmed through two artillery volleys before a third killed three of them and four horses with one cannonball. But Forrest kept on, assailing Union brigadier Jacob Lauman's brigade of Stephen A. Hurlbut's division at the point where Hurlbut's right connected with Prentiss. To Forrest's own right, the Twenty-sixth Alabama Infantry wanted to advance, and "the gallant Colonel Forrest offered his support," the Alabamans' commander would report. But underbrush slowed or halted Forrest's horses. The infantrymen went on to grab some spiked, abandoned Ohio cannons before heavy fire forced them back into a field. Forrest withdrew into the same field.[8]

As Forrest had charged the Hornet's Nest, the Confederates incurred a hard loss farther to the right. General Albert Sidney Johnston—rallying reluctant Tennessee, Missouri, and Arkansas units—had already had a boot sole ripped loose by one bullet and sustained wounds by shrapnel in the hip and another bullet in the thigh. His horse had been bloodied. Most important, he had taken another shot he may not have noticed. It cut an artery in a leg numbed by an old dueling wound. Having sent his surgeon off to care for wounded men of both sides in an adjacent hollow, the Confederate western commander fell and quickly bled to death.[9]

Forrest did not stay long in the field with the Twenty-sixth Alabama. Major Gilbert Rambaut, a Forrest commissary officer, would recall that his colonel got orders to screen a battery and move it up—likely to the left, into the front line of cannon gathering to blast Prentiss out of the Sunken Road. The troopers then "rested for a while." Probably between 4 and 5 p.m., "there came an order from our right to bring on the cavalry."[10]

The Hornet's Nest defense was collapsing. Hammered by fifty-three cannon massed in two positions, the long Union line that had hung on for six hours through several piecemeal assaults at various points finally contracted around the Sunken Road and broke. By then, attacks right and left had pushed the ends of the salient back so far that they nearly met. Under a charge on the center led by George Maney, some Federals inside the salient began pulling back. Others hung on, and still others turned to sprint to escape the closing trap. Most of the sprinters got crowded into an area soon known as Hell's Hollow.[11]

The extent of the carnage was unprecedented in America. The advancing attackers could hardly step on earth, rather than fallen comrades, as they swarmed over the ground in front of the Sunken Road. At the road and past it, most of the corpses were Union. Around this time a ball entered the right side of the head of Federal division commander and Fort Donelson veteran Brigadier General William H. L. Wallace, who was commanding here. It exited his left eye. He lived, in and out of consciousness and delirium, for four days.

Prentiss now saw that further resistance invited annihilation. He urged his men to surrender. White flags appeared in front of Confederate infantry commanders on the attackers' right, and they sent for various cavalry in the area to take the droves of prisoners to the rear. In the left-center, where Forrest now was, resistance continued a few minutes longer before Prentiss handed his sword to a subordinate of General Polk. Polk ordered the cavalry to pursue "such of the enemy as were fleeing."[12]

Forrest pushed his troopers into a gallop northeastward. Union troops dropped their weapons as the horsemen perforated their dissolving lines, but the Confederates kept going to the Union rear, getting between the Federals and the Tennessee River. Confederate cavalry had headed off a large body of the Hornet's Nest's escaping defenders. "From the number of men who had surrendered," Major Rambaut would remember, "I was of the impression that our forces had captured the whole army."[13]

According to Prentiss, who was among them, the captives numbered 2,200, including many wounded. On the right, cavalry started them toward the rear, where Alabama infantrymen were to march them to Corinth.[14]

The mopping-up process took irreplaceable time that the Confederates would soon need. Rambaut remembers that firing ceased on Forrest's part of the field for "probably two hours." While likely exaggerated, Rambaut's memory illustrates that the lull was prolonged.

Forrest apparently left to others the job of rounding up unresisting captives and rushed on looking for further damage to do farther on. His and some other cavalry—Rambaut among them—hurried to the bank of the Tennessee south of Pittsburg Landing. Rambaut recalled crawling to the river's edge and looking over to see two Federal gunboats that had been firing at an unseen enemy one hundred feet above them. The sailors and their officers pressed into the boats' bows, trying to discern what was happening up there.[15]

To his left, toward Pittsburg Landing, Forrest noticed something else: the Union defense between him and the landing was all but nonexistent. He took his men in that direction and, according to Rambaut, soon caught sight, from the heights to the south of the landing, of the chaos in the Union rear—"wagons, horses and artillery in the river and crowding the banks, while the men were endeavoring to escape by climbing up the sides of the transports." Forrest began skirmishing and sent a message back to Polk that a strong and fast advance on the right would drive the Federals into the river.[16]

This window of opportunity, if it was one, closed. Near 6 p.m., Bragg, commanding on the right, ordered the move that Forrest had requested of Polk perhaps as much as an hour earlier: a charge by the 4,000 or so Confederates on Bragg's part of the field "to drive the enemy into the river," in the words of General James Chalmers. General Jones Withers, even though some of his units had yet to receive ammunition, sent his whole division forward into a deep ravine, the ammunition-less advancing with fixed bayonets. Above stood the final hill, from atop which they could charge down onto Pittsburg Landing with its milling thousands of Union fugitives.

But it was no go. "In attempting to mount the last ridge," Chalmers reported, "we were met by a fire from a whole line protected by infantry and assisted by shells from the gunboats." Forty-one cannon aided by infantry units—the Sixth Iowa, for one—had rushed in from the collapsing Union lines for a last stand along the road leading down to the river. The thrown-together mass now erupted in thunderous flame. Bragg and Withers sent for help and ordered Withers's men forward into the hail of Federal lead. But Polk, to the left, ordered the troops in the ravine to retreat in his direction, away from the river, to avoid the concentrated fire. Chalmers apparently missed this order: "Our men struggled vainly to ascend the hill, which was very steep, making charge after charge without success."[17]

Forrest, too, was in the ravine. Polk had already ordered the cavalry to comparative cover there. But Forrest's men, now dismounted, joined Chalmers, whose brigade was in its sixth head-on clash of the day and still struggling to comply with Bragg's now obsolete order to advance. But the Confederates were "too much exhausted to storm the batteries on the hill," Chalmers reported, although they "continued to fight until night closed hostilities on both sides." Beauregard ordered them to camp beyond easy range of gunboat fire.[18]

Forrest was alarmed, and not just that the victory had not been finalized. He looked around in vain for Willie. His fifteen-year-old son and the boy's two young companions had been with him all day—until now.[19]

6

APRIL 6, AFTERNOON—GRANT

"I Haven't Despaired of Whipping Them Yet"

L ittle had gone right for Grant in the morning, and most of the afternoon was worse.

The Union's only luck lay in the delivery of the Confederate assault. Jerky and piecemeal, it repeatedly balked and wavered as commanders on the ground reworked Beauregard's unwieldy battle plan. Ill-trained, hungry volunteer troops had to cross terrain gashed by ravines, thickets, swamps, flooded creeks, fierce Federal resistance, and battlefield horror unprecedented in America.

The Confederates were determined though. During the morning, Federals with Sherman and McClernand, northwest of Prentiss and Hurlbut, had their right hammered loose from its Owl Creek anchor. They fell back toward the mobbed banks of the Tennessee and Snake Creek, into which Owl Creek emptied just north of Pittsburg Landing. McClernand requested help, and Grant sent the Iowa regiments he had drafted to stem the straggling. More panicked runaways swelled the horde extending north from the landing.[1]

Noon came and went. There had been no word, let alone sighting, of the reinforcements Grant had ordered forward that morning. Bull Nelson's division of Buell's army, supposedly marching down the east bank of the Tennessee from Savannah, and Lew Wallace's division from Grant's own force, summoned at 11 a.m. for what was presumably a two-hour march from the Crump's Landing area, remained absent. Grant could not know it, but the third Federal division he had ordered forward, Brigadier

Thomas Wood's, was still at Savannah. Grant had directed it to board boats there, but it had arrived to find none.

The outlook kept worsening. Grant sent off a tense message intended for Nelson. It sounded very like another he had written seeking aid from a gunboat captain during his hour of deepest crisis at Fort Donelson. Hurry, he wrote Nelson. The army had been under "spirited" attack, and arrival of "fresh troops on the field now would have a powerful effect, both by inspiring our men and disheartening the enemy." Nelson should lose no time in crossing the river, "leaving all your baggage on the east bank." Early arrival "might possibly save the day for us."[2]

The first reinforcement to arrive at Pittsburg Landing, around 1 p.m., was Major General Buell with a single staff member. Buell knew the urgency of the situation, having intercepted the dispatch urging Nelson to hurry up, but his arrival turned out to be not even symbolic succor.[3]

The two generals, their relationship tense under the best of circumstances, now faced each other in the heat of crisis. They met on Grant's steamboat, the *Tigress*, at the edge of the Tennessee River sometime be-

MAJOR GENERAL DON CARLOS BUELL

tween 1 and 2 p.m. Buell did not appear downcast to see his recently elevated superior in trouble. Grant, perhaps to break the ice, showed Buell his saber scabbard, which had been dented by a shell fragment earlier in the day. The scabbard had prevented a serious wound. Buell later wrote disdainfully that he "took little notice." He asked Grant about the state of the battle and requested that steamboats be sent back to Savannah to pick up Major General George Crittenden's just-arriving division. Then, a disputed story goes, Buell eyed the 5,000 to 7,000 crazed fugitives crowding the landing and asked what arrangements Grant had made to retreat. Grant replied that he had made none. "I haven't despaired of whipping them yet," he reportedly said.[4]

That sentence would become part of Grant lore. Buell maintained years later that it was never uttered, claiming that loyal, and sometimes creative, Grant aide John Rawlins had invented the purported exchange. Buell would add that on this day, he saw nothing of Grant's supposedly characteristic steeliness. Buell's observation may be partly correct, at least regarding the view he took of Grant at the time. Though possibly an attempt to overcome reticence in the face of Buell's coldness, Grant's showing him the damaged scabbard does seem boyishly digressive from the crisis around them. Whatever its cause, it made Grant seem rattled, an impression Buell was glad to receive.

Buell's suggestion of retreat may appear unnecessary, given that his own army was on its way, but Buell knew something Grant didn't. For several hours, Buell had held at Savannah the very division of Nelson's that Grant had ordered to hurry to the battlefield. Having no idea of the situation's urgency, Buell only released Nelson to start down the Tennessee's east bank when Buell and his chief of staff boarded a battlefield-bound steamboat at noon or after. A Nelson subordinate reported starting at 1 p.m. And while Grant had ordered Nelson to get a local guide, none was available. Nelson had to send a cavalry detail just to find a route down the low, partially flooded east bank—all of which cost Nelson more valuable time.

At Savannah, Buell had bided his time, watching for transport boats he thought Grant might send back from Pittsburg Landing. Like other Federals at the Union headquarters, Buell appeared little concerned. In his sickbed at Savannah, old General Charles Ferguson Smith laughed off the battle sounds as "a hot picket skirmish," and a naval officer guessed it was just gunboats peppering the riverbank to prevent positioning of Confederate artillery.

But while Buell had tarried, the men Nelson sent to scout out a route, having gotten nearer the din, had become filled with anxiety. They returned at noon from a ride so frantic it had killed some of their horses. They had found no route. A local finally told Nelson of another road. It would accommodate infantry and cavalry, the man said, but not artillery or wagons.[5]

Buell had finally loosed Nelson and headed toward Pittsburg Landing on a fast steamer. On the way, he met another craft racing north with Grant's urgent message to Nelson. And before Buell reached the landing, he saw Union fugitives swimming Snake Creek to put it between them and the battle. Habitually defensive minded and now surrounded by runaways bawling disaster, Buell likely wondered if Grant could hold until Nelson arrived. So Buell possibly did make an inquiry about withdrawal. Grant's memoirs say the scene at Pittsburg Landing probably "impressed General Buell with the idea that a line of retreat would be a good thing just then." But, he added, "the distant rear of an army engaged in battle is not the best place from which to judge correctly what is going on in front."[6]

"I haven't despaired of whipping them yet." This would have been the perfect afternoon for despair. Despite his higher rank, Grant's control over Buell and Buell's units was nominal at best. But the officer who gave him the greatest anxiety was his own subordinate, Lew Wallace. The Indiana governor's son and his division of more than 5,000 effectives remained absent, despite their orders to rush to the battlefield.

Wallace seemed to have vanished. The newly appointed major general—his three brigades scattered at least nine miles north of the battlefield, at Crump's Landing and points three and five miles west of there—had first been summoned as soon as Grant reached Pittsburg shortly after their early-morning conference near Crump's Landing. Grant had called for Wallace again at noon and yet again at 2:30. But the first order did not arrive until 11 a.m., and at their face-to-face meeting that morning, Grant, with typical optimism, had given Wallace no hint of a problem. So instead of marching his westward units back to Crump's and bringing his force on to Pittsburg by the road along the river, Wallace fed his men a fast lunch and marched for Shiloh Church. Around 2 p.m., Grant aide William Rowley arrived and said the camps around the church had been overrun. Wallace—only now learning Grant was in trouble—turned back to the river road. But instead of putting his erstwhile rear in front, he marched his more-experienced advance units through the rear ones so they would reach the fighting first.[7]

Mid-afternoon passed with no sign of Wallace. On the Federal right, Sherman and McClernand had countercharged in the late morning during one of the Confederate lulls and retaken nearly a half mile of ground. In the afternoon, though, they had to give it back again. By 3 p.m. they occupied much the same position to which they had been pushed at midday.[8]

Around 4 p.m., Hurlbut's southern end of the Hornet's Nest line began to falter. The Confederates had transferred much of their muscle from the Federal right in front of Sherman and McClernand to the center and left, and Grant faced the mounting possibility that Lew Wallace would not arrive. He put his chief of staff, Colonel Joseph D. Webster, to gathering artillery and arraying it on the ridge just south of the road leading down to Pittsburg Landing. Soon forty-one guns overlooked a hundred-foot gorge on the Federal left. But, for the moment, the guns nearest the river were nearly naked of supporting infantry.

At the Union line's opposite end, two regiments from Missouri and Ohio reanchored Sherman's right and clung to the Snake Creek Bridge, the sole remaining avenue by which Lew Wallace could reach the battlefield. Then, in the mid-afternoon Grant had to order even the Ohio regiment to the left to aid Hurlbut. At 4:30 he revisited the landing to plead with the straggling mob to return to the fight. When they refused, he loosed cavalry to try to drive them there with the flats of their sabers, to no avail.[9]

Confederate myopia saved Grant. Beauregard wasted hours blasting the defenders out of the Hornet's Nest instead of pouring past their flanks and surrounding them. At 5 p.m., as Confederate cannon finally blew the last of Prentiss's and Hurlbut's men out of the Sunken Road, Union reinforcements began arriving. Men of Colonel Jacob Ammen's brigade of Nelson's division, begrimed with mud from the swamps they had had to cross on their overland scramble from Savannah, burst from the woods on the far side of the Tennessee. They still had to cut a road to the bank, and no transport steamers were yet on that side of the river to meet them, but at least they were finally there.

Nelson himself did not stand on ceremony. A huge, profane former naval officer, he commandeered some merchant steamboats that were hugging the east bank to escape Confederate fire. Taking an initial boatload of two hundred Indiana troops, Nelson crossed the river, ordering the craft's captain to steam straight for the skulkers in the water. He landed about 5:20 p.m. and accorded similar sneers to the fugitives ashore, directing his mounted officers to descend the gangplank with sabers drawn and "trample these bastards into the mud." Continuing to bellow, he brought his three companies up the landing road onto the ridge overlooking the ravine. There, at Buell's order, they took places around the weakly supported cannons that Webster was hurrying into line. On the ridge, Nelson conferred with Grant and Buell. A cannonball interrupted the conversation by taking the head off a Grant aide, splattering Grant with brains.[10]

At 6 p.m., dusk settled over the bloodiest battlefield American history had yet seen. Around 7,000 Federals lay killed and wounded, maimed and slain in every possible manner and lying and dying in contorted heaps, while another 10,000 wailed in panic at the waterside. But Grant had not lost. His final line of cannon and infantry was a thin ribbon stretching not much more than a mile from the ridge to the west of the landing out onto the Savannah-Hamburg Road toward the Snake Creek Bridge. It was two miles behind where his troops had begun the day, but it had breasted the last fitful Confederate assaults. To a newspaperman who seemed fearful that the Confederates might overrun them in the dark, Grant said no, the enemy could not break their lines, which were finally swelling with reinforcements. He added a sentence that likely made the journalist blink.

"Tomorrow," he said, "we shall attack . . . with fresh troops and drive them."[11]

Grant apparently had seen Buell only twice that afternoon, possibly by choice. The Army of the Ohio commander was not very helpful. Sherman later claimed Buell had acted true to his typically cautious nature

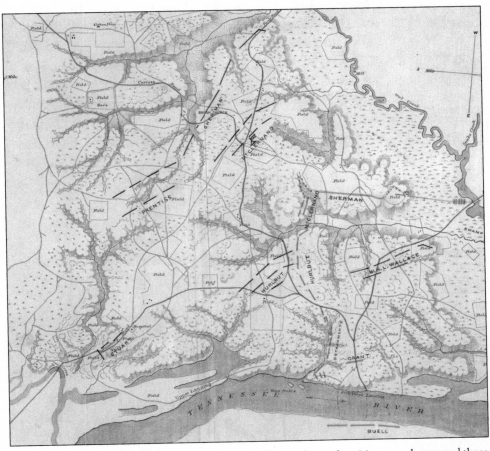

SHILOH'S FIRST DAY: This period map reflects (1) Sherman's initial position near the top and those to which he and his troops fell back during the day; (2) the Sunken Road near "Prentiss"; (3) Forrest's first post at Lick Creek Ford near the bottom left; and (4) Grant's final line just left of the road up from the river landing and Forrest's final position facing the gorge just left of Grant's line.

and resisted bringing any more of his army than Nelson's lead elements across the Tennessee because of the dicey "looks of things."[12]

But some of what Grant did see of his aloof, contemptuous fellow general reflected the differences between the two men. Grant later claimed that after their first brief meeting around 2 p.m., he noticed Buell shouting at the skulkers along the river and threatening to have the gunboats shell them. Grant's contrasting actions—eventually begging the fugitives to fight and then rounding them up with cavalry—separate him at this point in the war from Buell and most of the Union high command. Whereas Buell felt distrust and contempt for volunteers, Grant did not consider blasting them with cannons. His recent rank notwithstanding, he was more like them than like Buell—and he knew it. He could imagine what it must have been like to witness a battle as large as Shiloh through the eyes of men who had never participated in armed combat before. "Most of these men afterward proved themselves as gallant as any of those who saved the battle from which they had deserted," Grant would write.[13]

At Shiloh, Grant could only intuit, rather than know, that the Federal deserters would later prove their worth. But his postwar spelling out of the disparity between his own and Buell's views of volunteers reflects a lifelong philosophy. In a later article he suggested that Buell, looking down on volunteers as somehow different from professional soldiers, "did not distinguish sufficiently" what the difference consisted of. Wartime volunteer soldiers were "men who risked life for a principle, and often men of . . . independence of character." Peacetime professionals, as a rule, were "only men who could not do as well in any other occupation."

He knew, of course, what he was talking about. That last line perfectly described his antebellum self.[14]

7

APRIL 6, NIGHT—FORREST

"We'll Be Whipped Like Hell"

Forrest ignored Beauregard's order to the frazzled Confederates to rest until daylight. He was not a man to sleep much until a fight ended. In cheerless darkness haunted by the agonies of thousands of wounded, he became a nocturnal hunter. First, he had to find Willie.

Lieutenant William Montgomery Forrest apparently retained, in his mid-teens, some impetuous, unsoldierly boyishness. Now he and the two teenaged companions his father had procured for him some days earlier—progeny of Episcopal bishop James H. Otey, a fellow resident of Memphis, and Brigadier General Daniel S. Donelson, the Tennessee legislature's recent Speaker of the House—were missing in this colossal battle, perhaps separated from Forrest's staff during the dash to the river following General Prentiss's surrender at the Hornet's Nest.

Forrest searched in vain; the boys ultimately showed up on their own. They turned over to the provost marshal a few Federal prisoners—skulkers, surely—whom they had captured after charging them with blazing shotguns in a ravine near the river. So the boys were safe, the relieved colonel could tell Willie's mother.[1]

Forrest was a family man in the clannish way of rural Americans or Old Country immigrants. There were a lot of Forrests, and they were close. Around the time the Shiloh colonel turned twenty-one, his uncle Jonathan provided the sharp young farmer his entrée into the outside world: a junior partnership in the uncle's modest mercantile, livery, and livestock-trading business in Hernando, Mississippi. Forrest eventually offered a similar leg up to his younger brothers. The closest to him in age, John, partially paralyzed in the Mexican War, ran the Memphis slave jail that was the base of the Forrest business. The other brothers—Bill, Aaron, Jesse, and Jeffrey—also apparently worked in the firm, Bill in St. Louis and the others in Memphis or in its satellite office downriver in Vicksburg. The youngest sibling, Jeffrey, twenty-three at the start of the war, had lived for much of his youth in Forrest's home, reared alongside his nephew, Willie.[2]

It was likely more than the custom of the time that motivated Forrest, the eldest brother, to take so many siblings under his wing. Nathan Bedford Forrest had a twin sister who did not survive to adulthood. Nothing he said about his sister remains, but she was named Frances, or Fanny, after a maternal aunt. It seems significant that Forrest named his own daughter Fanny. (That daughter, like his sister, died young; fever killed her at age six.) The relationship between male and female twins is thought to include something of protector and protected; the male losing his twin can be left with a void and tend to seek others to protect. Forrest acted that way, and not just within his family. After shepherding his mother and siblings following the death of his father and drawing a gun in behalf of his uncle on the Hernando town square, he became constable in Hernando and, within a few more years, a rising and similarly bellicose defender of Memphians in need. Twice in the spring and summer of 1857 alone, the *Memphis Daily Appeal* cited him as a member of small municipal committees to dissuade and dispel lynch mobs that formed to avenge the murder of a Memphis businessman by a gambler.[3]

If Forrest's relationship to a dead twin sister explains some of his motivations, so may his business career. He advanced from glorified sharecropper to self-proclaimed millionaire in less than two decades. In an antebellum agricultural way, he seems to have embodied in significant measure the traits of rags-to-riches Northern industrial titans—the robber barons of the later part of the century. These tended to be puritanical and pious, discreet in their private lives, and well controlled, lusting mostly after money rather than sex. Most rose from childhood poverty, which made them serious in mind and demeanor. The ubiquitous Protestant

Bible inculcated self-discipline and counseled Old Testament ruthlessness, lack of trust, familial insularity, trickery, and the supreme moral worth of thrift, drive, and avoidance of waste.[4]

Forrest resembled this robber baron type much more so than not. Dozens of Confederates who rode with and knew him before and after the war characterized him as sympathetic and genial, severe when necessary, temperate, and possessing "no small vices." He was, wrote one, "not given to levity or common-place small talk, but was frank, candid, and sincere." His temper, on the other hand, was not well controlled. Under stress, his language was legendarily intemperate. And he had one vice that some accounted large: gambling big sums on cards, even bad cards, fearlessly bluffing opponents. In business, he was a loner, restlessly changing partners as his fortune grew. But his employees or junior partners, being family members, tended to be retained.[5]

For a man on America's southwestern frontier, Forrest was unusually disciplined. He shunned not only tobacco but whisky. He had no time for frivolity or hangovers. Except for gambling and high-stakes trading of real estate and human property, he had a marked degree of frugality, a habit he likely learned as much from making do with little on the farm as from the family Bible. Despite his tendency toward profanity, he showed respect for men of God. Without joining a church, he attracted to his ranks the ministers of several and encouraged them to preach and to say grace over meals in his camps. He often credited his survival of myriad combats to the prayers of his wife and his mother.[6]

<hr />

When Willie and his young friends returned from their shotgun exploit in the Shiloh ravine, they may have mentioned seeing or hearing a commotion down near the river. Or maybe what happened next proceeded solely from Forrest's own restless drive to always know what was happening.

Ignoring the onset of night and a dismal, general rain, he ordered scouts to don captured Union overcoats and sneak behind Federal lines near the river. They returned with bad news. Arriving steamboats were disgorging large numbers of fresh Federal troops at Pittsburg Landing, swelling the ranks of the milling fugitives gathered there.[7]

Forrest assigned his troops to bivouac that night in the camps that Stephen A. Hurlbut and William H. L. Wallace had abandoned on the Confederate right. The nearest general officer with whom Forrest had had most recent contact was Brigadier James R. Chalmers of Mississippi, whose infantry he had aided in the sunset push against the ridge crowned with the row of Federal cannon. When, on orders from headquarters, troops to the left of him began pulling back into the abandoned Federal camps for the night, Chalmers, farthest to the right, was last to go. He bivouacked near the Federal lines.[8]

Beauregard, whose plans had so complicated and delayed the Confederate advance, had been ill for weeks and was near exhaustion. Late in the day, he had heard from officers in nearby Alabama that General Buell's column had been diverted toward Huntsville. At about 9 p.m., he also heard that Grant was evacuating Pittsburg Landing. The latter report, possibly based on inaccurate conjecture about steamboats ferrying Buell's troops into Pittsburg Landing, came from a man who had shown a capacity to be cavalier in such matters. Chief Engineer Jeremy Gilmer was already due some of the blame for not placing heavy cannons at Fort Heiman opposite Fort Henry, an omission that probably cost the Confederates the Henry battle. Gilmer also did not push Nashville to fortify itself, leaving it indefensible after the fall of Fort Donelson.[9]

Gilmer's intelligence jibed with the report from Alabama. True, some of Buell's troops were headed for Huntsville, but only one division. Other information was deliberately false, fed to the Confederates by their prisoners. General Bragg wrote his wife that the captured General Prentiss, who knew from Grant that Buell's army and Lew Wallace's division were on their way, indicated to Beauregard that the Federals were skedaddling across the Tennessee River. Beauregard, Bragg told his spouse, "tho't it best no doubt to spare our men and allow them to go."[10]

Forrest, however, had just received eyewitness information that the Federals were not attempting to escape. Rather, they were arriving from across and down the Tennessee in forbidding numbers. Even as Beauregard interrogated Prentiss, the Federal reinforcements were shoving aside thousands of riverbank skulkers and fattening Grant's lines at the landing.

Around midnight Forrest awoke Chalmers with word of the Federal reinforcements. Chalmers, a diminutive, Charleston-educated Mississippi district attorney and son of an influential antebellum politician, may not have been happy about it. Forrest asked where he could find Beauregard or corps commanders Braxton Bragg and William Hardee. Chalmers professed ignorance and asked what information Forrest had, "if any." With patent directness, Forrest barked what his scouts had seen. He added his view that the whole Confederate army needed to resume its attack immediately and drive the half-disorganized Federals into the river—or retreat like rabbits. Otherwise, he added, "we'll be whipped like hell." Chalmers told him to find someone of higher rank.[11]

Forrest tried to do that. Around 1 a.m. he found Breckinridge and General Hardee perhaps a half mile northwest of his camp, but his persistence produced little satisfaction. Hardee, celebrated author of the preeminent Civil War tactics manual, was even less helpful than Chalmers. Hardee obviously did not think Forrest's report was worth being awakened for; he probably had heard at headquarters that Buell was headed to Alabama. He told Forrest to find Beauregard. But even though he himself had reported to Beauregard earlier that evening in Sherman's abandoned tent a quarter mile away, Hardee seems, for whatever reason, not to have given Forrest any specifics on how to get there.[12]

So, in the woods and thickets, the cold downpour, and darkness slashed regularly by lightning and gunboat fire, Forrest never found headquarters. Anybody trying to find anybody without exact instructions in this place on this night likely could not have done it. Forrest at least found Breckinridge and Hardee, which made him luckier than Colonel Robert P. Trabue, commanding Breckinridge's First Brigade. Trabue reported that he rode from dark until 11 p.m. trying to find any general at all to report to, then sent an aide riding for the rest of the night on the same mission, with no success—and Trabue, unlike Forrest, was in the Shiloh Church–Sunken Road corridor where Beauregard, Bragg, Breckinridge, and Hardee all had bedded down. On this night the Confederate command structure was in the dark in more ways than one.[13]

Forrest went back to his camp and at 2 a.m. sent out more scouts. They returned with the same news: hordes of fresh Federals continued to swell

Grant's lines. Again Forrest sought out generals Chalmers and Hardee, with similar results. Hardee told him to go back to his unit and "keep up a strong, vigilant picket line."[14]

Forrest gave up a couple of hours before dawn. Hardee did not notify Beauregard of Forrest's news, and neither Hardee nor Chalmers mentioned the cavalryman's visits in their official reports. Chalmers, for his part, only recalled them a quarter century later.[15]

8

APRIL 6, NIGHT—GRANT

"Lick 'Em Tomorrow"

At dusk, Grant knew he had survived. Within another hour, he knew something else that only an extraordinarily bellicose mind could have comprehended. Although 7,000 of his men had been killed, wounded, or captured, he was going to win.

With darkness falling, Lieutenant Colonel James B. McPherson asked if they should plan a retreat. No, Grant said. He was going to launch a dawn attack "and whip them." He explained to another subordinate, "The enemy has done all he can do today. Tomorrow morning, with General Lew Wallace's division and fresh troops of the Army of the Ohio, now crossing the river, we will soon finish him up."[1]

As bizarre as this must have sounded, it was typical Grant: dogged optimism based in hard reality. At 7:15 p.m. Wallace's 6,000 men slogged in from their roundabout hike. Bull Nelson's 6,000 had been piling off steamboats ferrying them across the Tennessee since an hour or more before that. Around 9:00 another Buell division, Major General Thomas Crittenden's, began arriving on steamboats from Savannah. A total of 20,000 fresh Union troops would be on hand the next morning. Many of the new arrivals, it is true, were under Buell's command, but Grant believed—and, given Buell's demeanor, doubtless hoped—that with the Confederates unreinforced and fought-out, Wallace's men would be all he needed.

What Buell did with his own army, which was forming for battle to the left of Grant's, Grant likely did not know. Buell similarly concerned himself with his own army; he did not look upon Grant "as my commander," he

MAJOR GENERAL LEW WALLACE

later wrote. Grant plainly had had his fill of Buell's lordliness. After dark, he made personal visits to all but one of his division commanders—and none of Buell's—and ordered them to "throw out heavy lines of skirmishers the next morning" at first light. The division commander he did not visit was Lew Wallace, whom both he and Lieutenant Colonel McPherson could not locate and who apparently could not find Grant. Grant seemingly did not confer at all with Buell, whose men were filing in on the undermanned Federal left, on the ridge overlooking the ravine.[2]

The night dragged. Grant's ankle throbbed. "The drenching rain would have precluded the possibility of sleep without this additional cause," he wrote. About 10 p.m. the downpour set in. He refused to find shelter on the *Tigress* after this hellish day. He did consider entering the log house at the landing but found it had become a hospital. Choosing not to attempt to sleep as surgeons sawed arms and legs off screaming men ("the sight was more unendurable than encountering the enemy's fire," he recalled), he returned to the dripping semishelter of a tree.[3]

Near midnight, Sherman encountered him there. Grant's collar was up, his hat brim low. He held a lantern, and his teeth were clenched on a cigar of the type admirers had sent him since Fort Donelson. The rain was pouring, and lightning flashes and rolling thunder competed with the fire and crash of salvoes from the gunboats in the river.

Sherman was there to suggest putting the river between themselves and the Confederates. He had followed the order to prepare his men for a dawn offensive and found it nearly impossible. The troops were dispirited, hopeless, mentally beaten. But Grant's dogged positivism gave Sherman pause. "Well, Grant," he began more tentatively, "we've had the devil's own day, haven't we?"

"Yes," Grant said. Then he quickly blocked the conversational path down which Sherman planned to head: "Lick 'em tomorrow, though."[4]

Grant explained. Their situation resembled that on the final day at Fort Donelson, after a Confederate onslaught raged from dawn into the afternoon. The Confederates had taken much ground but had not pushed through to triumph. Victory had hung in the balance between two exhausted armies, Grant said, adding that he had realized then that the one which retook the initiative would win. So he had attacked—and won. The same would happen here.[5]

9

APRIL 7—FORREST

Prophet Vindicated

Three hours after his second rousting of General Hardee, Forrest saw his early-morning prophecy begin to materialize.

On the Confederate right, his pickets—mostly clad in blue overcoats they had scavenged from the overrun Union camps—captured about fifty Federals in the rainy predawn. The captives confirmed what Forrest and his scouts had known since midnight: Buell's men had been coming ashore at Pittsburg Landing all night.

Around 5:30 a.m. Forrest himself was with the pickets as Bull Nelson's Federals counterattacked. Fighting, the cavalrymen withdrew toward the former Federal camps in what was now the Confederate army's right-center.[1]

Behind Forrest's retreating force, Confederate commanders dealt with disarray. Overnight they had made the same error that other Confederate commanders had made against Grant at Fort Donelson. They assumed they had won. So they pulled back and postponed an attempt to reorganize their intermixed commands until daylight. It was a tall job. They had sustained some 8,000 casualties. At least another 10,000 men were unaccounted for, many still looting the Union camps and sleeping off the liquor they had found there. More, having lost their units in the Shiloh thickets, had celebrated their army's presumed victory by starting back to Corinth.

Beauregard could field only 20,000 men, at best, on April 7. The sole reinforcement he had received overnight was the Forty-seventh Tennessee Infantry, six hundred new recruits who had marched all night from their

GENERAL P. G. T. BEAUREGARD

Tennessee training camp and did not arrive until 8 a.m. So at dawn Beauregard and his generals found themselves as surprised and hard-pressed as their foes had been twenty-four hours earlier. The supposedly whipped Federals were attacking.

Command control was makeshift. Brigadier generals Patrick R. Cleburne and Alexander P. Stewart were just two of the prominent subordinate commanders who had gotten separated from the bulk of their units and were leading remnants of their own men and a patchwork of others. A mistake in orders, or in understanding them, had sent General Cheatham and his comparatively organized division retreating four miles from Pittsburg Landing. Cheatham's men were camped on the site of their preattack bivouac.[2]

This morning, Forrest's men held their slowly retiring line intact against Bull Nelson's advance for an hour and a half. At 7 a.m. infantrymen of Chalmers's brigade, with elements of several other units, rushed in to relieve the cavalry. Forrest then got orders to form a straggler line to stop unauthorized retreating. At 11 a.m. more orders shifted his men farther left, where he dismounted some of his companies to fight as infantry. This tactic, still uncommon in America, Forrest had already used at Fort Donelson and in the ravine fronting Pittsburg Landing the previous day.[3]

Union pressure persisted all morning and well into afternoon. Because of the disorganization of his command, Beauregard had to scramble to cobble together a defense. Until around 10:30 a.m., he later claimed, he could field only some 10,000 infantry and artillery under Breckinridge and Hardee on his right and center against Buell's fresh troops. On the left Bragg had to face Grant's 20,000 or so with only about 7,500. By 11:30 Beauregard had to pull some of Bragg's men away to plug the hole in his line left by Cheatham's complete withdrawal from the battlefield overnight.[4]

The vastly outnumbered Confederates contended for the plundered Union camps as fiercely and tenaciously as the Federals had defended them the day before. It was useless, though. The South had missed whatever chance it might have had at Shiloh, and at mid-afternoon Beauregard acknowledged the fact. Around 3 p.m. he ordered a retreat. Forrest's cavalry helped cover the rear.[5]

A hastily gathered Southern army that was rushed into combat half ready had fought and nearly beaten a force heavily leavened with veterans from the Federal victory at Fort Donelson. But one of the Confederates' most highly regarded generals, Braxton Bragg, who during the battle had decimated some of his own brigades by insisting on assaulting strong positions with outflanked or badly outnumbered units, characteristically seemed not to notice his own mistakes. Instead, always ready to look down his nose at volunteers, he threw the whole blame on the democratic system that the American—and perhaps especially Dixie's—elite viewed with contempt and fear. He would write a few days later that some of his troops and the civilian officers elected to command their companies and regiments had run out of ammunition during the battle but had been "too lazy to hunt the enemy's camps" for "millions of cartridges" that lay all around them there.

"Our failure is *entirely* due to a want of discipline and a want of [trained] officers," he decreed. "Universal suffrage, furloughs and whisky have ruined us."[6]

10

APRIL 7—GRANT

Another Prophecy Fulfilled

As April 7 dawned, Grant grabbed the initiative. His Army of the Tennessee to the right and Buell's Army of the Ohio to the left advanced over lightly defended ground the Confederates had all but abandoned in search of camps the previous evening.

The ease of it mystified Grant. He wondered if the Confederates had sought the shelter of the captured Federal camps to escape the downpour and the nightlong barrages of the gunboats. Had roles been reversed, he never would have done it. Like most men in the ranks on both sides, he had spent most of his years depending on his wits for survival. To trade a dry night's sleep for ground that might need reconquering with bullets and bayonets risked wasting a lot of blood.[1]

Grant attacked with troops who were tired but still combat ready. Except for Benjamin Prentiss's division and William H. L. Wallace's brigade, most of Grant's troops, although severely depleted, remained semiorganized. Buell's and Lew Wallace's were completely intact. They rushed forward trying to shut their eyes and ears to myriad horrors around them. The battle ground was grotesque with the previous day's human debris. Dead men and assorted parts of others had been flung about in every pose, the whole ghoulish mosaic alive and pulsating with agony as masses of intermingled wounded groaned and crawled, crying out to horrified onlookers.[2]

The Confederates did not fight like overmatched men who realized they had lost. Here and there they launched charges that drove back the

Federals. They likely did not know for sure that they had lost until past noon. Then it became obvious to all that, contrary to what they had been told the previous evening by every source except the insistent Colonel Forrest, Grant had indeed been reinforced—overwhelmingly. At 3 p.m. the Confederates began withdrawing under fire. Within two hours they had all but left the field.[3]

Grant let them go. He did not seem to care how far they went, sending not even cavalry to see. They might be waiting for him, lying in ambush somewhere down the roads to Corinth. It was raining again, those roads were "almost impassable," and his units, except maybe for Lew Wallace's division, were so shot up and frazzled that, Grant later wrote, he "had not the heart to order men who had fought so desperately for two days, lying in the mud and rain whenever not fighting, . . . to pursue." Nor did he ask Buell to do it. He later all but acknowledged being cowed by Buell, writing that he was so newly senior to the Army of the Ohio chief, who "had been for some time past a department commander, while I commanded only a district," that he did not feel like asking Buell to do anything.[4]

Grant had seen enough fighting in the past forty-eight hours. Americans killed or wounded in those two days all but doubled the total casualties in the war's four major battles to date: Manassas, Wilson's Creek, Fort Donelson, and Pea Ridge. And Grant had more reason for pursuing minimally: Major General Henry Halleck had ordered it. Grant expected Halleck to arrive on April 8, and Halleck's instructions suggested that it was not prudent to go beyond some point "which we can reach and return in a day." Halleck had reinstated Grant to command of his army just three weeks before Shiloh, and the sin that got him relieved after Fort Donelson had been the mere appearance of disobedience. He had inadvertently made an unauthorized visit to Nashville to reconnoiter the Confederate retreat after informing headquarters that he was going if he got no orders to the contrary; his message, though, was delayed in arriving, and the trip without express permission made Halleck furious. Halleck was similarly upset about not receiving regular reports sent by Grant that were held up by hitches in mail delivery.

This time, Grant obeyed.[5]

Grant's achievement thus far at Shiloh was already important in ways he could not know. The lesson he gave Sherman on the ghastly overnight of April 6 to 7—that the side attacking first after a spent assault wins—would be critical. It began making, or remaking, the man who would become renowned as the war's second-greatest Union general.

All his prior life, Sherman had appeared to need the backstop that fate snatched from him at age nine: a father. At Shiloh he began finding a surrogate, one two years younger than himself. But it would be a two-way street. Old General Smith lay abed in Savannah, rotting away from the infection in his leg. With his sole peer-confidant dying, Grant needed another. Sherman, meanwhile, needed one whose strength of will could dispel his deep doubts that this war to reunite America was winnable.

The tall, nervous redhead had been three classes ahead of Grant at West Point. There, the plebe had seemed so unexceptional that Sherman barely remembered him. He was scarcely more impressed at seeing Grant again in the 1850s in St. Louis, where Sherman was a struggling banker and Grant a shabby farmer and occasional street seller of wood. But during the Fort Donelson battle, Grant got Sherman's attention. Senior to Grant, Sherman had been sent by Halleck to Paducah, Kentucky, to push aid on to Donelson. Halleck wanted to send him even farther forward, to replace Grant. But Sherman declined the latter job, doubting both himself and the Union's capacity to restore itself. But he wanted to believe. With the boats that he pushed hard upriver, he sent unusually supportive letters to Grant. "I will do everything in my power to hurry forward to you reinforcements and supplies, and if I could be of service to you myself would gladly come, without making any question of rank," Sherman wrote. In a second note that same day, he added, "Command me in any way." The messages took Grant aback. Such subservience had little military precedent.[6]

The two Ohio natives seemed like opposites. Sherman was tall, wildly demonstrative, a frequently provocative blusterer; Grant was mild and diminutive, a near sphinx. Sherman hailed from the upper class, Grant from well below.[7]

BRIGADIER GENERAL WILLIAM T. SHERMAN

But life's scourges had already lashed both men before the great leveler of this war swept over them. Each had experienced the psychological devastation of failure and poverty. Sherman's birth father, a respectable lawyer and judge, had suffered financial disaster and died penniless when the son was nine. Most of the eleven Sherman children were farmed out to relatives and friends, and young Cump, short for Tecumseh, trudged next door to live with the rich Ewings. The poor nonrelation grew up privileged in this lofty second family, into which he then married. But he seems never to have overcome a fear of the kind of financial calamity that collapsed his boyhood world. Like Grant, he had left the old army and failed—at banking and business—before doing time in a concern owned by his foster father. Grant, who hit bottom working for his father, at least was the man's actual son.[8]

Sherman had labored under a military cloud as dark as Grant's. But Grant at least was not crazy, as Sherman had been alleged to be in Kentucky in the summer and fall of 1861. Sherman needed to get to a battlefield to erase his Kentucky repute. Grant, surrounded by actual or suspected enemies in his ranks, surely saw in Sherman's Washington connections—his foster father had been US secretary of the interior and a brother was a sitting US senator from Ohio—a possible counterbalance to the clout of such ambitious subordinates as John McClernand and Lew Wallace and his doubting superiors Halleck in St. Louis and General in Chief George McClellan in Washington. McClellan had been livid at seeing Grant drunk in the old army, and Halleck was sitting on those shameful charges, likely inspired by McClernand, that Grant's thirst was chronic.[9]

So Grant and Sherman needed each other. Neither yet knew how much.

11

APRIL 8—FORREST

"Shoot That Man!"

The day after Shiloh, with the Confederates streaming back toward Corinth, Grant finally told Sherman to pursue. He wanted more of a gingerly probe than an attempt to run them to ground, but even that was delayed by a phantom battle. An Ohio unit testing rifles after another night's rain triggered more shooting as Federals traumatized by American history's most horrific battle up to that time rushed whole brigades into line. For fifteen minutes, they blazed away at empty woods.[1]

Near noon, Sherman got going. With two brigades, he headed down Ridge Road to perhaps two miles from the crossroads that had so snarled the Confederate march to Pittsburg Landing on April 5. At the crossroads, called Mickey after the adjacent farm of James Michie, the dregs of Beauregard's Confederate infantry—1,200 frazzled men of Breckinridge's corps—had reached a house converted into a hospital. The facility contained about four hundred wounded. Arms, legs, hands, and feet littered its yard.[2]

Sherman's advance had passed abandoned camps containing dead and wounded. White-and-yellow hospital flags flew over them. Now, two miles from the crossroads, they saw another a half mile or so farther on. Here Breckinridge's cavalry rear guard had gathered more wounded, and toward their makeshift aid station trudged a line of dismounted men leading horses. The Federals proceeded warily. They approached a patch of recently cut timber scattered for two hundred yards around a winding creek. It was the site of the skirmish that had brought Grant out to wrench his ankle on the rainy night of April 4. Beyond the felled trees, the enemy now was crossing a rain-soaked cotton field toward a rise. When the Federal cavalry reported the sight to Sherman, he ordered forward 240 skirmishers—two companies of the Seventy-seventh Ohio Infantry—and posted cavalry to their rear to charge the Confederates at contact. Behind the horsemen he positioned the rest of the Seventy-seventh Ohio. He deemed the total force enough, in his words, to "clean the camp."[3]

The creek and strewn logs were slowing the Federal advance when, suddenly, Confederate cavalrymen burst from behind a ridge. Brandishing shotguns and pistols and yelling, they charged pell-mell and broke the Federal skirmish line. Sherman reported that the Union cavalry galloped rearward, and the Ohio infantrymen "broke, threw away their muskets, and fled."

Sherman watched in dismay. The Ohioans fired prematurely, and the colonel of the Seventy-seventh reported that the headlong Confederate charge gave his men no time to reload. They tried to stand with fixed bayonets, but Dixie shotguns blew them backward. When they turned to run, the pursuers rode them down. Sherman himself turned tail. The Ohioans' colonel reported that fifty-seven of his men were killed, wounded, or captured.

When the rear brigade formed for battle to stop the rout, the Confederates slowed to round up prisoners. One tall Confederate did not stop. He crashed against and into the bayonet-bristling battle line. "Kill him!" Federals shouted. "Shoot that man!" "Stick him!" "Knock him off his horse!"

The solitary rider was Forrest. Either his horse had run away with him, or, more likely, battle fervor had made him oblivious. He was unaware that his comrades had not followed until he chased the fleeing skirmishers and cavalry to the battle line, and they turned to fight. Only then did he yank his reins. Realizing his fix, he turned and spurred his mount toward safety, clearing a path with his pistol. His horse was shot but kept moving. One of the nearest Federal soldiers rammed a musket against the rider's right side and fired. The ball lifted Forrest from the saddle and lodged near his spine. With his right leg limp in the stirrup, he held on and vanished, Sherman later recalled, "into the woods to the south."

By then, the remnant of Breckinridge's infantry had abandoned the camp and hospital at Mickey, farther to Sherman's front. The Union cavalry, sent a mile or more beyond the Seventy-seventh Ohio, entered Mickey with caution. Sherman ordered burial of his dead, gathered up his wounded, counted his missing, and got a pledge from a hospital doctor in Mickey that Union wounded there would be treated until ambulances could come next day. He got back to camp after nightfall.[4]

F orrest's lonely dash into massed Federals at what became known as Fallen Timbers would become one of his most fabled exploits. As years passed, it would be enhanced. One version would say he stopped only one minié ball because he had snatched a Federal up onto the horse behind him to ward off shots in the back, casting the man aside when out of range. All versions would portray him as leading the charge and masterminding the ambush—all versions, that is, except every official one.[5]

Some 350 Confederate cavalry made the charge alongside Forrest that day, only about forty of them Forrest's. Kentuckians led by Captain John Hunt Morgan and Mississippians under Colonel Wirt Adams also participated, but two-thirds, or 220, were members of the Eighth Texas of Colonel John Wharton. Wharton's wounding on April 7 put Major Thomas Harrison over the Texans on this day. Hard fighters, they called themselves Terry's Texas Rangers after their first colonel, who died in battle in 1861.[6]

Wharton's report briefly referred to the "brilliant charge gallantly led" by Harrison, not mentioning Forrest. Harrison reported he made the charge after consulting Forrest, but the report made plain that Harrison did not consider Forrest his commander. From Harrison's report it is not clear who proposed the charge, a fact that suggests Forrest did. One of Forrest's homemade precepts was that, with charges, it was better to give than receive. Harrison referred to Forrest's unit merely as "one of the companies cooperating with me" and indicated he ordered the retreat that left Forrest on his own—without mentioning Forrest at that point at all. He said he did so because his men had exhausted the ammunition in their weapons and did not have sabers. Harrison reported capturing forty-three prisoners, killing between forty and fifty Federals, wounding many others, and incurring nine casualties. He added, seemingly offhand, "I cannot state the loss of the companies co-operating with me. Colonel Forrest, I learn, was slightly wounded."[7]

Harrison plainly had little to do with Forrest after their initial "consultation," and his report indicates disdain for the Tennessean. Harrison's background surely contributed to this; he and Wharton were both Houston-area attorneys leading a distinguished regiment. They likely considered themselves superior to the Memphis ex–slave trader best-known so far in this war for fleeing Fort Donelson with the scorned brigadiers John Floyd and Gideon Pillow.[8]

Even if the charge was Harrison's idea, it would have been characteristic of Forrest to go flying independently to the front of the fight.[9]

It was typical, too, that Forrest would gallop into an enemy mob with such abandon that he neglected to notice his men were not following. Forrest came from fearless stock. His mother once took a panther's mauling rather than drop a basket of baby chickens a neighbor gave her. On what was then called the southwest frontier, settlers could force themselves to be brave, to challenge danger and vanquish it, protecting themselves and their own or dying fast—or they could cower and permit themselves and their own to die slowly by letting others take all they had. Fast was better. While he surely felt fear in deadly circumstances, Forrest habitually sublimated his fright in ubiquitous bellicosity whenever challenged—whether on the battlefield or in the street.[10]

He had in fact devoted much thought to fear and to learning to deal with it. In boyhood, a half-broken colt had thrown him off its back into a pack of vicious dogs. He recalled expecting to be torn to pieces—only to see the dogs scatter, terrified of this human mass hurled so suddenly among them. Seeing they were as afraid as he, he realized that the difference between the fearful and the feared is psychological. So Forrest developed his habit of all-out aggression to deal with foes. His second in command, Lieutenant Colonel David C. Kelley, wrote that early in the war Forrest in a fight was "so fierce . . . that he was almost equally dangerous to friend or foe, and . . . seemed . . . too wildly excitable to be capable of judicious command."[11]

But the passion Forrest fought with was partly for show. His goal, he would one day explain to a fellow Confederate, was to shock, stagger, and demoralize opponents by fiercely throwing everything he had at them at the outset. Then, allowing them no respite, he would furiously continue to attack until he was "killing, capturing, and driving them with . . . little difficulty." Usually, though, he put it more succinctly: "Git 'em skeered, then keep the skeer on 'em."[12]

12

APRIL 8—GRANT

"This Man . . . Fights"

By the time Sherman got back to camp from the Fallen Timbers battle on April 8, whispers of the butchery at Pittsburg Landing had reached Washington. A wire to the *New York Herald*'s capital bureau the next morning confirmed them. The Senate halted regular business to read the *Herald* report of "the bloodiest battle of modern times." It said the Confederates had retreated, and the *New York Times* reported a "glorious victory" for the North. Grant returned to the national hero's spotlight that he had occupied after Fort Donelson.[1]

Then came the casualty list. Nearly 24,000 Americans—Federals and Confederates—were dead, wounded, or missing at Shiloh. A firestorm of outrage swept the North. Both truth and lies fed the flames. The main truth, contrary to Grant's protests, was that his army had been unready for the all-out Confederate attack. The lies were almost innumerable. The *New York Tribune* stormed that Grant had devoted no more thought to readiness than to "a Fourth of July Frolic." A novella-length article by reporter Whitelaw Reid in the *Cincinnati Gazette* claimed Grant's troops were so cavalierly unguarded that some had been bayoneted in their tents.[2]

Some of the lies were Grant's. He had warned Julia in a letter on April 15 that "I will come in again for . . . abuse from persons who were not here," but in fact many of his detractors were there. These he dismissed as having disgraced themselves in the fighting; they were criticizing him now, he said, to deflect infamy from themselves. This letter highlighted Grant's least attractive trait, one ubiquitous among officers on both sides. This battler whom a fellow Mexican War veteran described as a "man of fire" because of his cool efficiency where bullets flew was not so unflinching under public criticism. Like many of his more timid peers, he tended in such circumstances to get creative with facts.[3]

As criticism of Grant mounted in the aftermath of Shiloh, he resorted to blatant misrepresentation in order to defend himself. He told his congressional patron, Illinois representative Elihu Washburne, that at Shiloh he had had 30,000 men against 70,000 Confederates; to a prospective subordinate he wrote that "the papers are giving me fits" despite his army of 35,000's having battled Confederates numbering "over 80,000" on April 6. With Lew Wallace's division missing for the first day of the battle, Grant's own numbers could be rounded down to around 40,000, but the Confederates never totaled much more than that, and Grant surely knew it. He also claimed so much skirmishing was going on for two days before Shiloh that he "could have brought on the battle either Friday or Saturday if I had chosen" but elected "to keep it off until Buell arrived." Only in a letter to his father twenty days after the battle would he admit he had no idea the Confederates would attack in force.[4]

Widespread whispers attributed the disaster to Grant's old nemesis: alcohol. He was drunk in Savannah when the Confederate fury struck his army, these rumors maintained. The arrival of Buell, many held just as incorrectly, had alone saved Grant from annihilation; in truth, just four frazzled Confederate brigades had made the final attack, which they soon abandoned at seeing Grant's cannons, while only twelve Buell companies crossed the river in time to be of any help. But Buell took credit nevertheless. His report highlighted the chaos at Pittsburg Landing and indicated, without quite saying so, that the arrival of Colonel Jacob Ammen's brigade of Bull Nelson's division had been vital in fighting off the first day's final Confederate attack.[5]

Grant's wily second in command, ex-congressman turned general John McClernand, was similarly quick with the verbal dagger. He ignored the chain of command and wrote a report directly to his long-term Illinois acquaintance and sometime-associate, President Abraham Lincoln. This letter overstated McClernand's role in the battle and focused blame on Grant for the inordinate slaughter and failure to mount more than token pursuit of the Confederates.[6]

Lincoln asked Secretary of War Edwin Stanton to investigate whether any misdeeds by Grant had contributed to the Shiloh carnage. Stanton telegraphed Halleck, who typically sidestepped. He did not name Grant, saying only that the totals of killed and wounded reflected the leadership of officers "utterly unfit for their places" and reserving opinion as to misconduct by specific individuals until he had received all battle reports. He added that great victories are rarely won without many casualties. But to Major General Ethan Allen Hitchcock, whom he had tried throughout the Henry-Donelson campaign to get promoted into Grant's job, Halleck trashed Grant. The high-toned Hitchcock, one of the prides of West Point, responded in kind, denouncing Grant as "little more than a common gambler and drunkard" deserving of censure and oblivion.[7]

Publicly, though, Halleck stayed mum. Perhaps he felt guilty for delaying and minding other business in St. Louis while assuring Grant throughout late March and early April that he was on his way to Pittsburg Landing to take field command of the Grant and Buell armies—a measure that, he doubtless felt, would have avoided the Shiloh horror. The professorial Halleck preferred houses and armchairs to tents and camp stools, but he finally hurried to Shiloh, leaving St. Louis on April 9 and arriving two days later. He found a vast graveyard, with monsoon-scale rains washing thin layers of mud off hundreds of half-buried corpses.[8]

Halleck then began doing what he did best: paperwork. He issued orders tightening up guard duty, instituting drills, bettering latrine facilities, and establishing rigorous bureaucratic standards throughout the chain of command. Each departmental communication "should relate to one matter only, and be properly folded and indorsed," he decreed. Grant got special attention. "Your army is not now in condition to resist an attack," Halleck wrote his subordinate with marked belatedness on April 14. "It must be made so without delay."[9]

Grant apparently was glad Halleck had taken over. Believing his chief had interceded with Lincoln to overturn his post-Donelson removal, he claimed to welcome the prospect of Halleck's arrival, terming him in a letter to Julia "one of the greatest men of the age." On April 25, he wrote Julia that he was happy to surrender the top command to Halleck. He hoped the newspapers would leave him alone henceforth. He said he avoided reading them and "consequently save myself much uncomfortable feeling."[10]

Almost immediately, though, Halleck cast Grant into limbo. Once again, as after Fort Donelson, he took away Grant's command of his army. This time, though, Halleck named his unloved subordinate, now the second-ranking officer in the department, his second in command. It was a position with few duties. Halleck possibly did this to avoid again upsetting Lincoln, which his previous removal of Grant had appeared to do. He may also have realized, if only half consciously, that never having been in combat himself, he needed Grant's experience and battlefield aplomb.

Whatever his reason, it was just the right move. Soon after Shiloh, Pennsylvania Republican Alexander K. McClure went to the president to argue that Grant was an inept sot who embarrassed the war effort and should be dismissed. According to the sometimes creative memory of McClure, Lincoln replied, "I can't spare this man: he fights." But the president's wish to keep Grant in a decision-making role was not so firm. When Halleck kicked him upstairs, the White House did not protest. Lincoln's behavior was classically political, keeping Grant viable for the future while responding to public outrage over Shiloh's rivers of blood.[11]

Halleck handed the Army of the Tennessee to a much more highly respected junior of Grant's. Recently promoted Major General George H. Thomas, a career soldier who had spent his final year at West Point as Grant was in his first, had been victor in the obscure but important battle back in January at Logan's Crossroads, or Mill Springs, Kentucky. Grant's erstwhile army, now Thomas's, was one of three corps gathered into a 110,000-man horde under Halleck's direct supervision. Its task would be to capture Corinth.[12]

III

MISSISSIPPI
AND KENTUCKY:
TIDAL EBBS AND FLOWS

13

MID-APRIL–LATE JUNE 1862—
GRANT FROM CORINTH
TO MEMPHIS

"I Am in the Way"

Shiloh was the most decisive, but by no means the only, Union gain in the spring of 1862. Federal forces were on the march—or, in the case of the navy, afloat—seemingly everywhere.

In Virginia, Abraham Lincoln finally had his endlessly cautious and procrastinating general in chief, George McClellan, moving. McClellan's Army of the Potomac had forced Confederate evacuation of Yorktown on the peninsula between the York and James Rivers sixty miles southeast of Richmond; that army now inched warily toward the Confederate capital. Union troops occupied the naval ports of Norfolk and Portsmouth in Virginia as well as Beaufort in North Carolina, Port Royal in South Carolina, and, on the Gulf of Mexico, crucial New Orleans. The president declared all these ports again open for commerce—Union commerce. And notes of slavery's death dirge were sounding. Congress voted to abolish it in the District of Columbia, and, in an act Lincoln the politician temporarily disapproved of, a Union general at Hilton Head, South Carolina, freed slaves there as well as in captured areas in Georgia and Florida.

But the Federals could have done more, much more. Their efforts east and west were hobbled by the perfectionism and timidity of McClellan and western-theater commander Henry Halleck. Holding the critical railroad junction of Corinth, Mississippi, P. G. T. Beauregard's was the only notable Confederate force shielding Mississippi and Alabama; yet Halleck moved his huge army toward Beauregard as if dreading a collision. Determined not to be surprised the way Grant had been at Shiloh, the famed military intellectual ordered his horde entrenched every night, reducing marching time to near nothing. Daily forward progress over the nineteen miles averaged three-fourths of a mile, turning a one-day ride into an all but endless odyssey.

Grant, supplanted by George H. Thomas, had little to do. His new position as second in command of the Army of the Tennessee carried few duties, and Halleck made sure that whatever Grant did do got close supervision. He ordered that Grant's headquarters be near his own.[1]

Grant chafed as the army set its deliberate pace toward what promised to be a major battle at Corinth. Twelve days after the order establishing his new post, he wrote Halleck to complain that his position felt superfluous. That he had to write at all, rather than just speak to Halleck in person, suggests the thickness of his limbo's walls. He told Halleck he was determined to have the situation corrected as soon as the impending crisis of battle was past. He complained that to the rest of the army, it looked as if he were under arrest because Halleck had been sending orders directly to the commanders of the right wing and the reserve, the two corps supposedly under Grant. Grant noted Halleck's assurance, back in March, that he had protected Grant from higher-ups. He said he was certain Halleck now meant him no harm but was obeying orders. He plainly meant from Lincoln, Secretary of War Edwin Stanton, and McClellan. He asked to be relieved or have his present duty defined so "there can be no mistaking it."

The next day, Halleck wrote back. Grant, he said, should leave command matters to him. Halleck's headquarters would send its orders directly to whomever it pleased, and Grant's position as second in command of the full army was the specific spot to which his rank entitled him. As for Grant's suspicions of injustice, Halleck only reinforced what he had told him in the brief and temporary removal in the aftermath of Fort Donelson. Since February, Halleck said, he had "done everything in my power" to defend Grant; if Grant trusted him so little that Halleck had to explain further, explaining would be useless.[2]

Grant's avowed intention to have his present situation corrected was no empty threat. He laid groundwork for a new assignment. He wrote Julia that he was "thinking of going home, and to Washington." He edged closer to a personal relationship with his one Washington supporter, Illinois congressman Elihu Washburne. He offered to write Washburne reports of army affairs. But they would be confidential, he said, "not to make public use of."[3]

Grant later condemned Halleck's Corinth pace and timid tactics, but at the time he justified the army's dawdle in letters home. Moving a large army over poor roads worsened by months of rain was difficult, he said. He looked forward to the last great battle in the west. Its aftermath, he said, would free him to request transfer or resign.

Halleck's haughtiness was continual. When at one point in the seemingly endless march toward Corinth they reached a strong position on a substantial creek, Grant suggested that a secondary force could hold that spot while Halleck moved a large body to the right and took the city from the flank. Halleck's response made plain that he wanted no advice. "I felt that possibly I had suggested an unmilitary movement," Grant recalled. Halleck replied in such an "insulting and indignant manner" that Grant struggled to hold his temper, his chief of staff later recalled.[4]

So the army's inching along continued. In a letter of May 13, Grant reported to Julia that they were "now encamped . . . within hearing of the enemies drums at Corinth." Two and a half weeks later they remained outside the city.

They could hear trains chugging into Corinth to Confederate cheers. Halleck feared they heralded reinforcements, but Grant suspected otherwise. Railroad men told him they could put their ears to the rails leading into the city and discern not only which way trains were moving but whether they were loaded. They said the trains entering Corinth were empty; those leaving carried troops. But Halleck believed that the trains and cheers meant he was about to be attacked. On the overnight of May 29 to 30, Major General John Pope, commanding the Union left east of Corinth, reported he expected that very thing the next morning, and Halleck shifted troops to support him. No attack came. On May 30, with suspicion dawning that the Confederates had gone, Halleck pushed into the town in line of battle. Corinth was all but empty, stripped of not only Confederate defenders but every useful military article. The attack preparations Pope had thought he heard were final Confederate arrangements to retreat fifty miles south to Tupelo.[5]

Grant knew from his capture of an all-but-empty Fort Henry in February what the public reaction would be. He wrote Congressman Washburne that "much unjust criticism" would swirl, "but future effects will prove it a great victory." Sure enough, the *Chicago Tribune* branded Halleck's achievement a "barren triumph." In his assessment to Washburne, Grant may have been attempting to be politic. A day earlier he had written Julia a seemingly more candid opinion of the upshot of Halleck's "capture" of Corinth: "The rebels . . . will turn up some where and have to be whipped yet."

That observation differentiated Grant not just from Halleck but also from virtually everybody in the Union high command. Most of its officers, especially Grant's fellow West Pointers, shared Halleck's aversion to blood, an element with which the tanner's son was highly familiar. Halleck told Pope, who was pursuing Beauregard, that he only wanted to push the Confederates far enough south to allow the Federals to use the railroads across northern Mississippi and Alabama. Halleck wrote his wife that he had gained a "most important military point . . . with very little loss of life. I have won the victory without the battle!"[6]

Halleck and too many other West Point theorists of his time approached war with a minimalist mind-set. To them, it was an academic exercise, with its textbooks studying conflicts fought by small professional armies, sometimes mercenaries, whose numbers because of lack of size were hoarded. Grant, by contrast, had to know in his bones—from hard experience with Missouri farm life alongside the working-class kind of men who marched in the Confederate armies—that this was no exercise. Wars as increasingly bitter as this one were different from those in the textbooks, the armies exponentially larger and fiercer. This war was national, reaching into every town and hamlet to affect practically every able-bodied man from North and South. In such a war, triumph could come only from capturing or annihilating armies, not towns. One of those men in the other army, Nathan Bedford Forrest, perhaps put Grant's conviction most succinctly: "War means fightin', and fightin' means killin'." This war would want more than maneuver. It would require blood, and lots of it.

Lew Wallace, riding by one day soon after the occupation of Corinth, saw a tent off to itself with a solitary figure in front: Grant. Wallace likely was not saddened at this evidence of the misfortune of his former commander. Grant had not endorsed Wallace's Shiloh report and its account of the roundabout march from Crump's Landing. In Grant's mind, that had cost his army the use of Wallace's division on the first day of the battle.[7]

Halleck had made no move to give Grant more responsibility. In early June the impatient underling still had nothing more consequential to do than he had during the crawl to Corinth: write a few promotion recommendations and communicate with home. He had time to treat all sorts of topics. He informed Julia of the money he was sending her and complained now and then at the amounts she required. Several times he mentioned a "five-shooter" pistol he had gotten for his little son Jess. He also showed conflicting inclinations regarding the burning social

MAJOR GENERAL HENRY W. HALLECK

question of the day. Julia's father had given a relative some slaves, and Grant now advised her to tell her father to do the same with all his others "to avoid the possibility of their being sold."

In making this recommendation, Grant seemed mindful of the best interests of the slaves. He told Julia he did not want her "to have any of them, as it is not probable we will ever live in a slave state again"—and added that he would not like to see them abandoned to the highest bidder in an auction by a slave trader.[8]

Weary of his limbo, Grant had almost immediately decided to go home. Three days after the Federal occupation of Corinth, General William T. Sherman heard the news at Halleck's headquarters and asked why Grant was leaving. Halleck claimed not to know. Sherman rode over to Grant's solitary tent to see.[9]

Sherman's chances for advancement would have been better had he dissociated himself from Grant. Likely because of his Washington connections, Sherman was a favorite of Halleck, who must have looked askance at Sherman's developing attachment to Grant. Sherman had emerged from Shiloh to public acclaim, but he likely was not seeking advancement at this point. Shunning Grant would have cost him a crucial source of personal strength. During the weeks following Fort Donelson, Sherman and Grant had gotten closer. During the maelstrom of Shiloh, Grant's firm expression of faith in ultimate victory on the horrid night of April 6 had been a driftwood log that kept Sherman's skeptical head above water.

Press abuse of Grant following the battle pushed the two men closer. At Shiloh, they had been the generals most culpable for ignoring the approach of the Confederate attackers. Yet, contrary to prevailing practice among their high-ranking comrades, they had not turned on each other. They had stood back to back, praising each other, disputing the claims of Major General Don Carlos Buell and others, and maintaining—against all evidence—that the army had not been surprised by the scope of the Confederate assault.

Grant seemed to want, if not exactly need, military soul mates, and he was finally finding them. In addition to Sherman, there were two prospects on his staff. One, Major John Rawlins, was becoming so trusted that Grant allowed this blustering, impassioned subordinate a privilege accorded no other: that of challenging his drinking. The other,

Colonel James B. McPherson, Halleck had sent on the Fort Donelson expedition as a spy to monitor Grant's imbibing, but McPherson—another Ohioan from far beneath the elite—had instead sided with Grant almost overnight. Rawlins, Grant wrote Julia, "would make one of the best General officers to be found in the country," and McPherson was "one of the nicest gentlemen you ever saw."[10]

Grant's attachment to Sherman, which would become more consequential nationally than his attachment to the other two, was also growing. Shiloh and its aftermath had forged a bond far stronger than the two had enjoyed before. In a letter to Julia on May 4, Grant paid homage to his revered friend and advisor General Charles Ferguson Smith, who had just died from illness contracted in the wake of the Donelson campaign, then immediately turned to his ripening friendship with Sherman as if he regarded it as similarly important: "In Gen. Sherman the country has an able and gallant defender and your husband a true friend."

By then, Grant had an inkling of how truly he wrote. Just a day or so earlier, Sherman had ridden from Halleck's headquarters to find Grant packing. Sherman asked why. "Sherman, you know I am in the way here," Grant replied. "I have stood it as long as I can." Where he was going? "St. Louis," Sherman remembered him replying, although Grant's letters to Julia indicate the destination was Covington, Kentucky, where she and the rest of the family were. Sherman asked if he had business there. "Not a bit."

Sherman begged Grant to stay. He would be miserable anywhere else while the army advanced, Sherman said. And his fate could change. Hadn't Sherman's, after newspapers branded him "crazy"? He made Grant promise not to leave before letting him know. But if he did go, Sherman would like to have Grant's "escort": his personal security staff.

Grant was surprised and moved by the appeal, a powerful proffer of friendship that he seems to have returned in kind. Grant wrote Julia on June 9 that "when I talked of going home and leaving my command here there was quite a feeling among . . . Gen. officers below me, against my going." A few sentences later, he said that despite Sherman's promotion to major general following Shiloh, "I have never done half justice by him." He added three sentences on Sherman's Shiloh heroism.

Grant heeded Sherman's counsel and cancelled his leave. Sherman seemed overjoyed. He said leaving would not have erased Grant's feeling "that injustice has been done you." He apologized for asking for Grant's escort, which could have been construed as an attempt to gain from Grant's fall from grace. Perhaps out of the discomfort of that, Sherman began one of the over-the-top diatribes to which his nervous nature made him subject. Grant's Fort Donelson victory was more consequential than Saratoga in the American Revolution, he said. The "irresponsible, corrupt and malicious" press had caused everything from the war to Grant's now controversial image. Grant's Donelson fame had produced jealous attempts to pull him from the "pinnacle" he had attained. "By patience and silence we can . . . in due time make them feel that in defaming others they have destroyed themselves," he said—the "we" underlining his allegiance to Grant. The mischief-making power of these "envious rivals" was waning, Sherman continued, and soon they would "drop back into the abyss of infamy they deserve."[11]

As Sherman forecast, Grant's luck began to change—and amazingly soon. Halleck, having taken care not to pursue Beauregard hard enough to catch him, now turned to his passion: administration. Making the same mistake he had made after Fort Donelson and then Shiloh, he decided that he needed not to pursue but to consolidate federal gains. So he transformed his horde into occupation troops. He divided the Corinth force into its original three parts and again placed Grant in command of his old Army of the Tennessee. Despite Grant's rank as second to Halleck in the western theater, he could have continued to be ignored had an out-of-the-way thing not happened: Major General George H. Thomas, whom Halleck had given Grant's army, asked to return to the command of just his former division under Don Carlos Buell. Thomas thus opened the door for Grant's return.

This act was odd. Thomas, a career officer with presumably normal ambition, had requested reduction to leadership of one division instead of five. The mystery is complicated by the laconic personal demeanor he shared with Grant; he never explained his decision. The two men somewhat resembled each other in a few other ways too: their disinterest in showy uniforms and sartorial assertion of rank, as well as a shy and self-effacing manner and racial open-mindedness very unusual for their day. In most other respects, however, the two differed nearly as much as Grant and the era's aristocratic ideal, Robert E. Lee.[12]

Like Lee, a prewar friend of his, Thomas was actually a second-tier Tidewater Virginian born of a father who died young. He was reared on a farm worked by twelve to fifteen slaves and, like Lee, attended private school and exhibited courtliness of manner, proud high-mindedness, and a somewhat aloof reticence. At West Point, Thomas graduated twelfth, six places behind Sherman, who was his roommate, and three years ahead of Grant. In Mexico, he was promoted to captain for repeated gallantry. After that war, he stayed in the army and taught cavalry and artillery tactics at West Point, fought Indians in Texas, and served as major and fourth in command (behind Colonel Albert Sidney Johnston, Lieutenant Colonel Lee, and Major William J. Hardee) in the famous US Second Cavalry. Grant and he surely knew each other, slightly, from their shared year at West Point and from serving in the same comparatively small army in Mexico, but that was as close as they ever got.[13]

Some have depicted Thomas's request for de facto demotion in June 1862 at Corinth as stemming from respect for Grant's superior rank. That is perhaps true. Thomas, like Grant, had a stronger-than-usual sense of rectitude, and he probably had heard rumors that Grant resented being kicked upstairs and losing his army. Thomas may well have also heard by way of Grant's former subordinates that Grant resented him for taking his old position; some of these subordinates possibly evinced loyalty to their former chief. Thomas was surely increasingly sensitive, as the Corinth force was divided back into three armies, to Grant's superior rank, which would seem to entitle him to regain command of an again independent Army of the Tennessee. Requesting return to his own former command likely extricated Thomas from an unpleasant situation.[14]

So Grant was restored to his old command. The trio of armies was then dispersed to try to cover and pacify southern Tennessee and northern Mississippi and Alabama. Grant's job was to guard the West Tennessee and northern Mississippi railroads that could bring forward supplies for moves farther southward. With Halleck in no hurry to advance, Grant's was arguably regarded as the least important of the three commands. Major

General John Pope and his Army of the Mississippi were assigned the critical rail hub of Corinth, crossing point of the Memphis & Charleston and the Mobile & Ohio tracks. Buell went east with his Army of the Ohio to try to take Chattanooga, Confederate anchor of East Tennessee and rail gateway to the Deep South. Buell also got the task of repairing and guarding the Memphis & Charleston line eastward, making the slow Buell even slower.

Then Abraham Lincoln, desperate for eastern victories, summoned Halleck east on July 11 to command all the Federal armies. McClellan, finally forced to fight, had lost the epic June 25 to July 1 Seven Days' Battles in front of Richmond. The president, wearying of the insolent young general's imperious demands and incessant delays, replaced him.

Grant meanwhile was doubly happy. Halleck, in addition to handing him back his army, had given him permission to move his headquarters to Memphis, where Julia could join him. As he did so, Grant made a sage observation. He noted that the three-fourths of white Southerners who owned no slaves were not all eager to die for this new nation few had had much voice in forming. "In my mind," he wrote Julia, "there is no question but that this war could be ended at once if the whole Southern people could express their unbiased feeling untrammeled by leaders. . . . [Hostility] is kept up however by crying Abolitionist against us."[15]

14

JUNE–JULY 13, 1862—
FORREST AT MURFREESBORO

"I Will Have Every Man Put to the Sword"

The western Confederacy's borders were shriveling. The losses at Fort Donelson in February and Shiloh in April, then the retreat from Corinth in May, swept away the outflanked Mississippi River bastions of Island No. 10, Fort Pillow, and Memphis. Now, in June, one of the three Federal armies from Corinth was headed for Chattanooga, threatening East Tennessee and its vital Virginia-to-Georgia railroad. One of the other two Federal armies still occupied Corinth, a hub of the Memphis & Charleston and Mississippi Central lines. The third army, Grant's, was fanning out to the west and north along the captured tracks in West Tennessee and northern Mississippi. The outnumbered Confederates somehow had to stop the myriad Union incursions before they gutted Dixie and ended the war.[1]

Consolidating his forces at Tupelo, Beauregard got an idea—perhaps from Jefferson Davis. Davis, outraged that Beauregard had failed at Shiloh and then abandoned Corinth, pelted him with insulting questions. For example, why had he not cut Federal communications and retaken Nashville?

Beauregard sent for Forrest. The Confederate commander later explained that he had heard of the Tennessean's dismounted fighting on Shiloh's second day and his exploit at Fallen Timbers. He later claimed to admire Forrest's "coolness and daring" and "determined to do all he could to increase, if possible, his sphere of usefulness." If sincere, this atypical comment possibly stemmed from Beauregard's roots in Louisiana's socially fluid bayous and a feeling of kinship for a fiery temperament resembling his own. Then again, Beauregard may have intended his remarks—made after the war—to capitalize on Forrest's later fame and make himself look prescient. In June 1862, he may well have seen Forrest as his most expendable cavalry officer.

And a cavalry officer was needed elsewhere. The goad from Davis likely helped Beauregard see that a behind-the-lines strike at Union communications, or anything else that might halt the Federal onrush, had become imperative. The commander of crucial East Tennessee, Major General Edmund Kirby Smith at Knoxville, was under mounting pressure from Federals in Kentucky to his north and Don Carlos Buell's advance toward Chattanooga to his south. Smith begged Beauregard for aid against Buell's threat to Chattanooga.

Smith needed a commander of mounted troops to reconcile cavalry colonels in southeastern Tennessee quarreling over seniority. Rich Louisiana planter John S. Scott was the ranking officer; his First Louisiana brimmed with the cream of bayou society. He, lawyer John Wharton of the Eighth Texas, and West Point–trained career soldier John Adams refused even to bivouac in the same vicinity.[2]

So a staff member of Adams requested Forrest. Colonel James E. Saunders, an Alabaman in his sixties, journeyed to Mississippi to tell Beauregard about the squabbling colonels. Saunders had seen Forrest in a cavalry clash at Sacramento, Kentucky, the previous December, in which Forrest had personally killed three Federal officers in combat. Impressed by what he had seen, Saunders now urged Beauregard to send Forrest to Chattanooga to resolve the impasse.[3]

Beauregard had to push Forrest to accept a new command. Having raised and outfitted his regiment at much personal expense, he hated to give it up in order to take an assignment elsewhere. Beauregard promised to send Forrest's troops to rejoin him as soon as they could be spared. Beauregard also said he was recommending Forrest for brigadier general, which would rank him above the Chattanooga colonels. Forrest likely viewed the promotion with mixed feelings. Well aware of his lack of polish, he tended to shrink from coming into closer contact with well-educated men like those comprising the high command. Finally, though, he agreed.[4]

The general-to-be was still healing. Forrest had been in the Corinth neighborhood for the brilliant evacuation that tricked Halleck. After sustaining his post-Shiloh wound—a bullet that barely missed his spine— at the hands of Sherman's cautious pursuers, Forrest got a sixty-day leave to recuperate at home in Memphis. A scant three weeks later, though, he was back in the saddle, rejoining his regiment to settle commissary problems and, probably, expecting to participate in the next great clash of the western armies.

But the Federal bullet was still in his right hip. When he jumped a log on his horse while reconnoitering near Corinth, the projectile moved. The pain was so intense that he ordered J. B. Cowan, his staff physician and relative by marriage, to cut it out. Unable to extract the ball on the first try, Cowan had to resort to a second. The ordeal put his patient in bed for another two weeks.[5]

Forrest had convalesced in camp rather than in a Corinth hospital. The Mississippi town was overrun by Shiloh wounded who were surviving or dying in agony and filth. They occupied every building large enough to shelter more than a handful, each structure crammed with horrors and echoing with dying groans and screams from amputation rooms. Nurse Kate Cumming, a cultivated Scottish immigrant from Mobile, tended patients overflowing the Tishomingo Hotel. She found them "mutilated in every imaginable way," emitting a collective stink that at first made her "giddy and sick." She and other female volunteers were forced to "walk— and, when we give the men anything, kneel—in blood and water." The drinking water around Corinth was pestilential and often deadly.[6]

Forrest must have been as glad as other Confederates to abandon the Corinth area's illness and gloom. But the destination he had committed himself to was not inviting either.

Forrest carried with him to Chattanooga an order dated June 9 directing him to "assume command of the cavalry regiments . . . commanded respectively by Colonels Scott, Wharton, and Adams."[7] Beauregard might as well have written it in disappearing ink. When Forrest arrived in Chattanooga and gave the three colonels copies of his directive, their recalcitrance worsened. Scott refused to be commanded by this rustic junior who had been recommended for, but not yet promoted to, brigadier. And East Tennessee commander General Kirby Smith, despite having called on Beauregard for all the help he could send, may have resented that the Creole general sent him an untrained colonel whose lack of seniority only aggravated his personnel woes.[8]

On July 5, Smith compromised. He ordered his Chattanooga commander, Brigadier General Henry Heth, to divide the Chattanooga cavalry between Scott and Forrest. They must cooperate, he directed, but could "act . . . on different routes." If Heth could not split the cavalry, however, "Scott, as senior officer, must command."

Forrest doubtless balked. He had not given up his own regiment and ridden all the way across northern Alabama to have his promised ascendancy ignored. Smith reconsidered. The next day, July 6, the he retracted his order and told Heth to send Scott's regiment north to Kingston to replace the unit there, the First Georgia. That regiment—whose colonel, J. J. Morrison, was junior to Forrest—was ordered to join Forrest "without delay." Smith also instructed Heth to prepare the Eighth Texas, a small Kentucky detachment, and the Second Georgia, a new unit only recently arrived in Chattanooga, "to go to Middle Tennessee under Colonel Forrest."[9]

It was a motley crew. Only the Eighth Texas impressed Forrest. He had charged with some of the Texans at Fallen Timbers, and their commander, Colonel Wharton, by consenting to serve under him, at least apparently preferred him to Scott.

Forrest got moving. On July 7, just a day after Kirby Smith's second order, Federal troops reported large numbers of Confederate cavalry under leaders including Forrest on the road forty to sixty miles northwest of Chattanooga. Forrest's troops already had crossed one mountain range and were astride a second. The Union commanders worried that these Confederates might be heading for the Louisville-Nashville rail line, its important station at Wartrace, or possibly even farther north, toward the large Federal camp at Murfreesboro.[10]

Forrest may not yet have been certain of his target himself. No dispatch from Kirby Smith or Heth identifies one, and a letter written by Tennessee governor Isham G. Harris soon afterward says the governor and antebellum Nashville congressman Andrew Ewing were at Altamont and Beersheba Springs, just northwest of Chattanooga, "planning the Forrest raid"—an indication that Forrest was, for the moment, operating without specific instructions.[11]

The Federals, by contrast, were soon excellently informed of Forrest's target. They learned its exact location on July 10, and their source could not have been unlikelier. On that date, in one of the war's odder incidents, wily Confederate colonel John Hunt Morgan—beginning a raid into Kentucky—personally dictated a bogus telegram to Union authorities in Louisville reporting that Forrest had attacked Murfreesboro that day, routing Federal forces, and was moving on Nashville "in concert with" Morgan. The eloquent profanity with which Forrest might have reacted, had he learned of Morgan's spur-of-the-moment wire, can only be imagined. By then, Murfreesboro had in fact become his long ride's destination.[12]

Surely Morgan would never have sent the telegram had he known how close to the truth it was. Most Confederates knew only that Forrest was headed far behind enemy lines. And Forrest's fellow officers at Chattanooga shook their heads. One told another that letting the untrained Tennessean lead largely untried troops behind the lines was "rash . . . and likely to lead to disaster."

Had they known Forrest's object, his doubters could only have shaken their heads harder. Sitting thirty miles southeast of Nashville and seventy northwest of Chattanooga, Murfreesboro had been under Federal occupation for more than four months and was becoming a major supply depot for Buell's Chattanooga drive. The Union's Murfreesboro garrison was about the size of Forrest's force, and Federals in Nashville to the north and Wartrace fifteen miles to the south were well able to reinforce it rapidly by rail.[13]

Confederate planners had scouted the risks. During those early days of July, Murfreesboro resident John Spence, a fifty-two-year-old businessman, saw or heard of lone strangers "in citizen garb, strolling through the woods" around town. Residents thought these visitors belonged to the cavalry of Lieutenant Colonel James W. Starnes, an antebellum Tennessee physician whose unit had been rumored to be active around nearby McMinnville.

If challenged by a Federal, such a stranger would say he was seeking a cow or pig that had wandered from his farm. The occupying Federal, hailing from Minnesota or Michigan or Pennsylvania, and thus having no strong local connections, would have no way of knowing the self-described farmer was not local and no longer even a farmer. Thus, out-of-uniform Confederate cavalrymen learned the number of Federals at Murfreesboro and where they were camped.[14]

Locals generally sympathized with the Confederate spies. Federal soldiers made life unpleasant for civilians. Apparently because of escalating Federal reprisals, John Spence, initially a strong antisecessionist, had become a Confederate adherent. According to him, daily Federal forage trains into the countryside took whatever they wanted. The trains' mounted guards often returned with stolen chickens and turkeys swinging from their saddles. The foragers, Spence said, often persuaded blacks "to run off" to the Federal camps, and significant numbers of slaves were doing so. Owners could get them back only by taking an oath of Union allegiance.

Federal behavior sometimes deliberately antagonized local citizens. According to Spence, Federal lieutenant colonel John G. Parkhurst of the Ninth Michigan assumed the title of the town's military governor and staged a mock parade around the Rutherford County courthouse, dragging from his horse's tail a makeshift Confederate flag.

Murfreesboro residents longed for Confederate deliverance, but uneventful months passed. The occupiers grew lax. Federal enlisted men played ball and marbles, and evening dances were held in the streets, attended by some of the local belles.[15]

But the Murfreesboro leadership was in flux. In May the post commander, Colonel William W. Duffield of the Ninth Michigan, had been ordered to Kentucky, and the command devolved onto Colonel Henry C. Lester of the Third Minnesota. Lester soon divided his forces into two camps at least two miles apart—because of water shortage, he claimed. But Duffield, who arrived back in Murfreesboro on July 11, said the division had resulted from jealousy among the officers. The primary antagonists were Parkhurst, filling in for Duffield at the head of the Michiganders, and Lester. At root, John Spence indicated, was disagreement over which Union officer would govern the city. Spence implied that the residents preferred Lester, suggesting that he was more lenient.[16]

Disturbing incidents occurred. A Union scouting party ran into a band of Confederate partisans—or perhaps the hovering, inquisitive cavalry. Spence wrote that the Southerners surprised the Federals and killed one. The Federals assumed the ambushers were local bushwhackers and cracked down. They searched residences for guns and arrested a dozen citizens. According to Spence, two of the twelve were to be selected and hanged for the killing of the Union soldier. Spence may not have learned the whole of it. A spy using the name James Paul and a Confederate captain, William A. Richardson, who had escaped a Northern prison, were reputedly also among the condemned, along with five others who lived in the area of rural Rutherford County where the Union soldier was slain. Spence's description makes two things clear: at this time his hometown was resentful, and its Union occupiers feared no return of Confederate troops on a significant scale.[17]

—•—

Beneath a searing July sun, Federal general Don Carlos Buell was plodding across northern Alabama. He had a big job, which he had made bigger. He was repairing not only the Memphis & Charleston tracks from Memphis, as General Henry Halleck had ordered, but also the Louisville-Nashville line, which continued south from Nashville by two routes to the northern Alabama towns of Decatur and Stevenson. Buell was leery of Halleck's implied instruction to supply his army by rail from Memphis to the west, using tracks crossing four hostile states. A less vulnerable plan, Buell thought, would be to resupply from the north at Louisville on the Ohio River via the Louisville-Nashville line. So he was repairing—and stationing guard detachments along—these tracks too. He also delayed any push on Chattanooga proper until the Louisville-Nashville route had been repaired, presumably by end of the second week of July.[18]

Guarding both routes required large numbers of Buell's 40,000 men. And during the first week of July, John Morgan's raid into Kentucky with

1,000 Confederate cavalrymen prompted Union commanders in the Blue-grass State to clamor for reinforcements. Buell sent two regiments from Murfreesboro, his strongest station between Nashville and Chattanooga. If he had to follow them with an entire division, he said, further advance toward East Tennessee would be out of the question.[19]

The Federals completed repairs to the Louisville-Nashville-Alabama tracks on July 12. This closed a twenty-three-mile break at which supplies had to be offloaded, hauled by wagon, then reloaded onto train cars. The first shipment of expedited provisions for Buell's Chattanooga-bound army was scheduled for the next day, July 13.

A July 11 train from Nashville into Murfreesboro had brought two Federal officers: the returning Colonel Duffield and thirty-six-year-old Brigadier Thomas T. Crittenden, the new post commander. Crittenden and Duffield planned immediate changes for Murfreesboro. They especially wanted to reconsolidate the garrison's separated units, saying that the Parkhurst camp, serviced by huge springs at a plantation belonging to the Maney family, had enough water to supply three times the number of troops present at Murfreesboro. Despite Lester's blasé assertion that no substantial Confederate force was closer than Chattanooga, Crittenden doubled the number of pickets around the city. Lester neglected, however, to disclose two important details: Confederate cavalry had been on the increase around McMinnville forty miles to the east, and Lester had been allowing Federal pickets to withdraw from the roads each evening after nightfall. Such laxness was idiocy, but Crittenden could not change a system about which he knew nothing.[20]

That same day, July 11, Forrest's Confederates entered McMinnville. The First Georgia rode in from Kingston to join the Eighth Texas, Second Georgia, and two smaller units of Tennesseans and Kentuckians. Together, Forrest's disparate command now numbered 1,400 men.[21]

The march from Chattanooga across two mountain ranges had been forced and exhausting, but Forrest rested only overnight at McMinnville. The cavalry already there doubtless informed him that Murfreesboro's Federal camps were widely separated; Crittenden and Duffield, having just arrived, had yet to institute their plan to consolidate. In the early afternoon of July 12, Forrest pushed on west to Woodbury, where he stopped to feed mounts around 11 p.m.

The women of Woodbury brought out food for the men and, in anguish, reported that a Federal patrol had dragooned many male residents into the Murfreesboro jail on July 11 amid dire threats of hanging. The prisoners would soon be free, Forrest promised. He also announced that on the next day, July 13, he had been born forty-one years before in the nearby county of Bedford. He expected to celebrate the morrow with a significant present from his men: Murfreesboro.[22]

He quickly pushed on. In the middle of the night, his brigade crossed the Rutherford County line and approached the hamlet of Readyville (pronounced "Reedyville"). They rode in silence, but whispers of their coming preceded them. At the brick home of Colonel Charles Ready, the family's women—along with slaves Malindy, Aunt Winnie, and Uncle Martin—had, like the women of Woodbury, prepared food for the troopers. Colonel Ready's young granddaughter helped hand it out.

To the young girl, the troopers' unpolished commander was an instant hero, a tall man coming to rescue her jailed kinsmen. Her admiration quickly became more personal. Out of deference for females, or his reputed regard for young people, or just the heightened consciousness of the wonder of life that can grip a man facing battle, he gave the girl a compliment she never forgot.

"Your face," he said, "is as beautiful as the moonlight."[23]

A round 4:30 a.m., Forrest's scouts reported pickets just ahead on the town's eastern outskirts. Lester's lack of orders had left nocturnal vigilance, if there was to be any, up to individual commanders. One of the in-town units—the Ninth Michigan or the Pennsylvania cavalry—had posted fifteen of its men along the Murfreesboro-Woodbury highway on which Forrest's men were now approaching.

Forrest detailed a few Texas Rangers to take the fifteen pickets with no noise. The Texans veered off into a field, skirted the picket post, then reentered the road, turned, and trotted back from the town side. In the predawn, the Federals took the approaching horsemen for other Federals until the Texans were on them with drawn pistols. From the captives, Forrest learned that General Thomas Crittenden had arrived and taken command, but the Federal camps were still separated. Each was also well removed from the courthouse square, where Crittenden occupied a hotel and a Michigan company guarded the jail on the second floor of the courthouse.[24]

Forrest conferred with subordinates, then issued orders. Wharton's Texans were to charge the Seventh Pennsylvania Cavalry's camp just ahead to the right of the road. Most of the Texans and some men of the Second Georgia would dash on to attack the five companies of the Ninth Michigan, whose tents were pitched near the Maney estate and its great springs more than a half mile north of town. Forrest himself would lead the rest of the troops a mile or so farther west toward the public square. Near it they would separate again. A company of Texas Rangers would storm the buildings around the courthouse in search of General Crittenden. Some companies of the First and Second Georgia would assault the single company of Michigan troops camped on the square guarding the jail. The Georgians were also to liberate the prisoners held there.

Forrest's plan also provided protection for these operations. Colonel J. K. Lawton and much of his Second Georgia would be held in the rear as a reserve, and Forrest—after breaking off from the Texas Rangers and the Georgia infantrymen in the vicinity of the courthouse—would lead a third column to seal off roads northwest to Nashville and north to Lebanon, the likeliest routes of Federal reinforcement. That would wall off the Third Minnesota, holding it in its camp a mile and a half northwest of the courthouse. Colonel Lester's nine Minnesota companies, aided by the four guns of Captain John M. Hewett's battery of Kentucky Light Artillery, made up the strongest Federal unit at Murfreesboro, and Forrest meant to keep them isolated while he reduced the others.[25]

Forrest plotted a fight the way an attorney plots a court case. He prepared in advance his response to each opposition alternative. But rule one was psychological: "Git 'em skeered." Federal reveille was at 5 a.m.; only cooks would be fully awake before then. Forrest wanted to surprise the others in their tents.

Just past 4:30, a carefully kept Confederate silence exploded. Whoops, gunfire, and thunderous hoofbeats descended on Murfreesboro like a summer storm. "I first saw the enemy when charging on my camp," Major James Seibert of the Seventh Pennsylvania reported.[26]

Wharton's Texans were "yelling like Indians," one of the Federals recalled. They dashed in among the Pennsylvanians' tent supports and got

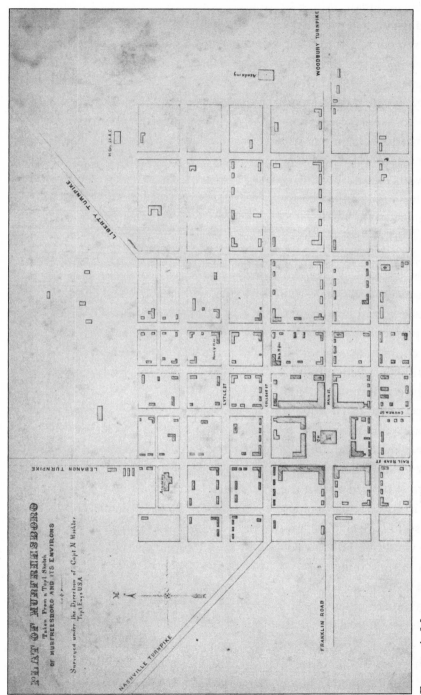

FORREST'S MURFREESBORO RAID: This period map by a US Army engineer shows the courthouse square at the bottom center; the approximate location of the Maney estate, which is possibly represented by the rectangle at the top center between the Lebanon and Liberty turnpikes; and the location of Colonel Henry Lester's Minnesotans out the Nashville Turnpike to the far left.

entangled in long, thick ropes stretched between trees as hitching places for the Union mounts. Shooting and yipping, they fought through the ropes and torched the tents. Union cavalrymen "hardly had time to get out," let alone arm themselves and mount their horses, a member of the Ninth Michigan Infantry would remember. The half-dressed or undressed unfortunates, traumatized, offered scant resistance. Most were captured in camp, Major Seibert reported. But Seibert and a few others made it to the Ninth Michigan companies on the Maney property north of town. Seibert reported losing five killed and twenty wounded out of eighty troopers. Most of the rest became Confederate captives.[27]

Then snags developed for the Confederates. To get to the Ninth Michigan at the Maney estate from downtown, they had to ride north more than a half mile on what amounted to the Maney driveway. There, among tents along the fence bordering the extensive front lawn, Michigan private Charles Bennett of Company G had risen early, at about 4:15. He was washing himself near where cooks were chopping wood for their fires when he heard "the clatter and roar of cavalry on the gallop."

"I ran to each tent in our company yelling, 'Turn out, the Rebels are coming,'" Bennett wrote in his journal. By the time he reached the second tent, the aroused bugler had sounded the alarm, and a drummer was beating the long roll of warning.

Bennett heard shooting from the direction of Woodbury pike. The shots woke more Federals, but too late. Wharton's troopers were on them. The bugler was still in his tent, trying to dress, Private Bennett wrote, when a bullet to the head killed him. The captain of Company K abandoned his troops and fled.[28]

Lieutenant Colonel Parkhurst reported that before his men could form, the Texans "with terrible yells, dashed upon us from three directions . . . with double-barreled shotguns and Colt's navy revolvers. Some of my men gave way under this charge." Those Federals who did not break fell back toward the middle of the camp and rallied, some in just underwear. For perhaps twenty minutes, the combat became "nearly hand-to-hand," remembered Parkhurst's commander, Duffield. Somebody, likely Wharton himself, shot Duffield in the left thigh—and, Duffield would note in his report, the "right testicle"—as the Federal commander urged his men to rally.

Wharton likely did not yet know that he was understrength. Forrest had taken more Texans toward the public square than his plan called for. As two dozen of his Confederate troopers died or were wounded on the Maney grounds, Wharton ran out of muscle. Parkhurst had more men, and his rifles overmatched the Confederate pistols and shotguns. The Federals wounded Wharton in the arm and stopped the Texans at the center of the camp. They turned away from the rifle fire, and the Ninth Michigan's Company C chased them three hundred yards in the direction they had come.

Most of the Wharton contingent retreated toward the Woodbury pike. A few dismounted and tried in vain to charge again. But they could do no more than hold the Federals at Maney's.[29]

Forrest's theft of some of Wharton's Rangers had occurred on the fly. H. W. Graber, a Texan riding in the Rangers' column, wrote that as they were following Wharton into the side street leading toward the Maney estate, Forrest found that his Georgia and Tennessee troops had not come up. So he ordered the rear of Wharton's column—"about fifty or sixty men"—to peel off and go with him to assail the formidable Third Minnesota northwest of town. Forrest's spontaneous order put Graber among the first four horsemen in Forrest's borrowed column, riding just to the left of Forrest himself.

Forrest's plan had been to avoid the courthouse and proceed through town to the Minnesota camps on the Nashville pike, but circumstances again intervened. As they passed in sight of the courthouse, two Federals on its upper floor saw them and raised weapons. Forrest and Graber saw them and fired first—with well-nigh tragic results. When Forrest's pistol went off, his horse bolted to the left, "almost in front of me just as I fired," Graber wrote. The Texan "very nearly" shot Forrest in the head.[30]

Graber heard firing north of town, signaling Wharton's attack on the Ninth Michigan. Joyous townspeople, including half-dressed women and girls, were rushing into the streets. Forrest plainly presumed that the absent Georgians and Tennesseans had lost their way in the commotion and would find their assigned positions besieging the courthouse. So he and the fifty or so Rangers, except a few shot by guards as they bypassed the courthouse, poured through the square toward the other side of town and the Third Minnesota.[31]

On the courthouse's second floor, prisoner William Richardson stood on a box to peer out a narrow jail window. His fellow inmate, the spy calling himself James Paul, had shaken Richardson awake to hear the hoofbeats. Before the two saw horses and riders, they heard the high, keening rebel yell. Then some of the charging troopers—those Forrest had suddenly dragooned—rushed by, while others halted in front of the jail to confront the Federals in the courthouse square.[32]

The commotion in town had alerted the Minnesotans. Captain John M. Hewett's Battery B, First Kentucky Light Artillery, had camped just southeast of the Third Minnesota. Hearing firing downtown, Hewett ordered his horses harnessed before hurrying back to the infantry. He told Colonel Lester he was ready to advance into town. Lester told him to wait for the riflemen. When the Third Minnesota arrived in front of Hewett's camp and Hewett asked Lester "in what order we would advance on the town," the bad blood between Lester and Parkhurst resurfaced. Rather than rush to Parkhurst's aid, Lester said they were not going into town. They would move forward a half mile, position themselves on a hill in a sage field to their left front, and await orders. They proceeded to do so, then sat there, listening to the fight in town, for nearly thirty minutes. Finally, they sighted Confederates a half mile or more to their left. Hewett's battery opened fire.

The Confederates "instantly dispersed," Hewett wrote. The account by Graber, who was on the other end of the barrage, agrees. It adds that Forrest, who had led Graber to the area, had disappeared.[33]

Forrest galloped pell-mell northwestward. He lost his way and had to stop at a house for directions to the Minnesota camp.[34]

He had reached the target area as Hewett's cannons opened up. When they did, they underlined what Forrest doubtless knew: he needed more troops to keep the Minnesotans in place while he dealt with the smaller Federal force at the courthouse. So he had immediately turned and galloped back to town to send his reserve—Lawton and some Georgia, Tennessee, and Kentucky troopers, all stationed just east of the square along the Woodbury pike—to attack and occupy Lester.[35]

At the square, Forrest found his men in a sniping standoff, dodging cross fire. Here, as at Maney's farm, blood was flowing. The attackers endured heavy fire from the windows of the courthouse and hotel. Some Georgians and a few Texas Rangers were pinned down between the Ninth Michigan's B Company in the courthouse and General Crittenden's staff seventy-five yards across the street in a hotel. Crittenden was trying to get a civilian-clad courier out to Duffield at the Maney plantation to coordinate with the Michigan troops, but it was no use. The Confederates had surrounded his quarters as soon as they entered the square.[36]

Numbers of townspeople tried to aid the Confederates. Parkhurst reported that assailants of his position at the Maney farm included "a large number of citizens of Rutherford County, many of whom had recently taken the oath of allegiance to the United States Government." For some time, Murfreesboro had reputedly been under a standing order from Parkhurst that, in event of enemy attack, his Michigan troops were to fire on all citizens—men, women, and children—who took to the streets. The order, diarist John Spence wrote, was now carried out. Federal bullets killed one civilian and wounded another.[37]

The stalemate on the square ended first. Before 8 a.m., Forrest put aide James Saunders, the Alabama colonel who had urged Beauregard to assign Forrest to Chattanooga, in command of a remnant of Texas Rangers. He sent them against General Crittenden's staff and other Federals in buildings around the square. At the same time, he ordered Colonel Morrison and part of the First Georgia to storm the courthouse. Several Georgians fell dead or wounded crossing the street, but their comrades rushed the courthouse doors. In front of each of two groups charging from opposite sides of the building, Forrest put a single file of troopers. The first man of each group carried an axe, and Forrest ordered that both axes be kept in the air, no matter how many men fell carrying them, until they reached the doors and battered them open. They soon did. The Federals withdrew to the building's second story, where they continued firing at anybody in the street, soldiers and civilians alike.

On the other side of the square, Colonel Saunders was initially unable to find Crittenden in the hotel or other buildings. The colonel hurried back outside and, remounting to search elsewhere, took a musket ball to a lung.[38]

In the besieged courthouse, the Federals were now on the same floor as the jail. When the Confederates demanded surrender and were refused, the Georgians threatened to torch the first floor. The Federals continued to resist until, Forrest's report says, the courthouse "was fired." With smoke rising, a detachment of the Second Georgia, already having overwhelmed the town's telegraph office and captured the telegrapher, charged up the stairs. That ended it. The Ninth Michigan's B Company had held the Confederates at bay for perhaps three hours—killing twelve of them, Federals reported, and wounding eighteen. Now, though, they were out of options. From the hotel, Crittenden's staff watched the courthouse capitulate. The general's staff then surrendered to Saunders's Texans.[39]

For the men in jail, horror remained in store. Overjoyed at seeing the whooping Confederates thunder into the square at dawn, they had then listened for hours to the fighting that ensued. Prisoner Richardson said that when their rescue seemed sure, several Federals came to their cell door and fired in at them; the inmates avoided the bullets by crouching in an out-of-the-way corner. Then, as the Federals surrendered to the Confederates storming the stairs, a laggard Union guard struck a match to paper, pushed it under loose planks in the floor of the hallway in front of the cell, and departed with the keys. Only by means of an iron bar did desperate rescuers manage to bend a bottom corner of the heavy, locked metal door enough to allow the prisoners to lie on the floor, squeeze out, and avoid roasting.

At this point, Richardson remembered, Forrest "dashed up" to the jail cell. Perhaps worried that setting fire to the first floor—likely under his orders—had harmed the inmates, he asked if the prisoners were safe. The officer in charge, the Second Georgia's Lieutenant Colonel Arthur Hood, said yes, but added that the Federals had tried to burn the inmates alive.

"Never mind, we'll get them," Forrest replied. Richardson said Forrest's eyes looked as if they were "on fire," his face flushed dark with obvious passion.

In a few minutes, the Federals from the courthouse and the hotel were lined up in the street, and Forrest turned to Richardson. He asked him to identify those who had behaved "inhumanly" toward the prisoners. Disregarding the soldiers who shot into the cell, Richardson said he wished to designate just the man who had lit the fire to incinerate them, then pointed him out.[40]

According to Graber, the man was brought to Forrest, who "pulled out his pistol and killed him on the spot."

Forrest galloped out the Nashville pike again. He had to make sure the nine Minnesota companies with their battery of artillery could not join the five Michigan companies at the Maney estate.[41]

The troopers he had dispatched from town had kept the Minnesotans in position, but that was all. Artillery captain Hewett reported that after his fire dispersed the first Confederates he saw that day—the initial detachment led by Forrest—he put a section of his guns on the turnpike. The pieces were barely in place when he saw a larger enemy force, Forrest's Lawton-led reserve, advancing from town. A few artillery shells drove them into some woods, which Hewett then shelled.[42]

Forrest now took over for Lawton, still hunkered down in the woods. He sent some Georgia troopers to feign a forward movement, then led most of his force on a wide swing to the right to attack the camps the Minnesotans had left. It took three charges to dislodge a hundred-man rear guard sheltered by wagons and rock ledges. After the second lunge failed and the cavalrymen, still new recruits, fell quickly back, Forrest gathered these troops. In a rage, he challenged their manliness and said that he would never tolerate premature departure from a field of battle. If they had not known it before, they now saw that they served a commander who would shoot them if need be. The third charge carried. The cavalrymen killed or captured the rear guardsmen and fired the tents and reserve ammunition. The billowing smoke attracted the attention of Captain Hewett. He shelled and finally drove out the attackers, but his shells could hardly extinguish the conflagration, free the captives, or save the ammunition.[43]

Hewett had just finished bombarding the burning camps when two hundred or more Southerners charged his battery from in front. He drove them into the woods, where they disappeared. But Forrest had accomplished what he came to do. His destruction of the Minnesotans' camps and supplies weakened them and further demoralized Lester. Now he headed for the Maney plantation.[44]

At the Michigan camp, the Texans and part of the First Georgia had periodically made sham shows of bellicosity. Parkhurst had replaced the wounded Duffield and stabilized his situation. His Federals piled hay bales and arranged supply wagons to block the half-mile Maney driveway. He had fashioned, Parkhurst thought, "quite a formidable position."

Parkhurst soon learned, however, that no aid was coming from across town. Hearing that Lester had not advanced his Minnesotans, Parkhurst sent him word by courier of the fighting at the Maney estate. He said his position was good, and he could hold it if reinforced. Hearing nothing back, he ordered off another courier.[45]

The bad blood between Parkhurst and Lester now became a hemorrhage. It likely also augmented the already demoralized Lester's mounting paranoia. Probably around 9 a.m., Parkhurst heard that Lester had ordered his two couriers arrested "as spies." When a Lester scout eventually arrived at Maney's, Parkhurst wrote out another plea for aid and an explanation of his position. When Lester's scout returned from Parkhurst's camp, he reported Confederates in force on the Lebanon road between Lester and Parkhurst. Lester decided that getting his troops through to join Parkhurst was impossible. He stayed where he was.[46]

With Lester atop his hill and Parkhurst behind his barricades, Forrest faced another standoff. His men had now been in Murfreesboro for seven hours, and his officers were nervous. Their troops had shut down the Murfreesboro telegraph office and cut its wires, but Federal garrisons north and south, alarmed by the dead wire, could rush troops in by train. Subordinates urged Forrest to be content with what he had accomplished and quit the town.

No, Forrest said, perhaps recalling Donelson and Shiloh and the disasters that had followed unfinished Confederate victories there. Yet, he knew the same thing his officers did: he had to make something decisive happen soon.[47]

Hours earlier, as Captain Hewett's guns scattered Forrest's band of Texans in front of the Third Minnesota, a comrade had hailed Ranger H. W. Graber.

Reeling in his saddle, his arm shattered by a shell, the man begged Graber not to leave him. Graber grabbed the bridle of the man's horse and hurried mount and rider into the woods. He continued until he came to a house, whose resident hitched up a buggy. With Graber following, the civilian drove the injured trooper on a swing around the town. Out the Woodbury road, they found Rangers who had withdrawn from the attack at Maney's and Forrest's initial, outmanned move against Lester. Gathered around the wounded Colonel Wharton and some captives, the Texans were forming ranks when a messenger arrived from an angry Forrest: Get back up town! Even Federals soon heard he had considered court-martialing Wharton for leaving the field.[48]

At Maney's following his destruction of the Minnesotans' camp, Forrest had dismounted his Tennessee and Kentucky troopers and ordered them to skirmish with the Federal front while he sent units of the Second Georgia to the Federal right. He told the Georgians to prepare for a dismounted charge. Then he had the Second Georgia's Colonel Lawton write out an ultimatum and took it forward himself under a white flag. The note's language was formal, but hardly genteel.

COLONEL: I must demand an unconditional surrender of your force as prisoners of war or I will have every man put to the sword. You are aware of the overpowering force I have at my command, and this demand is made to prevent the effusion of blood. I am, colonel, very respectfully, your obedient servant,

N. B. FORREST,
Brigadier-General of Cavalry, C. S. Army[49]

Surrender or die. Shaken, Parkhurst sent the note to Duffield. The gallant colonel, despite his wound to the groin, had led his troops while they fought off the initial Confederate attack. But now, lying in the Maney mansion in intense pain, he left to Parkhurst the decision about how to answer Forrest. While Duffield read the note, Parkhurst grew even less sanguine. He claimed to have learned that Forrest had all but one squadron of his forces now surrounding the Michiganders and obviously intended to carry out his threat.[50]

If Parkhurst really knew what he claimed to about Forrest's numbers, he could only have got the information—true or otherwise—from Forrest himself. The Confederates did look imposing. In addition to Texans, Georgians, and a crowd of Murfreesboro's private citizens, Parkhurst saw "quite a number of negroes . . . armed and equipped," who "took part in the several engagements with my forces during the day." These were likely the enslaved teamsters, cooks, and so on normally attached to Confederate troops.

Without help from Lester, the Ninth Michigan's position was dire. Parkhurst now had just 134 able-bodied men, including the few Pennsylvania cavalrymen who had managed to make it from their camp to his. He gathered his officers for a conference.[51]

Suddenly their situation worsened further. The hard-riding cowboys and Indian fighters of the Eighth Texas, summoned back to town from the Woodbury road, raced into view. The fearsome sight created an effect "most fortunate," Forrest would remember. He did not squander this gift of fate. According to Graber, Forrest verbally warned Parkhurst that if the Confederates had to make another charge, the Federals would bear the blame for what happened—and "he had five hundred Texas Rangers he couldn't control in a fight."[52]

Parkhurst's report says the assembled Union officers thought better of continuing to resist. To a man, they voted for surrender.[53]

I t was now into afternoon. More time passed as Forrest's troopers disarmed Parkhurst's men, collected or burned their supplies, and headed the captives toward Woodbury.

Northwest of town, Federal artillery captain John Hewett was plainly disgusted with Colonel Lester. For several hours after the burning of the Minnesota camps, Hewett saw few Confederates, and those he did see made no move to attack. Yet Lester, described in a subsequent official Federal document as "stupid with fear," remained where he was. When the sound of fighting in town ended, he had sent a second scout "to try to get news from our friends." This man was unable to get through Confederates guarding the Lebanon road, but around 2 p.m. a Michigan soldier coming from the opposite direction did. He reported that his regiment had surrendered. Lester then fell back to a farmhouse, purportedly to make a last stand behind its fence.[54]

The Minnesotans were settling in behind the fence when a flag-of-truce party rode up. Sent from Maney's at the stated order of Duffield, it directed Lester to come there for a conference. Lester mounted and left with the party.[55]

Lester's ride would show history, if not Lester himself, just how cunning Forrest could be. Cantering into town and out Lytle Avenue to Maney's, Lester had to have seen Confederate troopers marching in heavy force behind two different stands of woods along the route. He could not know that these seemingly separate Confederate units were actually the same men marching and countermarching. Lester thought Murfreesboro was crawling with Confederates. Riding back out of town after conferring with Duffield, he again passed the two patches of woods behind which even more Confederates marched to simulate overwhelming numbers.[56]

Lester never reported what he saw along the road. Nor did he mention Forrest's surrender-or-die ultimatum. His report said only that Duffield told him the Confederates had "overwhelming force," and even if they had not damaged the railroad tracks, no reinforcements would be coming because Federal forces at Nashville were gone on an "expedition." Lester also reported that Duffield suggested he put the idea of capitulation to his subordinates. He claimed he did, with most recommending surrender. He obviously did not consult Hewett, whose report was clipped and outraged: "Returning, he surrendered the entire command. Up to the moment of surrender the utmost confidence was evinced by the officers and men."[57]

Lester said he surrendered at 3:30 p.m. By then, Forrest had his men gathering up all the supplies they could carry and burning the rest. He reported by dispatch to Major General J. P. McCown at Chattanooga that he had captured 1,200 Federals, taken $300,000 worth of supplies, and burned $200,000 more in matériel, along with the Murfreesboro railroad depot. Frugal by long habit, he counted and reported the rest of his haul: at least 50 wagons, 4 pieces of artillery, and 450 or more horses and mules. In a report to General Kirby Smith, he said he knew of losing only about twenty-five killed and forty to sixty wounded, although not all his unit commanders had yet reported. He said the Federals had sustained "about 75 killed . . . [and] 125 wounded."[58]

Forrest put the Minnesota prisoners on the road to McMinnville, behind those from Michigan and Pennsylvania. According to Private Charles Bennett of the Ninth Michigan, many of the officers and men were permitted to ride the captured horses and mules; Bennett may not have realized that this was likely because Forrest did not have sufficient troops to manage the animals as well as guard the prisoners. Lieutenant Colonel Parkhurst, though, was not as happy as Bennett. Having dished out harshness to Murfreesboro residents, he now got a taste of his own fare. Despite Forrest's presurrender assurance that the prisoners could keep their private possessions, the Confederates took "everything not worn upon our backs." And Forrest, who doubtless had talked to local residents, personally took Parkhurst's horse.

The Federal noncommissioned officers and privates were released at McMinnville on a pledge not to rejoin Union units until properly exchanged, a general for a general down to a private for a private. Officers were sent to Knoxville, then on to incarceration in a "filthy" cotton gin at Madison, Georgia—where, Parkhurst reported, guards charged them $2 a day for food.[59]

As for Forrest, he left Murfreesboro having added to the tally of men he had killed in this young war, although he probably did not include them among the thirty Union combatants he claimed at war's end. During the charge on the Third Minnesota camps, he had reportedly drawn his pistol and dropped an African American firing at him from behind a wagon so accurately that a shot had clipped his hatband. Even if the man was uniformed, Forrest likely regarded him as a fugitive slave; the so-called contrabands flocking out of bondage and trying to accompany their deliverers were still far from being enlisted in the army or even generally welcomed within Federal lines.

Forrest's other personal victim, at least according to Texas Ranger H. W. Graber, was the courthouse jailer who had tried to burn his prisoners alive. When the name of the arsonist guard was called out in a subsequent formation of captives, nobody answered. After the name was called a second time, Forrest himself spoke up.

"Pass on," he said. "It's all right."[60]

15

JULY–EARLY OCTOBER 1862—
GRANT IN NORTH MISSISSIPPI

"The Most Anxious Period of the War"

On July 13, the day Forrest's birthday torches singed the Federal fist at Murfreesboro, the Grant family was at Columbus, Kentucky, hurrying off a Mississippi River steamboat. Heeding an abrupt and mysterious summons from Memphis to return to army headquarters at Corinth, Grant wished to avoid endangering his wife and children by crossing ultrahostile North Mississippi. So he took the boat north from Memphis to Columbus, then a Mobile & Ohio train back south to Corinth. There, three weeks after resuming leadership of the Army of the Tennessee, he found himself promoted still further. Halleck gave him command of all northern Mississippi, West Tennessee, and western Kentucky.[1]

This smile of fortune came about more by default than favor. Halleck had left for Washington, chosen by Lincoln to relieve McClellan as chief of all the Union armies. And Halleck had no time to reactivate the lengthy process of replacing his second in command. So Grant inherited the Corinth job.

Well, two-thirds of it. Halleck generally respected Major General Don Carlos Buell, and he knew Buell-Grant relations were icy. So Buell, whose Army of the Ohio was headed east toward Chattanooga, would continue to report to Halleck. Grant, however, would oversee the Army of the Mississippi as well as command his Army of the Tennessee. So

Brigadier General William S. Rosecrans, new commander of the Army of the Mississippi, now was to report to Grant. Rosecrans had just replaced Major General John Pope, who had been called to Washington on June 26 to command a new Army of Virginia.

The South, it is said, never smiled after Shiloh. The Union victory there opened the Deep South to invasion from the north, and by June, Federals moving north up the Mississippi River from the Gulf of Mexico had captured not only New Orleans but also Baton Rouge. That narrowed Confederate control of America's primary river to the area around Vicksburg, Mississippi.

That bluff-crowning city was doubly strategic. In addition to being the Confederates' last real bastion on the Father of Waters, it was the western terminus of a railroad link to important Confederate munitions factories at Selma, Alabama. With the Union now controlling the more northern Memphis & Charleston line, the tracks out of Vicksburg connecting with a line in Louisiana comprised the Confederacy's last means of rapidly transporting foodstuffs, matériel, and armies eastward from the southwest.

But Forrest's Murfreesboro coup in July momentarily stalled further Confederate contraction. Buell—having reached Huntsville, Alabama, on his trek toward Chattanooga—was furious. He cashiered the timid Colonel Lester and termed the Federal dereliction of duty at Murfreesboro one of the most disgraceful "in the history of wars." He informed Halleck that a dozen regiments had already been guarding the newly completed rail line that Forrest had just closed once again. Repairs would require another two weeks, during which Buell could not even consider advancing on Chattanooga. Instead, he would have to detail still more guards for the tracks.[2]

Rather than the brief sprint both sides had signed up for, the war was morphing into a marathon. Hints of its increasing ugliness had emerged in late June 1862, as Grant had headquartered in Memphis to accommodate a visit from Julia.

The preeminent city in West Tennessee, Memphis seethed with the same civilian resentment that the Federal occupiers of Murfreesboro had faced, except worse. Grant soon junked a forbearing policy toward Confederate sympathizers. That policy—instituted in the hope that average Southerners were lukewarm on secession and thus not dangerous—had signally failed. Most Memphians appeared steadfastly rebellious. The city's clergymen insisted on praying for Jefferson Davis each Sabbath, and citizens refused to attend a formerly well-patronized church where a loyalist minister had been installed to preach to Union troops.[3]

On July 1, Grant closed the disloyal *Memphis Avalanche*, which resurfaced a few days later as a repentant *Memphis Bulletin*. He announced on July 3 that Federal losses of matériel to guerrillas would be replaced by personal property taken from Confederate sympathizers in the neighborhoods where the losses occurred. The same day, he decreed that guerrillas operating outside the regular Confederate command structure would not be treated as prisoners of war. On July 14, lacking enough troops to control "violent" Confederate kin, he ordered an evacuation southward by all Memphis families of Confederate soldiers or officials.[4]

More wrenching measures loomed. In mid-July, a day or so after receiving two-thirds of Halleck's former job, Grant wrote to Illinois congressman Elihu Washburne saying that he had hoped for a different one: "the taking of Vicksburg." The Mississippi town was the obvious next, mammoth prize for Federals in the West. Its capture would open the Mississippi to Union gunboats from end to end, cut Dixie in two, and close to Confederate use the Vicksburg railroad. Taking Vicksburg, Grant later reflected, would be "equal to the amputation of a limb" in its effect on the enemy.[5]

Washburne's reply was momentous in the advice it offered. The congressman said he had "learned with great pleasure" that Grant had been reinstated and given a widened command. He added that the Northern public—and, by inference, officials of the Lincoln administration and many members of Congress—would see Grant's return as "the precursor of more . . . vigorous operations." He then endorsed the kind of policy Grant had instituted in Memphis. Average US citizens, he said, "want to see *war*. This matter of guarding rebel property, of protecting secessionists . . . is 'played out' in public estimation."

Washburne then proposed that Grant wield a harsher hand against secessionist sympathizers, making them suffer economically for their disloyalty. He suggested, by inference, that Grant begin uprooting the South's long-controversial economic foundation. He should promote the decamping of slaves from disloyal Southern owners and be aware that the Lincoln administration was leaning toward enlisting fugitive slaves as soldiers. Most Americans would have found the latter unthinkable a few months before. A Midwestern transplant hailing from Maine, Washburne could not have known the depth of horror and rage what he was outlining could engender in the Caucasian South, where armed African American insurrection had been a nightmare equated for centuries with doom. The Lincoln administration, Washburne said, had finally agreed with "the people" that blacks must henceforth be put to work—laboring or fighting—for the North instead of the South, and the general who best instituted this new idea would "be held in the highest estimation."

"The idea that a man can be in the rebel army, leaving his negroes and property behind him to be protected by our troops, is to me shocking," Washburne continued. "If the constitution or slavery must perish, let slavery go to the wall."[6]

Grant knew from working fields alongside slaves—as well as with Caucasian Southern subsistence farmers—the wrenching nature of this concept. But he could also see its military benefit. The latter, along with longstanding sympathy for the enslaved, now began to drive a progression in his attitude.

Grant had initially opposed on military grounds the encouragement of slave escapes. He thought it would stiffen Southern opposition and add to the Union army's task. In mid-June, he had written home complaining of "negro stealing" by soldiers, saying it helped Confederate leaders whip up hysteria by painting Federals as abolitionists. But in mid-July, with the Grants occupying the plantation house of a Confederate sympathizer named Francis W. Whitfield on the outskirts of Corinth, Grant asked Halleck if he could "let . . . go" slave women and children that Whitfield wanted to send to relatives farther south. Significantly, this request slightly predated Washburne's letter. And in early August, having had time to digest Washburne's views, Grant guardedly wrote his slavery-hating father, who could not be trusted to keep their correspondence private, that he had no personal preference "with regard to the negro, either to effect his freedom or to continue his bondage. If

Congress pass any law and the president approves it, I am willing to execute it." He said he did not believe a soldier should even discuss "the propriety of laws and official orders."[7]

Two weeks later, in mid-August, a letter from Grant to his sister expressed growing comfort with the army's de facto "negro stealing," which he said was making the war "oppressive to the Southern people." Slaves were getting restless, following back to camp every detachment of soldiers that went out. He had begun employing blacks "as teamsters, Hospital attendants, company cooks &c. thus saving soldiers to carry the musket." He added a note reminiscent of the feelings he had shown in 1859 (but never discussed) in freeing, rather than selling, the only slave he ever owned.

"I don't know what is to become of these poor people in the end," he wrote, but he rejoiced that taking them weakened the enemy.[8]

G rant needed all the help he could get. He soon barely had enough troops to defend his Department of West Tennessee. Halleck ordered him to send two divisions to Buell, then another, and then a fourth. Grant's 80,000 men shrank to 46,000.

He could barely defend what he held. He wrote his sister Mary in mid-August that his job was to "keep open" the Mississippi, Tennessee, and Cumberland Rivers, as well as railroad tracks from Columbus, Kentucky, to Corinth, Mississippi; from Corinth to Decatur, Alabama; and from Jackson, Tennessee, to Bolivar, Tennessee. Guerrillas hovered everywhere. His men were kept busy whipping them every day, he wrote.

Confederate activity in fact appeared threatening, he wrote Mary, and he did not exaggerate. South of him, Confederate general Earl Van Dorn, by combining his forces with those of General Sterling Price, could amass an army nearly the size of Grant's own, and to the north Confederate cavalry bands were bedeviling his supply routes. In mid-August he sent his family to St. Louis after less than a month in the Whitfield plantation house.

That raised another problem. Where could Julia live long enough for the children to attend school for the term starting in September? The wife of Grant staffer William Hillyer occupied a "nice" St. Louis residence and was alone, "and it may be that she and Julia will keep house together," he wrote. Julia, though, preferred Covington, Kentucky, where Grant's parents lived—perhaps so the in-laws could help with the children.[9]

Another worry was simultaneously personal and military. Congressman turned brigadier John McClernand, commanding the First Division of the Army of the Tennessee at Jackson, Tennessee, had an infuriating habit of sidestepping the chain of command. Grant already disliked and feared McClernand for befriending and praising William J. Kountz, who had filed the drunkenness charges against Grant back in January. A former congressman, McClernand was also a shameless self-promoter, writing letters baldly aimed at self-advancement to the president and other high government officials. On July 9, he had asked Grant's congressman friend, Washburne, to recommend him for command of a corps comprising two divisions of new Illinois troops. And he wanted a transfer east, away from Halleck and Grant. That request was nipped in the bud when, just two days later, Halleck himself was called east to supervise all the Federal armies; thus, McClernand could no longer escape Halleck's supervision by going there. In August Halleck rebuked McClernand for sending Lincoln a request for a leave unapproved by Grant. He had violated army regulations, Halleck told him, adding that it was not the first time.

Grant's annoyance grew. McClernand's White House ties remained dangerous, but Grant now knew that he at least need not fear McClernand's ingratiating himself with Halleck. He had been around his chief long enough to know Halleck despised civilian interference in military matters; for that reason, he cared less for the militarily unschooled recent politician than he did for Grant.

But McClernand kept pushing. When another officer turned up to investigate destruction of government property in his district, McClernand threatened large consequences if anyone again encroached on what he maintained was his territory. At the same time, he charged Brigadier General James B. McPherson, fast becoming one of Grant's most trusted lieutenants, with letting the railroads ship civilian goods in preference to military matériel; McPherson fired back that he was doing all possible to prevent such smuggling and would pay no attention to complaints from "Officers who know nothing about the circumstances and . . . misstate facts." Again, when Major General Edward O. C. Ord entered Bolivar, McClernand indignantly inquired of Grant on whose authority Ord had come. This time Grant tartly informed him that as commander he would order any officer wherever in his department he wished. McClernand countered hotly, protesting Grant's "boast of authority."[10]

And McClernand's scheming was by no means the only ongoing annoyance. There was always the hypersensitive Halleck to deal with. The Union's new general in chief required careful deference, despite which he nonetheless periodically burst into fits of waspish rage, then resented it when Grant took offense. On June 29, two weeks before Lincoln ordered Halleck east, a band of Confederates had captured a supply train and its Federal guard detachment, and Grant reported hearing from behind Confederate lines that 30,000 enemy were at Abbeville, Mississippi, intending to march on LaGrange, Tennessee, as soon as a bridge over the Tallahatchie River was repaired. Halleck replied, "You say thirty thousand rebels at Shelbyville to attack LaGrange. Where is Shelbyville? I can't find it on any map." Furthermore, he believed no such attack to be imminent. Why did Grant not obtain "*facts*? It looks . . . like a mere stampede." After making this implied slur on Grant's courage, he instructed Grant to investigate loss of the train "and ascertain facts. I mean to make somebody responsible for so gross a negligence."

Grant replied angrily. He corrected Halleck's mistaking Abbeville for Shelbyville and added that he heeded "as little of . . . floating rumors" as anybody. Indeed, he had sent for cavalry to make an investigation of the train incident before Halleck demanded it. And, Grant added, "stampeding is not my weakness." Halleck waited nearly a week, then responded as if it were Grant who was overreacting. In ordering him to investigate the loss of the train, he said, he had not implied that Grant was at fault. He had only directed a gathering of the facts, "and you take offense at the order, as intended to reflect upon you! Nor did I suppose for a minute that you were stampeded; for I know that is not in your nature. . . . I was very much surprised at the tone of your dispatch, and the ill feeling manifested in it . . . toward one who has so often befriended you."[11]

Such were dealings with Henry Halleck.

Then there was the other war—the one with the Confederates. Charged with protecting undermanned outposts dotting ultrahostile northern

Mississippi and western Tennessee, Grant could only watch the enemy grab the initiative.

On July 23, Grant notified Halleck that Confederates were departing Tupelo, Mississippi—"in what direction or for what purpose is not . . . certain." Rumor, however, had it that a heavy Confederate column had moved on July 7 toward Chattanooga. Grant began to suspect that the best western Confederates were heading to Virginia to aid Lee while the rest would try to hold him and Buell in check. But his July 23 dispatch also contained other odd information. He had learned from spies that at Tupelo, Confederate major general Sterling Price of Missouri had made a speech to his troops promising to return them to Missouri by way of Kentucky.

Grant kept watching. On July 29 he reported that Union colonel Phil Sheridan had driven six hundred Confederates from Ripley, Mississippi, and captured a captain and thirty interesting letters. Some were from Richmond, but most were from members of the Twenty-sixth Alabama Infantry. These indicated that a significant number of troops were going by rail from Tupelo roundabout through Mobile, Alabama, to Chattanooga. Meanwhile, wagons were hauling their equipage cross-country to the rail station at Rome, Georgia.[12]

Three weeks later, a closer threat emerged. Thirty-two thousand Confederates left behind in Mississippi—halved between Price at Tupelo and Van Dorn at Vicksburg—were uniting to attack. The question was where. Meanwhile, 3,500 Confederate cavalry under Colonels Frank Armstrong and William H. Jackson had linked up in northern Mississippi and sped northwest toward Bolivar, Tennessee. Grant and his subordinates, puzzling over the upshot, inked much paper during August's last days. On August 30, six Federal cavalry companies and a section of artillery clashed repeatedly with Armstrong and Jackson a few miles out of Bolivar. Armstrong was erroneously reported killed. A Union lieutenant colonel died leading a saber charge.[13]

The carnage from mid-July to mid-September equaled that of most of the famous battles of the Mexican War, Grant later recalled. The little Bolivar-Jackson campaign, all but forgotten today, was a mini-bloodbath for the Confederate attackers. But Armstrong's cavalry thrust accomplished much. By his account, he had destroyed all bridges and a "mile of trestle work" between Jackson and Bolivar, killed two Union colonels and one lieutenant colonel, and captured 8 other officers and 213 prisoners. This drew much of Grant's attention north, away from the targets Price and Van Dorn were eyeing.[14]

Grant had connections to both Confederate commanders. Price had been governor of Missouri when Grant was struggling at farming there. And Van Dorn, eight months older than Grant, had been one class ahead of him at West Point. An elegant Mississippi plantation dandy and ladies' man, Van Dorn likely would not have had—or wanted—much association with Grant. Grant probably felt the same about Van Dorn.

The day after the Bolivar fight, August 31, the mystery surrounding Confederate intentions in Grant's department cleared a bit. Michigan cavalry captured a Confederate courier from Chattanooga carrying mail saying that Major General Braxton Bragg was now in command there. Major General William J. Hardee was Bragg's top subordinate, and Beauregard was not present at all. Most important, Bragg's troops were said to be on the march, headed for Nashville. Reportedly numbering 70,000, they were traveling light, carrying no tents and accompanied by just one wagon per hundred troops.[15]

The captured letters did not mention epic plans Bragg had for Price and Van Dorn. He wanted these two Mississippi subordinates to deal with Rosecrans at Corinth and Sherman at Memphis, then march their armies north. They were to join Bragg in a grandiose sweep whose aim was breathtaking. It meant to flank the Federals out of Nashville from the northeast, force Buell to drop the Chattanooga drive and defend northern Kentucky, whip Buell in the Bluegrass State, and push the Union all the way back to the Ohio River.[16]

Bragg had neglected one factor, though. To deal with Rosecrans and Sherman, Price and Van Dorn would also have to confront the Federal department commander: Grant. Bragg, hero artillerist of the Mexican War and four years Grant's senior, likely misjudged the ex-captain with whom he had participated in several of the same Mexican battles. Stampeding was not Grant's weakness, as he had lately reminded Halleck, and now, ringed by foes in enemy territory, he would show how true that was.[17]

B ands of Confederate and guerrilla cavalry were striking Federal out-posts across West Tennessee and northern Mississippi in the first half of September, but with no discernible pattern. Their goals remained unclear to Grant for the first half of September. On August 31, on the Tennessee River south of Fort Henry, two hundred Confederates captured and burned a transport steamer loaded with coal to fuel Federal gunboats. Another two hundred Confederates attacked a forty-man bridge guard post near Humboldt northwest of Jackson. They burned the camp and set the bridge afire before being chased farther down the track by counterattacking guards. Their target had been a freight train bound for Holly Springs, Mississippi, but two fugitive slaves from the hamlet where the Confederates camped the previous night had stolen away and warned Federal mounted infantry. The horsemen kept the attackers off a larger bridge south of Humboldt. The Confederates fired into, but could not stop, the train.[18]

Then, in mid-September, the Confederate aim began taking shape. They appeared to be massing on the Alabama border near Iuka, Mississippi, hardly more than twenty miles from Corinth. From Iuka, Colonel Robert Murphy of the Eighth Wisconsin Infantry reported by courier that Armstrong's cavalrymen had attacked him on September 13. Two Confederates taken prisoner during the clash had told him infantry was a day or two behind them. Murphy said he had fended off that morning's attack, but telegraph wires had reportedly been cut. When the attackers reappeared the same day, Murphy withdrew, leaving behind commissary supplies that he should have burned.[19]

Three days later, a large reconnaissance force from Rosecrans's Army of the Mississippi set out from Burnsville, just west of Iuka, to see how many Confederates were gathering there. Numbering three infantry regiments and two sniper companies, plus cavalry and artillery, Rosecrans's troops ran into Confederate pickets six miles from Iuka. They drove the pickets backward under increasing fire until, at the edge of woods less than two miles from town, they detected enemy activity on their right flank. The Federal commander, Colonel Joseph Mower, retreated to a hill and decided to camp there—until a Confederate deserter came in and reported that Iuka contained at least 12,000 Confederates under Price.

The Confederates planned to flank the Union position after dark, the deserter said. Mower changed plans and ordered his Federals back to Burnsville.[20]

Grant now knew where the nearest enemy force was—Price's half of it, anyway. But Grant could only guess what the Confederates were up to. One report, Grant wrote Halleck, had Price aiming to cross the Tennessee River to the north and head for Kentucky. Another had Van Dorn and Price combining to attack Corinth from opposite directions, southwest and northeast. According to a third, Price would cross the Tennessee toward Nashville, and Van Dorn would attack Corinth if Grant moved any troops from Corinth to pursue Price.[21]

Whatever the plan, Grant aimed to wreck it. Figuring that with infantry and artillery Van Dorn would need four days to reach Corinth from his Vicksburg base, Grant decided to attack Price first. A few weeks earlier Halleck had cautioned against any move that might weaken the Federal defense, but on September 17 the general in chief had new priorities. He ordered Grant to use all possible means to keep Price in Mississippi. Allowing him to join Bragg in Tennessee or Kentucky, Halleck said, would spell disaster.

There was also a risk that Price and Van Dorn would combine to attack Grant. Grant accordingly brought 3,400 troops from Bolivar and stationed detachments south and southeast of Corinth to guard against a cavalry dash. Then he ordered Rosecrans to march 9,000 men toward Iuka via two roads from the southwest and the south, while Ord moved another 8,000 on Iuka from the northwest. Halleck and other West Point book soldiers shrank from launching an attack with less than three-to-one odds, but Grant told Halleck he considered the 17,000 total troops in the Rosecrans-Ord force equal to or greater than the Confederate numbers. His Mexican War hero, Zachary Taylor, had often ignored the West Point ratio. For Grant, too, equal was enough.[22]

On September 18, Grant moved out with Ord by train to Burnsville, halfway to Iuka. Beating Van Dorn to the target was crucial, but while Ord encountered Armstrong's cavalry and pushed it from the northwest to within four miles of Iuka on September 18, part of Rosecrans's command took a wrong road, and he remained well short of his southern attack sites. Rosecrans suggested Ord strike first "and draw their attention that way" to give Rosecrans time to approach and attack from the opposite side of town. This idea strained plausibility. It required part of Rosecrans's force to rush twenty miles and still have the energy to attack.[23]

Grant received Rosecrans's dispatch in the wee hours of September 19. Thinking Rosecrans was closer to Iuka, he had ordered him to advance as fast as possible and do all the damage he and Ord could on September 19 because Van Dorn might arrive the next day. Rosecrans's late dispatch necessitated redrawing Ord's instructions. Rejecting Rosecrans's suggestions, Grant directed Ord not to open the battle but instead to wait until he heard Rosecrans's guns.

As September 19 wore into afternoon, Ord heard nothing. He rode back to see Grant at Burnsville at about 4 p.m. He had hardly left when, around 4:30 p.m., the commander of his advance units, Brigadier Leonard Ross, saw "dense smoke" rising over Iuka. From seven miles off, Ross thought Price was retreating and burning his supplies. But Ord and Grant, miles away from Ross, did not know this as they conferred. The two agreed that Rosecrans could not get in position in time to attack that day. Grant told Ord to push the Confederate pickets backward onto Price's primary force but to bring on no battle unless he heard firing from the south. Only around 6 p.m. did a dispatch from Ross reach Ord reporting the thick smoke over Iuka and Ross's interpretation of it as evidence of a Confederate retreat.[24]

Ross could not have been more mistaken. The smoke was Price ambushing Rosecrans. Price, who had participated in the considerable trans-Mississippi battles of Elkhorn Tavern and Wilson's Creek, described the ensuing struggle as "the hardest-fought fight . . . I have ever witnessed." But a hard wind from the west prevented Ross or Ord from hearing the battle's roar.[25]

Earlier that afternoon, Rosecrans had pushed Confederate cavalry and sharpshooters six miles toward Iuka in a steady skirmish. Hurrying to open his attack while there remained enough daylight, he either forgot, or chose not, to divide his column and send some of it farther east to block the Fulton Road, the second of two thoroughfares running south from Iuka. He took his whole force up the nearer, more westerly Jacinto Road.

At about 4:30 p.m., a mile or so from the town, just past a log church at a hill-crowning crossroads closed in by trees and briary underbrush, a withering volley of musket and artillery fire stopped Rosecrans. Then four regiments of Confederates sprang out of a ravine and charged his right front in three lines two men deep. Crowded into the road by trees, underbrush, and steep ravines on either side, the Federals at first could field a front line only three regiments wide.

It was inordinately vicious. There was no room for the Federals to maneuver or retreat. An Ohio battery lost all its officers and most of its horses and men before being captured by the Confederates. Then it was retaken, lost again, and again retaken, its gun carriage riddled with musket balls. Two fresh Union regiments rushed in to stop a Confederate push, shoved the attackers back, then withstood three charges in which "in several instances the enemy was received on the point of the bayonet and then shot off." Some Confederates were pistol shot in the face by Federal officers at point-blank range. An Iowa unit made three bayonet charges, the last because their ammunition was gone. They had expended some of it in fury against their own comrades, who after falling back had fired into them. An Iowa captain, left in the lurch by his vanishing colonel, was himself put out of action when his bullet-struck, dying horse bashed him against a tree trunk.[26]

As dusk fell on the Jacinto Road, it was hard to discern who had won— or even if the battle was over. Rosecrans was holding on, but, in his own mind, just barely. At 10:30 p.m., from two miles south of Iuka, Rosecrans sent Grant a dispatch indicating grave concern, if not outright fright. "You must attack in the morning and *in force*," he wrote. "Push in onto them until we can have time to do something. We will try to get a position on our right which will take Iuka."[27]

Rosecrans may or may not have meant that he planned to send some troops onto the Fulton Road at this point; if so, it was too late. His dispatch did not arrive until 8:30 a.m. on September 20. Grant hurried to Iuka to find that Price had departed overnight by the route Rosecrans had neglected. "This was the first I knew of the Fulton road being left open," Grant told Halleck. But at least the Confederates had headed south, not toward Tennessee or Kentucky to join Bragg.[28]

The principal fighting, lasting a bare three hours between 4:30 p.m. and dusk, had involved most of Price's army of 15,000 and hardly more than a Federal division, but the casualties were dreadful. The Federals reported

790 lost, while the Confederates admitted losing 901—and the Confederate total omitted the missing.[29]

+———+

Two weeks after the vicious standoff at Iuka, Van Dorn and Price combined their forces and struck.

Grant, then headquartering at Jackson, Tennessee, had his men as ready as possible, considering they were stretched paper-thin and uncertain where the blow might fall. Van Dorn had been at LaGrange, Tennessee; Price, southeast at Ripley, Mississippi. The two had thrown a cavalry curtain between them, the mounted Confederates maintaining a tight twenty-five-mile line stretching from northwest to southwest of Corinth. Grant, seeing that the screen made it possible for Van Dorn to move his and Price's troops undetected between LaGrange and Ripley, began to suspect the target. He ordered Rosecrans to concentrate his troops at Corinth and positioned potential reinforcements. He sent two regiments from Bolivar to a bridge six miles south toward the Ripley-LaGrange line and told General Stephen A. Hurlbut at Bolivar to try to strike the rear of any large Confederate force heading for Corinth from the west. He provided for other contingencies, too, but he was becoming certain the objective was Corinth. He told Rosecrans to expect an attack from the north cutting resupply routes and communications with Grant at Jackson.

Rosecrans hurried troops northwestward to blunt the coming blow. There was no attack on October 2, only skirmishing north and west of Corinth, and Grant used the time to send four regiments by train down to Corinth from Bolivar. He ordered two more to join the pair already dispatched to the bridge south of Bolivar. Becoming ever surer of the Confederate object, he put these combined four regiments under McPherson and sent them hastening from the bridge to Corinth. Then the trains stopped, and the Corinth telegraph went dead.[30]

Colonel John Oliver commanded the first troops Rosecrans had ordered northwest. On October 1, they had marched toward Chewalla north of the Tennessee border on the Memphis & Charleston Railroad. The next day they met a large Confederate force that pushed them backward until, with reinforcements, they charged and drove the Confederates backward. Then, coming upon a line of battle with artillery, they fell back. That night a flood of arriving Confederates poured southeastward into the top of a left-tilted *V* formed by the Memphis & Charleston Railroad, running northwest to Memphis, and the northbound Mobile & Ohio. The two tracks funneled the flood toward Corinth.

On the morning of October 3, the Confederates barreled down the Chewalla Road and in twenty minutes overwhelmed Federals in entrenchments Beauregard had dug there in May. Rosecrans sent a division rushing a mile and a half up the Mobile & Ohio tracks between the railroads to stem the tide. But hardly more than two hundred men held the point where this division linked up with the Union troops left on Chewalla Road. Van Dorn found the weak link and broke it.

October 3 was freakishly hot for that time of year, even in Mississippi. Thermometers registered ninety-four, and along with murderous artillery and musket fire, sunstroke and dehydration felled men on both sides. The Federals between the railroads, their center smashed, scrambled backward in continual withdrawals. But they got indispensable assistance from an unexpected source.

Van Dorn, in a failing characteristic of him, had done minimal reconnaissance, grossly underestimating the number of Federal cannon and the force needed to take them. Rosecrans's man in the middle was Colonel Thomas A. Davies, whose command included the cannon. His ammunition repeatedly ran low and was replenished by a six-mule team running into Corinth. His cannoneers' faces were blackened by gunpowder, their horses leaving a bloodstream in the road while units on their left withdrew, but Davies and his cannons held their position for a critical ninety minutes. By day's end they had fallen back five times, and the Confederates got close enough to shell Corinth. But the Federal left held onto two fortified artillery bastions north and northwest of the town, and, thanks in great part to Davies, Van Dorn could not drive between Rosecrans's two wings.[31]

Grant was in the dark back in Jackson, Tennessee, as he had anticipated he would be. Couriers had to go roundabout in a seven-hour trek because

Van Dorn and Price were between Jackson and Corinth. So Grant's reports from Rosecrans were few and late. One said Oliver's brigade had "acted feebly" and incorrectly implied that Davies's left had been driven backward for the same reason: "Our men did not act or fight well." Rosecrans added that a usually reliable scout remained sure the main Confederate target was Bolivar.

Grant had not bought it. Corinth, the rail hub and Union base in northern Mississippi, was obviously a much more attractive prize to Van Dorn than Bolivar, and the Confederate attack there presented Grant with an opportunity almost as alluring: a chance to take the Corinth attackers in the rear and possibly crush them. So he had ordered Hurlbut's division to march from Bolivar toward Corinth on October 3 and sent Rosecrans a roundabout message conveying how badly he wanted to get at Van Dorn.[32]

"Genl. Hurlbut will move today towards the enemy," he wrote. "We should attack if they do not. Do it soon. . . . Fight!"

Typically, no question of defeat clouded Grant's mind. He directed Rosecrans to pursue the enemy "the moment" he began to retreat. And if, in retreat, Van Dorn attacked and drove back Ord, who also was coming down from Bolivar, Rosecrans was to hound Van Dorn's rear all the way to Bolivar if need be.[33]

That night, Rosecrans continued to show his slight regard for Davies. Assigning positions for October 4, he granted Davies's request to have his men—who had borne so much of the brunt of the fighting the day before—moved out of the center. But Rosecrans did not move him far, despite Davies's warning that he "must not depend on my command" on October 4. Even with the move, Davies remained near the center.

The Federals would pay for Rosecrans's refusal to heed Davies's admonition. The next morning, Rosecrans watched in self-described "personal mortification" as a renewed Confederate attack routed Davies. Again facing an overpowering charge, some of Davies's "wearied and jaded troops yielded and fell back, scattering among the houses" of Corinth, leaving exposed artillery to be taken by the Confederates.[34]

But Missouri infantry posted along a ridge behind the front line of cannons fixed bayonets and delivered hot musket fire into the yelling, exultant Confederate horde. An uncaptured Wisconsin battery double-shotted its guns with canister, large projectiles made up of nearly fifty smaller ones per round—or one hundred per double shot—that separated like the contents of a shotgun shell when fired. The Wisconsin gunners fired 507 rounds and—working with the Missouri infantrymen—turned back repeated Confederate charges. They prevented the hauling off or spiking of the captured Federal guns, then recaptured them with a bayonet charge.

Some of the Confederate attackers made it into Corinth's courthouse square, but there most of Davies's men rallied. Federal volleys, together with a charge by reinforcements, drove the Southerners into flight. They left behind flags, dead, wounded, and some three hundred prisoners. Price reportedly wept seeing his men mowed down by the Federal cannons.[35]

The losses on both sides had been enormous. Of the 22,000 Confederates and 20,000 Federals who participated in the Battle of Corinth, some 1,100 were officially reported killed: 623 Federals and 515 Confederates. More than 5,000 more were wounded, and 1,600 were missing. Price's men had been driven into retreat. He and Van Dorn had also escaped with the remainder of their men, fleeing across the Hatchie River to the southwest.

The narrow Union victories at Iuka and Corinth were incomplete but notable. Grant was disappointed that Rosecrans did not follow instructions and stay on the Confederates' heels. With Ord closing in from the north and Rosecrans to the south, they might have crushed Van Dorn. But Grant had kept two armies from joining Bragg and so thinned their ranks that they would never launch a campaign in Mississippi again.[36]

The Iuka and Corinth battles weakened Grant's trust in Rosecrans. The latter had shown himself prone to snap judgments based on sloppy reconnaissance. Price had escaped down that uncovered road at Iuka, and he and Van Dorn had departed Corinth without pursuit, contrary to Grant's direct order. And, as Grant surely soon heard, Price and Van Dorn were both able to escape Corinth at least partly because Rosecrans was venting his spleen at his own exhausted men.

Davies, too, had had more than enough of Rosecrans. Almost three weeks after the battle, Davies all but dressed down his commander in an official letter. He reminded Rosecrans that on the afternoon of October 4, with the retreating Confederates barely out of sight, Rosecrans had said "upon the battle-field, among the piles of dead and groans of the wounded" felled by Davies's men, that Davies's men "were a set of cowards; . . . that they had disgraced themselves, and no wonder the rebel army had thrown its whole force upon [them] during the two days' engagement." Rosecrans's accusation was "demoralizing" to Davies's men and had prompted press articles denigrating them, Davies wrote. Virtually demanding a public apology, he noted that he now had filed a report of all that his men had done. Rosecrans took the hint and apologized.[37]

16

JULY–NOVEMBER 1862— FORREST IN THE CENTRAL SOUTH

"Mounted on Racehorses"

While Grant kept Price and Van Dorn from joining Braxton Bragg in the autumn of 1862, Bragg was benefiting from the work of a new, underappreciated subordinate: Forrest. The cavalryman's Murfreesboro raid in mid-July had enabled Bragg to transfer a massive number of troops by rail from Tupelo through Mobile to Chattanooga. Loss of the Federal garrison at Murfreesboro halted Buell's drive on Chattanooga and fixated that general's defensive nature even more on protecting his rear. This gave Bragg time to gather his army at Chattanooga for a dramatic drive northward. This sweeping attempt to recapture Middle Tennessee and seize much of neutral Kentucky, coupled with Robert E. Lee's invasion of Maryland, would be the closest the Confederacy ever came to coordinated grand offensives east and west of the Appalachians.

The Murfreesboro surrender had climaxed a marathon of long-distance riding, fighting, and railroad destruction for Forrest's troopers. They departed the town late on July 13 needing rest, and he gave them four days. From camp on Mountain Creek north of McMinnville, they paroled 1,700 prisoners, made a place in their ranks for the pair of artillery pieces they had captured, and exchanged their worst horses for better Federal ones.

They also scouted new targets, of which they had noted a profusion. A captured and then paroled member of the Seventh Pennsylvania Cavalry claimed to have overheard John Morgan, James W. Starnes, and Forrest exulting over the Murfreesboro coup and plotting continued disruption of Buell's supply line. They planned to destroy a bridge and then, just as it was repaired, to destroy another one, and so on. By Confederate design, perhaps, the Pennsylvanian escaped to tell an officer at Nashville.[1]

It was a good plan. The Murfreesboro strike had shown that the Federals' Louisville-Alabama supply line, which Buell had regarded as safer than the longer one to Memphis, was just as dangerously vulnerable. The Murfreesboro destruction had so broken the flow of Union provisions that it forced Buell to put his men on half rations. Buell's chief of staff warned a subordinate that getting even that half was not certain; to others, he wired that Buell's troops would "starve at this rate." Halleck ordered General Bull Nelson to hurry north from Alabama to reorganize the shambles at Murfreesboro. At the same time, he summoned Major General George H. Thomas eastward to take Nelson's place in Buell's force in northern Alabama.[2]

The instigator of all this commotion soon set off to cause more. Forrest left the Mountain Creek camp on the afternoon of July 18, intending to overpower an Ohio regiment garrisoned at Lebanon, Tennessee, east of Nashville. When he got there at dawn on July 20, however, the Ohioans had left for Nashville the previous midnight, burning everything they could not carry.[3]

Forrest rode on into the suburbs of Nashville, which he and his cavalrymen set about terrorizing. Five miles out, he captured three Federal pickets, then turned southwest to the Nashville-Chattanooga rail line, took two more pickets, and cut telegraph wires. He skirmished heavily with strong guard details posted at three railroad bridges on the city's south side, then destroyed the bridges. He would report killing a total of ten Federals, wounding at least that many, nabbing ninety-seven prisoners, and burning supplies at a suburban railroad depot. When more Federal troops rushed toward him, he fell back to McMinnville, having sustained not a single casualty.

Forrest's fighting style was heavily psychological; it had to be to compensate for his lesser numbers. The Federals had become so spooked that he could have taken Nashville with a few thousand men, he reported, but he had only 1,400. Similar fear swept Murfreesboro, where Federal troops were now fortifying and trying to blockade the road to his McMinnville base. He said he saw the same consternation everywhere he looked. He regretted that the size of his force would not let him "avail myself of this terror."[4]

He did not scare everybody, though. Some, he just frustrated. Federals were wearing themselves out looking for him. General Bull Nelson, having rushed into Murfreesboro in the wake of Forrest's departure, discounted to Buell the fearful wires from Nashville. Nelson promised when other converging troops were in position, "I will have about 1,200 cavalry, and Mr. Forrest shall have no rest." But that did not convince everybody, including General Buell, who himself appeared affected by the widespread, debilitating panic generated by Forrest's activities. When Halleck warned Buell from Washington that the slow progress toward Chattanooga was unacceptable, Buell replied that "a vastly superior cavalry force" was bedeviling his supply line to such a degree that he had "to fortify every bridge" on more than three hundred miles of railroad. Nelson promised Buell that he would start after Forrest on July 28, but the 1,200 Union cavalrymen he expected did not arrive by then. And chasing Morgan and Forrest with infantry in a hot Tennessee summer was "hopeless," he wrote. The two Confederate cavalry demons were "mounted on racehorses."[5]

While Nelson awaited his reinforcements, Bragg's flowed in. On July 24, Bragg's troops from Tupelo began arriving in Chattanooga from their rail trek through Mobile. During that week and the following one, Forrest continued to divert Federal attention by repeatedly striking the Nashville-Chattanooga tracks. In early August, he received word that the Confederate Congress had approved his promotion to what he had been calling himself since his memorable birthday in Murfreesboro: brigadier general. The notification came from General Kirby Smith in Knoxville, who ordered Forrest to continue his depredations in Middle Tennessee while the last of Bragg's men chugged into Chattanooga to the southeast. Smith also indicated that new command arrangements were in the wind. Forrest, he wrote, should now copy Bragg on all his communications.

Bragg had recently succeeded an ill Beauregard to command of the Confederacy's largest western army. The new theater chief soon ordered Forrest to Chattanooga for a conference.

I n August, a misleadingly bland wire arrived in Chattanooga. It would prove the most fateful of Forrest's military life—and perhaps nearly so for the Confederate States of America. Addressed to Bragg from G. W. Randolph, the Confederate secretary of war, it informed the western commander that "Forrest and Withers are appointed brigadiers, and ordered to report to you."

In blue blood–controlled Dixie, possibly no high commander besides the far-sighted Lee or the iconoclastic Beauregard (if even he) would have heeded the opinions of such a coarse but brilliant commoner as Forrest. Still, it is hard to imagine a Confederate commander less so inclined than Braxton Bragg. Just as the new man on a job tends to overachieve in trying to fit in, Bragg, a plebeian who had blasted a path into the upper class as a Mexican War artillerist, now brandished that class's prerogatives with thoroughgoing egotism. His marriage into huge wealth on the strength of his Mexican glory only compounded his surpassing sense of self-worth. An adjunct aristocrat, he had become master of a large Louisiana sugar plantation and property that included more than two hundred slaves.

Like Forrest's blacksmith father, Bragg's, a carpenter, had worked with his hands. Each son had endured the snubs of the self-described "better class of people" in the community of his youth. Both men also were born of strong-willed mothers. There, though, the similarities ended. Bragg had been born in Warrenton, North Carolina, at a time when his father, who had bootstrapped his way upward, was constructing some of the upscale town's finer buildings. By the time youngest son Braxton had reached boyhood, his father owned twenty slaves. He was able to send Braxton, at age seven, to the fashionable Warrenton Male Academy. The boy would never have to soil or callus his hands with the kind of labor his father performed. Forrest, by contrast, had been born in humbler Chapel Hill, Tennessee, and his father's finances had gone "to wreck," as the son's authorized biography vaguely puts it. The family then fell from land ownership in comparatively settled Tennessee to lessee status in northern Mississippi, from which the government had only recently removed Native Americans. Bedford, the eldest son, labored dawn to dark clearing and tilling leased fields.[6]

The difference in their respective sides of the Appalachians would have been significant to Bragg. His North Carolina hometown, Warrenton, was located just a few miles from the Virginia border in his state's longest-settled eastern half, far from the wilderness of the western mountains. Tennessee, by contrast, was a more insular area offering fewer educational and cultural advantages. Bragg tended to view Tennesseans as backwoods rustics lacking in character and inclined toward shiftlessness and cowardice, much the way twentieth-century society often viewed so-called hillbillies. By the time Bragg approached manhood, his older brothers had raised the family into the lower levels of the upper class, one having become a congressman and the other a judge. A personality with a bent toward caustic criticism of others and rare self-examination buttressed, if anything, Bragg's consciousness of higher status. He wrote thousands of letters but never mentioned his mother, who was once briefly jailed for killing a slave because of alleged impertinence. Her son would rarely, if ever, accept shame or blame.[7]

Like every other Civil War West Pointer, Bragg would have heard Napoleonic precepts taught by famed professor Dennis Mahan. According to Mahan, an army must be professional, its commanders bold. Forts are valueless if they inspire a defensive mind-set. An enemy's country must be invaded to make him feel war's burdens. Obsession with opportunities to deceive the enemy, a firm resolve not to waste resources, rigorous intelligence gathering, and zealous guarding of security—all these were central tenets of Mahan's military philosophy, along with cavalry and bayonet charges and strong cautions, too often ignored by Civil War commanders, against attacking fortifications head-on.[8]

As a student at West Point, Bragg would likely have memorized these maxims. But he had a self-satisfied mind and an archly contentious attitude toward viewpoints other than his own. He never checked a book out of the academy's 8,000-volume library, and in the prewar army, he became the subject of an undoubtedly apocryphal story that points up a larger truth. Serving in a regiment, the story went, he held the position

of both company commander and quartermaster. As company commander, he purportedly requisitioned some supplies, then as quartermaster denied the requisition. He then disputed back and forth over it
until the regiment's commander supposedly said, "My God, Mr. Bragg,
you have quarreled with every officer in the army, and now you are quarreling with yourself." Such traits only assured his neglect of another
Mahan rule, which went over not just Bragg's head but those of countless other privileged young officers-to-be, especially ones from Dixie. It
warned cadets to act "like ordinary people, to court society in general,"
because in associating with everybody, rather than just other officers or
the upper crust, they would find and absorb "that floating capital, ideas
common to the mass, called common sense."[9]

Bragg and the Confederate high command forgot or ignored Mahan's
social advice. They seemed unable to comprehend that a person from the
"mass" could already know by instinct or personal experience the com-
monsense essentials of Mahan's strategic precepts. So, along with the
Mahan principle of cultivating common connections, Bragg and his fel-

GENERAL BRAXTON BRAGG

low aristocrats neglected to notice the capabilities of men such as Forrest. Of the bagging of Murfreesboro, Bragg wrote to Beauregard, a fellow Louisiana planter and close friend, "The whole affair, in proportion to numbers, [is] more brilliant than the grand battles where 'strategy' seems to have been the staple production on both sides."[10] Forrest had obviously planned the three-pronged Murfreesboro operation with care, then devised some of its elements on the fly. Bragg recognized the brilliance of the result, but he seemed to miss the mental ability that produced it. Professor Mahan presumably would not have done so.

On August 17, the day he received Randolph's wire assigning Forrest to his command, Bragg sent a dispatch requesting that the Tennessean cross the mountains to Chattanooga for a face-to-face meeting. Had it occurred, it probably would have been their second. The first appears to have happened a few days earlier.[11]

The mood of that initial conversation, for which Forrest also had to ride to Chattanooga, was likely cordial. Although the month was August, Bragg was in the springtime of his hopes, just starting his reign as commander of what would soon be redesignated the Army of Tennessee. He would have been patronizingly genial to a new, working-class subordinate—even one whose sometimes primitive English would have been off-putting. Forrest, for his part, would probably have been more than willing to accept the authority of an eminent superior such as Bragg, who was nationally famed for his performance during the Mexican War.

The Chattanooga round-trip, made during the second week of August, was two hundred miles, but Forrest made it in four days. His job, as he doubtless learned from Bragg, was to bedevil Federal forces and prevent them from advancing farther east. In holding them in central Tennessee, Forrest could help ensure that they would not get in the way of the campaign Bragg was mulling.[12]

Bragg's idea was to strike northward in concert with Kirby Smith from Knoxville and Van Dorn and Price from Mississippi. While the rickety rails of the South's already deteriorating railroads continued to bring the last of Bragg's units into Chattanooga from Tupelo, Bragg pondered whether to attack Nashville or adopt a suggestion from Kirby Smith. On

August 9, Smith had proposed that they make a joint invasion of Kentucky, recommending that they do it by separate routes and unite when they reached the Bluegrass State. Four days later, Smith hurried off from Knoxville toward eastern Kentucky, while Bragg still contemplated.

In his second dispatch to Forrest, on August 17, Bragg requested that Forrest provide an advance guard for Bragg's northward move. It had become "perfectly evident you cannot cope with the enemy in your front as he is now located," the general said. This seemed obvious to Bragg because of the number of Federal units that Buell was rushing into Middle Tennessee to safeguard Union supply lines from Forrest, John Morgan, and Bragg's developing northward thrust. With enemy presence mounting in Forrest's vicinity, Bragg continued, his cavalry could be of more use screening Bragg's front and western flank as the army headed up the Sequatchie Valley, then crossed the Cumberland Plateau westward into Middle Tennessee.

Bragg's dispatch also said something else of equal importance. It promised Forrest command of "the whole" of the cavalry of the Army of the Mississippi as soon as the mounted force arrived in Chattanooga. The pledge of such an important position would have become even more meaningful to Forrest's working-class pride. He had reluctantly left northern Mississippi only at Beauregard's urging, then had been confronted with aristocratic officers who refused to serve under him. Given the self-consciousness he felt because of his educational deficiencies, he doubtless viewed the prospect of becoming cavalry commander with some concern. Such a prospect required planning, so he would have had to tell a few trusted subordinates. The Murfreesboro raid had more than indicated that he was up to the new job, though, and within his inner circle, expectations must have risen dramatically.[13]

Bragg's dispatch said he would like to see Forrest in person. It appeared, though, only to propose—not order—Forrest's return to Chattanooga. Bragg seemed to suggest that Forrest leave only a token force in Middle Tennessee and bring most of his troopers into the Sequatchie, where they could prevent Federal incursions and prying reconnaissance from detecting the movement of Bragg's main force.[14]

Forrest was slow to respond. The August 17 dispatch appears to have taken a while to reach him. He had probably left the McMinnville neighborhood before Bragg's communication arrived there. The Federals had sent two regiments and Major General Thomas, a first-class commander, into McMinnville, and another Union general, Richard W. Johnson, had more troops ranging nearby west of Smithville. Others were hurrying into southeast-central Tennessee.[15]

Bragg sent Forrest another message on August 22. This one was abrupt and indicated displeasure. It ordered him to "act according to the instructions you have previously received" and prepare "your command for other service. The enemy is reported advancing up the Sequatchie Valley." Bragg's need of a cavalry screen was fast becoming more pressing.[16]

Forrest, though, was busy spreading havoc among Buell's supply lines. He was thus deflecting plenty of attention from Bragg's advance, just not in the area where Bragg most wanted it. On August 27, Forrest attacked a Union column near Woodbury and, after being repulsed there, threatened Federal railroad communications again at Manchester. He seems to have received Bragg's second dispatch around that time, for he next headed eastward, ostensibly to comply with Bragg's order.[17]

The Federals began closing in. Three large Union commands—at Winchester, Manchester, and McMinnville—crowded Forrest against the Cumberland Mountains, the western wall of the Sequatchie Valley. Riding to the top of a commanding peak in the early morning of August 29, he saw the trio of forces converging on him on three roads. A fourth was approaching too. On August 30, George Thomas alerted General Alexander McCook at Altamont, a village southeast of McMinnville on the Cumberland Plateau, that Forrest was headed toward him, and around the time of the mountaintop reconnaissance, Forrest learned from a scout that a McCook unit was already approaching from the east.

Forrest's road into the Sequatchie Valley was now blocked. In grave danger of being surrounded and overwhelmed, he remembered that his force had just passed a dry creek bed with banks high enough to hide mounted men. He ordered his troopers backward, and they snuck down that creek bed and away. He gave up trying to cross into the Sequatchie Valley at Altamont. In the presence of so many Federals and with his intended transmountain escape route closed, he determined to join Bragg's northbound army when it reached Sparta farther north, on the western slope of the Cumberland Mountains.[18]

Masking his intended move, he hurried westward. On August 29, the same day that he saw he was blocked at Altamont, he attacked a stockade guarding a railroad bridge at Morrison, a dozen miles southwest of McMinnville. Opposed by a detachment of the Eighteenth Ohio Infantry, he suffered daunting casualties estimated at nearly two hundred. He withdrew to the northeast toward Sparta, leaving behind a dozen dead.[19]

As Forrest maneuvered west of the Cumberlands, Bragg chose another cavalry commander east of them. Contradicting his August 17 dispatch promising Forrest the Army of the Mississippi's mounted troops from Tupelo, Bragg on August 27 ordered these newly arrived cavalrymen into the Sequatchie under a twenty-six-year-old converted infantry colonel. Joseph Wheeler, number nineteen in the West Point class of 1859, had commanded the Nineteenth Alabama Infantry at Shiloh. In an apparent interim action, Bragg had named Wheeler head of the Tupelo cavalry in July. He now handed Wheeler the command he had promised to Forrest.

At Bragg's order, Wheeler crossed the Tennessee River and rode up the Sequatchie Valley. Reaching Altamont on August 30, he surprised the McCook Federal unit that had obstructed Forrest's way across the mountain the day before. Then Wheeler dropped back into the valley and took up the duty Bragg had originally assigned to Forrest, covering the front and left flank of Bragg's army as it moved north.[20]

Forrest continued to have brushes with Union troops. The significance of these encounters varied from source to source. The Federals reported that they continually whipped Forrest, while he dismissed the incidents as skirmishes. The most convincing indication that Forrest "was handled pretty roughly" at the end of his six-week sojourn behind the lines is the fact that those words came from Thomas. One of the most experienced and level-headed Union commanders, he wrote Buell from McMinnville that Forrest was "whipped" on August 28 near Woodbury, "whipped again" the next day at Morrison, and "whipped" yet another time near Altamont as he tried to escape into the Sequatchie Valley. On turning back toward Woodbury, he was overtaken "and again badly whipped and dispersed," Thomas wrote. The unexcitable major general is unlikely to have inflated these claims, although subordinates reporting some of them to him may have done so.[21]

Whatever his punishment by Federal pursuers, Forrest accomplished most of his purposes. His aim at the time was not victory so much as occupying as many Federals as he could. At that, he was anything but whipped.

The Confederate advance had turned into a race. Bragg's northward thrust, flanking Buell's entire Louisville-Nashville-Alabama supply line, sent the Union general scrambling backward before his army could be cut off and defeated. He abandoned Alabama and marched hard for Nashville, then continued north toward Kentucky.

But Buell's fallback, although heartening to Confederates, did not repair all the damage the Union presence had done to secessionism in central Tennessee. This was especially true of slavery. Jefferson Davis had tried to shield as much Southern territory as possible in part to prevent slaves from fleeing their owners and actively or passively assisting the Union anywhere the Federals gained influence.[22]

The Confederate president's fears of slave disarray were now being realized. At Murfreesboro, even though Union troops had pulled out to head for northern Kentucky, the lasting damage was apparent. The farm of Confederate soldier Robert D. Jamison, away fighting with the Forty-fifth Tennessee Infantry, had escaped Federal foraging back in the summer, but not its effects. Jamison's twenty-two-year-old wife, Camilla, had trouble with refractory slaves. Several had fled, Camilla bitterly wrote, adding that she would not mind if others did. One named Erline had apparently left for the "glory land" to the north. The day the Federals departed Murfreesboro, Erline gathered "Becky, Susan, Dick, and Bob" and vanished. And Camilla's mother was missing six more, including a Harry, a Silas, and a Mariah. Camilla told her husband that if he encountered any of them, he should sell them to buyers farther south, "for I never want to see one of them again."[23]

◦━◦

On September 3, Forrest caught up with Bragg's army at Sparta, as he had planned. Over the next ten days, however, he would have slowly realized that he had been supplanted as Bragg's cavalry leader before serving a day in that post. Bragg's message of August 27 (likely the last Forrest had received, if, indeed, he did receive it) had said that Forrest was expected to cover the army's left and front. Yet near Glasgow, Kentucky, on September 12, he literally ran into Wheeler and found him doing the job supposedly assigned to Forrest—and at the head of the cavalry that had been promised him.

One can only wonder how much of a surprise this was. Bragg himself had not been at Sparta when Forrest got there, so the Tennessean had had to ride twenty miles farther southeast to report to his commander. There Bragg ordered him to harass the rear of Buell's northbound army, observe it closely, and screen Bragg's movements. Forrest's reaction soon afterward indicates that Bragg did not tell him Wheeler now commanded the cavalry. If Bragg did tell him, he probably did so in such a passing way that Forrest took it as a stopgap measure until he himself could arrive.[24]

Bragg and Buell were now entering the climactic heat of a race to northern Kentucky. Buell had snatched up every "cartridge or . . . ounce of provisions" at such bases as Murfreesboro before abandoning them. He was hurrying past Nashville toward Louisville, and Bragg was marching hard to cut him off. Forrest, meanwhile, complied with Bragg's orders and began dogging Buell's rear.

Forrest headed to McMinnville and then to Woodbury, aiming to overtake Buell at Murfreesboro. There he found that Federal soldiers had set the town's courthouse afire, but he arrived in time to save it. As Buell pushed his units up the road through Nashville, Forrest crossed the Cumberland River between Lebanon and the Tennessee capital and drove Federal protective cavalry back onto the Union rear. He then attacked the Federals at Tyree Springs on the Nashville-Louisville turnpike, halfway between Nashville and the Kentucky border. A little farther north, he again assailed them, this time with artillery. He later claimed to have delayed Buell's progress for four hours, requiring the Federals to form for battle. When they halted and shelled a position Forrest had taken in the cover of some woods, he sneaked his men away and into a roundabout ten-mile trot to get ahead of the Union column.[25]

The Federal delay may have been as much Wheeler's work as Forrest's. On the night of September 11, seven hundred of Wheeler's men had set an ambush in Buell's front just north of Woodburn, Kentucky, on the Bowling Green road. The Federals discovered the danger and turned back, Wheeler reported, but not before his men had captured a Union captain and several enlisted men. The hidden Confederates waited awhile longer, then withdrew two miles off the highway to rest and feed. At about 2 p.m., Federal cavalry and infantry came looking for them. A fraction of the seven hundred Confederates fell back fighting, hoping to draw the foe to the main body of Wheeler's troops and separate the Union infantry from its cavalry. The Federals refused the bait and retired, but they had lost time responding to Wheeler's threats.[26]

Hearing the firing, Forrest pushed forward, looking for the fight. Then scouts reported an enemy force approaching pell-mell from his right. Ordering his Eighth Texas to assail these troops head-on, he moved the rest of his men to attack from the flank. The Texans were preparing to charge when they discovered that the presumed enemy was Wheeler, whose men were as surprised as Forrest's. The flank attack was barely aborted in time to prevent friendly-fire losses. Forrest then learned from Wheeler that Wheeler had struck the Federals at the approximate point Forrest had gone to the front to hit. If their encounter here was strained, neither Forrest nor Wheeler commented on it. Wheeler's report dismissed the incident with a single, clipped sentence: "General Forrest came up in the rear while the fight was going on, but finding he could not engage the enemy to advantage he retired toward Glasgow."[27]

If his battlefield interactions with Wheeler did not embitter Forrest, plenty of other things about the young colonel would have. Wheeler's personality could not have helped their relationship. Fifteen years Forrest's junior, he stood five feet, five inches and was a human wisp of 120 pounds. He was humorless, aloof, and full of a stiff, pompous courtliness that the pragmatic Forrest would have regarded as silly in general and infuriating in particular. That, however, was not all. Nominally hailing from Augusta, Georgia, Wheeler had New England Yankee roots. His parents had come to the Peach State from Connecticut, where their son had attended a prep school. He had also lived for a time in New York City.[28]

Wheeler was much more like Bragg than Forrest. Indeed, the two West Pointers already had a history. Wheeler's first Confederate assignment had

been as a first lieutenant of artillery at Pensacola, Florida, under Bragg.
His antebellum combat experience had been limited to scouting with the
US Army against Indians in New Mexico. But at Pensacola he had in-
gratiated himself. In some ways, Wheeler was the perfect Bragg subordinate. Extraordinarily polite, genteel, and serious, he was the product of an
elite education, both civilian and military; he was also hyperenergetic and
eager to please.[29]

Wheeler's ambition initially created friction with his superior. His in-
troduction to Bragg had come when he bypassed the chain of command
and entered Bragg's Pensacola headquarters one evening. He volunteered
to mount and arm some captured siege guns that the commander had
been unable to get his politically appointed volunteer officers to render
operational. Bragg gave Wheeler permission to do it, and he did. But then
the young officer made a slight misstep. As a West Point graduate,
Wheeler was obviously overqualified to serve as a lieutenant in the state
forces of Georgia, but he became overzealous. With his cooperation, Alabama politicians coaxed such a spectacular promotion for him out of
Confederate secretary of war Leroy Pope Walker that Bragg complained.
Walker then resigned to become a brigadier general, so Bragg could only
protest to Walker's successor. Walker had vaulted the young lieutenant all
the way to colonel—a megapromotion that, Bragg grumbled, injured the
morale of those of his subordinates who possessed more distinguished
records in the old army. It also, Bragg said, drew attention to his own failed
efforts to get these other men promoted.[30]

Nevertheless, Wheeler remained colonel of the Nineteenth Alabama
Infantry. He fought heroically at Shiloh with the Nineteenth and saw a
third of his men killed or wounded there. He carried the unit's colors in
its final charge of the battle, and his brigade and division commanders,
along with corps commander Bragg, all praised his performance. In the reorganization that followed Bragg's succession of Beauregard, Bragg first
turned to one of his Pensacola favorites, infantry brigadier general James R.
Chalmers, to lead the unit's cavalry. But then, when Chalmers asked to
return to his infantry unit, Bragg drafted Wheeler, despite his distinctly
marginal credentials. Although his first assignment out of West Point had
been to the Cavalry School at Carlisle, Pennsylvania, Wheeler had ranked
fourth from the bottom of his West Point class. And although he was

about to become commander of all the cavalry of the Army of the Mississippi, his worst marks had been in cavalry tactics.[31]

On September 13, Bragg reached Glasgow, Kentucky. Forrest arrived there the same day, almost certainly intending to clarify the situation regarding Wheeler.

There is no account of the conversation. Since his September 3 meeting with Forrest south of Sparta, Bragg had had ten days to decide what to do about the command of his mounted troops—whether to leave them under Wheeler or transfer them to Forrest. Bragg was a harsh disciplinarian, and he likely intended to impress on Forrest the necessity of obeying orders, received or otherwise. He had first given Wheeler command of his cavalry out of necessity and also, apparently, out of irritation at Forrest's prolonged stay in Middle Tennessee when Federals blocked him from entering the Sequatchie Valley. Bragg was given to snap judgments followed by equally swift reversals, and now, faced with a man whose rank and exploits fully entitled him to head the cavalry, Bragg backed off a bit. On September 14 his headquarters issued orders dividing the cavalry into two brigades. They placed Forrest in command of mounted troops on the army's right wing under plodding General Leonidas Polk. Wheeler got the left under General William J. Hardee, a much-respected military author and professional soldier.

Under other circumstances, Forrest might not have felt abused. As John Morgan's second in command Basil Duke would write, Forrest did not appear to aspire to lofty positions—likely because, as Duke did not have to add, such heights would have made him more conscious of his cultural limitations. But working-class pride rarely permitted Forrest to ignore a slight, and Bragg's public disregard of his rank and reneging on the appointment to head the cavalry had all the hallmarks of one. It also made Bragg appear emphatically ungrateful for the work Forrest had done from Murfreesboro onward.

Over the next two weeks, Bragg continued to slight him. The right was the lesser wing. Its commander, Episcopal bishop Polk, was the army's least-experienced top general. The September 14 order transferred the

Eighth Texas Cavalry, one of Forrest's most valued units, to Wheeler. The next day, Hardee, commander of Bragg's right, temporarily ordered to Wheeler two units given to Forrest by Bragg the day before. Hardee then quickly reassigned the Texans back to Polk, but not specifically to Forrest. Also on September 15, Polk ordered Forrest to supply one of his remaining regiments to a right-wing division commander. Overnight, the five cavalry units under his command had shrunk to two.[32]

Why Bragg rethought his initial impulse to put Forrest in charge of his cavalry is not difficult to guess. It occurred so soon after their meeting on September 3 as to make Forrest's inability to get back across the Cumberland Plateau on time seem like an excuse. Bragg prided himself on his cultivation, and in their earlier, first encounter, he likely was put off by Forrest's lack of polish. Forrest's speech was backwoodsy, full of such words as "mout" for "might" and "fetch" for "bring." There may have been additional contributing factors. Two of Bragg's admiring colonels at Pensacola, now in his army as brigadiers, had known Forrest years before. Chalmers was a lawyer who remembered seeing Forrest as a young farmer, when he was tilling leased hill land. James Patton Anderson had boarded with the Forrests when Bedford was selling farm equipment. The portraits both men could draw of Forrest would have diminished him in Bragg's eyes. Bragg plainly looked down on him.[33]

Forrest's service in the Kentucky invasion lasted just a dozen more days. His performance was decidedly lackluster, but not as much so as Bragg's. Bragg beat Buell to central Kentucky, then dithered. And on September 19 at Munfordville, he moved his 30,000 troops aside and offered Buell's 38,000 Federals an open road to the safety of Louisville. Wheeler later recalled that Bragg permitted Buell to pass him on the Louisville road because Thomas's troops from Nashville had caught up with Buell's on September 19, swelling the retreating army. Wheeler said Bragg did not feel strong enough to take on the combined Federal commands without help from Kirby Smith's 10,000 troops, with whom he had yet to form a junction. Bragg, Wheeler said, presumed he would get a better chance to fight later.[34]

Quintessentially indecisive, Bragg had hamstrung himself. His army was suffering for lack of water and forage for its animals. In initially urging the campaign, Kirby Smith had volunteered to subordinate himself to Bragg, but Bragg had not ordered Smith's 10,000 men to Munfordville to help him fight Buell. He also was slow to adopt Smith's repeated recommendation that Bragg take Louisville, which on September 20 was defended by 6,000 Federals reportedly ready to abandon it. Had he followed Smith's advice, Buell and Thomas would have had to face entrenched Confederates when they got there. At Munfordville on the night of September 17, Bragg had left Tennessee governor Isham G. Harris with the impression that Bragg and Smith would unite to take Louisville "doubtless . . . within the next ten or twelve days." That, though, would not have beaten Buell and Thomas there. The Confederates would have had to fight their way into the fortified city against more than equal numbers.

On September 20, the day after Thomas caught up with Buell, Bragg moved east toward Kirby Smith's army at Lexington in the lush Bluegrass pastureland. At Bardstown on October 4, he would install a rump Confederate state government that had no prayer of surviving if the Confederate armies left.[35]

This first cusp of autumn was hot, the ground hardened by a parched summer. The bluegrass had turned brown, many springs to dust. They mirrored the desiccation of Confederate hopes. In Maryland on September 17, Robert E. Lee had failed to defeat George McClellan at Antietam Creek. The battle there had cost the Confederacy 10,318 irreplaceable casualties.

On the Bluegrass side of the Alleghenies, Kentuckians were not rising to embrace the Confederate standard. Kirby Smith wrote Bragg on September 17 that the locals did not want to see themselves and their land scarred by war; their "hearts are evidently with us, but their bluegrass and fat-grass are against us." Most of the surplus rifles Bragg and Smith had brought to arm new enlistees remained packed in wagons. General John C. Breckinridge, the Kentucky statesman and recent US vice president, had not arrived to help rally them, as Bragg had wished and presumed. In late September, Breckinridge was still in Mississippi with Van Dorn, who was pursuing his own agenda. When Breckinridge did move, under orders from Richmond, it was toward Knoxville to help keep East Tennessee unionists from revolting.[36]

Meanwhile, Forrest's patience with his superiors was wearing thin. On September 17 at Munfordville, he helped the Confederates capture 4,000 Federals after a three-day siege. There he began to complain. Many of his men's horses had been killed at Murfreesboro, he wrote Polk, and the

Confederacy owed them for the animals. He also filed a requisition for a variety of the small arms captured at Munfordville; they were "much" needed by his men, he said.[37]

The next night, September 18, Forrest's horse, exhausted by long and hard use, fell and rolled on its rider. The accident dislocated his right shoulder and bruised his whole body. Confined to a jolting wagon, he continued to be peppered with orders from Polk, who appeared oblivious to the depletion of Forrest's command. Forrest's primary grievance, however, seems to have been against the ultimate source of his troubles: Bragg. According to lore, Forrest began to complain publicly about this commander who had driven his army so hard to block the enemy's line of march and then done nothing after getting there.[38]

On September 20, as Bragg's army began stepping out of Buell's way and moving east toward Kirby Smith, Polk gave Forrest a profusion of orders. He was to throw a "strong force" in front of Bragg's wagon train, protect both flanks, gather provisions along the road, and destroy the railroad between Louisville and Elizabethtown, Kentucky, as well as a spur track to Lebanon, Kentucky. The assignment was preposterous, and two mornings later Forrest, aching at Bardstown, rebelled. He said his horses were in no condition to do all these things even if he had sufficient men. He would "do the best I can to protect the wagon-train." That was all.[39]

Polk paid no attention. On September 23 he ordered Forrest to position his "brigade"—the men assigned to Forrest now numbered nowhere near that—twelve miles from Bardstown, place detachments a dozen miles right and left, keep in "constant" touch with the pickets by courier, immediately report any enemy movements, destroy bridges and culverts on the Louisville-Bardstown rail line as far toward Louisville as he could, and do it all "as promptly as possible." At 10 p.m. that night, Forrest replied that he did not have a full company in his "brigade" because of guards and pickets that he already had supplied, but he would take from the remnants of his force enough men to obey the order. No enemy, he said, appeared closer than 10 miles.[40]

Forrest had not exaggerated the condition of his men and mounts. An order from Bragg that very day, September 23, indicates that. It required all cavalry horses to be inspected and all found permanently disabled or unlikely to recover in four weeks to be shot. As many replacement mounts as were available would be purchased locally, and riders unable to be re-mounted would become "sharpshooters."[41]

On September 25, Forrest was relieved of duty with Bragg's Kentucky army. He was allowed to keep just four companies of his original regiment. The rest of the cavalry of the right wing was put under Wheeler, enlarging his command. Bragg ordered Forrest to Middle Tennessee to scrape up a new force to guard Bragg's rear. At a meeting in Bardstown on September 27, Bragg told Forrest that all troops he was able to gather in Middle Tennessee would be his.[42]

Forrest wasted no time on the road. Trekking the 165 miles from Bardstown to Murfreesboro in five days, he arrived in early October. He hardly reached his new command before it came under attack.

On the night of October 6, Federals from Nashville marched to LaVergne, on the railroad between Murfreesboro and Nashville, and attacked a Confederate garrison of mostly raw recruits. These scattered. A day or so earlier, Forrest had sent forward a veteran Alabama infantry regiment, the Thirty-second, and it held its position until overwhelming Union numbers forced its retreat. With just his own cavalry battalion and Captain S. L. Freeman's artillery, Forrest pushed through the flood of fugitives to LaVergne. But by then the Federals had returned to Nashville, satisfied to have dispersed the Confederates.[43]

Forrest quickly rearranged. He formed the green survivors into stronger units, recruited others, and consolidated irregular remnants. The last-mentioned included the Fourth Tennessee Cavalry of Colonel James Starnes of Tullahoma. Starnes had fought under Forrest at Sacramento, Kentucky, and been active in the Murfreesboro-McMinnville region, cooperating with Forrest there. Other new units were the Eighth Tennessee of Colonel George Dibrell of Sparta, with whom Forrest's youngest brother, Jeffrey, served as major; the Ninth Tennessee of Colonel Jacob B. Biffle; and Colonel A. A. Russell's Fourth Alabama. Forrest spread the newer recruits among these.[44]

Forrest also sought help from his immediate superior, Major General Sam Jones in Knoxville. The day of the LaVergne debacle, he telegraphed Jones that the Federals were advancing. Jones ordered some troops to him, along with "arms, ammunition, and accouterments." On October 10, Jones wired that he had no more men to send and authorized Forrest to fall back to Tullahoma if need be, but he suggested that if the Federal force in Forrest's front was no larger than reported, "the cavalry ought to be able so to harass the enemy as to prevent their advancing to Murfreesboro." Intelligence was obviously conflicting. On October 16, Forrest sent forward 1,500 cavalry and a section of artillery to investigate a "strong rumor of evacuation of Nashville." Meanwhile, Jones sent him five infantry regiments. As many arms as he needed were also on the way, Jones promised. But Forrest's first, mediocre stint as a leader of combined infantry and cavalry lasted little more than two weeks. Jones informed him on October 20 that Major General Breckinridge was headed to Murfreesboro to take command.[45]

Forrest's service with Breckinridge was brief also. During it, he launched one notable operation, a heavy demonstration against Nashville, which had been all but abandoned by the departure northward of Buell and Thomas. In the overnight of November 4, Forrest led 3,000 cavalry and some Kentucky infantry on no less than seven roads into Nashville from the south and east. Just across the Cumberland River, Colonel John Hunt Morgan attacked with still another force. By 10 a.m., the Confederates had carried the outer fortifications and were within two miles of the city proper. Then Breckinridge apparently withdrew the attack's necessary infantry element on orders from Bragg, and the attack foundered.[46]

Bragg returned from Kentucky amid shattered Confederate hopes. He had fought Buell to a bloody draw on October 8 at Perryville, southeast of Louisville, and came hurrying back by way of East Tennessee. Whereas in September he had raced Buell for Louisville, in November he had to try to beat the Federals back to Middle Tennessee, which had become vulnerable because Earl Van Dorn and Sterling Price, held in Mississippi by the unproductive battles of Iuka and Corinth, had never arrived.

Bragg reached central Tennessee in mid-November. Headquartering at Tullahoma, roughly halfway between Chattanooga and Nashville, he installed Wheeler as permanent leader of his cavalry, naming him chief of the three mounted brigades that Bragg considered "regular"; he viewed Forrest's and Morgan's men as mere partisans. Wheeler took over Forrest's headquarters, and Bragg ordered Forrest west to Columbia, Tennessee, to prepare for his most dangerous assignment yet: a strike deep into occupied West Tennessee to relieve growing Federal pressure on Mississippi.[47]

The draw at Iuka and the incomplete Union victory at Corinth had done more than just keep Van Dorn and Price out of Bragg's Kentucky campaign. The two battles had so depleted these two generals' forces that they could no longer mount an offensive in Mississippi. The Federals were now dotting West Tennessee with rail-supported supply dumps and forwarding stations for ominous operations farther southward. During the autumn, matériel and newly recruited Midwestern regiments were hurried forward from Columbus, Kentucky, into bases and depots in southern Tennessee and northern Mississippi. Grand Junction, Tennessee, at the crossing of the Memphis & Charleston and the Mississippi Central railroads, was now a staging area for establishment of a huge supply base at Holly Springs in northern Mississippi. If Federal progress down the Mississippi Central was not stopped, Union troops would soon reach Mississippi's capital at Jackson. The statehouse was just forty-five miles east of vital Vicksburg, now the last major connection between the eastern Confederacy and the states of Louisiana, Arkansas, and Texas. If Vicksburg fell, the Confederacy would be cut in two, and Union troops and commerce could travel every mile of America's primary river.

Forrest's resentment was meanwhile hardening. Around December 1, 1862, a small and slender youth showed up at Forrest's headquarters carrying orders naming him Forrest's new chief of artillery. Lieutenant John W. Morton, son of a prominent Nashville physician, had commanded a gun crew intrepidly at Fort Donelson, braving fire that killed or wounded thirty-three of his forty-eight comrades. Now, released from the Johnson's Island prison and exchanged, he had wangled this appointment to join the fierce cavalryman who had disdained the Donelson surrender. But Forrest knew only one thing about Morton: that Bragg was using the young man to insult him again. Bragg was purporting to take from Forrest's command an experienced and gallant man and replace him with a stripling. The chief of artillery, Captain S. L. Freeman, was an antebellum attorney whose steady courage Forrest was coming to admire.

"I have a fine battery under Captain Freeman, and I don't propose to be interfered with by Bragg," Forrest defiantly told Morton. That was that. The aghast youth stumbled out, and Forrest wheeled on an aide to curse. "I don't know why in the hell Bragg sent that tallow-faced boy here to take charge of my artillery," he said. "I'll not stand it."[48]

He ordered an aide to fire off a letter of outrage to Forrest's new immediate superior, another comparative boy: Wheeler. Had there been any doubt about Forrest's attitude toward the man who had become head of Bragg's cavalry, there could be none now.[49]

IV

VICKSBURG:
IMPREGNABILITY DEFIED

17

OCTOBER–DECEMBER 1862— GRANT AT CORINTH

"You Have Command of All Troops and Permission to Fight"

Grant's patience was worn thin.

Newly minted major general William S. Rosecrans, commander of the Union's base at Corinth, was proving unmanageable. Back on September 19, he had arrived late at Iuka, Mississippi, to initiate the battle plan he himself had suggested. Then, hurrying to catch up, he had left open a road down which Confederate general Sterling Price's army escaped. Now, in early October, Rosecrans was slow to the chase as General Earl Van Dorn's winnowed ranks retreated from Corinth—this despite Grant's repeated orders to get on the Southerners' heels as soon as they broke, then dog them "to the wall."

When Rosecrans did move, he seemed to overcompensate. He repeatedly beseeched Grant to allow him to trail the shattered foe all the way down through central Mississippi to Mobile. Grant twice refused. Rosecrans nevertheless would not halt despite the fact that outposts across West Tennessee and northern Mississippi were dangerously vulnerable because Grant had borrowed every available man to aid Rosecrans at Corinth. Rosecrans had bungled his chance. He "did not start in pursuit till the morning of the 5th"—after the battle ended at 11 a.m. on October 4—then encumbered himself with a wagon train and took the wrong road, Grant later wrote.

"Two or three hours of pursuit on the day of battle, without anything except what the men carried . . . , would have been worth more than any pursuit commenced the next day," Grant asserted. He added that, even with the late start, if Rosecrans had taken the road Van Dorn took, he would have overtaken the Confederates in a swamp with a stream in front and Union troops under General Edward Ord holding the only bridge.[1]

On October 7, Grant wired Rosecrans to halt. "We can do nothing with our weak forces but fall back to our old places," he told him. The same day, Rosecrans wired back three times in almost confrontational disagreement. Grant likely felt himself being maneuvered toward a chain-of-command set-to with General Henry Halleck. He wired Washington; Halleck responded with typical equivocation, keeping his options open. Why not pursue? Halleck asked.[2]

Grant by now was wary of snares laid by better-connected colleagues. He already had sidestepped many. Halleck just above him and Major General John McClernand just below were both snakes in the grass, and General Lew Wallace too bore watching. Plus vague warnings from Halleck had indicated that unnamed higher-ups—Secretary of War Edwin Stanton? President Abraham Lincoln?—were always ready to fire him for his drinking, as if whisky and armies were mutually exclusive and none of his higher-born peers imbibed.

Grant had learned to meet perfidy with steely resolve. He now circumvented Rosecrans's trap. When Halleck seemed to take Rosecrans's side, Grant offered Halleck the accountability. He said he believed "disaster" was around the corner, but "if you say so," he would join Rosecrans's pursuing column himself. The question died.[3]

William Starke Rosecrans was another upwardly focused Grant subordinate who misjudged his commander. He had been a star of the class preceding Grant's at West Point, ranking fifth. Like Grant, he had stayed in the old army until 1854, and like Grant, he had encountered difficulty after leaving the military. At the war's outset, he had headed a struggling Cincinnati kerosene firm.

Unlike Grant, Rosecrans did not fight in the Mexican War. He had been occupied elsewhere in the engineer corps, whose prized places were open only to top West Point graduates. After South Carolina fired on Fort Sumter, Rosecrans obtained one of the spots Grant failed to get on the first staff of General George McClellan. He then went with McClellan to western Virginia in 1861. There, after McClellan went east to head the Army of the Potomac, Rosecrans finished the job of chasing Robert E. Lee's Confederates out of the heavily unionist part of the Old Dominion. That allowed formation of the new state of West Virginia.[4]

This success, though, did not keep Rosecrans ahead of Grant. In mid-February 1862, the victory at Fort Donelson, the Union's largest to date, vaulted Grant into a major generalship that outranked Rosecrans. Sent west from Virginia, Rosecrans arrived in Mississippi just before Halleck marched into empty Corinth. He commanded a wing in Major General John Pope's Army of the Mississippi, then took Pope's place when Pope headed east to command all the Virginia forces except McClellan's. Soon Halleck too was called east, and Rosecrans found himself reporting in Mississippi not to Halleck but, instead, to the unimpressive fellow Ohioan who had been one class behind him at West Point.

Chagrin at his new position may explain the disputatious tone of Rosecrans's October 7 protests against Grant's order to halt pursuit of Van Dorn. His dispatches sound like those of commander to subordinate. He wanted Bridadier General James McPherson to launch a diversionary operation against the foe, he wrote. He advised Grant where to send General William T. Sherman and what road should be protected to supply him. He repeatedly insisted that the enemy should be hounded to Mobile or Jackson and given "no rest day or night"—except, of course, for the head start Rosecrans had already provided. He "deeply" dissented from Grant's order. "We . . . should now push them to the wall," he wrote.[5]

Their relationship skidded downhill. Grant was the bulldog of the battlefield, the little brawler who refused to allow an inch of territory to be wrested from him without all-out combat. He was just as territorial about the prerogatives of his new high rank, not least because he knew others with long pedigrees hungered to snatch them.[6]

On October 21, Rosecrans sent a haranguing response to a question from Grant. Grant had inquired whether Rosecrans expected a shipment of cavalry rifles Grant had obtained from Washington, but Rosecrans seemingly deemed it up to him, rather than Grant, to decide which units received the weapons. Grant replied that he would distribute the arms where they were most needed and cautioned that Rosecrans was making a mistake in seeming to regard himself on the level of a department commander.

Rosecrans responded with a howl. Protesting the "tenor" and "injustice" of this dispatch, he claimed Grant had had no truer friend or more loyal lieutenant. Then he went over the top and used a word sure to evoke the worst possible reaction. He implied that Grant had been told tales by "mischief makers, *winesellers* & mousecatching politicians" and demanded to know who had turned Grant against him.[7]

Rosecrans's outbursts reached the ears of, and prompted discussion among, the staffs of other ranking officers. At least one implied that Grant should fire Rosecrans. On October 19 from Bolivar, Tennessee, Colonel M. D. Leggett of the Seventy-eighth Ohio wrote Grant aide John Rawlins that he was "pained" to see a subordinate make such a determined effort to add to undeserved popular prejudice against Grant. Leggett, apparently referring to talk by Rosecrans's staff about the battles of Iuka and Corinth, said he considered it an outrage for aides of a newly minted major general to try to take credit for Grant's victories and make "irresponsible assertions and mysterious insinuations. Major Genl. Rosecrans is undoubtedly an excellent officer—and I hope . . . that he is not a party in this hellish attempt to ruin Genl Grant—but the evidence is such that I cannot rid my mind of the conviction that he must be, at least, privy to the whole devilish scheme."[8]

Grant valued loyalty—partly, no doubt, because he had seen so little of it. Two days later, on October 21, he recommended Leggett and five other colonels for promotion to brigadier. Meanwhile, Rosecrans addressed a communication to "My Dear General" Halleck in Washington requesting transfer to General Don Carlos Buell's army, complaining of a "spirit of mischief among the mousing politicians on Grant's staff to get up in his mind a spirit of jealousy." He ended, though, with an ultimatum: if Grant did not frankly avow that he was satisfied with Rosecrans, "I shall consider that my ability to be useful in this department has ended."[9]

Two days later, on October 24, Halleck saw an opportunity in Rosecrans's dissatisfaction. By now, Buell had bested Major General Braxton Bragg at Perryville, Kentucky, but Bragg had managed to flee the state after the battle. Lincoln had long condemned Buell's continual sluggishness, and now he blamed him for allowing Bragg to escape. Halleck saw an out. Instead of just giving Rosecrans the place in Buell's army that he had requested, Halleck gave him that army itself.[10]

G rant's offensive possibilities were improving by late October. Midwest recruiting was swelling his ranks with new levies, and Rosecrans's transfer had allowed the promotion of Grant's obedient and loyal coordinator of rail transportation, James B. McPherson, to major general to take Rosecrans's place.

Grant itched to be moving again. He wired Halleck from Jackson, Tennessee, on November 2 that he had ordered five divisions southward to Grand Junction, nexus of the east-west Memphis & Charleston Railroad and the north-south Mississippi Central. His eventual goal was of course Vicksburg, the Confederate Gibraltar on the Mississippi River. For the Union war effort, the taking of Vicksburg and the consequent reopening of the Mississippi from the Midwest to the Gulf of Mexico would be priceless logistically—and, as Grant later put it, an amputation to the Confederacy. Grand Junction was an ideal jumping-off point into interior Mississippi, and Grant planned to use it. He said he would repair rails and telegraph wires on the way forward and proceed if possible at least to Holly Springs, fifteen miles south of the Mississippi border. He might even go as far south as Grenada, some eighty miles past Holly Springs.

Halleck was atypically enthusiastic. Dealing with Lincoln's chagrin at other generals' lassitude—McClellan's reluctance to contest Lee's retreat from Antietam and Buell's similar dawdle behind Bragg—Halleck welcomed offensive movement anywhere.

"I approve of your plan of advancing upon the enemy," Halleck replied on November 3. "I hope for an active campaign on the Mississippi this fall."[11]

With pushes from Halleck, regiments, brigades, and divisions of reinforcements for Grant kept flowing from the Midwest into Columbus, Kentucky. From there they poured down the Mobile & Ohio Railroad into West Tennessee. More steamed down the Mississippi past Columbus into Memphis. Grant relished these new arrivals, seeing in them the means to seize all-out initiative again. Wanting to make the slash southward that he thought should have immediately followed the battle of Shiloh, he began to envision a strike down the Mississippi Central Railroad through the center of the state to Vicksburg's land side, its back door.

Vicksburg was the second-largest town in Mississippi, trailing only Natchez, its neighbor seventy miles downstream. Situated on the next flood-safe bluff below Memphis 250 land miles to the north, it sat 200 feet above the river and boasted nearly 5,000 residents, three newspapers, five churches, and two hospitals. With the coming of war, the waterside approaches had been fortified for miles with frowning trenches and gun emplacements. These defenses would grow to include 171 cannons, most of them overlooking the river.[12]

Grant's plans aimed to capitalize on enemy disarray. Outnumbered Confederates, feeling the shrinkage of their ranks by the 5,000 casualties at Corinth, were reportedly withdrawing from Holly Springs. Their Mississippi commander, Van Dorn, had requested a court of inquiry into his alleged mishandling of the Corinth battle—through inadequate reconnaissance and purported drunkenness—and the court had weakly sustained him. But public outcry over his leadership prompted Jefferson Davis to reduce his command to cavalry alone and subordinate him to a new Mississippi commander, Pennsylvania-born Lieutenant General John Pemberton. Pemberton quickly countermanded the withdrawal from Holly Springs and ordered Confederate troops back into the town and north of it, to the south bank of the Coldwater River.[13]

Happy to have the Confederates await him on the Coldwater, Grant spent early November gathering supplies and troops north of the Tennessee-Mississippi border. He also sent reconnaissance parties south from LaGrange and Grand Junction. On November 8, near Lamar, Mississippi, on the road to Holly Springs, cavalry and infantry under McPherson skirmished with enemy cavalry. Flanking them and getting into their rear, they killed at least sixteen Confederates and captured more than a hundred. McPherson's advance reached the Coldwater.[14]

The next afternoon, November 9, McPherson himself arrived on the river's north bank. Across it he saw 10,000 Confederates in line of battle, with another 10,000 under Sterling Price reported just south of Holly Springs and 13,000 more at Abbeville nearby. The Confederates were plainly ready to fight, and McPherson, undermanned, fell back.

Grant was content to "let them lay" until another 20,000 troops under Sherman could join his developing campaign. Then, as he wrote another subordinate on November 9, he could loose Sherman in a flanking move from the west onto the Confederate rear or bring Sherman's troops to join him on his march down the Mississippi Central line. The final plan might depend on the progress of two other Federal moves purportedly underway, one upriver from New Orleans and another from Helena, Arkansas, against Grenada.[15]

The day after his lead units marched south from LaGrange toward Holly Springs, Grant took a subtler step, one that at bottom was fully as aggressive. It aimed to foster indigenous support for the Union.

On its face, his plan intended to aid loyal Southern civilians suffering the privations of war. General Orders No. 4—which Grant issued for implementation in his jurisdiction, the Department of the Tennessee—noted that many noncombatants in the area lacked food and clothing and a way to earn the means of getting them. It directed that persons not rebelling should not go hungry in a region lush with supplies. And the Union, which had not caused the war, should not bear the cost of feeding them. That burden, Grant's order said, should fall on those responsible: supporters of secession. So the bill would go to Confederate sympathizers. They would be assessed "money, foodstuffs, or forage."[16]

But General Orders No. 4 entailed more than was obvious at first glance. Who were all these Union loyalists who lacked food and clothes and had no way of earning a living? A minority of whites doubtless fit this description, but many more of the "suffering" noncombatants were almost certainly fugitive slaves. On October 29, Grant aide William Hillyer wrote Sherman in Memphis recommending that if Sherman found it "necessary to distribute food to the poor and destitute families, *or to unemployed contrabands*," he should pay for it with assessments on "better provided" secessionists.

Grant's order was timely. On September 22, as a whipped Lee retreated from Maryland, Lincoln had issued a preliminary proclamation of emancipation. Some declared the action a political sham, since it granted freedom—

as of January 1, 1863—only to slaves in territory under Confederate control. It was no sham, however. The slave mobs that followed the invading Union armies increased after Lincoln's preliminary proclamation. Any suggestion of a forward move by Federal troops brought more refugees from the area to be invaded. Grant wired Halleck on November 15 that they were "coming in by wagon loads."[17]

The fugitives constituted a huge burden for the army but also an invaluable military boon. The slaves provided information about Confederate moves and local back roads, creek fords, and terrain. As numerous as a second army, they were helpful in still more respects, and Grant began exploiting as many of these as he could. Able-bodied men were put to work as teamsters, cooks, and construction workers, while other males, females, and children above age ten picked corn and cotton on abandoned plantations.

Grant appointed Chaplain John Eaton of the Twenty-seventh Ohio Volunteer Infantry to supervise a huge camp for the former slaves at Grand Junction and supplied him with assistants and guards. Eaton was a New Hampshire native who had graduated from Dartmouth to become schools superintendent in Toledo, Ohio, then had left Toledo in 1859 to attend Andover Theological Seminary. He and Grant established pay scales for work by the former bondspeople. After the cotton was picked and the workers paid, the harvest was shipped north by the army quartermaster to be sold, with proceeds going to the federal treasury. Any owners remaining on their plantations could save their crops by hiring the work done at the same rates. The former slaves were suddenly earning wages in the same areas where for centuries their forebears had labored for nothing.[18]

But the refugees kept coming, and the sheer magnitude of the influx interfered with military movements. To free up the army, Grant began sending some north to Cairo. There a glaring flaw in the national character again asserted itself. Reflecting the indifference that had permitted human bondage to thrive in America for 243 years, the majority of Northerners evinced little more compassion for African Americans than did Southerners. Judge David Davis, one of Lincoln's closest advisers, wrote on October 14 to protest sending the unfortunates to Illinois. It would, he warned, "work great harm in the coming election." The bulk of antislavery politics in the North was founded on the principle that white workingmen should not have to compete with slave labor for a livelihood, that each man should live by his own labor. Most antislavery feeling consisted of enmity toward the slaveholder, not empathy for the slave, and even well-meaning people evincing the latter, including Lincoln himself at the time, thought freed slaves should be shipped to Africa, not brought north to try to survive in white-ruled society.[19]

But while the overwhelming majority of Northerners did not have the best interests of the former slaves at heart, the issuance of General Orders No. 4 indicates that Grant was not just attempting to remove an African American millstone from around his army's neck. He was acting on an impulse of humanity that he already had shown toward slaves. Part of his motivation for feeding, clothing, and employing them in the fall of 1862 likely grew out of guilt for having followed Congressman Elihu Washburne's July suggestion to draft them for military uses. The slaves' fate was uncertain by any measure in late 1862, emancipation or no, and not knowing whether their labors for the army would reap a happier destiny surely bothered Grant's sense of fairness. More than the Maine-born Washburne and other Northerners fixated on the blacks' usefulness in the war, Grant thought about the people themselves. Having labored alongside both slaves and whites in slaveholding territory, he knew how cloudy their future was.

Grant was not without his own ugly prejudice, though. In November and December 1862, he disclosed this fault in one of the most repulsively bigoted acts of his career.

"Refuse all [civilians] permits to come south of Jackson for the present," he wired Major General Stephen A. Hurlbut at Jackson, Tennessee, on November 9. "The Israelites especially should be kept out."[20]

Hurlbut and other Grant subordinates tried to make these orders less toxic, rephrasing them to bar all "civilians." Grant seemed not to notice their efforts. On November 10 he ordered Colonel Joseph Webster, in charge of rail transportation in Grant's department, to instruct conductors that "no Jews" could travel by rail southward. He described them as "such an intolerable nuisance that the Department must be purged from them." By December 17 the discrimination in these directives would reach an infamous crescendo in General Orders No. 11, which expelled "the Jews as a class" from his department.[21]

At the time, nativism was the norm among working-class white Americans. Grant may have absorbed it from his father or from other non-Jewish businessmen who competed with Semitic ones. The army was a prime repository of such attitudes. One of Grant's closer military friends before the war had been Kentuckian and future Confederate general Simon Bolivar Buckner. After resigning from the army to become a Chicago businessman in the mid-1850s, Buckner briefly ran an immigrant-decrying, Know Nothing Party–affiliated newspaper in the Windy City.[22]

But the abrupt and all-encompassing nature of Grant's General Orders No. 11 had more to do with his present circumstances than with his past. It resulted in part from disgust with traders of all backgrounds who followed the army like vultures, seeking to grab captured cotton at bargain prices, swindle soldiers, and exploit any other commercial opportunity. Grant had to contend with these obsessed profiteers, and like most front-line soldiers, he hated them. Most traders were not Jewish, but a number of the more prominent were. An indication of the kind of problems they gave Grant, and of the tension-raising levels of political clout they could wield, is found in a letter he wrote Congressman Washburne on November 7. Grant had read a false forecast in Illinois newspapers that Bloomington attorney Leonard Swett, a close Lincoln associate, was to receive a White House advisory position. Grant told Washburne he considered Swett "one of my bitterest enemies" because, during the 1861–1862 winter, when Grant was in charge at Cairo, he had prevented the cheating of soldiers and the federal government by "contractors and speculators" with whom Swett seemed to be allied.[23]

The context of General Orders No. 11 likely also had even more personal overtones. Just nine days before issuing it, he had revoked a similar order by Colonel John V. DuBois. What happened between December 8 and 17? On December 15, Grant—then at Oxford, Mississippi—learned that his father was at Holly Springs, fewer than thirty miles north. He surely learned within another day or so that Jesse Grant's purpose was not just to accompany Julia to see Ulysses; it was also to buy cotton for a Jewish firm in Cincinnati. Jesse's deal with Mack & Brothers was to work his son's department in return for a one-fourth share of profits. Jesse, who had derided his son as a failure until he became a general, had sought ever since to parlay the son's rise into personal promotion.[24]

Perhaps Jesse's entry into an arena that had already vexed his son to distraction was too much, causing the younger Grant to overreact. The son's desperation could well have been prompted by fear that newspapers, eager after Shiloh to print any rumor of his whisky consumption, might now also charge him with colluding with his father to profit from the war. That allegation would have been more mortifying to him than charges of drunkenness.

General Orders No. 11 died swiftly. Jewish leaders visited Abraham Lincoln. Legislation condemning the order was introduced in the House and Senate, failing in both but only barely in the House. The White House revoked the order within two weeks. Halleck wrote Grant that Lincoln likely would not have objected had the order restricted only Jewish merchants. But it banned "an entire religious class, some of whom are fighting in our ranks."[25]

General Orders No. 11 has been justly condemned. But a comparison of it with General Orders No. 4 probably gets closer to Grant's essence. The latter meant to aid a minority of families, white and black, who were near starvation. The former—although it resulted in undeniable suffering by Jewish people in such places as Paducah, where some thirty families were expelled within twenty-four hours—was intended to stop unethical enrichment of fat businessmen seeking to get fatter. Evident in both orders is the intent to protect the deserving less fortunate. In the case of the former, though, its execution was misguided and ugly.[26]

By mid-November, Grant's army was moving well into northern Mississippi. It was skirmishing often and collecting small gangs of disheartened captives. Significant numbers of Confederates from Kentucky, Tennessee, and Missouri, having seen their states abandoned by their armies, were deserting, pledging allegiance to the Union, and going home.[27]

Grant's plan was first to get past Holly Springs and Oxford to Grenada. Grenada connected with Memphis by rail and could provide a supply route much shorter than the tracks coming from Columbus, Kentucky.

By November 14, the Union advance had reached the Tallahatchie River south of Holly Springs. Grant wrote Sherman that mounted troops under Colonel Albert Lee of Kansas had met and driven back five regiments of Confederate cavalry. Lee had killed some 50 men and taken 250 prisoners, with a Federal loss of just 3 wounded. This had driven Confederate General Pemberton's cavalry out of Holly Springs and back to Pemberton's fortified line on the south bank of the Tallahatchie. To dislodge him, Grant expected to meet Sherman and 16,000 troops from Memphis at the Tallahatchie and then to begin opening the Memphis-Grenada rail line. He was awaiting word of Sherman's departure.[28]

Then, on November 15, Grant received a wire from Halleck, saying he could not supply twelve additional locomotives Grant had requested to activate the Memphis-Grenada line. The general in chief may have feared Grant's drawing men and attention away from the supply line back to Columbus, Kentucky, and the many Kentucky and West Tennessee outposts guarding it, in order to open the shorter Memphis-Grenada route. Nixing the latter, he mandated a two-pronged offensive. He restricted Grant's operations in the Mississippi interior to fast, short marches against significant enemy forces. And they must be combined with a stronger flanking thrust down the Mississippi River by Grant's units in Memphis.[29]

A week later, Grant received another wire from Halleck regarding the river operation. It asked how many men Grant had and how many he could float down the Mississippi to Vicksburg. Grant replied that his department contained a total of 72,000, 16,000 of whom could go downriver. But, he continued, Sherman had already left for the Tallahatchie with the troops from Memphis. Union troops in Arkansas had promised to threaten Grenada, and Federal gunboats were headed farther southward to the Yazoo River to prevent the building of enemy fortifications just north of Vicksburg. Should he scrap these efforts?

"Proposed movements approved," Halleck telegraphed on November 25. But "do not go too far."[30]

G rant-Halleck relations were improving. Since late October, each man had brooded over a worsening problem: their unhappy and treacherous subordinate Major General John McClernand. For Halleck, the choice between the bulldog West Pointer and the grasping politician in uniform was no contest. McClernand was by far the more dangerous.

The ex-congressman's ambition was overweening. It resembled the obsession of the hungriest Washington officeholder, the type with White House dreams. A longtime acquaintance of Lincoln, McClernand had seemed to covet Grant's job—if not Lincoln's—since fate threw the two generals together in autumn of 1861. One of McClernand's ugliest traits was a tendency to appropriate others' accomplishments as his own. He had claimed for his troops, and thus for himself, more credit than they were due after Belmont, then Fort Donelson, then Shiloh. Worse, he used the stolen glory to exploit his connections in Midwestern statehouses, Congress, and the White House. Lincoln, a Republican, prized McClernand's Democratic influence as a tool for forging a bipartisan Union war effort, and McClernand wielded this cachet like a club.

Despite his clout, though, McClernand had been frustrated. In the summer of 1862, he had schemed for transfer to the Army of the Potomac to escape Halleck and Grant—only to see Halleck promoted to general in chief and moved to Washington, with direct oversight of the Army of the Potomac. Now McClernand pushed another ploy. Taking a leave from his position as commander of the Army of the Tennessee's First Division, he trekked to Illinois and Washington. Sherman soon would write his senator brother, John, that McClernand was "trying to get elected to the U.S. Senate." General Sherman was doubtless correct, and McClernand meant to get there by raising an army of his own that he could lead to military-political glory. On October 21, Secretary of War Stanton issued a confidential order directing McClernand to recruit and organize volunteers and draftees in Indiana, Illinois, and Iowa, then dispatch them to Memphis. He was to use all of them not needed by Grant, the order said, "to clear the Mississippi River and open navigation to New Orleans." McClernand had bedazzled Lincoln with an alluring military and political prospect. Heartland merchants were clamoring for the reopening of the Father of Waters, and McClernand had promised to do it.[31]

Lincoln's approval of McClernand's scheme underscores something important about the president: his openness to contributions from anybody, West Pointer or not, aristocrat or commoner. That McClernand had neither a West Point education nor military training did not matter. West Pointers and aristocrats, after all, were mostly failing Lincoln by this point in the war. What mattered was that McClernand wanted to save the Union and might be able to help do it.

For Grant, these activities of his furloughed division commander were threatening. He soon heard ominous rumors about them. On October 29, an officer wired him that McClernand, without going through channels, had ordered the holding at Cairo of some rifles destined for Grant's army. Grant directed the officer to ignore the order. The same day Grant wired Sherman that newspaper and other reports indicated McClernand planned to take his new units to Helena, Arkansas. There, the information had it, McClernand would report to Major General Samuel Curtis, a Mexican War colonel and three-term Iowa congressman.[32]

Grant became alarmed. Knowing McClernand's ties to Lincoln, he wondered if the White House intended for a McClernand Mississippi campaign to trump Grant's. Pending McClernand's arrival from the Midwest, some of his new units already were showing up in Memphis, where Sherman was in command. Pretty certain that Halleck had little use for the ex-politician, Grant wired his chief on November 10 to ask if he, Grant, was expected to "lie still here while an expedition is fitted out from Memphis"? Or did Halleck want him to push as far south as possible? Was Sherman still his subordinate? Or were Sherman and his troops now "reserved for some special service?" And could Grant expect reinforcements for his projected drive toward Grenada? In other words, were these new troops, coming into Sherman's command post in Grant's department from McClernand in the Midwest, to be under Grant's supervision or McClernand's? Halleck's reply was swift and unequivocal: "You have command of all troops sent to your department, and have permission to fight the enemy where you please."[33]

That message arrived on November 11, the day before Grant's cavalry drove the Confederates out of Holly Springs. Two days later, on November 13, Grant ordered Sherman to march from Memphis toward Oxford with at least two divisions of infantry. Sherman brought three divisions, which almost certainly included some of McClernand's new levies. By November 29, Sherman had proceeded to Wyatt, Mississippi, twenty miles southwest of Holly Springs, and Grant had established Holly Springs as his southernmost supply depot. All of its matériel had to come by rail from Columbus, Kentucky, "a long line," Grant later noted, "to maintain in an enemy's country."[34]

Then Halleck reined Grant in. Grant had wired on December 4 to say he would cut the Mobile & Ohio Railroad south of Tupelo and asked how much farther south his chief wanted him to go. Should he hold the Confederates south of Grenada while moving a force from Memphis and Helena downriver to Vicksburg? Halleck replied on December 5 approving the destruction of the railroad but directing Grant not to try to hold territory south of Abbeville, Mississippi. And Sherman had to have his troops back in Memphis by December 20, Halleck warned.[35]

Grant and Halleck were now communicating almost in code, rarely mentioning whom this was all about. Grant wanted to get the river operation started from Memphis to Vicksburg under Sherman out of fear that McClernand would soon show up on the lower Mississippi to lead those troops himself. The obnoxious politician outranked Sherman and would be able to assume independent command. Halleck's mention of December 20 concerned the same thing. Halleck felt as nervous about McClernand's Washington clout as Grant—it threatened to make McClernand independent of not just Grant but also General in Chief Halleck—and Halleck obviously had a good idea of when McClernand would leave the Midwest for Memphis. It would be best for both of them if Grant could hijack McClernand's new army before McClernand arrived to command it.

On December 8, Grant grabbed the initiative. He ordered Sherman to take one of his three divisions back to Memphis, board steamers, pick up another 12,000 men—many recruited by McClernand—at Helena, Arkansas, and proceed downriver to a point north of Vicksburg. Grant also asked Sherman to "come over this evening" to Grant's Oxford, Mississippi, headquarters "and stay to-night or come in the morning" for the kind of chat Grant rarely sought with others. The subject doubtless would be McClernand. Grant's note said he would like to talk with Sherman about how to go at Vicksburg. His idea, he said, was for Sherman to strike it from the river in tandem with Grant, who would bring his own command down the Mississippi Central Railroad and keep much of Confederate general Pemberton's army preoccupied well north of the city. If Grant could not hold Pemberton north of Vicksburg, he would stay on the Confederate general's rear and follow him to the city's gates.[36]

Halleck did much to enable the Grant-Sherman Vicksburg operation. He extended Grant's authority to Helena and promoted McClernand's friend Curtis to command of the Department of the Missouri, getting him out of the way. So Helena and the trans-Mississippi forces based there were now temporarily in Grant's department and his to use as he wished. Brigadier General Frederick Steele, a member of Grant's West Point class of 1843, now commanded at Helena, and Grant notified his old classmate of his evolving plans.[37]

The next day, December 9, Halleck warned Grant that Lincoln "may insist upon designating a separate commander." They both knew who that would be. If it did not happen, however, Grant could name the commanders of the operation as "you deem best." Halleck added that he, like Grant, preferred Sherman as "the chief under you."[38]

If Grant wanted to oversee the attack on Vicksburg, he needed to strike first—exactly as he was now racing to do. Having arranged a deft theft of McClernand's army, he was readying a hard one-two punch at the western Confederacy. He would hold Pemberton in central Mississippi while the trusted Sherman floated downriver to Pemberton's rear and attacked Vicksburg.

Little did Grant know, though, that his own rear was now suddenly in danger. On December 15, 1,800 Confederate cavalrymen finished crossing the Tennessee River at Clifton, Tennessee, more than a hundred miles northeast of Oxford. They were heading for the Kentucky-to-Mississippi rail line that Grant considered "long . . . to maintain in an enemy's country."

At their head was a far deadlier general than McClernand or Pemberton. It was Forrest—in a rotten mood.

18

DECEMBER 1862—FORREST IN WEST TENNESSEE

"We Have Worked, Rode, and Fought Hard"

Mississippi was in disarray. The disheartenment that Grant and other Federals had perceived in its residents was not wishful Union spin.

As Grant readied his double-edged slash into the state's heart, an alarmed Mississippi lawmaker wrote Jefferson Davis to warn of its "listless despondency." Writing on December 9, Senator James Phelan urged the president to return home, "unfurl your banner at the head of the army," and deliver Mississippians from not only Grant but also the lackluster Pemberton and the discredited Van Dorn. A military court had just acquitted the latter of charges of bloody carelessness at Corinth, but Phelan said the state remained rife with "narratives of his negligence, whoring, and drunkenness" so damning that "a court-martial of angels would not relieve him of the charge."

Generalship and manpower were not the only difficulties facing Mississippi Confederates. They were not even foremost. Phelan reported that efforts to enforce the new conscription law in his state and neighboring Alabama were bungling, corrupt, and inciting resistance. Crowds of fighting-age males were "everywhere," unenrolled in the ranks. Populism was hardly a pet subject of the South's ruling oligarchy, but Senator Phelan raised it. He condemned the Confederacy's policy of letting substitutes carry rifles for able-bodied people wealthy enough to hire them, saying it had infuriated the poor.

Impartial imposition of conscription was essential to mollify the public rage, Phelan wrote. The system needed wholesale redress, and "the prominent, rich, and influential" should be driven into the army like everybody else. A new measure also exempted from service anyone owning twenty or more slaves, and Phelan said this favoritism for the wealthy was scandalous. The injustice of exempting slave owners was "denounced even by men whose position enables them to take advantage of it" and had reportedly "aroused a spirit of rebellion" among poor whites.[1]

Into this trans-Appalachian morass, Davis in late November threw Joseph E. Johnston. The fourth-highest-ranking Confederate behind Adjutant General Samuel Cooper, the late Albert Sidney Johnston, and Robert E. Lee, Johnston had spent the past several months recuperating from serious wounds incurred in Virginia on May 31 at the battle of Seven Pines. Named head of the Department of the West, Johnston became a supervisor with no army of his own. He could only advise as General John Pemberton in Mississippi cried for help from Tennessee to hold off Grant's horde. Johnston's geographical problem was thorny. If Grant or one of his subordinates captured Vicksburg, "we cannot dislodge him" because of the strength of Vicksburg's fortifications, Johnston wrote Adjutant General Cooper in Richmond.

But the Confederate leadership could not send aid to Pemberton without endangering its cause elsewhere. Sending Bragg from Middle Tennessee to Vicksburg would abandon the forage-rich country south of Nashville to Rosecrans's Union army. Johnston advised against sending Pemberton even a part of Bragg's army, fearing to decrease the 47,000 men with whom Bragg at Murfreesboro faced Rosecrans's 60,000 at Nashville. The Davis government had ordered General Theophilus Holmes in Arkansas to aid Pemberton, which Johnston favored instead.

But Davis ignored the advice of the man he had named department commander. He determined to reinforce Vicksburg even if it cost him Middle Tennessee. Arriving in Murfreesboro on December 12, he ordered 9,000 infantrymen detached from Bragg's army and sent to Pemberton. If necessary, the president told Bragg, he should fall back eighty miles south of Murfreesboro, behind the Tennessee River in Alabama.[2]

But all that would take time. The Tennessee River lay between Bragg and Pemberton, and Pemberton, under pressure from Grant and Sherman, was moving south toward Vicksburg, not north toward Bragg. Johnston sent a December 4 telegram to Bragg asking him to help delay Grant's further advance into Mississippi by loosing cavalry on Grant's supply lines.[3]

Communication in the west was so roundabout that, by the time Johnston's recommended cavalry solution reached Bragg, Bragg had come to the same conclusion on his own two weeks earlier. On November 21, he wired both Pemberton and the Davis government that he was sending "a large cavalry force under Forrest to create a diversion" by attacking Federal communications in West Tennessee. He apparently informed Forrest of the assignment around the same time. On November 24, he wrote Davis that he had ordered Forrest "to seek a crossing, which he is confident of finding, throw his command across the Tennessee River, and precipitate it" on Union supply routes. Two more weeks passed, though, before Bragg ordered Forrest to prepare to leave. Forrest himself may have caused the delay. He repeatedly requested better arms for his men. Most had only shotguns and pistols brought from home, and some carried flintless flintlock muskets. The former would be ineffective, and the latter useless, against the Federals' usual .58-caliber, bayonet-equipped Springfield percussion muskets or the similar British Enfield.[4]

Bragg meanwhile decided to give himself the same sort of assistance he was sending Mississippi. He ordered more cavalry under John Hunt Morgan, now a brigadier, to wreck the Louisville-Nashville rails supplying Rosecrans's Federals in the Tennessee capital. But Morgan's assignment, to destroy track and two five-hundred-foot trestles just south of Louisville, was not as difficult as Forrest's. Kentucky was not as hard to get into and out of as Federal-occupied West Tennessee. Forrest would have to cross the wide Tennessee River in territory inhabited by Union sympathizers, dodge contingents of Federals larger than his own, hack Grant's vital railroads to pieces, and get back across the Tennessee alive.[5]

On December 4, Bragg ordered Forrest to ready his mission. The weather was forbidding, which would make the crossing of the Tennessee River all the more treacherous. And Bragg gave Forrest none of the support he had requested. His troops would be the new, mostly untried, badly armed ones he had gathered around Murfreesboro and McMinnville while Bragg was returning from Kentucky. For their old shotguns they had just ten firing caps per man, and Forrest protested that pistols and largely flint-missing flintlocks were their only other weapons. Bragg did not care. Three weeks earlier he had reported having a surplus of rifles, tents, and other matériel, but he gave none of it to Forrest. Anything Forrest needed he would have to capture. Government supplies Bragg reserved for regular soldiers only, and he did not include Forrest in their ranks. Bragg wrote Jefferson Davis on November 24 that he had 5,000 cavalry in three "regular brigades" and an equal number under Forrest and Morgan. The latter were "on partisan service, for which, and which alone, their commanders are . . . suited."[6]

Bragg's distinction between Forrest's troops and those in the "regular" units was arbitrary and typically rigid. Forrest's fellow Bragg-designated "partisan," John Hunt Morgan, was a Kentucky aristocrat with whom Bragg was very friendly, and Morgan had requested the partisan designation. Forrest had not. Forrest's unvarnished machismo and seasoned maturity, compared with the obsequious boyishness and cultivation of Bragg's hand-picked successor to Forrest, Joe Wheeler, would only have reinforced Bragg's opinion that Forrest was barely a step above the status of guerrilla. The sycophantic Wheeler had charmed Bragg in Kentucky. His cavalry's defense of the retreat from the Bluegrass State had prompted Bragg, on October 11, to shower Wheeler with praise. He termed Wheeler's performance "brilliant," adding, "No cavalry force was more handsomely handled and no army better covered." Soon after Bragg's army arrived back in Tennessee, Bragg directed Forrest to report to Wheeler for orders. Forrest continued to obey Bragg's commands—most of them, anyway—but with ever more resentment.[7]

Forrest's rancor showed. His treatment of Lieutenant John Morton, the "tallow-faced boy" artillerist whom Bragg had named Forrest's chief of artillery, was one such manifestation. When Forrest angrily told Morton that he would not "be interfered with" by Bragg and that his current artillery chief would remain in that position, the chagrined Morton said he never meant to supplant anybody, he just wanted to serve with Forrest and go on the campaign into West Tennessee. He said he trusted that Forrest would soon capture guns he and his crew could operate. Forrest's disgust decreased slightly. Facing this chance to emphasize his contempt for both Bragg and Wheeler, he reiterated that his artillery chief, S. L. Freeman, would remain exactly that. He then challenged both Bragg and Wheeler by going out of his way to inform them of his disobedience of the order. He told Morton that, to remain with Forrest's cavalry at all, Morton needed to obtain Wheeler's approval. The cavalry chief was fifty-two miles away at LaVergne, so Forrest likely thought he had seen the last of the boy cannoneer. Instead, Morton left immediately for LaVergne, woke up Wheeler, got his signed permission, and galloped back to Columbia. He covered 104 miles in twenty-three hours.[8]

But Forrest obeyed Bragg's more important order, the one to prepare for his perilous raid into West Tennessee. He thought, long and hard, about how he would do it. He was given to solitary planning sessions, during which his concentration was remarkably impervious to distraction. A Forrest trooper who later became a judge and historian of a Forrest regiment would eventually recall that during these meditations Forrest would sit motionless, chin on chest, or walk in circles with his head down and his hands clasped beneath the tail of his coat. During one such ambling session before another West Tennessee raid later in the war, the judge recalled, Forrest strode in circles around a railroad station in West Point, Mississippi, lost in thought. An ill-advised person tried repeatedly to interrupt him with a request. Forrest finally reacted with a single blow from his fist, knocking the man unconscious. Without having uttered a word, Forrest stepped over the man and kept walking.[9]

Since his teens, Forrest had made it his business to know how to get things done. If he could not do something himself, he made sure to know—personally—somebody who could. Long treks in the operation of his slave business, monitoring countless auctions and estate sales, provided him with connections across lower- and middle-class Southern society from Kentucky to Texas. He made inroads into higher circles too. Heading the Memphis city council's finance committee, he was a frequent spokesman for Memphis & Charleston Railroad president Sam Tate, to whom he sold slaves in 1854.[10]

Forrest's wide-ranging contacts had become vital. In July 1861, two Kentuckians had helped him buy and smuggle out of Union-leaning Louisville five hundred Colt pistols, a hundred saddles, and other equipment to outfit his first regiment. Now he put similar friends to work arming his troops once again. He dispatched unnamed agents into Union-occupied West Tennessee in search of firing caps. He also sent a

party of carpenter-soldiers ahead to the Tennessee River to build and hide
two flatboats. Braxton Bragg had forced him to use all his ingenuity; luckily for the Confederacy, Forrest had been using it for most of his life.[11]

O n December 10 Bragg ordered Forrest to get going. He departed
Columbia the next day, a Friday, heading west with nearly 2,000
troopers, 500 of them all but unarmed. He covered the seventy miles in
two days.

Forrest arrived on the east bank of the Tennessee River just north of
Clifton on Sunday evening. He posted scouts up and down the bank to
watch for five Union gunboats that were patrolling the river, and while
the bulk of his men stood out of sight in a cold and dismal rain, scouts
pulled the flatboats from hiding places behind Double Island, beyond view
of the main channel. Then, twenty-five at a time, the men and their horses
filed onto the boats to cross a quarter mile of icy river.[12]

It took a long time, and they had to stay constantly on the lookout for
the Federal gunboats. "Working night and day," he would report, they "finished crossing on the 15th."[13]

He ordered the flatboats sunk in a slough where they could be raised
later, then led his troopers eight miles away from the river to camp for the
night. The rain subsided, and the men were able to build their first fires in
two frigid days and nights. They dried their clothes and cared for their
horses. They were unable to dry everything, though. Most of the few firing caps they had on hand had gotten wet in the rainy river crossing, so
now Forrest was worse off than ever. He had all but trapped himself behind enemy lines with much of his force out of ammunition. That day
and the next, they spent in hiding. Finally, on the evening of December 16,
one of his civilian connections arrived with 50,000 firing caps acquired by
the agents sent ahead the previous week. He felt "great relief."[14]

The intervening two days had not gone to waste. Forrest had little use
for most military ritual, but he enthusiastically adopted one: inspecting
his troops. It was in keeping with a habit engrained in him from youth.
Going into his family's leased fields at dawn without all the needed tools
squandered daylight and energy, both as valuable as money. With him,
though, an inspection was likely intended for more than the standard

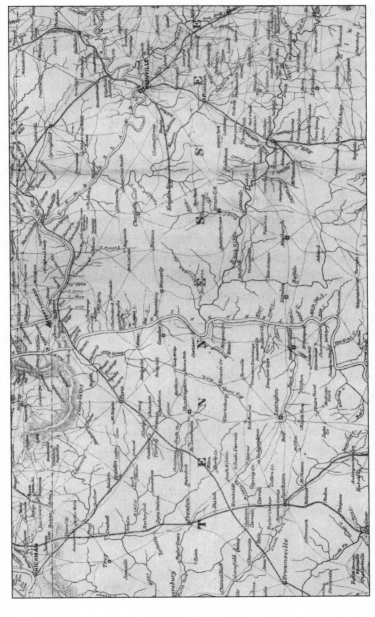

FORREST'S WEST TENNESSEE RAID: This 1863 map shows the territory Forrest covered in West Tennessee. He went from Clifton—which for some reason is here labeled "Carrollville"—to Lexington then to Jackson. From Jackson he rode north, capturing and wrecking outposts along the railroad to Union City, Tennessee, and Hickman, Kentucky, then turned back south along other railroad tracks to Dresden, Tennessee, and McKenzie. He took back roads to McLemoresville and farther south to Red Mound, where he fought the Battle of Parker's Crossroads before heading back to cross the Tennessee River at Clifton.

military purpose of making sure each man, horse, and piece of equipment was as prepared as possible. It also inventoried in Forrest's mind every resource he could call on in the moment of crisis.[15]

With the firing caps distributed, Forrest was ready. Most commanders entering enemy country with inferior numbers proceed with quiet caution; not Forrest. To accomplish his daunting assignment, he had to distract, misdirect, and confuse the Federals regarding his primary task—wrecking railroads and supply depots—and Bragg could not have assigned a more perfect man. His favorite ploy on the card table or the battlefield was the bluff; the stronger you acted, the more strength and wariness your enemy would assume he needed to defeat you. The extra time the foe took gathering strength you could spend running wild all around him.

The Federals had deduced that Forrest was coming. His Murfreesboro raid had given them a far greater appreciation of his ability than that held by his Confederate peers and superiors. The Federal generals now realized that their long Mississippi-to-Kentucky rail line was vulnerable at many points to his talent for destruction. As early as December 11, the day Forrest departed Columbia, Rosecrans at Nashville, noting Forrest's westward direction, wired Grant at Oxford, Mississippi, that railroad guards must "look out for Forrest." The next day, Brigadier General Jeremiah Sullivan at Jackson, Tennessee, reported that Forrest was moving via Waynesboro toward the river at Savannah. Sullivan ordered "all roads obstructed," adding, "I will try to force him south," closer to Grant. On December 15, the day Forrest finished crossing at Clifton, General Grenville M. Dodge at Corinth wired Sullivan that he had found no Confederates at Savannah and suggested Sullivan check Clifton. That day, a Union cavalry picket near Clifton detected Forrest's move and guessed his numbers to be "3,000 strong." That figure grew exponentially almost overnight. On December 17, Sullivan wired Grant that an "estimated 10,000" Confederate cavalry with artillery were reported across the Tennessee.[16]

Grant felt the danger and began trying to spring the West Tennessee trap Forrest appeared to have entered. On December 18, Grant asked the navy at Cairo for more gunboats to prevent Forrest from recrossing the Tennessee; in his request, he said Forrest's force, reported to number between 5,000 and 10,000 men, was nearing the Union base at Jackson. But

Grant did not wait for the gunboats. He directed Dodge at Corinth to entrain troops to Jackson and, together with those already there, to attack and drive Forrest back across the river. "Move to-night," he commanded. He also ordered Colonel William Lowe from Fort Henry, on the Tennessee near the Kentucky-Tennessee border, to come south on the river's west bank and prevent Forrest from bringing any more troops across. Lowe, leading 1,500 men, was also to attack the Forrest force already in West Tennessee at once, in conjunction with the Federals from Jackson. Grant informed Sullivan of all these orders and wrote, "I expect to get a good account from Jackson to-morrow."[17]

He did not. The next day brought bad news followed by a dead telegraph. At Lexington, Tennessee, Forrest had beaten and captured Sullivan's chief of cavalry, Colonel Robert Ingersoll, taking 148 members of Ingersoll's Eleventh Illinois Cavalry and two pieces of artillery. Sullivan managed to report, before the wire died, that he himself had held off the Confederates six miles from Jackson.[18]

Forrest by then had been riding hard. Moving toward Jackson fifty miles from Clifton, he had skirmished with Union scouts on December 17. The next afternoon he had run into Ingersoll's cavalry and pushed a company of Federals across a bridge over Beech Creek east of Lexington. Members of the Second West Tennessee Cavalry, comprising two hundred of Ingersoll's seven hundred men, formed for battle on the stream's west side. They were supported by two cannon of the Fourteenth Indiana Battery, which opened up and scattered their pursuers. When the Confederates attempted to position a cannon, Ingersoll reported, the Federal artillery knocked it off its wheels.[19]

If so, the cannon was quickly repaired. Commanding the gun Ingersoll claimed to have disabled was the "tallow-faced boy," John Morton. Before leaving Columbia, Morton had approached Forrest again and asked if, since his ten men as yet had no cannons, they might have muskets. Until additional artillery was captured, he thought they might ride with Colonel James Starnes's Fourth Tennessee, one of the consolidated units Forrest had formed after his return to Middle Tennessee from Kentucky in the fall. Forrest had no extra muskets. Thanks to Bragg, he did not have even enough for his cavalrymen. He frowned, then ordered Captain Freeman to lend the youth two of his half dozen field pieces. Forrest told Morton to take the two guns and join Starnes in the advance.

Morton was thus supporting Starnes's Fourth Tennessee in Forrest's vanguard as it approached the Beech Creek Bridge. Forrest sent twenty men forward to drive back the Federal pickets. Ingersoll's Federals, now shooting from the creek's other side, had disabled the bridge by removing most of the cross-planking after they crossed, and Morton rode onto its east end to assess the repair required to get his battery across. His horse shied to one side in the Federal fire and stepped on the end of a plank. The board flipped, catapulting horse and rider into the steep-banked stream. After comrades rushed to pull them out, the Confederates planked the bridge with nearby fence rails. In twenty minutes they were clattering across.[20]

With Starnes's men crossing Beech Creek, Forrest groped for Ingersoll's retreat route. He left Starnes to drive the Federals from their position at the creek and galloped more than two-thirds of his force—Colonel George Dibrell's Eighth Tennessee, Colonel Jacob B. Biffle's Ninth, and Captain Frank Gurley's four companies of the Fourth Alabama—to the right and down the so-called Lower Road toward Lexington.

Ingersoll discovered the move. He realized that some of the West Tennessee cavalry he had assigned to torch another creek bridge on the Lower Road had failed to do it. Leaving a few men at Beech Creek, he withdrew his guns and most of two other regiments, the Eleventh Illinois and the Fifth Ohio, to a ridge on the Lower Road. He also dispatched many of the Second West Tennessee horsemen to the Lower Road to delay Forrest. But Forrest arrived at the ridge at nearly the same time Ingersoll did. "The enemy were pouring in on all directions," Ingersoll reported.[21]

Forrest had ordered Gurley's four veteran Alabama companies to take the lead and charge the first Federals they saw. Occupying the foe with Gurley's men, he now formed the rest of his troops and led an assault against the Federal left. The Union line broke under his onslaught, and he changed direction to his own left, feeling for the Federal flank. There he put to flight the horsemen of the Second West Tennessee. Ordered to oppose his advance down the Lower Road, they "did not fire a single gun," Ingersoll reported, and Forrest's flank attack scattered them. Ingersoll reported that they withdrew chaotically, running and pursued, and would not obey his order to halt. The green Fifth Ohio, having never been drilled or shot at, also fled.[22]

Of the Federal resistance, the section of Indiana cannons and the Eleventh Illinois Infantry alone remained. The climax was brief, the defenders far outnumbered but stubborn. The Illinoisans charged and twice drove the Confederates from the Union guns. The Indiana artillerists stayed at their posts—some dying there—as Gurley's men surged into their very faces. An Alabama private, the first of Gurley's men to reach the cannons, was touching one of them when it fired, cutting him in half. But then it was over, the surviving Indianans captured along with their guns. Lieutenant Morton swiftly appropriated two of their three-inch steel-rifled Rodman cannon.[23]

Starnes's and Dibrell's men had galloped off after the fleeing Federals. They pursued through Lexington and kept going all the afternoon and evening of December 18. After nightfall, Dibrell reached the Jackson suburbs, twenty-five miles from the initial skirmish at Beech Creek. On the roads east of town, Forrest ordered his troopers to drive Federal pickets into the cannon-studded works surrounding Jackson, a regional Union base. He did not have numbers enough to attack, but the Federals did not know it. Ingersoll's fugitives were spreading reports of hordes of Confederate cavalry, infantry, and artillery massing around Jackson. Parts of the Eighth, Twelfth, and Fourteenth Iowa, heading home from Corinth on a Christmas furlough, were hurried off a train at Jackson and ordered to defend "to the last extremity" the supply-filled depot. If overwhelmed, they were to "blow up the buildings and retire to the court-house."[24]

Having hemmed the Jackson Federals into their perimeter, Forrest meant to keep them there. That night, he built fake campfires at Spring Creek, four miles from town. Then he sent night-riding parties to slash Federal communications north and south.

He ordered Dibrell to circle eight miles north, cut telegraph wire, and capture Carroll Station on the Mobile & Ohio; that would block the arrival of any Union reinforcements from Columbus, Kentucky. He sent Colonel A. A. Russell of the Fourth Alabama sweeping around to Jackson's south side, destroying bridges on Mobile & Ohio tracks connecting Jackson with Grant's left wing at Corinth. Major N. N. Cox's Second Battalion got a similar assignment on the Tennessee & Ohio, which ran through Bolivar to Grant's headquarters at Oxford, Mississippi.[25]

On December 19, the Confederates rampaged around Jackson. Dibrell, delayed by ignorant guides, just missed capturing a train at the Carroll Station. His advance arrived in time to fire into the cars as they rolled past. He did not leave empty-handed, though. He charged the stockade at the station and captured 101 occupants, plus rifles, ammunition, and tents. The Confederates with flintlocks swapped their arms for better Federal ones. They stacked the flintlocks inside the stockade, with other supplies too heavy to remove, and torched the structure. They then tore up tracks and rejoined Forrest at Spring Creek near dawn on December 20. The forays south and southwest were also productive. Cox's men hushed Grant's telegraph wire.[26]

While Dibrell, Russell, and Cox raided around the city, Forrest had menaced Jackson itself. At his direction, some four hundred men of Colonel Biffle's Ninth Tennessee, two companies of Kentuckians under Colonel T. G. Woodward, and two of Captain Freeman's guns advanced toward the town on the morning of December 19.

The Federals inside the city could only wonder at what was happening outside. The raids were islanding Jackson, and the Federals were more than nervous. Brigadier General Jeremiah Sullivan had already wired Grant, on the evening of December 18, that Confederate numbers were reported at 10,000 to 20,000, with more crossing the Tennessee River. The following morning, Sullivan heard that Carroll Station had been burned and its men captured—and that bridges had been torched twelve miles south on the Mobile & Ohio toward Corinth, with "a large force" crossing those tracks to head for the more southwesterly rail line to Bolivar and Oxford.

Heading out to find Forrest in the morning, Sullivan ran into Biffle and Woodward as they approached Jackson. Freeman's guns drove the Federals back into their defenses, and the skirmish continued until late afternoon. Then the Thirty-ninth and Twenty-seventh Ohio arrived by train from Oxford before the Confederates could damage that route, and at about 3 p.m. Sullivan sent six Union regiments against the Confederates. These Federals claimed to have driven the Confederates back before camping for the night six miles out of Jackson.[27]

Forrest's withdrawal may have resulted as much from his own decision as from Sullivan's counterattack. He needed to be tearing up more rails and burning more train stations before the Federals could combine. He had been informed that reinforcements Grant sent from Oxford and ordered from elsewhere had increased Jackson's defenders to at least 9,000, so Forrest pulled back and headed toward his mission's primary objective: the rails and stations denuded by the Union consolidation at Jackson. His first objects were Humboldt, a crossing nineteen miles to the north-northwest, and Trenton a dozen miles beyond.

Early on December 20, he issued orders toward that end. Colonel Russell's Fourth Alabama would protect the rear at Spring Creek. Dibrell would destroy a railroad bridge between Humboldt and Jackson. Starnes would attack Humboldt. Biffle would circle to the north side of Trenton, the main Federal base between Jackson and Columbus, and threaten it from the rear. Then Forrest, his escort, and Cox's Second Tennessee Cavalry Battalion would dash into the town.[28]

The smaller raids yielded varied, although generally favorable, results. Dibrell's attempt to destroy the blockhouse and trestles between Humboldt and Jackson failed. The structures were surrounded by creeks and a swamp, stymieing Morton's guns. Starnes's attack on Humboldt fared better. His 750 men burned a trestle bridge and the depot and stockade there and took more than a hundred prisoners, most of them wounded or sick; Humboldt's Union garrison, except for the ill and convalescing men, had been withdrawn to Jackson a day or two earlier. The Confederates did not hold the town for long, but they made their short visit memorable. Union colonel George P. Ihrie arrived in the area just at nightfall and reported that with three companies of Federals he attacked and retook Humboldt, causing the Confederates to flee toward Trenton and "forget some of their plunder." They did not forget much. The booty they made away with included four caissons, the accompanying horses, 500 stands of rifles, and 300,000 rounds of ammunition.[29]

Forrest's attack on Trenton, while Biffle prevented a Federal retreat up the railroad, was much more of a rout, despite the Union commander's stubborn defense. Colonel Jacob Fry of the Sixty-first Illinois had seen his once-strong position cannibalized by superiors concentrating on defending Jackson. When Forrest's entry into West Tennessee was first noised, Fry had selected a hill overlooking the depot and thrown up enough earthworks and rifle pits, he thought, to accommodate 1,500 troops. He had then had to abandon these defenses. On December 18 Sullivan had called Fry's five hundred able-bodied troops to Jackson, leaving Fry with only convalescents.

Fry had given rifles to the ambulatory ill, then ordered the little platform of the Trenton train station barricaded with cotton bales and hogsheads of tobacco. Off a train coming through from Columbus to Jackson, he snatched another twenty men returning from hospitals. On the morning of December 20, he had heard that Forrest's whole force was camped twenty miles away at Spring Creek. Fry's men, ill and all, numbered 250. Fry did not know it, but Forrest's own force numbered little more—just 275. The Confederates, however, looked like more. They included Freeman's six cannons and some wagonloads of captured materiél. In addition, Biffle's 400 men were positioned as a blocking force north of the town. Fry telegraphed his situation to Jackson. Then the wire went dead. Nonetheless, he thought he could hold out against anything but artillery.[30]

At noon on December 20, scouts reported Forrest within a few miles and closing fast. Fry put sharpshooters atop a brick building across the street from the depot and more in a building commanding another street. Around 3 p.m. Forrest galloped into town in two columns. His personally led escort of sixty men came from Fry's right, with Major Cox's 160-man battalion arriving from the left. A Federal fusillade killed two Confederates and wounded seven more, and Forrest drew back two hundred yards to the southeast. He then dismounted his men and put them in houses as sharpshooters.

Sure he was surrounded, Fry expected a charge from all sides and thought he could handle it—until he saw his nightmare: artillery. The Confederates positioned six cannon on the heights overlooking the town, two within his new earthworks. They fired sixteen shells, one into the ammunition-filled depot, and Fry decided Forrest could level "stockade, depot, and all in thirty minutes."

Fry consulted his officers. All favored surrender. When several makeshift white flags appeared around the depot perimeter, Forrest sent forward his adjutant, Captain J. P. Strange. The discussion became contracted, and

Forrest strode up. When Fry asked for terms, Forrest barked one word: "unconditional."[31]

Forrest then displayed two sides of his nature in rapid succession. He returned Fry's proffered sword, which had been in Fry's family for two decades, and said he hoped its next use would be in a better cause. But he had hardly said that when he saw smoke coming from the depot. Too much time had elapsed for Confederate shelling to have ignited it; it was obviously a Union attempt to destroy the supplies. Forrest hurried to the depot door with his saber drawn to keep the captive Federals from rushing out. Then Adjutant Strange drew a pistol, and together they ordered the prisoners to put out the flames—or die. Forrest warned Fry that he would punish another such attempt "in the most summary manner."[32]

Forrest now had more prisoners than he could herd. At Trenton alone the Confederates gathered seven hundred captives: four hundred soldiers, many of them sick, and three hundred African Americans aiding them. Forrest would report that the Trenton captures also included "a large quantity of stores, arms, ammunition and provisions," as well as "several hundred horses, few of which were of any value." As usual, he counted each item captured. The additional spoil included 13 wagons and ambulances, 7 caissons, 20,000 artillery rounds, and 400,000 rounds of small arms ammunition.[33]

Combined with those at Trenton, prisoners taken at Humboldt and Lexington and in the railroad wrecking around Jackson swelled Forrest's total captured to more than half his brigade. Needing to dispose of this captive mob that would slow his pace, he paroled it—after crafting the stories its men would tell on reaching Union lines.

Now Forrest again showed his Confederates—but not their Union prisoners—his talent for trickery. From the beginning he had paraded, rather than crept, into West Tennessee. His men told civilians they encountered that their numbers were legion—enough, one soldier told a wondering female onlooker, to put a soldier behind every tree in West Tennessee "and two or three behind the biggest ones." Forrest also apparently sent out bogus Confederate couriers to be captured. Union general Grenville Dodge, hurrying from Corinth, reported capturing one from General George Maney, who carried a message telling Forrest to "hold" Jackson and keep Grant's communications broken; this, of course,

encouraged Federal concentration at Jackson rather than on the railroads
Forrest meant to smash. Dodge also captured another supposedly sent
by cavalry Colonel Philip D. Roddey in Alabama informing Forrest he
was awaiting orders, suggesting that Forrest had access to other forces
besides his own. All such fakery multiplied Forrest's overall strength and
threat in Union minds.[34]

Now, to impress the captives he would parole at Trenton, he undertook
other ruses. As his officers filled out parole papers, he had couriers ride up
announcing the purported approach of Confederate commands that were
not within a hundred miles. These phony dispatches asked for orders and
made progress reports. Forrest's genius for fabrication knew few bounds.
Somewhere since crossing the Tennessee he had captured kettledrums, routinely used to aid the march of infantry. Any other cavalry officer doubtless would have directed that they be burned as useless. Forrest, by contrast,
ordered them carried along. Now he had them beaten at various locations
within the captives' hearing as they were readied for parole. After nightfall,
he ordered a detachment of dismounted cavalrymen to march into and out
of sight of his campfires at different points, each appearance seeming to be
that of a new infantry unit.[35]

On the morning of December 21, Forrest paroled four or five hundred
Tennessee prisoners, sending them out to spread their stories of a full-
fledged Confederate army. Eight or nine hundred parolees hailing from
farther north he sent marching toward Columbus, Kentucky, under a flag
of truce. What he did with the African Americans captured at Trenton remains unspecified. Confederate policy was to return them to their masters,
but he hardly had time to sort that out, operating as he was in enemy territory. Possibly he entrusted them to Confederate-sympathizing planters
in the area—he did that with the unserviceable captured horses—or perhaps he turned them loose to spread more tales of his counterfeit legions.
Whatever he did in that regard, he soon afterward torched the Trenton
depot along with all its surplus matériel, including six hundred bales of
cotton, two hundred barrels of pork, and hogsheads of tobacco that had
anchored the makeshift Federal breastworks.[36]

Although he had declined Fry's sword, Forrest nevertheless departed
Trenton with a new one. He appropriated for himself from the loot a hand-
some blade of Damascus steel. It was a model used by US Dragoons, but

what he did with it illustrates his view of the conventions of armed conflict. He filed its back edge—kept dull, per army custom—to the razor-like sheen of the front one, so that he could slay and maim with a backstroke as well as a forward slash. The developers of the conventions had probably never thought of that or encountered a warrior whose bellicosity demanded every possible chance to kill and wound. A natural lefthander but ambidextrous, Forrest strapped the blade to his left side and drew it with his right hand. But he could swing it—hard—with either arm.[37]

On December 21, the day after the raid on Trenton, Forrest pushed on north toward Union City, another rail hub. On the way, he destroyed more than twenty miles of Mobile & Ohio track, further decimating the connection between Grant's left wing at Corinth and its Columbus, Kentucky, supply source. At Rutherford Station he captured two Union companies; at Kenton Station, he took a colonel of the One Hundred Nineteenth Illinois plus twenty-two men left in a hospital.[38]

At Trenton, a 430-man cavalry battalion under Colonel T. Alonzo Napier had joined the Confederates. Forrest's swelled ranks, magnified by his tricks into a pseudo-horde, threw the lower Midwest into paranoiac convulsions as they approached the Kentucky border. Brigadier General Thomas A. Davies, commanding 5,000 Federals at Columbus, Kentucky, first heard that General Sullivan had ordered the Union City garrison to Jackson, then that Humboldt, Trenton, and Rutherford had fallen. On this intelligence he ordered the two companies at Kenton to retreat to Columbus. Cut off from Grant, Davies wired Halleck in Washington for instructions. Davies claimed to have reliable information that Forrest had 7,000 cavalry plus ten field guns and a backing of heavy infantry. Halleck in three different wires ordered him "to hold Columbus at all hazards."

As Forrest gobbled up the wounded and sick men left at the Rutherford and Kenton stations north of Trenton on December 22, Federal consternation descended into terror. Davies tried to save as much matériel as he could from the marauding Confederates. He loaded the mountains of supplies at Columbus onto troop transport steamers and sent them to Memphis. With Forrest reported heading for Hickman just north of the Kentucky border, Davies withdrew the 150-man Hickman garrison, then sent the gunboat *Fair Play* racing to the town to save its heavy artillery. The gunboat scared off Confederates trying to mount two sixty-four-pounder Union cannon, and Davies dispatched a regiment "to roll the guns into the river." He believed the Federal base at Island No. 10 in the Mississippi between Columbus and Memphis, with all its armament and ammunition, was in direst danger, so he ordered the guns there dismantled and rendered useless.[39]

The Confederates at Hickman were indeed Forrest's. Most of his command was still in northwest Tennessee, wrecking bridges and long trestles across fifteen swampy miles between the northern and southern forks of the Obion River. Not all of his command, though. On the night of December 23—from Union City, Tennessee, some fifteen miles south—he sent forty men to within twelve miles of Columbus at Moscow, Kentucky, just east of Hickman. Using a typical Forrest tactic, the detachment routed a party of entrenched Federals by yelling for phantom artillery to be brought up and trained on the Union position. The Federals quickly decamped toward Columbus while the Confederates destroyed the Moscow railroad bridge.[40]

By then, Forrest had captured Union City with more trickery. On the morning of December 22, he heard that a Federal force 10,000 strong had left Jackson heading east to block his routes back to the Tennessee River. But, as at Murfreesboro, he had not come here to do half a job. The Mobile & Ohio tracks divided at Union City, one set running northeast to Paducah and the other north to Columbus, and their junction was too good a target to ignore. Ninety-four Federals had just arrived there from Columbus, sent down by General Davies, when Forrest approached with four hundred Confederates. Marching less than five minutes ahead of them was their drove of nine hundred, Columbus-headed parolees.

Forrest seems to have used the prisoners wisely. He later claimed the Federals first took them for Confederates, multiplying the size of his force in their eyes. By contrast, the Federal commander, Captain Samuel Logan of the Fifty-fourth Illinois, reported that Forrest advanced the prisoners under a flag of truce and, while doing so, surrounded the Union force with his cavalry and artillery. Either way, Forrest ordered his artillery advanced and shells rammed home; then he demanded an immediate, unconditional surrender. Logan estimated Forrest's strength at 1,500 and deemed it "folly" to resist. He gave up without firing a shot.[41]

Three days later, on a dreary Christmas morning in a hard rain, Forrest left Union City and at last turned southeast, back toward Clifton. But he was determined to make even his escape productive, laying waste to more bridges and trestles along the Northwestern Railroad to McKenzie. Late on December 26, his column reached Dresden, Tennessee, and camped there overnight. Pushing on toward McKenzie the next morning, he sent Biffle's Ninth Tennessee south to harry a Union column reported heading belatedly to Dresden to cut him off. His main force—burdened with his artillery, more captives, and a wagon train of captured supplies—continued southward. He aimed to elude larger Federal troops to attack one more large Union supply depot, Bethel Station on the Mobile & Ohio south of Jackson.

But Forrest now had to outwit nature and topography as well as Federals. At dusk on December 28, another cold and sleeting day, he was a few miles south of McKenzie near the lower end of the Obion bottoms. There he found all usable bridges destroyed. The enemy and Forrest's own work of area-wide destruction had left him only a long, rotting structure in a swamp on a seldom-taken road to McLemoresville. He put his tired troopers to carpentry work, reinforcing punky planks and timbers with newly cut support logs forked at the top end to cradle and brace the timbers. He himself wielded an axe. Well after dark, with the shoring up completed, the cavalry clattered over, and Forrest himself drove the first wagon across to show that their handiwork had done the job. It had not. The next two wagons slid off the sleet-slick, wobbling span into the frigid swamp. Much of his command despaired of saving the wagons and guns, but Forrest plied his usual stress-induced profanity and assigned twenty men to each team of horses and fifty to each cannon. He ordered the deeper points of the swamp chocked with timber and even sacks of prized flour and coffee from his plunder wagons. The cold, muddy troopers got the guns and vehicles dragged to the east bank of the Obion's south fork by 3 a.m. Forrest then moved them on four more miles to McLemoresville before stopping to rest and feed.[42]

While his men rested on the morning of December 29, many Federals were obeying Grant's order to get between Forrest and the Tennessee River. These included three brigades from Jackson and the 1,500 men coming south from Fort Henry. The bulk of General Dodge's Union force from Mississippi, minus cavalry, had returned there on December 23 on urgent orders from Grant—because Grant had suffered another smash to his supply lines on December 20. On that day, the same on which Forrest took Trenton, General Earl Van Dorn raided and burned Grant's Mississippi supply base at Holly Springs. Dodge's cavalry still roved south and east of Lexington, however, and gunboats still prowled the Tennessee. As Forrest fought mud in the Obion bottoms, a brigade from Jackson commanded by Colonel Cyrus Dunham passed just five miles south of him on the road from Trenton to Huntingdon. Not knowing Forrest was near, Dunham passed on.[43]

Federal forces of significant size were not all Forrest had to worry about. As at Clifton, he was again nearing territory where Confederate sympathies were scarce. Such pockets dotted the Confederacy and were plentiful in Tennessee. The Tennessee River's banks from Kentucky to Alabama bristled with hills tended by poor farmers unfriendly to slavery and its proponents. Around Huntingdon, some ten miles east of McLemoresville, such supporters welcomed Federal troops rushing north from Mississippi without "shelter, rations, and cooking utensils." Residents feted them with impressive quantities of pork, cornmeal, and similar sustenance.[44]

Forrest's mud-begrimed troopers were not so lucky. He rested them briefly at McLemoresville, but by mid-morning on December 29, his scouts reported thousands of Federals at Huntingdon. These were two of the three Jackson-based brigades of General Jeremiah Sullivan—Cyrus Dunham's and another led by Colonel John Fuller. Hearing the Federals had vacated Lexington under the impression that he was headed for the river east of Huntingdon or farther north, Forrest rode back toward Clifton, where he had originally crossed. In continual rain he took a rolling, muddy back road that struck the Huntingdon-Lexington highway at Parker's Crossroads, fourteen miles south of Huntingdon.[45]

Forrest's men and animals were exhausted, and he gave them a day off on December 30 amid the gathering danger. He sent out his brother, Captain Bill Forrest, to scout northward on the Huntingdon-Lexington highway. Bill led a small company of so-called Independents informally known as the "Forty Thieves," a hard group of unenlisted and unpaid civilian guerrillas who, living off their plunder of unionists and the kindness of secession sympathizers, merited the attitude Bragg took toward Forrest's whole command. That evening the Thieves met the vanguard of Colonel Dunham's Federal brigade. This was the unit that had passed south of Forrest, heading east from Trenton to Huntingdon the day before, while Forrest's men were still in the Obion bottoms. The Thieves encountered them at Clarksburg, nine miles south of Huntingdon, but sixty-five troopers of the Eighteenth Illinois Mounted Infantry dismounted and bested the Thieves, who left three of their number dead on the field. Dunham's whole brigade moved south from Huntingdon that evening and bivouacked at Clarksburg for the night, and Bill Forrest sent a courier reporting this fact to his brother. Bill's elder sibling sent back orders to delay Dunham as long as possible and report often. Meanwhile, he let most of his men rest through the night.[46]

Forrest now knew that, to make it back to safety, he would have to fight his largest battle since crossing the Tennessee. Because he had sent detachments under Biffle and Starnes off toward Trenton and Huntingdon to prevent Federal pursuers from reaching his position, Forrest had about 2,000 men with him. Still, his force equaled or surpassed the numbers of either Dunham at Clarksburg or the brigade remaining at Huntingdon with Sullivan, commanded by Fuller. Forrest determined to hit the two Union colonels piecemeal.[47]

Dunham, like Forrest, knew where his opponent was. Each expected to fight the other around the crossroads at the farm of a family named Parker, where the byroad Forrest was traveling intersected the Huntingdon-Lexington highway less than a mile north of the community of Red Mound. But Dunham made an unfortunate assumption. He took it for granted that Forrest was trying only to escape the converging Federal armies via Lexington to Clifton and the river. He sent word back to Sullivan at Huntingdon that Forrest had 8,000 men and twelve guns and that he, Dunham, would try to "force a fight out of him." If he really meant to do that, he had to have assumed that Forrest was very frightened. Even so, Dunham obviously needed and expected help from Huntingdon.[48]

At 4 a.m. on December 31, Forrest ordered his men into their saddles to head for Parker's. A mile away, he could hear small arms and artillery fire and knew Dunham had reached the intersection first. Dunham was chasing Confederate pickets from the timber and outbuildings around a house belonging to a Dr. Williams northwest of the crossroads.

At about 10 a.m., Forrest formed for battle. He dismounted Russell's Fourth Alabama and Dibrell's Eighth Tennessee and sent them forward as skirmishers, then hurried a second band of scouts to Clarksburg, six miles north on the Huntingdon-Lexington Road. He expected these to join Bill Forrest to delay, and warn of, more Federals coming down the road.[49]

He rushed up his guns to challenge Dunham's. He led one, a twelve-pounder supervised by Sergeant Nat Baxter Jr., a half mile forward. Dismounting, he walked to the top of a low hill and showed Baxter where to set up. The site was daunting. Baxter saw a thick battle line of Federals four hundred yards off with only a hundred or two Confederate skirmishers scattered in trees and fence rows between it and his gun. Behind him were only two or three hundred friendly cavalry.[50]

At Forrest's order, Baxter opened fire. Dunham had seen Dibrell's skirmishers deploying behind the little hill's crest, and he had pulled his own men back to their regiment in the cover of the Williams house. The rest of Forrest's artillery, five more cannons directly commanded by Captain Freeman and two by Lieutenant Morton, spread out left of Baxter and joined in the barrage. They challenged Dunham's three guns, part of the Seventh Wisconsin.

The resulting duel was intense but brief. Baxter's gun dismounted one of the Wisconsin cannons, killing or disabling its horses. Troops of the Fiftieth Indiana withdrew the piece under the heavy Confederate fire. With his guns largely ineffective—perhaps because they had gone into the fight with little ammunition—Dunham ordered his cannoneers to cease firing and his forces there to withdraw to his main column at the crossroads.[51]

The crossroads was not far enough, as it turned out. Forrest departed from conventional military theory by using artillery the way he used infantry, taking its cannons as close to the enemy as he took the rifles of his dismounted cavalrymen. He pursued a retreating foe with cannons as well as horsemen, and that happened now as Freeman's six guns and Morton's two kept on the heels of the withdrawing Federals. So, finding himself still hammered by Forrest's cannons, Dunham withdrew farther, to a ridge a half mile south of Parker's. Seeing the Confederates descend on the crossroads, he sent two companies of the Fiftieth Indiana back to impede them. The Indianans moved up and opened fire, then fell back in the face of the comparative horde of oncoming Confederates. Continuing to push, Forrest drove forward with the cannons and his dismounted cavalrymen front and center. Two or three hundred troopers on horseback, divided equally, guarded his flanks. The new Confederate battle line near the crossroads put Morton's two guns in the middle, with three each of Freeman's to Morton's right and left. All were a few strides in front of the dismounted cavalrymen, six hundred yards from the Federals.[52]

Fighting cavalrymen as infantry was becoming a Forrest habit. It let them find cover more easily, take better aim, and deliver more devastating fire. This tactic had occasionally been practiced against Plains Indians in the 1850s, but Forrest likely knew nothing of that. His placing of cannons up front, all but unsupported, was even more original. Others sometimes credited Morton, but Morton said the idea was Forrest's; he himself just saw its sense. The closer a cannon came, the more accurate and daunting it was. At Parker's Crossroads, however, Forrest had a more immediate reason for leaning heavily on his artillery. Expecting to fight Fuller's Federal brigade after finishing with Dunham's, he was hoarding his human resources and sustaining as few casualties as possible so as to have optimum strength available to meet Fuller.

He may have had a specific reason, too, for putting Morton's battery in the center of his advancing line. The "tallow-faced boy" was, after all, still a new member of Forrest's unit, and in the center—Forrest's own position—Forrest could watch Morton's performance under fire. Now, out in front of the Confederate center, in a peach orchard and open field facing Dunham's ridge south of the crossroads, Forrest gave Morton a curt order: "Give 'em hell."[53]

Morton fired. The Confederate guns drove the Federals off the ridge and down into some woods behind it. Dunham complained that a Confederate battery to his right, probably Morton's, enfiladed his line with "terrible" fire. The Federals were stubborn, though. Between 10:30 a.m. and noon, they made three charges at the Confederate guns. Two of these got within eighty and sixty yards of the targets, but that was all. In one, the Confederates countercharged and took two disabled Federal cannons ringed by dead and wounded men and horses.[54]

The Federals again fixed bayonets to charge the enfilading guns. Suddenly Colonel Napier attacked the Union right rear "furiously" with a "heavy dismounted force," Dunham would recall. Napier forgot or did not know of his chief's aim to let cannons do most of the labor. The assault, breasting fire all the way to a fence covering the prone Federals, cost Napier his life and those of several men in his battalion.[55]

By the time Napier's assault failed, another mass of Confederates was moving along the east-west byroad in Dunham's front. They were crossing the Huntingdon-Lexington Road, heading to the Federal right. Dunham misconstrued their aim. They were moving in the general direction of the Tennessee River, and Dunham still thought Forrest was trying to escape. Actually, Forrest was surrounding him.

Dunham had no sooner fought off Napier than Russell's dismounted Fourth Alabama attacked his right rear. Then Dunham's tenuous circumstances turned dire. In the early afternoon, 250 mounted troopers under Starnes rushed back from their detached duty at Huntingdon, and Forrest sent them to the right to find and attack the Federal rear. They soon thundered up the Huntingdon-Lexington Road from the south and got between the Federals and their wagons, parked in a hollow 150 yards behind the Union left.[56]

The disparate attacks were shaking the Federal line. Around noon, about half of the green Thirty-ninth Iowa on the Federal left, pounded by Confederate cannon fire, had broken to the rear. When Russell and Starnes struck, the Iowans broke again. They fled into a cornfield west of the road, chased by canister. The Confederates now got other assistance: Biffle, hurrying back from his detached duty near Trenton. The initial breaking of the Thirty-ninth Iowa had provided Forrest with a throng of prisoners and a developing hole in Dunham's left front. Behind the position the Iowans vacated, a company of the One Hundred Twenty-second Illinois, assigned to guard the Federal wagon train, fought off Starnes. Dunham lost his wagons, anyway, though; separated from the bulk of Dunham's force, spooked Federal teamsters fled with the vehicles and were captured.[57]

Amid the flight of the Iowans into the cornfield to the left and the Confederate attacks on the Federal right and rear, Sergeant Nat Baxter Jr. had seen white flags "all along the Union line." Needing to reorganize his badly mixed men and refill their cartridge boxes, Forrest sent forward a flag of truce. Dunham came out to meet it. One of Forrest's aides told Dunham that Forrest understood Dunham had surrendered. According to Dunham, he replied that he had "never thought of surrendering" and that any white flag was unauthorized. The aide left but soon returned; Forrest demanded unconditional surrender. Dunham said that if Forrest thought he could "take me, he can come and try."[58]

Indeed, Forrest had already taken Dunham's only three pieces of artillery and isolated his wagon train. He soon reported that Dunham offered to withdraw if allowed to bury his dead. Forrest refused, thinking surrender imminent. Men on both sides apparently thought the same. During the parley, they mingled as if the Confederates had already won. Forrest's adjutant, Major J. P. Strange, took charge of the Federal wagons and inventoried booty. Artillerist Baxter strolled forward to talk with a Union officer. Observers reported Dunham had not fired a shot for as much as half an hour. The day "seemed inevitably lost," wrote one.[59]

The problem for Forrest was that these observers were Federal.

Forrest was negotiating with Dunham when disaster struck him from behind. With his commander riding with the rear guard, Colonel Fuller of Sullivan's Second Brigade had been marching from Huntingdon when he heard the fighting involving Dunham, Sullivan's other brigade. Instead of allowing Forrest to finish Dunham and then turn on Fuller's brigade, as Forrest had intended, Fuller had taken the initiative, hurried forward, and attacked Forrest's rear.

Fuller struck at 1:30 p.m. During his approach, a unionist resident had informed him that cannons and rifles heard in the distance belonged to Dunham and Forrest and that Dunham "needed aid." Fuller rushed to the field and struck with artillery and the bayonets of three Ohio regiments: the Thirty-ninth and three more guns of the Seventh Wisconsin Battery west of the Huntingdon Road, and the Twenty-seventh and Sixty-third regiments to the east.[60]

Fuller's men were capturing horses and their holders and bearing down on Forrest's cannons. When a staff officer galloped up, yelling that Federals were in their rear, Forrest did not believe him. He raced back there and saw the horse holders running willy-nilly from, and some surrendering to, an enveloping Union line. The Sixty-third and Twenty-seventh Ohio were marching at double-quick pace down the Huntingdon Road. For the only time in the entire war, Forrest was totally surprised.[61]

The trouble had started at Clarksburg. The second scout party Forrest sent there had misunderstood its orders, which were to watch the Huntingdon Road and warn of any Union reinforcements coming down it. Perhaps these orders were garbled in transmission between Forrest and the aide who dispensed them. Captain William McLemore had understood that his hundred-man detachment was to link up with Bill Forrest, make a reconnaissance, then return to the Confederates at Parker's Crossroads. Reconnoitering and angling to Clarksburg by back roads had taken a while, and near the town McLemore learned that Bill Forrest had withdrawn during the night in the face of a heavy Federal force. McLemore's men then heard the sound of fighting a half dozen miles behind them at Parker's crossroads and saw Federal cavalry, probably Fuller's rear guard, galloping south on the Huntingdon Road. McLemore started back toward Forrest, but by the time he could return—also by secondary routes—he found Union troops between him and his commander.[62]

The Confederate rear was in chaos as Forrest rode up. The onrushing Ohioans were overwhelming three of his slimly supported cannons. Horses pulling three more caissons ran madly away with their pieces. Determined to save as many guns as possible, Forrest ordered the runaways ridden down, brought under control, and hauled away at breakneck speed. He collared every trooper he could hail and told him to turn and face the foes bearing down on the flying caissons. Seeing Sergeant Baxter running after one of the vehicles, Forrest ordered him to join the general's escort and fifty more men under Major Jeffrey Forrest in a charge to save the guns. Baxter replied that he had not so much as a knife. Forrest said Baxter should join the countercharge anyway: "I want to make as big a show as possible." Dashing at the Federals with his patchwork force, Forrest slowed their advance and saved five of the cannons.[63]

Forrest's spontaneous tactics at Parker's Crossroads became famous. One order supposedly issued by Forrest during the moment of crisis— "Charge both ways!"—is doubtless apocryphal, but its sense is substantially true. Forrest did charge to his rear to save five guns, and his men did charge Dunham, just not from Dunham's front. Russell and Starnes, seeing Forrest's predicament, instead resumed attacking Dunham's rear and got his attention—apparently all of it. Two Union officers later complained that Dunham did not fire a shot at Forrest's men as they galloped across his front and off to the west of the road. Colonel Z. S. Spaulding of the Twenty-seventh Ohio, in the center of the counterattacking line, reported that his riflemen had little time to do more than empty a few Confederate saddles before Forrest had made off with the reclaimed cannons.[64]

Lieutenant Morton, bloody from a saber wound in the thigh, helped spirit away the guns. Riding beside Forrest as they circled the Federal left and exited the field southward, he saw his chief deep in thought. Forrest was doubtless pondering why McLemore had not warned him of Fuller's approach. Suddenly a minié ball sang past Morton's temple, and Forrest's head dropped to his chest. Alarmed, the lieutenant touched Forrest's shoulder. "General, are you hurt much?" he asked. Forrest raised his head, took off his hat, and they both stared at a hole in its brim.

"No," Forrest replied. "But didn't it come damn close?"[65]

The Federals had significantly bloodied Forrest at Parker's Crossroads. He approximated his losses as 25 killed, 75 wounded, and 250 captured—along with three cannons, four caissons, two ambulances, and five wagons containing 75,000 rounds of ammunition. Even this was an underestimation. Sullivan reported taking 300-plus prisoners and more than 350 horses. The reported Union casualties totaled 27 killed, 140 wounded, and 70 missing.

His losses notwithstanding, Forrest had been lucky. Sullivan, one of whose subordinates wryly praised his "genius for tardiness," had halted his column twice on the way to Parker's and was himself nearly captured by

Bill Forrest's Thieves. Only Fuller's repeated advances without orders got the second Federal brigade to the crossroads in time to save Dunham.[66]

Forrest's good fortune held after the battle. Sullivan's pursuit exemplified the Federal general's "genius." Two hours after Forrest's men fled, Sullivan mistook the approach of McLemore, who was finally returning from Clarksburg, for a Forrest counterattack. Sullivan threw out guards and did not pursue until the next morning. His men then marched only fourteen miles—two miles beyond Lexington—and camped for the night.[67]

By then Forrest was long gone. He had hurried the twelve miles to Lexington and sent his wagon train and prisoners on ahead while briefly resting and tending his wounded. Then, at 2 a.m. on New Year's Day, in dismal rain, he took the road to Clifton. En route, he paroled three hundred prisoners taken since departing Union City, eighty-three of them seized at Parker's.

The escape was briefly stymied when his advance ran into the Sixth Tennessee Union cavalry. It blocked the road. But around noon, when the main Confederate column came up, Forrest ordered Dibrell's Eighth Tennessee to charge. They routed the Federals, and that night he ferried his main body across the Tennessee. McLemore and another separated detachment crossed at points north of Clifton.[68]

He had not just made it out of West Tennessee. He had done so largely triumphant.

Forrest left West Tennessee with more than he brought. Even without his 300 captured cavalrymen, he led more men back to Bragg than the 2,000 he had left with, thanks to the addition of 100 recruits and the Napier battalion that joined him at Union City. And he had made captives of at least 1,439 Federals, the number for which he turned in official paroles, and suffered no more than 500 casualties.

As Forrest reported to Bragg from Clifton, "we have worked, rode, and fought hard." Truly. In terrible weather, his seventeen-day operation spanned three hundred miles and decimated rail and telegraph communications vital to Grant's campaign to get to Vicksburg through central Mississippi. Forrest also had made veterans of largely green troopers and armed them with Federal weapons. And he had preoccupied every Federal in West

Tennessee, allowing none to reinforce Rosecrans as Rosecrans and Bragg fought between December 31 and January 2 to a titanic standstill at Stones River that ended in another Bragg retreat.[69]

Most important, Forrest's work—combined with Van Dorn's December 20 raid on Holly Springs—had cut a leg from under Grant's Mississippi plan. Forrest's wreckage of four miles of trestle and track in the Obion bottoms would keep the Mobile & Ohio from full operation until March 7. By then, Grant's army would have ceased using it altogether between Columbus and Jackson. Perhaps the greatest testament to Forrest's feat would come from Grant himself. Grant later wrote that the raid had severed his northern communications for more than a week and stopped his rations and forage for two weeks. It shook his faith in maintaining such a long supply line through hostile territory ever again.

Now Grant would have to revamp his Vicksburg plan—and try to alert Sherman, who, with no idea how much his chief's communications had been damaged, was floating down the Mississippi expecting help in attacking the Dixie Gibraltar.[70]

19

DECEMBER 1862–FEBRUARY 1, 1863—GRANT IN MEMPHIS

"General McClernand . . .
Is Unmanageable and Incompetent"

Forrest and Van Dorn had smashed Grant's plan. The Union commander had intended to assail Confederate general John Pemberton's army and hold it in central Mississippi while Sherman swung down the river from Memphis and assaulted Vicksburg. But in less than three December weeks, Van Dorn had torched the cached Union supplies at Holly Springs, and Forrest had wrecked the rails that could bring more. Together, the two had islanded Grant's army for more than two weeks. He had little choice but to withdraw from along the Mississippi Central Railroad.

So now the other half of Grant's scheme was in peril. No longer under threat, Pemberton's 25,000 Confederates at Grenada, Mississippi, were free to rush the 150 rail miles southeast to Vicksburg to meet and defeat Sherman's 32,000 Federals steaming downriver. And the Confederates' wholesale slashing of telegraph wires across northern Mississippi and West Tennessee prevented Grant from even informing Sherman about what had happened.

Sherman soon knew, though, that something was wrong. Almost as soon as Forrest crossed into West Tennessee, Sherman heard about it and divined the Confederate's aim: "to draw us back from our purpose of going to Vicksburg," he wrote General Willis A. Gorman in Helena, Arkansas, on December 17. Sherman thought that Forrest might indeed delay Grant—but not stop him. Sherman's soldierly impulse was to do the reverse of what the enemy wanted, so he got going. He presumed, he wrote, that time was "everything to us."[1]

And not just to outfox Pemberton in Mississippi. There was also power-hungry John McClernand in Illinois. Sherman was as eager as Grant to foil the ex-congressman. Since October, McClernand had been recruiting Midwesterners and sending them to Memphis. Secretly but plainly backed by the White House, he expected to lead them on his own Vicksburg operation, trumping Sherman's and beating Grant to a victory.

The downriver half of Grant's disintegrating Vicksburg project would be Sherman's first independent operation since his nationally noted Kentucky paranoia of 1861. Both personal and professional dimensions were at play now. McClernand represented almost everything Sherman loathed: cut-throat politics, headline hunting, obsessive ambition, and civilian intrusion on the turf of soldiers. The two men resembled each other in volubility and overt nervousness, but little else. To McClernand, style was substance. To the apolitical Sherman, style was nothing, substance everything; it explained his attachment to Grant. He seemed to delight in eviscerating political hypocrisy and obfuscation with direct, cynical, and often outrageous speech. But McClernand, a Democrat possibly angling to succeed his Republican president, was dangerous: a snake who struck at all in his path. Grant aide John Rawlins had not been far off in branding McClernand a "damned, slinking, Judas bastard."[2]

So Sherman from the outset had been an enthusiastic accomplice in Grant's bid to scotch the McClernand plot. On December 20, at Grant's bidding, Sherman hijacked the recruits McClernand had been sending to Memphis for his own intended Vicksburg drive. Sherman melded them into two Memphis divisions that accompanied a third from the Tallahatchie foray, then rushed the three out of Memphis. Totaling some 20,000 men, they were off downriver on an armada of transports and gunboats before McClernand could leave Illinois. Sherman left so fast that he forgot some pontoon parts he would need in the Vicksburg area's boot-swallowing swamps.[3]

He picked up more strength on the way. At Helena, Arkansas, and Friars Point, Mississippi, on December 21, he took aboard a fourth division—another 13,000 men—under Brigadier General Frederick Steele. At Friars Point, Sherman learned troubling news. Twenty-five men claiming to be sole survivors from the Union depot at Holly Springs had escaped to Memphis saying the big supply depot had fallen. Sherman wrote to Grant. He did not know, he said, "what faith to put in such a report, but suppose whatever may be the case you will attend to it." Continuing to be certain that any damage to Grant's supply lines was intended to stop Federal progress in Mississippi, Sherman was determined not to let that happen. Two days later, in an order to his division commanders, he wrote that the attack on Holly Springs only made their own mission more important.[4]

So Sherman kept going. On December 22, while Forrest was still slashing his way through West Tennessee and Grant was withdrawing from northern Mississippi into southwestern Tennessee, Sherman's expedition arrived at Milliken's Bend, Louisiana, ten miles northwest of Vicksburg. To protect his rear and block any aid that Confederates in Louisiana might send to the citadel, he ordered a brigade several miles west to destroy tracks and trestles of the Shreveport-Vicksburg Railroad. He then pushed on to the mouth of the Yazoo River, a tributary running from the northeast into the Mississippi west of Vicksburg, well in front of the city's northern defenses. Sherman steamed up the Yazoo twelve miles. There he faced the north end of the fourteen-mile Vicksburg trenches. They ran atop the Chickasaw Bluffs rising out of the Yazoo Valley.[5]

Even up here along the Yazoo, the defenses were daunting. At Sherman's disembarkation site, the Yazoo combined with the Chickasaw Bayou and a bend of the Mississippi well behind him to enclose a huge, rough rectangle about nine miles long and six miles wide. This maze of bayous and swamps offered two narrow avenues to get at the hill-crowning fortifications: a causeway bridge corduroyed with logs and, a mile south of the bridge, a sand spit ford, both crossing Chickasaw Bayou. Confederate artillery and rifle pits frowned on each. Just to get to these crossings, Sherman's men would have to attack through three miles of swamp, abatis, enemy pickets and skirmishers, and a deep, fifteen-foot-wide bayou. The water was bordered by swaths of quicksand that widened the barrier by a factor of as much as five or six. At both bridge and ford, the attackers would have to mass into two all-but-sitting targets. Those who survived the crossings would charge onto a dry, open shelf fronting the so-called Yazoo Valley Road. It ran from Vicksburg north to Yazoo City behind an earthen bank at the foot of a levee twenty-plus feet high. Behind the levee rose the Walnut Hills, the ridge backing the Chickasaw Bluffs. The hills were lined with more rifle pits and guns.[6]

There was little time to seek alternatives. Sherman's information indicated the Confederates numbered about 15,000 and could be reinforced at a rate of 4,000 a day by railroad from Grenada if Grant could not keep Pemberton occupied there. "Not one word," he wrote, "could I hear from General Grant, who was supposed to be pushing south."[7]

Sherman had heard, of course, that the Holly Springs depot had fallen, which perhaps should have given him pause. But he had few other options. As far as he knew, Grant was out there somewhere holding—or at least pushing—Pemberton, and McClernand was expected to be heading south from Illinois at any time. And Sherman's confidence had also been bolstered by recent intelligence. After landing on the Yazoo, he heard from a black man in the vicinity that a Federal force had arrived in Yazoo City. Sherman made no investigation of the report—he had little way to do that from where he was—but he presumed that the rumored approaching Federals were Grant's, so he hurried to keep his end of their bargain. If the Yazoo City force was Grant, it meant Pemberton was retreating to Vicksburg, with Grant, as called for by their original plan, pursuing as closely as possible. So Pemberton had to be closer to Vicksburg than Grant or Sherman had expected or wanted.[8]

Sherman rushed ahead. On December 27 and 28, reconnoitering as they went, his men pushed Confederate skirmishers across the three miles of swamp leading to the crossings. A hellish nightlong storm of heavy rain pelted his unsheltered, ill-clad troops. Soaked and shivering, they got Sherman's orders to attack the bluffs the following morning.[9]

Sherman's plan was by the West Point book. He would launch a diversionary strike toward Vicksburg in front of his right, while sending his main assault to break the Confederate center. General George W. Morgan's troops would cross the corduroy bridge in the primary attack while General

A. J. Smith's division would cross the sandy ford to Morgan's right. When either force broke the Confederate line, its men could turn right toward the town of Vicksburg or left to decimate the Confederate right. The latter, if accomplished, would make a critical lodgment nearer Yazoo City and, Sherman presumed, nearer to Grant's approaching army.[10]

After noon on December 28, Morgan thought he found a route safer than the corduroy bridge. Midway between the bridge and the ford, the bayou ran deep and wide, so the Confederates had left that area undefended. Morgan proposed bridging this point under cover of darkness and crossing there before the Confederates could react. Sherman approved. But during the stormy night, the engineers unwittingly bridged a nearer stretch of water that lay parallel to the one Morgan and Sherman intended. When day dawned and Morgan discovered the blunder, he informed Sherman that the engineers could remedy the error in two hours by taking up the bridge they had lain in the dark and laying it again across the correct pool. That pool, though, was wider than the first, and in the rush from Memphis, they had forgotten to bring enough pontoon linkage and flooring. They would have to cut trees to extend the new bridge the proper distance. As they started cutting the timber, they came under fire from Confederates hurrying to fill this gap in their line. Sherman refused to wait any longer. During the night, trains had been heard arriving in Vicksburg. Every lost minute threatened greater resistance.[11]

Sherman's tension was high, and it showed that morning in one of his controversial career's most flammable remarks. With the bridge-building scheme now useless and junked, the sole route left for Morgan's advance—the corduroy bridge—promised to exact a high cost in blood. Just beyond the crossing lay swampy ground that would further slow the bridge-bunched troops amid a vortex of fire. Morgan asked Sherman to have a look. For silent minutes, Morgan later remembered, Sherman studied the terrain. Then he pointed toward the daunting bluffs beyond the bridge and refused to change the plan. "That is the route to take!" he decreed and turned back toward his headquarters at a plantation in the rear. Soon an order arrived for Morgan. The aide carrying it said Sherman's words were, "Tell Morgan to give the signal for the assault. We will lose five thousand men before we can take Vicksburg and may as well lose them here as anywhere else."[12]

Sherman was between a rock and a hard place. He had promised Grant he would attack, and he needed to do it before Pemberton's reinforcements further filled the Vicksburg lines. As far as Sherman knew, McClernand could arrive at any moment. If that happened before Sherman attacked, Sherman would have to hand his army to the ex-politician without trying for the victory he and Grant needed. Not trying would be more than an abandonment of both commanders' personal aspirations; it would also elevate the headline-hungry McClernand's marginal competence to where it could threaten the fate of the nation. Sherman had to attack, odds—and hopelessness—be damned.

But Sherman's plan unknowingly threw his army's strength at the strongest point in the Chickasaw Bluffs defenses. The majority of the Confederate defenders fronted Morgan at the corduroy bridge: seven regiments of infantry backed by artillery, all entrenched to the eyes on higher ground. General Smith's rightward lunge at the sandy ford was intended "to prevent a concentration on Morgan," but the Confederate muscle was already concentrated on Morgan. Facing Smith at the sand-spit ford were just two regiments, along with a single battery. These, though, were exceptionally situated.

The terrain at the ford made the Confederate position there as forbidding as the one at the bridge. The sand spit and the high bayou bank beyond were impossibly narrow; the latter offered an upward path only wide enough for two men to charge abreast. Division commander David Stuart had learned from reconnaissance that Confederate rifle pits overlooked the narrow path up the far bayou bank. Confederates there, he feared, could "drop every man who attempted to ascend it as fast as he appeared." Stuart thought the Federals might be able to reach the far bank across the ford, but they could not possibly ascend it. He explained his misgivings to his superiors, but to no avail.

Morgan's discarded suggestion had been the best move. Opposite the spot where Morgan had wanted to bridge, there remained an undefended quarter mile separating just two regiments of Georgia infantry. But rather than hitting this weakest spot in the Confederate line, Sherman had ordered Morgan to lead his men across the corduroy bridge and into the massed might of the enemy defenses.[13]

The Federals who had to do it knew that attacking across the corduroy bridge was suicide. When brigade commander John F. DeCourcy received Morgan's order to form his troops, DeCourcy rode to him and asked if he was about to order a charge. Morgan said he was. "My poor brigade," De-Courcy said. "Your order will be obeyed, General."[14]

It was—with doomed heroism. The attackers' valor was squandered in five hours of slaughter. DeCourcy's men crossed the bayou, deployed on an open half mile of ground sloping upward to the Confederate trenches, and charged into a storm of fire from the front, both sides, and previously undetected Confederates to their left rear. Two more of Morgan's regiments pressed forward in support, but because of the constriction at the crossing point, they could not arrive before the men in front fell back. The hails of cross fire around and beyond the bridge were murderous.[15]

Hearing Morgan's firing nearly a mile away, Smith began his diversion. He sent the regiment in his center, the Sixth Missouri, charging across the bayou. Once over the ford, however, the Missourians could only take cover beneath the flood-hollowed bank beyond. Unwilling to ascend the narrow path into certain slaughter, they tried to dig through the bank. The digging achieved nothing, which was just as well; the Confederates soon reinforced the two regiments holding this part of their line with a third, the Sixtieth Tennessee. After dark, Smith withdrew the Missourians.[16]

Most of the carnage had occurred at the corduroy bridge. Casualty tallies for the three days—two spent crossing the bayou and one on the final assault—would give DeCourcy's Sixteenth Ohio 311 men killed, wounded, or missing. The Fifty-fourth Indiana lost 264; the Twenty-second Kentucky, 107; the Forty-second Ohio, 42. Morgan reported that the flag of the Sixteenth Ohio was "shot to tatters, only shreds remaining on the staff," while that of the Twenty-second Kentucky was "not less dripping with blood."[17]

Not all the Union colors made it back across the bayou. Troops under Confederate general Stephen Lee, who commanded in front of the bridge, reported taking four regimental flags, more than three hundred prisoners, and five hundred stands of small arms. Sherman's losses over the three days totaled 1,776. Confederate losses during the same period were reported as just 187.[18]

Sherman had had his fill of Chickasaw Bayou. He and gunboat commander Admiral David Porter decided to move farther up the Yazoo and
attack the far right of the Confederate line on December 31, hoping to
connect with Grant. Sherman was so desperate that he proposed a night attack, but upon their arrival at the site upriver, a thick fog so hampered the
vessels that Porter deemed any assault, night or day, "too hazardous to try."

All the while, Confederate reinforcement had continued. Sherman
heard trains arriving and leaving. Then he heard a rumor that Grant had
retreated, which "became confirmed by my receiving no intelligence from
him." He decided it was time to give up this bloody sally on Vicksburg.[19]

Two days later, as Sherman steamed back upriver, a very unhappy
General McClernand ran him to ground.

G rant had covered his tracks in the McClernand affair. Outwardly, he
  appeared merely to have deferred to superiors on the question of
McClernand's place in the Vicksburg campaign. On December 18, he
wrote McClernand the latest instructions from Washington the same day
he himself had received them. These included Halleck's order that all
Vicksburg-bound troops be under Grant and divided into four corps. Halleck went on to specify that Lincoln wanted McClernand's new army to
be "part" of the troops over which Grant had supervisory authority; Mc-
Clernand could have active command, but under Grant. Halleck, himself
wary and contemptuous of McClernand, had obviously persuaded Lincoln that the Union could not have a new army operating outside its chain
of command.[20]

While seeming only to follow orders, Grant skillfully obstructed Mc-
Clernand. He knew that the political general was still in Illinois and
could not get to Memphis before Sherman left with McClernand's
troops. Sherman had written Grant on December 12 that he expected
to leave Memphis on December 18. So when writing McClernand on
the latter date, Grant could be all but certain that by the time McClernand received his letter, Sherman would have left Memphis and thus
would be out of range of McClernand's higher rank when he did show
up. And until the political general did arrive in Memphis, McClernand
would not even know Sherman had gone.

As it happened, the interval between Sherman's departure and Mc-Clernand's receipt of Grant's letter was longer than Grant could have hoped for. Thanks to the Van Dorn-Forrest savaging of communications, McClernand did not receive the letter until December 29. He found it awaiting him in Memphis when he arrived.[21]

When he did turn up, he had to have been thunderstruck to find he had no army. He would not have been surprised, though, to find himself still under Grant's overall command. Halleck had sent him a copy of the orders he sent Grant; McClernand had gotten them while still in Springfield, Illinois, on December 22. The command structure they outlined was, of course, not what Lincoln had promised McClernand, and the ex-congressman faced yet another frustration within twenty-four hours. On December 23, he had to prod Halleck just to cut travel orders authorizing him to go to Memphis, let alone launch a Vicksburg campaign.[22]

McClernand saw his scheme unraveling. He had planned to use his clout with Lincoln to outflank Halleck and Grant and descend on Vicksburg with an independent army. He had envisioned arriving in Memphis in

MAJOR GENERAL JOHN A. McCLERNAND

pomp, accompanied by a train of not only military subordinates but also, improbably, attendants to his campaign-christening December 23 nuptials; that day, the same one on which he received Halleck's authorization to proceed to Memphis, he had married his deceased wife's young sister. Now, rather than posturing in front of his wedding party, the fifty-one-year-old politico had to chase down and capture the expedition he had doubtless boasted he would lead.[23]

McClernand was certain he knew the authors of his embarrassment and that they included not just Grant and Sherman. He was sure the two would not have acted without first consulting Halleck. So McClernand focused his hottest ire on the general in chief. On January 3, a day after catching up with Sherman at the mouth of the Yazoo, he formally protested in a letter to Secretary of War Stanton. McClernand informed Stanton he was writing to "establish . . . the fact that either through the intention of the General-in-Chief or a strange occurrence of accidents, the authority of the President and yourself, as evidenced by your acts, has been set at naught, and I have been deprived of the command that had been committed to me." Four days later, on January 7, he wrote Lincoln with no such restraint, blasting Halleck as possessing no "genius, justice, generosity, or policy."[24]

McClernand had correctly identified the pivotal actor in the charade. Halleck's revulsion at politicians intruding in army business was strong, and his preference for West Pointers over unaccredited commanders was more so.

Meanwhile, perhaps aided by the ongoing McClernand drama, the Grant-Halleck relationship continued to warm. The improvement also seemed in direct proportion to Halleck's increased dealings with the commanders of his other key armies: the balky, West Point–trained prima donnas George McClellan, Don Carlos Buell, and William Rosecrans. It likely did not hurt, either, that Grant cultivated his superior's favor. Grant had heard in early December from his congressional patron, Illinois congressman Washburne, that Halleck had spoken favorably of him and had said he would aid Grant in "anything" Grant wanted regarding changes to his staff. On December 14, Grant thanked Halleck for his expression of confidence. He also confided his views of his individual staff members, his subordinate generals, positions that needed filling, and the officers he thought should get them.

In the same letter, Grant did not miss the golden chance to voice his disdain for McClernand. He said his wing and division commanders were good and that he hoped no officer would be sent him that out-ranked them—then added, "I would regard it as particularly unfortunate to have either McClernand or [Lew] Wallace sent to me. The latter I could manage if he had less rank, but the former is unmanageable and incompetent."[25]

Thus, by late December Halleck and Grant were in solid agreement regarding McClernand. They were also actively cooperating to keep him from leading a Union campaign against Vicksburg. When McClernand caught up with Sherman at the Yazoo and found Sherman already had led a Vicksburg strike, he let his displeasure show in a foul humor directed toward both Sherman and Admiral Porter.[26]

It may have occurred to McClernand, however, that Halleck and Grant had done him an unwitting favor. By rushing Sherman ahead downriver, they had gotten Sherman—not McClernand—besmirched with the blood of Chickasaw Bayou. In the effort there, Sherman had "probably done all in the present case that anyone could have done," McClernand wrote Secretary Stanton, damning with faint praise. He then rushed on to blame Sherman, Grant, and Halleck for the defeat. He said Grant had not co-operated with the Chickasaw Bayou attack (which was true, but only because Van Dorn and Forrest had prevented him), and the composition of the tools and troops in the assault had been badly planned and "essentially defective."[27]

McClernand was hardly Grant's sole ongoing problem. In January 1863, Halleck ordered him to repair the railroads smashed by Forrest and Van Dorn. The general in chief wanted the Mobile & Ohio tracks fixed across Tennessee to Columbus, Kentucky. That was not all. Grant also was ordered to withdraw his army to the Corinth-Memphis line and fashion a new supply route. First he reopened the Memphis & Charleston rails to Corinth, but this did not remedy his supply problem. Forrest's rail and trestle wrecking had marooned too many cars on the

Mobile & Ohio in Tennessee and Kentucky; there were not enough left on the Memphis-Corinth line to feed Grant's men. To do that, he had to resort to gathering forage and meat from civilians in the countryside.[28]

Then there were the contrabands. Fugitive slaves from Mississippi, Tennessee, and Kentucky continued to overwhelm his department's commanders. Grant did not know what to do with all those he could not employ with the army as cooks, laborers, laundresses, and so on. He wrote Halleck on January 6 that he had authorized an Ohio philanthropist to take all who were at Columbus to his state at government expense. "Would like to dispose of more same way."[29]

The officer commanding at Columbus wired Grant that the condition of the fugitives thronging that Kentucky town was "terrible." Sympathy for them, though, was hard to find. Eleven days after Grant's note to Halleck, Secretary of War Stanton got a letter from a New Yorker, possibly a Republican political operative, warning that if Grant shipped large numbers of these needy blacks into Cincinnati, it would be "very impolitic." Stanton directed that Grant countermand his order. Grant aide John Rawlins tried to do that, but too late. The commander at Columbus wired Rawlins that "the Tennessee contrabands were forwarded to Cairo Ill . . . as follows[:] 212 men, 200 women, and 203 children." It turned out that these six hundred were "still at Cairo without proper shelter." Rawlins ordered them left at Cairo or sent back to Columbus, "whichever place they can be of most use and best cared for."[30]

While Grant juggled refugees and railroads, McClernand found himself a battlefield. Supplanting Sherman on January 4, the Illinoisan renamed his force the Army of the Mississippi and looked for a place to attack. Steaming down from Memphis in pursuit of Sherman, McClernand had voiced to Brigadier General Willis Gorman at Helena the need to reduce a Confederate stronghold forty miles up the Arkansas River. Arkansas Post, as it was known, had loosed attacks on Union supply boats on the Mississippi. While Sherman was at Chickasaw Bayou, Confederates had captured one, the *Blue Wing*, that was carrying needed coal.[31]

Sherman and McClernand both claimed authorship of the Arkansas Post attack, and both had reason. McClernand needed to christen his new military administration with a quick triumph to make headlines in Illinois and Washington. Sherman, who had the same idea before McClernand arrived, was in worse need. The public and press were condemning him for the casualty-ridden repulse at Chickasaw Bayou. Lincoln and the whole North—having just suffered appalling losses at Fredericksburg, Virginia, and in the draw at Stones River in Tennessee—ached for a turn of fortune. After the debacle at Chickasaw Bayou, Sherman's, and now McClernand's, army needed a victory more than ever. Even Grant would acknowledge this after learning Sherman had advocated the move against Arkansas Post.[32]

Not initially, however. When on January 11 he received a letter from McClernand announcing his intent to attack, Grant wired Halleck terming it "a wild-goose chase." He also rebuked McClernand and refused to approve the move. It would, he wrote, incur unacceptable losses and diverge from the quest for "the one great result, the capture of Vicksburg." Grant seemingly could not hide his anger and chagrin over his failed ploy to take Vicksburg before McClernand's arrival. Even now, though, he remained wary in dealing with the ultrapolitical general. "Unless you are acting under authority not derived from me," Grant wrote, "keep your command where it can soonest be assembled for the renewal of the attack on Vicksburg."[33]

Grant had thought General Nathaniel Banks would arrive soon from New Orleans to cooperate against Vicksburg and had previously ordered McClernand and Sherman to await news of Banks's approach. But McClernand and Sherman were at Milliken's Bend, closer to New Orleans than Grant, and they had heard nothing to suggest Banks was coming. So McClernand, not having received Grant's January 11 letter forbidding it, pushed his army up the Arkansas River.

On January 12, McClernand attacked the 5,000 Confederates at Arkansas Post with some 30,000 infantry, 3 navy ironclads, and 6 other gunboats. The four-hour battle cost the Federals 1,000-plus casualties, but they captured 5,000 Confederates, 18 pieces of artillery, and 5,000 small arms. "Glorious! Glorious! My star is ever in the ascendant! I'll make a splendid report!" McClernand crowed. So, anyway, claimed Sherman, whose dislike of McClernand had turned to hate after a few days under the ex-congressman's leadership.

Pressure on Sherman was mounting. Enduring renewed questions from the press about his sanity because of the seemingly suicidal assault on Chickasaw Bayou, he again showed signs of the paranoia he had exhibited in Kentucky in 1861. He wrote his wife, Ellen, that Lincoln's placement of McClernand over him was meant "to ruin me for McClernand's personal glory." Slipping toward depression, he accused journalists of spying and supplying information to the enemy. He went so far as to initiate the only court-martial of a reporter—Thomas Knox of the *New York Herald*—in American history.[34]

Sherman's turmoil reflected the effect McClernand was having on Grant's officers generally. Grant needed to intervene—and, out of the blue, he got orders to do just that. On January 12, in response to Grant's "goose chase" telegram, Halleck wired back a one-sentence godsend: "You are hereby authorized to relieve General McClernand from command of the expedition against Vicksburg, giving it to the next in rank or taking it yourself."[35]

This directive was no huge departure from Halleck's December 18 order placing McClernand's downriver army under Grant's overall command, but it was less veiled. It openly invited Grant to take hands-on charge of the McClernand force. Grant must have been overjoyed, but he did not overreact. McClernand was still, after all, an associate of the president.

Unbeknownst to Grant, though, Lincoln was tiring of McClernand and his tattling, self-serving letters. The president received another after McClernand got Grant's communications disapproving the Arkansas Post attack. On January 16, the egomaniacal ex-congressman wrote Lincoln that his victory at Arkansas Post "is gall and wormwood to the clique of West Pointers who have been persecuting me for months." He added an all but outright command: "Do not let me be destroyed, or, what is worse, dishonored."[36]

McClernand was not just the victim of a West Point clique, as he loudly claimed. He was disliked by nearly everybody. And Grant, despite being a West Pointer, had himself been victimized by the "clique." Having such an unimpressive academic record, family background, personal appearance, and history, he had been almost as much a target of West Point prejudice as McClernand. True, he had finally reached an accommodation with Halleck, and he was liked by two other outstanding West Pointers in his lieutenants, Sherman and McPherson. But Halleck and McClellan had so underestimated Grant in 1861 and most of 1862 that only the luck and timing of his indispensable victories had prevented his permanent removal from army leadership. McClernand's howls notwithstanding, Grant remained an utter anomaly among the West Point elitists who made up the Union high command.[37]

The fact that Grant was part of it at all, though, sharply differentiated Northern and Southern soldiery. Lincoln's relationships with non–West Pointer McClernand and Grant differed dramatically from Jefferson Davis's relations with Bragg and Forrest. After Fort Donelson and Shiloh made Grant the Union's most victorious general, Lincoln appeared to care little about his education or social level, just as he appeared to care little about McClernand's lack of military education. The Union president was smart enough, and plebeian enough, to seek help anywhere he might find it.

Lincoln was too busy now, though, to coddle the pestiferous McClernand any longer. Their bipartisan connection was reaching the point of diminishing returns. The president's written reply to McClernand's plea observed that in the army the ex-politician was attempting to help not only the country but also himself. Lincoln bluntly advised against "open war with Gen. Halleck." Reading these words, McClernand's blood must have iced over. He had already suspected he was nearing peril. The same day he had written his pleading letter to the president, he also wrote a friend in Illinois, "I may be standing on the brink of official ruin." This instinct was uncharacteristically prescient.[38]

Grant wasted no time. On January 13, the day he got Halleck's wire suggesting he take personal command of the Vicksburg drive, he wrote McPherson that he would do just that. The confidential message reflected the thirty-four-year-old McPherson's rapid ascent into the tiny circle of Grant's most trusted subordinates, the only others being his chief of staff, John Rawlins, and Sherman.

McPherson was a top-of-his-class West Point engineer, but that had nothing to do with why Grant liked and trusted him. The two came from common ground in more than the geographic sense: both had been born on Ohio farms, spent time struggling to make a living, and performed

common work as storekeepers. Perhaps most important, McPherson—
initially sent to Grant by Halleck to watch out for whisky—identified with
and admired Grant and disliked McClernand. Grant amply rewarded
McPherson's loyalty. A lieutenant colonel when he came to Grant in February at Fort Donelson, by October McPherson was a major general.

On December 20, two days after Halleck decreed that McClernand's
command of the Vicksburg expedition must be under Grant's direction,
McPherson had urged Grant to consider directing it in person. He had
also asked to go along. Now, on January 13, Grant informed McPherson
he was taking his advice. On January 15, he ordered the grateful subordinate to accompany him.[39]

Grant did not, however, immediately tell McClernand he was taking
hands-on control of the Vicksburg campaign. He had loose ends to tie
up. He dropped the attempt to move south along the Mississippi Central
Railroad and sent three divisions out of interior Mississippi into Memphis.
He also abandoned the Forrest-wrecked Mobile & Ohio Railroad north
of Jackson and instead readied the Memphis-Corinth tracks, so as to
maintain a substantial Union presence in northern Mississippi. And he
named Major General Charles Hamilton, one of his West Point classmates, commander of the Memphis district in his absence.

Grant finally visited the downriver expedition on January 18. There he
consulted with McClernand, Sherman, and naval commander David
Porter, but he still did not mention to McClernand that his presence
would soon be permanent. He likely wanted to forestall the general's in-
evitable howl to Washington until he was ready. But on January 20, back
in Memphis, he wrote Halleck, "I found there was not sufficient confidence felt in Gen. McClernand as a commander, either by the Army or the
Navy, to insure him success."[40]

A week later, Grant departed Memphis for good. On January 28, he
arrived at Young's Point, Louisiana, located on an eastward bulge in the
Mississippi's western shoreline opposite Vicksburg. There, he inspected
a canal he had ordered dug across the neck of the bulge, connecting with
the Mississippi on either side. He wanted to see if it would allow his army
to bypass the towering bluff that commanded the river in front of the
town. If the scheme worked, he could attack the Gibraltar from its less
defended southern side. But the force of the water diverted into the canal

was insufficient to wash it to the width and depth needed, and he began looking for other routes.

He waited two more days—until he was fully ready—before informing McClernand that he was not just there to visit this time. On January 30 his staff issued General Orders No. 13, under which he assumed "immediate command of the expedition against Vicksburg." It restricted McClernand's authority to command of a single corps.[41]

McClernand squalled. He charged that General Orders No. 13 disobeyed previous orders from Lincoln, Stanton, and Halleck. Grant's reply was swift and curt. While he regarded the president as the army's commander in chief and would obey his every directive, he said, he had received no order precluding him from taking direct command of the Vicksburg expedition—and he had received one from Halleck authorizing it.[42]

The next day, McClernand demanded that his protest be forwarded to Washington. Why is unclear. He had already received letters from Lincoln and Stanton subtly backing Halleck. It was likely a bluff intended to cause Grant to reconsider. So far, a prudent wariness of the ex-congressman's influence had tempered Grant's dealings with McClernand, who perhaps hoped Grant might choose not to face off with him under scrutiny from Washington.[43]

Whatever McClernand was thinking, his ploy failed. Grant did not know about Lincoln's chilly letter to McClernand, but he did know Halleck was backing him this time. He surely also suspected Halleck would not have supported him if Halleck thought the Lincoln-McClernand bond was still tight. So he complied with the politico's request and sent Halleck's office a copy of everything—General Orders No. 13 and the resultant exchanges between McClernand and himself. Grant accompanied the package with a letter of explanation. He said that had Sherman been left in command of the force on the lower Mississippi, he would not have felt the need to go there in person. But he had no confidence in McClernand's ability to do the job. However, he added, he was "respectfully submit[ting] this whole matter to the Gen. in Chief and the President."[44]

McClernand must have quaked when he heard.

20

JANUARY 3–FEBRUARY 3, 1863— FORREST AT DOVER

"I Will Go into My Coffin Before I Will Fight Under You Again"

Forrest's savaging of the West Tennessee railroads, along with Van Dorn's fiery raid on the Union supply depot at Holly Springs, had wrecked Grant's first try for Vicksburg. Forrest returned to Columbia, Tennessee, anchor of Bragg's left wing, in early January facing a new year more promising than his commander's. Forrest, after all, had excelled in the last days of 1862. Bragg had not.

Bragg had retreated from Murfreesboro in the wake of his epic draw at Stones River between December 31 and January 2, and Southern disappointment was intense. He had formulated an all-but-impossible battle plan, had fought a bloody stalemate in forbidding weather, then had withdrawn from the field when Federal commander William S. Rosecrans would not. The Confederates had pulled back south of Duck River, headquartering at Tullahoma and abandoning another large swath of forage-rich Middle Tennessee. Bragg appeared unsure of himself and asked subordinates if he should resign. This seeming insecurity, however, was apparently disingenuous. He shortly began to blame the Stones River mistakes on generals who had answered his question in the affirmative. His detractors, civilian and military, proliferated. An admired Kentucky brigadier, Roger Hanson, had gone into his final Stones River assault saying Bragg should be shot. Luckily for Bragg, Hanson—who limped from an antebellum duel—was the one who now stopped a bullet, receiving a mortal wound in the charge.[1]

But Bragg was not the only unfortunate facing a grim new year. The war's macrocosm offered a mixed, dispiriting picture to both sides. The Union army had endured senseless butchery in a defeat at Fredericksburg, Virginia, in November and in another at Chickasaw Bluffs, Mississippi, in late December. In Richmond, Jefferson Davis learned that many of his generals—and higher-ranking ones than Roger Hanson—were coming to regard Bragg's abilities with contempt and the man himself with hate. Albert Sidney Johnston's son Preston said Bragg possessed "the instincts of a drill-sergeant but not the genius of a general." Edmund Kirby Smith had vowed following the Kentucky debacle never to work under Bragg again. Bragg, never accepting blame, tried to turn the Stones River censure onto Leonidas Polk and John C. Breckinridge, who returned his enmity in spades.[2]

So it was to bolster himself in Davis's eyes, rather than to advance Forrest, that Bragg wrote to the Confederacy's president on January 8 and praised Forrest's raid. He recalled that he had ordered Forrest into West Tennessee to strike Grant's supply lines, and it had worked in "brilliant" fashion, even though Forrest's troops were mostly "new" and "imperfectly armed and equipped." Bragg did not mention that they were in that condition because Bragg himself had refused to arm and equip them. And he only turned to the subject of Forrest after lavishing praise on John Hunt Morgan for Morgan's tardy and less decisive strike into northern Kentucky. The lesser nature of the Morgan effort was not the Kentuckian's fault. Throughout much of November and December, instead of putting Morgan—a personal friend—to work, Bragg had allowed the thirty-seven-year-old widower to spend most of that time in Murfreesboro with his eighteen-year-old fiancée, preparing for their December 14 wedding, which Bragg attended. A weeklong local honeymoon followed.

The principal departure from Morgan's November–December romantic idyll occurred on December 7. Bragg's dispatch to Jefferson Davis accurately described the event of that day as a "brilliant affair" at Hartsville, Tennessee, just fifty miles from Murfreesboro. The Kentuckian lost fewer than 150 casualties there while capturing more than 2,000 Federals, whom he whisked away under the noses of a larger Federal force nearby.

Two weeks later, on December 21, Bragg finally ordered Morgan to leave his new bride and strike behind Federal lines into northern Kentucky. There, as Bragg wrote, "distance and long repose" had lulled the foe into complacence, and the Kentuckian destroyed two long Louisville & Nashville Railroad bridges. But the feat did not matter nearly so much as it would have if conducted three weeks earlier, because in the interim the Federals had not been as complacent as Bragg and Morgan. Federal supply trains whose tracks had been wrecked during Bragg's Kentucky sojourn had been up and running again since November 26, and the Federals kept the rails hot. They stockpiled matériel at Nashville for nearly a month before Bragg even learned that the Louisville & Nashville line was operational again. Yet Bragg wrote that Morgan's "brilliant effort" merited the Confederacy's "admiration and gratitude."[3]

While Bragg wrote his slanted report, Forrest rested and reorganized his men and horses. Bragg ordered him to continue guarding the Army of Tennessee's left wing. Some of Forrest's troopers, meanwhile, were ordered out on an offensive foray. During the second week of January, these men braved frigid temperatures and continual sleet and snow to participate in a raid under cavalry commander Joe Wheeler. The effort captured a light gunboat and four transports on the Cumberland River northwest of Nashville and destroyed bridges by which the Federals had been hauling supplies cross-country. The weather was so punishing, though, that some of these troops suffered frostbite, and a few froze to death.[4]

Forrest did not accompany that Wheeler raid. Two weeks after it returned, he possibly went on leave, or tried to. That may explain his ignorance, late in the month, of the departure of a large detachment of his men on a second Wheeler raid. He apparently learned of it only when ordered to report to Bragg's headquarters on January 26. There, he found that at least eight hundred of his troopers had already left—again in bitterly cold weather—for the Fort Donelson area. Bragg ordered Forrest to overtake the column and lead his men under Wheeler's command.[5]

To have so many of his men sent on an expedition without his knowledge was bad enough, but at headquarters Forrest likely learned something else that rankled him. On January 20, Bragg recommended Wheeler for major general. It was a mere formality—Wheeler was already chief of cavalry—but for appearances' sake, Wheeler needed to outrank Forrest. So as a basis for the promotion, Bragg seized on Wheeler's comparatively minor capture of the gunboat and four steamboats on the Cumberland. Bragg would have been better advised to cite Wheeler's coup two days preceding the battle at Stones River, when he had completely circled the Federal army in two days and nights, destroying four hundred loaded supply wagons and capturing six hundred prisoners, plus rifles sufficient to arm a brigade. Yet it was for the gunboat and steamboats, Bragg told the Confederate Congress, that Wheeler should be rewarded with a promotion.[6]

News of Wheeler's imminent elevation must have stung as Forrest rode hard northward into ominous, dreary freeze. Wheeler was brave and daring, but the raid for which Bragg recommended his promotion paled in comparison to the latest ones by Morgan and especially Forrest, whose exploits preceded the Wheeler boat captures by only days. Forrest had two icy days of riding to dwell on all this before catching up with his men at Palmyra, Tennessee, on the Cumberland. They had headed to this little town northwest of Nashville under Brigadier General John Wharton, who was also leading 2,000 men of his own. But Wheeler had caught up and taken charge by the time Forrest got there.

It was a seat-of-the-pants operation all too typical of Wheeler. He had issued orders for the raid from Bragg's headquarters at Tullahoma and overtaken it himself on the road a few miles north of Franklin. His report says he undertook the operation "in obedience to instructions," but he likely suggested it, since it aimed to repeat and enlarge upon his early-January steamboat captures. Bragg probably approved the idea because Morgan's raid had just stopped all Federal trains from Louisville to Nashville. If the Confederates could now halt Nashville's incoming river traffic as well, Bragg must have thought, they might break the Federal grip on Middle Tennessee. That was unlikely, Nashville's depots having been filled with supplies during Morgan's romantic interlude. But Bragg did not know that.[7]

Arriving at Palmyra, Forrest accosted Wheeler. He had found his men short of food, cooking utensils, and, most important, ammunition. Wondering if the rest of the command was similarly lacking, he apparently requested an inspection, which disclosed that Forrest's men carried just fifteen rounds per man; Wharton's, twenty.

Wheeler was doubtless surprised. He later claimed to have ordered the troops out "with a full complement of ammunition." He refused to blame any of his subordinates for the deficiency, but the fault may have been Wharton's. General Wharton was the erstwhile colonel of the Eighth Texas Cavalry and a prewar Houston lawyer. Bragg had designated him one of the Army of Tennessee's "regular" cavalry commanders, along with Wheeler's fellow West Pointers John Pegram and Abraham Buford. Wheeler reported that "they," seemingly meaning Wharton and his staff, tried to collect the needed ammunition until receiving the order to march, then apparently thought they should set out rather than wait any longer. Wharton, if it was his decision, likely presumed they would be able to re-supply themselves from a captured Federal transport vessel.[8]

But no vessel appeared. The Federals had discovered the Confederate presence along the Cumberland and halted boat traffic. The dearth of supplies now asserted itself. Forage for 2,800 mounts was scarce around Palmyra. The north side of the river might have been more favorable, but the Federals had destroyed all ferry craft. Wheeler faced two choices:

MAJOR GENERAL JOSEPH WHEELER

return to headquarters empty-handed from a 150-mile foray or attack something else. He settled on Dover, the fortified town adjacent to now abandoned Fort Donelson. It lay twenty miles northwest of Palmyra on the same side of the Cumberland, and local sources assured Wheeler it would be an easy capture. "After maturely considering the matter, we concluded that nothing could be lost by attack upon the garrison at Dover," he reported, rather offhandedly.[9]

Who "we" was, Wheeler did not say. From all other accounts, Forrest argued against the idea. He secretly told two staff officers that if he were killed in the battle, he wanted them to inform posterity he had opposed it. On the other hand, Wharton, now a Bragg "regular" after earlier service under Forrest, may have sided with Wheeler. Six months earlier, Forrest had voiced hot displeasure with Wharton at Murfreesboro after Wharton, wounded early in the battle, had withdrawn many of his Texans from the fight. Some of Wharton's resentment may have lingered, because he, like Forrest, had a temper. Two years later, he would be shot to death by a fellow Confederate officer in Houston after Wharton, unarmed, slapped the officer and called him a liar.[10]

Forrest would have had good reasons to oppose the attack. The Confederates' ammunition supply was low. The Dover garrison was fortified. Wheeler's force was a hundred miles behind Federal lines. If they took Dover, they did not have supplies enough to hold it against gunboats plying the Cumberland and the nearly 2,000 Federals twelve miles west at Fort Henry. They would have to block the Fort Henry Road just to protect their own rear while attacking. Unless the fort surrendered without a fight, they would have to exhaust their ammunition in an assault and march away several hundred prisoners with little or no means of controlling them. None of these considerations dissuaded Wheeler.

The Confederates approached Dover on February 3. On the way, they captured most members of a Union cavalry detachment, but four escaped to warn the Federal garrison that the Confederates were coming.[11]

Forrest came northward up the River Road, down which he had escaped the Fort Donelson surrender almost exactly a year earlier. Wharton took a more westerly path, likely the Forge Road, from which he could also reach and block the most direct road to Fort Henry. Dover sat atop a hill overlooking the Cumberland. The Federals had abandoned Fort Donelson, atop the next hill a mile north, likely because defending both it and the town required too many men. Around Dover they had dug trenches and gun emplacements, but surrounding ridges offered points from which enterprising enemy artillerists might pound the town's defenses with plunging and enfilading fire.

The Confederates pushed Federal skirmishers into Dover's entrenchments around 1 p.m. The attackers were in position by 1:30, and Wheeler sent the Dover commander an ultimatum signed by all three generals, doubtless to emphasize and exaggerate his strength of numbers. The note refined Forrest's Murfreesboro threat of annihilation by asserting that if the Federals refused surrender, they must "abide the consequences." It also bluffed larger numbers by describing Forrest and Wharton as each commanding a division. The one-sentence reply of the Federal commander, Colonel Abner Harding of the Eighty-third Illinois Infantry, sounded a bit equivocal but was negative. Harding declined to surrender his forces "without an effort to defend them."[12]

The Confederates opened with cannons they hauled up the higher ridges to the east, south, and west of town. They then heavily shelled a Federal battery at the eastern end of the Federal rifle pits, their hot fire giving no hint that their supply of shells, like that of their small arms, was short: about fifty per gun.

Harding's six hundred men were outnumbered more than four to one, but most of his nine companies occupied a ravine just west of Dover, out of the cannon fire. The Confederate shells played havoc with the Federal artillery, though. Lieutenant Morton zeroed in on a thirty-two-pounder siege gun supported by field artillery in the yard of the courthouse. A keystone of the Federal defenses, the thirty-two-pounder was mounted on a swivel carriage so that it could be turned in whatever direction was needed. The Confederates hurled "storms of iron hail" on it, Harding reported. He added that his guns, most of them under the immediate command of a lieutenant colonel named Smith, suffered such severe loss of men and horses that he had trouble withdrawing them.[13]

Amid the shelling, Wheeler ordered an attack on foot. He had accompanied Forrest's column, so he issued the order to Forrest, then turned to ride to Wharton. Suddenly, while Wharton was massing his larger force south and west of the Federal position in anticipation of Wheeler's directive to move forward, Harding ordered a cannon and a supporting infantry company to leave the east end of his rifle pits and reinforce troops in a cemetery on the town's west side. To get there, the gun had to hurry a short distance north beside the river, then turn into a street running uphill past the courthouse. Harding also transferred another gun from the southwest corner of his lines to the courthouse. All this movement likely precipitated what happened next.[14]

Wheeler had hardly turned to leave Forrest and go to Wharton when Forrest disobeyed Wheeler's order. Harding had just moved the two guns—one from the rifle pits to the cemetery and the other from the southwest trenches to the courthouse—when, he reported, "the enemy made demonstrations for a charge along the low ground near the river." Seeing this, Harding ordered a gun at the courthouse toward the river to try to stop the incipient assault. At that moment Forrest, "thinking the enemy were leaving the place, and being anxious to rush in quickly," ordered the troopers Wheeler had just ordered dismounted to remount and charge, Wheeler reported. But the Federal fire was so intense that the charge was beaten back.[15]

The hurried simultaneous movements of Union guns and troops along and toward the river had doubtless looked like an attempt to flee. Knowing his men had little ammunition and believing Wheeler's plan foolhardy, Forrest would have wanted to exploit any opportunity. Whatever specifically prompted his charge, he aimed to cut off the presumed retreat and then follow the intercepted Federals as they rushed back into their fortifications. His first charge had failed, but not for long. The Confederates "soon rallied," Harding reported. "Led on by Forrest himself, they again moved forward in a solid, motley mass."

This time Forrest and his men got into Dover itself and galloped up a street. Harding reported that they came from the south, "filling the whole open space with mounted men and the air with yells of triumph." But their presumption of victory was short-lived. Harding's men double-loaded the courthouse siege gun with canister and, Harding reported, tore "one man to atoms and two horses, within 10 feet of the muzzle." Harding then ordered his infantry out of their protective ravine to the southwest. They came running to meet the enemy at the crest of the ridge with a volley from their three hundred Springfield rifles. That and the siege gun's canister perforated the Confederate ranks and silenced the rebel yell. The Federals then mopped up with fixed bayonets, capturing some forty prisoners.[16]

Forrest had gone down, his horse shot beneath him. His men, thinking he had been killed, fled. He followed them back to their original position, hurrying there on foot. Then he reissued Wheeler's original order to dismount and led the men in another attack. He himself remained mounted and had another horse killed under him as they again got into the town. They ran Union sharpshooters from some houses on the east side and took those positions themselves. Here, Wheeler reported, they could fire down on the enemy. Wharton's men had meanwhile driven the Federals into their fortifications on the town's west side. The Confederates overran a battery there, "killing and wounding many of the enemy, and capturing prisoners, small-arms . . . munitions and stores," Wheeler reported. By sundown, the Federal siege gun and other Federal artillery had been spiked and abandoned to Wharton's men. Yet the Confederates quit firing, confusing Harding and his Federals.[17]

"We lay there in breathless suspense, expecting a last but possibly a successful charge of the enemy," Harding reported, "but determined to fight it to the bitter end."[18]

Almost from the fight's beginning, various Confederate regimental commanders had reported to Wheeler that they were out of ammunition. By nightfall, all of them were. Most of the Federals were in nearly the same fix, but they had a fresh supply in their rifle pits beside the river. Three dug-in companies that were all but cut off from the rest of the garrison held this cache. To resupply themselves, several Federal companies suddenly vaulted out of their fortifications in the gathering dusk and raced down to the rifle pits. Their accompanying yell, Harding reported, "sent the rebels running in every direction."[19]

The Federal rush back to the trenches containing the ammunition appeared to Forrest's Confederates to be headed somewhere else: toward where a fourth of Forrest's men held his troops' horses. Fearing a Union attempt to stampede or capture their mounts, Forrest's men fled the houses in town and ran back to try to protect them, Wheeler reported.

Forrest, once back there, then mounted up his men and withdrew from the battle. Had he not withdrawn, Wheeler wrote, "the garrison would have surrendered in a very few minutes."[20]

Wheeler was either intentionally ignoring his own errors or revealing a markedly illogical mind. The Confederate troopers did outnumber Harding's men about five to one, and the Federals had lost their artillery and been all but driven from their primary positions. But they also had just refilled their cartridge boxes. If Harding's six hundred remaining troops had been about to surrender, perhaps an advance by Wharton's 2,000 men coming from the south and west could have compelled it. But Harding's men were not intending to surrender, and Wharton's cartridge boxes, like Forrest's, were empty.

Instead of occupying the cusp of victory, the Confederates stood on the brink of disaster. Wheeler admitted that his entire command was out of ammunition but said Wharton occupied the west side of Dover and "had a secure position not more than 90 yards from the main rifle-pits of the enemy." How Wharton could have further improved that position without ammunition (cavalrymen did not carry bayonets), he did not explain. Neither did he say how Forrest could have capitalized on his position in the houses, no matter how good it was, with empty cartridge boxes. The ammunition problem, meanwhile, was made exponentially worse by developments on other fronts. Advance elements of Federal reinforcements from the west had already attacked Confederates blocking the Fort Henry Road. More Federal aid was coming up the Cumberland on gunboats alerted by steamboats on which Harding had sent away the town's women and children before the battle.[21]

Wheeler's report also neglects to mention the battle's humiliating end. Harding noted that Union detachments kept firing until 8 p.m., when the Confederates requested a cessation. "They sent in a flag of truce, again demanding the surrender of the post, telling us that they had not brought into action more than half of their forces," Harding wrote.

"We declined. . . . They then left."[22]

Later that night, the three Confederate generals thawed out in a roadside cabin. They were in a hamlet called Yellow Creek Furnace four miles out of Dover and well off the river. In the distance, they heard gunboats shelling the darkness along the Cumberland banks. Forrest, bruised and aching from his horse falls, had overturned a cane-bottom chair and lay on the floor on a rainproof coat, his head raised by the chair's back. His booted feet warmed on the hearth, where Wharton sat. Wheeler was composing and dictating the report he would send to Bragg.[23]

The document underestimated the Confederate killed and wounded at about one hundred and bloated the Federal loss to "equal to ours." Actually, Forrest alone lost two hundred and Wharton an additional sixty. Colonel William W. Lowe of the Fifth Iowa Cavalry, commanding the Fort Henry–Fort Donelson district, reported that the next day the Federals found 135 dead Confederates on the field and made prisoners of 50 wounded. In stark contrast, Harding reported the Federal loss as just thirteen killed, fifty-one wounded, and forty-six captured.[24]

Now, as Wheeler wrote his version of the story, a voice outside the cabin asked for Forrest. He rose from the floor and went into the freezing night. There a staff member, Charles W. Anderson, sat still mounted, nearly frozen to his saddle. Anderson had headed a detachment left behind to bring off a caisson and shells captured by Wharton, along with ambulatory wounded. They had done it under gunboat fire, which proved harmless. Forrest helped Anderson down from his horse and led him inside. He strode to a bed where two other officers lay, jerked their blankets off, and ordered them out. Then Forrest gave Anderson the officers' place in the bed and returned to his spot on the floor.

Anderson watched and listened as the generals discussed Wheeler's report. Wharton began talking about the situation on his side of Dover during one of Forrest's charges. He said his men went forward at the signal, but most gave way under "severe" Federal fire. As they fell back, he noticed the Federals in his front running across to the defenses' opposite side to deal with Forrest. Under all the Federal fire, Wharton said, Forrest "must have suffered severely."

Forrest surely wondered why Wharton had not charged again when he saw much of the garrison in his front hurrying away. But Forrest said only—with great heat—that he found no fault with his troops. They had done their duty as always, he observed, perhaps questioning whether Wharton's had.

"General Forrest, my report does ample justice to yourself and your men," Wheeler interjected.

Forrest was in no mood. He exploded.

"General Wheeler, I advised against this attack and said all a subordinate officer should have said against it," he said, "and nothing you can now say or do will bring back my brave men lying dead or wounded and freezing around that fort to-night."[25]

Wheeler tried to cool him. As commander, he said, he himself took the "responsibility for this failure," a declaration belied by the report's assertion that the Federals would have surrendered had Forrest's men not run back to their horses. Forrest grew angrier. According to a staff surgeon present, he responded to Wheeler with distraught contempt. Wheeler could tell that to the relatives of Forrest's dead troopers, he said.

"I will tell you this one thing with all due respect, and you may take my sword now if you want it," he said, eyes afire. "I will go into my coffin before I will fight under you again, and you can put that in your report to General Bragg."[26]

Despite this outright rebellion, Wheeler could hardly allow the resignation of a man some might regard as the Confederacy's most accomplished western warrior. Wheeler said he "exceedingly" regretted Forrest's offer of his sword and that he himself bore all responsibility for the defeat—which assertion, of course, was not borne out in his report. But Wheeler's mild response to the overt defiance of his older subordinate hints that Bragg's cavalry commander realized Forrest deserved to hold that position himself. Indeed, Forrest had been publicly and repeatedly humiliated, denied a position to which rank entitled him and which Bragg initially promised him. General James Chalmers, a Bragg intimate and admirer who eventually became Forrest's second in command, would say after the war that had Bragg chosen Forrest instead of Wheeler as cavalry chief, Wheeler would have enthusiastically accepted the subordinate position.

"Bragg simply made the wrong choice and had to live with it," Chalmers said.[27]

As for Forrest, he would have regretted nothing he said to Wheeler at Yellow Creek Tavern. Any regret he would have felt would have been for his fallen troops and how he had wasted so many of them by participating in Wheeler's ill-founded attack. He also surely smarted over his uncharacteristic battlefield mistakes—produced by an on-the-fly operation that permitted none of his usual careful planning.

Anderson said that Forrest, just before offering Wheeler his saber, told his diminutive commander that he meant no disrespect and that Wheeler knew the affection Forrest had for him; this, though, has the ring of a postwar closing of ranks. There is little indication that Forrest had any positive feeling for Wheeler at that time. Evidences of personal regard between the two men did eventually surface—but only much later.[28]

The war would be over.

21

FEBRUARY–APRIL 1863— GRANT IN LOUISIANA

"Weather, Roads, and Water All Against Me"

By the time Grant had assumed personal command of the Vicksburg expedition in late January 1863, the war's—and America's—political character had begun to change. Lincoln's signing of the final Emancipation Proclamation at the beginning of the month overjoyed the Union's abolitionist minority, but it cooled the ardor of unionist sentiment across the South, Midwest, and lower Northeast as well as in pockets of the South. The ranks of Grant's army exhibited the chill with apathy, defiance, and sometimes disloyalty.

Take the One Hundred Ninth Illinois Infantry, for example. Recruited in the southern part of Lincoln's home state shortly before preliminary announcement of the proclamation back in September, the regiment reportedly contained just seven men who identified themselves as Republicans, four of whom opposed emancipation. At Columbus, Kentucky, in October 1862, the unit proved so reluctant to fight against slavery that some of its members apparently let Confederate prisoners escape. During the Confederate capture of Holly Springs, Mississippi, in December, others tried to surrender despite the fact they were guarding an area the enemy did not attack.

After the Holly Springs raid, Grant ordered a court-martial, which convicted nine of the Illinoisans on shameful charges. All but one were officers. A lieutenant colonel had deserted in the face of the enemy, trying to get captured. A captain had encouraged his men to desert. Another captain tried to persuade men of his regiment that they were included in the Holly Springs surrender despite knowing otherwise. A third captain said "in the hearing of his men, in the presence of the enemy, that he would not fight if attacked," and a fourth hatched a plan to get his regiment surrendered to the raiding Confederates. A second lieutenant persuaded a secessionist civilian to write fraudulent paroles for him and some of his men, so that they would seem to have been captured and released into temporary noncombatant status; another lieutenant feigned illness to get himself hospitalized and surrendered in Holly Springs. A first lieutenant spoke "in an improper manner of the War and the President," and a commissary sergeant vowed never to fire a gun and voiced hope that the report, soon substantiated, that Confederates had slaughtered General Ambrose Burnside's troops at Fredericksburg, Virginia, would prove true.

On February 1, Grant ordered that the convicted officers of the One Hundred Ninth Illinois be dismissed from the army. But he also exonerated the regiment itself, saying its sins had been caused by those found guilty. For offenses such as the One Hundred Ninth's, Grant almost always blamed officers. Unlike many West Point–trained generals on both sides, his first impulse was not to stand a few low-ranking recent civilians in front of a firing squad. Grant seemed to identify with enlisted men; as a lieutenant in Mexico, he had jumped into waist-high water to work alongside some of them. He demanded discipline from his troops but held officers responsible for maintaining it.[1]

Grant, technically a professional, empathized with the citizen-soldier. Contrary to the howling of McClernand and a few others about victimization by a West Point cabal, Grant tended to side with and promote colonels and brigadiers with civilian backgrounds. His letters in February 1863 indicate he felt non–West Pointers generally showed more ability and inclination to fight. On February 9, he wrote with uncharacteristic heat to Lincoln about having seen a list of names sent to the US Senate for confirmation of promotion to brigadier or major general. Outraged that West Point–educated Napoleon B. Buford, a Kentucky aristocrat, had been recommended for major general, he wrote that Buford "would scarcely make a respectable Hospital nurse if put in petticoats, and certain[ly] is unfit for any other military position."[2]

Grant's revulsion for Buford contrasted starkly with his feeling for several commanders of less distinguished background. Buford had disobeyed orders from Grant and McClernand on the battlefield at Belmont in November 1861, nearly got his regiment captured, and was excluded from the Fort Henry–Fort Donelson expedition. Yet Washington clout got him command of the Cairo supply base, displacing General James M. Tuttle, who had led the first Union regiment into Confederate trenches at Fort Donelson and did much to hold the Union line in the Hornet's Nest at Shiloh. To Grant, combat performance was almost everything, and he valued Tuttle accordingly.[3]

Tuttle was not a West Pointer. Neither was Brigadier General John A. Logan, the first man Grant recommended to Lincoln in the letter condemning Buford. Grant went on to name a half dozen more officers deserving promotion. Only one had seen the inside of a West Point classroom, and that one, Marcellus M. Crocker, had dropped out after two years to become an attorney in Iowa. Of all these, the highest praise went to Logan, and it left little doubt as to the quality Grant most valued. Logan was a prewar southern Illinois congressman known as "Black Jack" for his dark eyes, hair, and complexion. He was best-known, though, for his courage on the battlefield. He had started out as colonel of the hard-fighting Thirty-first Illinois, which sustained 176 casualties at Fort Donelson. One was Logan himself.[4]

"There is not a more patriotic soldier, braver man or one more deserving in this Dept. than Gen. Logan," Grant wrote.[5]

Grant's lowest opinion was reserved for war profiteers. With these, he was iron-fisted. He held that the federal government, rather than private businessmen, should get all profits from the sale of captured Confederate cotton. On February 8, he ordered Brigadier General John McArthur, new commander at Lake Providence, Louisiana, to "positively prohibit . . . speculators from going into the country to purchase and bring in cotton. Enforce that Article of War which says that any person, citizen or soldier, passing beyond the outer pickets shall be shot. These people with the army are more damaging than the small pox." One of the more recent of these pests, to Grant's undoubted shame, had been his own father.[6]

The Mississippi was rising. Grant was living on a steamboat on the river north of Vicksburg, but, he told Julia in a January 31 letter, he would go into camp as soon as he fastened on a plan of action. The Vicksburg area, he added, was "a terrible place at this stage of water. The river is higher than the land, and it takes all the efforts of the troops to keep the water out." It was drowning the lowland opposite the Vicksburg bluffs and their miles of Confederate cannon emplacements. Flood or no, the price in blood of approaching the defenses on Vicksburg's side of the river anywhere near the town from the north was prohibitive in the extreme. And Sherman's repulsed December assault had proved that the cannon-bristling hills were insurmountable even if Grant could get at them.

The best chance was to get south of Vicksburg on the river's Louisiana side, then cross over into Mississippi and attack the town from the rear. The west bank, however, was a virtual swamp. A sliver of knife-shaped Louisiana lowland jabbed northeast in front of Vicksburg, shoving the river into a hairpin curve from which it then turned to run south past the town. The hilt of the knife seemed a likely site for a canal that could let boats detour downriver out of range of Vicksburg's guns, and Federals had begun to dig one the previous summer. If Grant's forces could divert enough of the river into this projected mile-long, twenty-yard-wide trough, they could float troops across the knife's handle and reenter the river below Vicksburg. Now, though, most of northeast Louisiana appeared in danger of inundation. Grant urged General Gorman at Helena, Arkansas, to send boats "as soon as they can possibly get here" because it "may become necessary to move our forces from here to higher ground."[7]

Then Grant got a look at the canal and despaired. He "lost all faith in it ever leading to any practical results," he wrote Halleck in Washington in early February. On both ends, he explained, the site was perpendicular to the river current, which caused the new waterway to begin and end in eddies. The river could force little water into the ditch, and any that did enter had trouble exiting. Worse, Confederates were already fortifying bluffs overlooking the exit site and posting cannon on bluffs at Warrenton, the next waterside town south of Vicksburg. So digging here promised marginal success at best. At the same time, it was causing Confederates to divide forces and disperse their cannon over more territory. Rethinking,

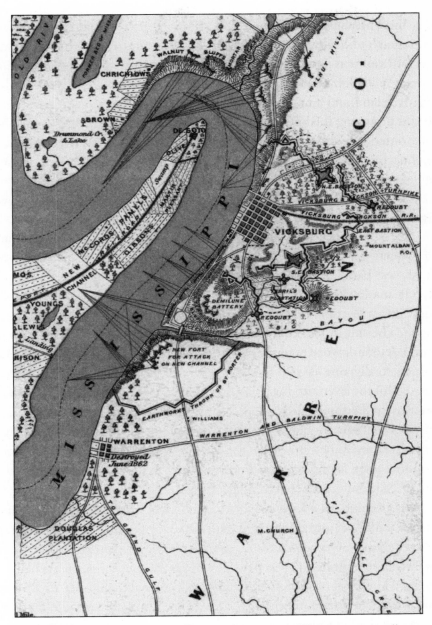

THE MISSISSIPPI "GIBRALTAR": The fortifications of Vicksburg eventually ran along the Mississippi and its tributaries from the Walnut Hills north of the city to the town of Warrenton nearly fifteen miles south of it. This map from the period shows the "New Channel," which Grant ordered dug to try to bypass the city.

Grant proposed alternate, simultaneous attack routes. The first was through Yazoo Pass, which left the Mississippi three hundred miles on the winding river north of Vicksburg and wound inland to the Coldwater River, then the Tallahatchie, and finally the confluence of the Tallahatchie and the Yalobusha, forming the Yazoo. Up the Yalobusha lay Grenada and crucial railroad bridges. Down the Yazoo sat Yazoo City, where Confederates were reportedly building gunboats. On down the Yazoo towered Haynes Bluff at the north end of the Vicksburg trenches. If Union troops got that far, Grant thought, they would outflank the Confederate river batteries and Vicksburg's massive fortifications.[8]

Two other routes also looked promising. Each could use networks of rivers and bayous on the Louisiana side to depart the Mississippi north of Vicksburg and reenter it south of Warrenton. One proceeded from Lake Providence and reconnected with the Mississippi via the Red River well south of Natchez. Another, much shorter, left the Mississippi at Milliken's Bend north of Vicksburg and took Willow and Roundaway Bayous to return to the Mississippi south of Warrenton at New Carthage. The latter looked more viable than the canal and "would have been accomplished with much less labor if commenced before the water had got all over the country." But political and public impatience did not allow Grant to wait for the flood to recede. Lincoln liked the canal idea, so, despite his own skepticism, Grant pushed ahead with the excavation while plotting alternatives. He wrote Halleck that he was making new intake and outflow mouths to try to better employ the force of the river current.[9]

Initial prospects along the alternate routes were encouraging. On February 2, the day that he wrote Halleck about the three alternatives, Grant received a heartening report on the Yazoo Pass. Lieutenant Colonel James Harrison Wilson said he had arrived at a levee across the pass around noon that day, had men digging by 2 p.m., and expected to open a navigable waterway by evening of February 3. Wilson reported that the difference in the water levels outside and inside the levee was eight and a half feet, promising a powerful current and "fine results." On February 4, Wilson reported troops had blasted a channel through the levee twenty feet wide and five feet deep, and four hours later the resulting flash flood had washed the opening to a width of forty yards. Water was "pouring through like nothing else I ever saw except Niagara Falls," he exulted. "Logs, trees and great masses of earth were torn away with the greatest ease. The work is a perfect success."[10]

The outlook for the route from Lake Providence to Red River was also rosy. On February 3, Lieutenant Colonel George Deitzler at Lake Providence wrote that the water there, too, was eight feet lower than the river. Within a week, Deitzler thought, they could make a hundred-foot gap in the levee between the river and the lake, creating a channel five feet deep linking the two. Then gunboats and small steamboats could navigate a bayou, Baxter's, ten to fifteen miles to another bayou, Macon. When the Mississippi inrush finished raising the level of Lake Providence, Deitzler wrote, Baxter's Bayou would float large boats. "Once in Bayou Macon," he added, "we shall have a clean coast to Red River."[11]

On the river's east side, Grant ordered six hundred infantrymen onto shallow-draft gunboats and sent them toward Yazoo Pass. He hoped to capture enemy transport vessels in the Yazoo and its tributaries, destroy two gunboats under construction there, and burn two Grenada bridges on railroad lines to Memphis and Columbus, Kentucky. He told Rear Admiral David Porter that Confederates were repairing both lines and making such progress on the one to Columbus that, unless the relevant Grenada bridge was destroyed, he might at any time have to take much of his force on the Mississippi and march it inland to protect the Yazoo expedition.[12]

Grant gave similar attention to the Louisiana side of the river. On February 5 he wrote General James McPherson at Memphis to hurry his Seventeenth Army Corps to Lake Providence, which Grant had decided offered the best route. Enclosing a map showing the route linking the Tensas, Washita, Black, and Red Rivers to the Mississippi, he said all were navigable almost the whole way. He thought that less than a quarter of such digging as had already been done across the river from Vicksburg would connect the Mississippi and Lake Providence and wash a channel.[13]

Then things slowed. McPherson and his sixteen-hundred-man division were marooned in Memphis by a lack of transport steamers. Grant himself suffered a setback. He wrote Julia in Memphis on February 11 that the previous evening he had put his teeth in some water in a wash basin, and the servant attending his stateroom, "finding water in the basin,

threw it out into the river teeth and all." He asked Julia to get an officer
to find his dentist and make arrangements for a new dental impression.[14]

G rant's problems proliferated. On February 13, he wrote Major General Hurlbut advising him to rescind an order banning the Southern-
sympathizing *Chicago Times* from Sixteenth Corps camps at Memphis.
Grant, though no proponent of press intrusion into army matters, doubted
that halting distribution of the *Times* in a single corps would accomplish
the main purpose of keeping it from reaching the Confederates—because
they could get it "through other channels." And banning it would only give
it more notoriety and probably increase its sales.[15]

Grant's action enraged the *Times's* principal competitor, the Lincoln-
backing *Chicago Tribune*. Editor Joseph Medill wrote Congressman Washburne that by this order "your man Grant . . . shows himself to be little
better than a secesh [secessionist]." Medill claimed the *Times* had quickly
shipped 3,000 copies into Grant's department "to breed more mutiny and
demoralization." The editor said he had heard "from a hundred sources"
that Grant's army was approaching "a state of insubordination" and that he
had lost the confidence of the "loyal officers and privates." Medill added
that out of consideration for Washburne, the *Tribune* had gone lightly on
Grant: "We could have made him stink in the nostrils of the public like an
old fish had we properly criticized his military blunders." Citing Grant's
sending of "crazy Sherman" to Chickasaw Bayou, he added, "Was there
ever a more weak and imbecile campaign."[16]

Medill, a devout antislavery proponent, saw a spirit of insubordination
in Grant's army but seemed not to see emancipation's role in creating it.
Grant, by contrast, saw emancipation-engendered treason flourishing in
Medill's backyard. To Julia he wrote on February 14 that his expectation
of taking Vicksburg remained "unshaken" if Midwesterners in his army
and back home were supportive. But if disgruntled soldiers such as those
in the One Hundred Ninth Illinois chose to quit and go home, there
would be no getting them back because disloyal citizens in the Midwest
would "protect them in their desertion."[17]

The worst influence on troop morale, however, was not emancipation,
in Grant's view. He wrote letters to Halleck and the federal paymaster

complaining that his men had gone unpaid for many months. Soldiers' families were doubtless suffering for lack of this income. The paymaster replied on March 1 that he had received enough money to give five divisions of Grant's troops back pay owed through October 31, 1862. Other Federal officers then warned him not to risk bringing such a sum— $4 million—downriver into the combat zone. On March 4, the men remained unpaid. Aide John Rawlins issued an order for paymasters to be arrested and brought to Grant's downriver bases to do their job.[18]

Pressures on Grant were myriad. Officers sought discharge for minor ailments, apparently to engage in cotton smuggling. Soldiers paid $13 per month could not be trusted to resist bribery. Railroad employees took illegal payments reportedly as large as $1,000 a month to sneak war matériel to the Confederates. Then there were guerrillas. Admiral Porter exchanged angry letters with Confederate general John Pemberton over Porter's order that people shooting into vessels from riverbanks would not be treated as soldiers. Plus vessels for them to shoot into were scarce, many having been taken by General Rosecrans to the Tennessee and the Cumberland. As far away as Chicago, Grant's agents sought boats small enough for use on bayous and Mississippi tributaries.

Halleck's job was in jeopardy, as he was increasingly seen as a do-nothing. In January, he refused to honor President Lincoln's urging that he make a personal inspection of General Burnside's Virginia front and get Burnside to advance; Halleck offered his resignation rather than interfere with a commander's own assessment of his situation on the ground. Lincoln did not accept the resignation, but Halleck's fate, and that of the republic, increasingly depended on Grant's Mississippi campaign because of the inactivity or defeat of other commanders. Most notably, Rosecrans had refused to follow up the Confederate retreat from Stones River in early January; Burnside's troops had been slaughtered at Fredericksburg, Virginia, in mid-December; and Sherman's attempted assault at Chickasaw Bayou had been decisively repulsed in late December. Amid Lincoln's multiple frustrations, Grant and his Vicksburg expedition increasingly looked like the best hope, equivocal though it was. At least Grant, unlike the others, was continuing to attack his problems.[19]

Grant's letters voiced continual hope that the canal digging would work. He had wanted his men paid quickly in part because, as he told Hurlbut

on March 4, he expected "to make a move very soon which may delay pay-
ments for some time." But flooding and an unexpected need to clear many
trees that overhung or grew in the bayou channels caused serial delays.
The trees had to be cut off beneath the surface. The water was so high
and the mud so deep that digging crews could barely get themselves, let
alone equipment, to the sites.

As usual when Grant was stymied, private reports of his drinking circu-
lated. "On the 13th of March 1863 Genl. Grant . . . was Gloriously drunk
and in bed sick all next day," said one. That claim went to President Lincoln
himself—from Grant's old Cairo enemy William J. Kountz, accompanying
a letter from McClernand.[20]

McClernand was just one of the subordinate snakes in the grass whom
Grant had to worry about. Major General Charles Hamilton, a Grant
classmate at West Point who had been in command at Memphis before
Hurlbut arrived there from Cairo in early February, connived to keep his
post over Hurlbut when that general did arrive. In February, apparently referring to McClernand's effort to lead the Mississippi expedition before
Grant took personal command, Hamilton obsequiously wrote Grant that
taking Vicksburg "is your right . . . as the most successful general of the
war." Two days later, Hamilton wrote a Wisconsin senator that "Grant is
a drunkard." Adding that Julia had been a continual visitor at Grant's various headquarters in West Tennessee and Mississippi for months to keep
him sober, Hamilton said that on an occasion when Grant left her behind, he was "beastly drunk" for several days, "utterly incapable of doing
anything." Hamilton said he and their mutual West Point classmate,
Brigadier General Isaac F. Quinby, had watched Grant "day & night . . .
keeping liquor away from him," until they could telegraph Julia and get her
there to take care of him. He cautioned the senator that his letter was confidential because "Grant is a warm friend of mine."[21]

Grant proceeded shrewdly in the face of the continual whisper campaign against him. His dealings with politically powerful opponents and
subordinates had often contrasted sharply with his battlefield fire, but his
self-assurance was growing. On February 21, he relieved Brigadier General
Willis A. Gorman at Helena. Gorman was a former Indiana congressman
and governor of the Minnesota Territory who had been praised for military competence in the Virginia theater. At Helena, though, he reportedly

had a gunboat guarding his son's commercial cotton-gathering enterprise. As the cotton rightly belonged to the government, Grant replaced Gorman at Helena and busted him to division command.[22]

Soon Grant relieved Charles Hamilton as well. After quarreling over rank with Hurlbut, his senior as major general by two days, Hamilton had asked that he be allowed to report to Grant rather than Hurlbut. Instead, Grant put Hamilton under McClernand. That should have signified to Hamilton that he was on thin ice, but he then made a worse slip. Noticing that he was senior to Seventeenth Corps commander McPherson, Hamilton suggested that the Seventeenth Corps was rightly his and said he was having McPherson's date of rank checked in Washington. Grant reacted quickly. He asked Halleck to remove Hamilton from the department and send the matter to Lincoln. Hamilton resigned.[23]

During this period, McClernand also erred unforgivably. Back in the Midwest gathering troops, he had resumed associating with one of Grant's bitterest enemies: William J. Kountz, the former chief of river transportation who in January 1862 had formally lodged inflammatory charges of drunkenness against Grant. McClernand had very likely abetted those charges since Kountz apparently was not in Cairo when some or all of the alleged incidents occurred. Additionally, McClernand had requested Kountz's assignment to Cairo and then praised his work there. Now, more than a year later, Grant heard that Kountz was back in McClernand's camps, and Chief of Staff John Rawlins shot McClernand a curt note: "If W. J. Kountz, late a Quartermaster, is at Millikens Bend you will please [ascertain] by what authority . . . and on what business and report . . . to . . . Headquarters."

McClernand feigned ignorance, responding that he understood Kountz had been at Grant's headquarters but had left by northbound steamboat the same day Kountz arrived. Actually, Kountz had come down on proper authority. Secretary of War Stanton had issued orders, at Kountz's request, for him to join McClernand. And McClernand had written Kountz that his services were needed in Louisiana, where "I expect soon to move by water." Rawlins's note, however, prompted McClernand to bid Kountz a swift farewell.

Not swift enough, though. McClernand had crossed a Rubicon. Grant brooked no perfidy in the area of his drinking, and this time McClernand's backstabbing was all but overt. The ex-congressman's military future now depended on whether his remaining Washington clout could topple Grant—before Grant toppled him.[24]

G rant's own career was approaching another crisis: the kind of polit-ical danger he had barely survived before and after Fort Donelson and again following Shiloh. McClernand was much disliked in the army, but he had strong—and, as the Mississippi stalemate wore on, growing—support in Congress and the Midwest. Grant's people feared Lincoln would yield to the malaise and replace their man with McClernand.

The pressure kept mounting. Halleck wrote Grant on March 20 that the "eyes and hopes of the whole country are now directed to your army." The increasing Northern desperation infected even staunch *Chicago Tribune* ed-itor Joseph Medill, who wrote House Speaker Schuyler Colfax that he sometimes thought they should settle for the best achievable boundary with the Confederacy. He complained that the effects of the war—mounting combat casualties, war-enabling taxation, "continued closure of the Missis-sippi," sky-high fees "for carrying the farmers' products eastward" in com-parison to the cheaper prewar route down the Father of Waters—"all combine to produce . . . despondency and desperation."[25]

Yet Grant's ploys continued failing. By March 22, reaching Vicksburg from the north, the safest direction, looked unlikely. The Yazoo efforts had taken so long that the Confederates had managed to fortify the main routes, block the channel, and repel the gunboats. A third route, through Steele's Bayou, was dangerously narrow and slow. Plus the Mississippi was now receding, decreasing the depths of the canals and threatening to trap Grant's boats. His only chance of reaching Vicksburg now from the north, he thought, was to assault the scowling bluffs on Pemberton's far right. Then he found he could not even do that. He inspected the site with Sher-man and Rear Admiral David Porter on April 1 and found the cliffs over-looked too little land on which to debark and operate. An assault would entail "immense sacrifice of life if not . . . defeat," he informed Porter.[26]

Press sniping increased to volleys. With Grant's campaign seemingly running out of options, correspondents howled for an advance—led by Mc-Clernand. A *Cincinnati Gazette* reporter described the army as "thoroughly disgusted, disheartened, demoralized" because its commanders were "such men as Grant and Sherman." The *Gazette* editor wrote US Treasury Secretary Salmon Chase that Grant—"foolish, drunken, stupid"—was "an ass" who was wasting their great Midwestern army. Another prominent newspaperman, the *Cincinnati Commercial*'s Murat Halstead, informed Chase that Grant was a complete "jackass." Chase took the letters to Lincoln.[27]

Even some of Grant's supporters wavered. No less than US Representative Washburne's brother, now a brigadier general in the Vicksburg effort, wrote his sibling that he feared Grant's desperation would spawn a "calamity: . . . He knows that he has got to do something or off goes his head." He apparently "intends to attack in front. . . . I hear that he has a plan . . . yet to be tried in which he has great confidence."[28]

Grant did have an as-yet-untried idea. On March 22, he wrote Sherman that up to then he had hardly considered any scheme besides outflanking the bluffs north of Vicksburg, but he now was formulating another. Its outline, he said, had been in the back of his mind since mid-January. Now he fleshed it out, poring over maps for a week. Late one night, McPherson urged him to throw the "burden" off his mind for an hour or two and join him for a drink. Grant refused. All he wanted, he said, was another dozen cigars and solitude.

The plan he hatched frightened subordinates. With the Mississippi falling, he believed he could march troops via "a good wagon road" from Milliken's Bend thirty-seven miles south to New Carthage, Louisiana. From there he could go farther south to link up with General Nathaniel Banks at Port Hudson. They could then capture that important town "and everything from there to Warrenton just below Vicksburg." At New Carthage, he would also be halfway between the Mississippi towns of Warrenton and Grand Gulf, each offering roads to both Vicksburg and the state capital, Jackson. To reach either town, though, he would have to get his troops across the Mississippi. And the boats to ferry and supply them were all north of Vicksburg. To get these gunboats, transport steamers, and barges into position, he would have to run them past the miles of Vicksburg guns.[29]

Federal boats had dared those guns before. They had gotten some five craft past them over the preceding couple of months. But on March 25 Grant had seen the Vicksburg cannons destroy the iron-prowed "ram"

Lancaster and damage another, the *Switzerland*. Brigadier General Alfred Ellet, commander of the Marine Brigade, had rashly sent the two vessels down by day. Admiral Porter warned Grant that even if the Confederates did not shoot his ships out of the water, the low-powered ironclads, essential to protect any marine convoy, could not get back upriver against the current. If Grant ordered such a move, he would be irrevocably committed to that route.[30]

Sherman blanched. He feared Grant's ruin—and resultant McClernand ascendance to the Mississippi command. Grant's plan violated every military maxim, Sherman said. He urged Grant to require every corps commander to submit ideas as to how to proceed. That way, no one—meaning McClernand—could later claim to have proposed anything he did not advocate at the time. Sherman reiterated his own idea: go back to Memphis and come at Vicksburg from interior Mississippi, down the Mississippi Central Railroad and through Jackson—the route Forrest and Van Dorn had slashed and burned in December.[31]

Grant had more iron inside him than Sherman, and his background gave him a far better feel for average Americans. His lifelong preoccupation with them, rather than with the comparatively insulated upper class, had made him more conscious of how near the Northern citizen in the street and behind the plow was to the breaking point. He had been, and at heart still was, such a citizen himself; West Point and thirteen years as an army officer had not changed his essence. After the army's four-month Louisiana sojourn, the home front would not abide withdrawing from Milliken's Bend and starting over. Northern support for the war could collapse. Sherman, with a senator brother and an even more prominent foster father, lived at the top of Northern society and took for granted that authority in America proceeded from there down. "Grant trembles at the approaching thunders of popular criticism," he wrote his wife, Ellen, as if those thunders accompanied no lightning. Grant, having spent most of his life nearer the bottom, was much more attuned to the reality that in national crises, the anger, terror, and will of the people tended to rule their leaders; that intuition pervaded his biography. If he could not strike Vicksburg in time, the Union might well lose all will to fight.[32]

Grant often took Sherman's advice; not now. His only general who supported the plan with enthusiasm was McClernand, the semicompetent who stood to profit if it failed. Unlike virtually all other high-ranking Union generals, Grant dared trust his own, solitary self in the face of ruin. He had done it in the late 1850s in his star-crossed farm fields and in the streets of St. Louis peddling wood. He had persevered in the face of looming disaster by second nature, and he did it again now.[33]

In early April, Grant cast the die.

He sent McClernand first west and then southeast, following a winding wagon road through inland Louisiana. This route left the Mississippi above Vicksburg and returned to the river's banks below the city. The politician-general was to shepherd a massive force along this route: 20,000 troops, 6 million rounds of small arms ammunition, and 10 six-gun artillery batteries with 300 rounds per gun. By McClernand's figures, it would take the 150 available wagons three trips and thirteen days to get the load to New Carthage. There, according to Grant's plan, McClernand would meet however many provision-laden, gunboat-guarded transports and barges survived the fire of the miles of Vicksburg guns.[34]

The plan's second phase commenced on the dark night of April 16. Admiral Porter ordered seven gunboats, three transports, and a dozen barges out into the channel to dare the wall of fire. Grant and his family watched. Julia and the children, visiting at Milliken's Bend, were aboard as the headquarters boat *Henry von Phul* pulled to the upper mouth of the useless canal fronting Vicksburg. Fred Dent Grant, twelve, watched his father puff the habitual cigar, eyes glowing intensely. Aide James Harrison Wilson held on his lap one of the smaller Grant children, who whimpered and held tighter to Wilson's neck with every cannon blast. The Confederate guns on the bank and the Union ones on the gunboats combined to make 525 of these great booms, according to War Department official Charles Dana. What Grant saw must have looked like fifty Fourths of July—but the glow Fred saw in his father's eyes reflected more than cannon blasts. The Confederates torched huge fires for visibility when they heard the convoy coming past. On the Vicksburg bank, they ignited barrels of tar and great piles of pine logs as daring skiff-borne lookouts sped to the Louisiana side and fired entire houses.[35]

Each vessel required twenty minutes to pass the guns. In the disarray, smoke, and confusion, the boats and barges spun in a complete circle once or even twice like slow-motion tops. Some crashed into each other and lost parts of their protective piles of cotton and hay bales. Some of the cotton, set ablaze by the Confederate cannons, fell overboard and bobbed on the current, making scores of floating bonfires.[36]

But it might have been worse. The convoy's descent had taken Pemberton by surprise. He and his officers were at a gala thrown because Grant was thought to be giving up, withdrawing northward following his repeated failures; Confederates had seen Federals retreating from Yazoo Pass. Also benefiting Grant, many of the Vicksburg guns—located atop the bluffs as well as two or three dozen yards above the water line—were protected by such high, thick fortifications that they had trouble firing steeply downward. The shells slid forward in the muzzles before ignition, decreasing the shots' velocity. Union convoy commanders foresaw that advantage and hugged the Mississippi side of the river.[37]

The protective measures worked. All but two of the vessels made it down, the only exceptions being a coal barge that sank and the transport steamboat *Henry Clay*, which exploded under Confederate fire. But the success was not at first apparent from downriver. On the morning of April 17, the first thing McClernand's lookouts on the New Carthage levee saw floating toward them on the current seemed a harbinger of doom: numbers of flaming cotton bales and the battered pilothouse of the *Henry Clay*. Confederate adherents along the banks were gleeful, but not for long. At 12:20 p.m., in the wake of three barges, the black, beloved ironclads hove into view. The sight was electrifying. Union officers yelled, danced, and began drinking.[38]

Grant's forces were now on the vulnerable side of Vicksburg with means to cross the river. They also had all necessary accessories when, a few days later, another nocturnal run of the Mississippi lost just one of six steamboats, and six of twelve barges passed the gauntlet with cargo completely undamaged. This second lunge, along with wagon freight hauled down the Milliken's Bend–New Carthage Road, got all Grant's men and provisions into position to launch their move toward Vicksburg's back door.[39]

When April ended, Grant himself was downriver. At the plantation of a Louisiana family named Perkins, he assessed targets across the Mississippi forty to fifty miles south of Vicksburg, between the town of Grand Gulf and the village of Rodney.

Grant also ordered the fanning out of diversionary forays to protect his amphibious invasion. Sherman steamed north with 20,000 men to threaten the Haynes Bluff area on the Yazoo River above Vicksburg. A cavalry raid was launched from Grand Junction, Tennessee, through the interior of Mississippi under Grant's best leader of mounted troops, Colonel Benjamin Grierson, to cut Vicksburg's eastward rail communications. Grant's department also lent Rosecrans in Nashville nearly 8,000 troops under Brigadier General Grenville Dodge to disguise a second, even more dangerous rail-cutting raid across northern Alabama under Colonel Abel Streight.[40]

With combat looming, Grant had sent Julia home, along with all the children except Fred. On April 28, the day after his forty-first birthday, he wrote her with typical, understated satisfaction that he had "been fretting here" readying an attack on Grand Gulf "with weather, water, and roads all against me. Tomorrow morning at furtherest will see the work commenced."

This letter's preoccupation with a host of domestic details connotes a shrugging, plebeian trust in the gods of battle and Grant's own grit. He instructed Julia on business she should take care of in St. Louis. He apologized for not writing her sister, Emma; "tell her I think just as much of her as though I wrote every week." He said he and Fred were soon to "be off in a tug witnessing the naval attack upon the land batteries and the debarkation of troops." And finally, with little more intensity than if he were informing her when he would be home for dinner, he wrote, "You had better not return to Memphis until you hear of me in Vicksburg."[41]

Sherman's letters home were more animated on the subject. Sherman could only see Grant's violation of an elementary West Point axiom. Grant had all but isolated his army. Its resupply was possible only by hazardous runs past Vicksburg's cannons or by wagons hauled down a dirt road vulnerable to guerrillas and floods; at its lowest points, the route's surface was just twenty inches above surrounding swamps. And now the army was about to head across the wide Mississippi into a hostile interior, even farther from aid. Nearly two weeks earlier, after watching the boats glide past the Vicksburg guns on April 16, a very troubled Sherman had written his wife that "I tremble for the result" of Grant's plan. He added, "I look upon the whole thing as one of the most hazardous and desperate moves of this or any other war."[42]

MARCH 4–MAY 3—FORREST IN MIDDLE TENNESSEE AND NORTH ALABAMA

"Shoot at Everything Blue and Keep Up the Skeer"

The attack on Dover had been a disaster, and its aftermath was humiliating. Wheeler's force, without ammunition, had to flee the debacle in freezing weather ahead of Union pursuers.

Chased by Federals from Fort Henry to the west and Franklin to the southeast, Wheeler's Confederates hurried almost due south, well west of the direct route. They had to push for a Duck River crossing at Centerville before they could turn east toward Confederate-held Columbia. They barely made it. They had to leave the icy roads and take to fields and woods in some places, then scrounge means of ferrying troops across the flood-swollen Duck. The cold was intense. The current swept away one man testing whether the river was fordable on horseback, and when citizens pulled him—still alive—from the river, his clothes froze on his body within minutes. Along the route, pursuers captured thirty of Forrest's battle-depleted troop, including two staff members.[1]

Forrest set about replenishing and refitting his shattered command. Bragg's headquarters meanwhile ordered the transfer of a valued Forrest unit—the seven hundred men of Colonel A. A. Russell's Fourth Alabama—to Wheeler. Two battalions of guerrillas, totaling nine companies, replaced them and, along with two more guerrilla companies, were cobbled together to form the Eleventh Tennessee Cavalry. The consolidation provoked protests so strong within the units that Forrest felt forced to arrest several officers and confine them at Columbia. In keeping with his heavy reliance on inspections, he instituted twice-weekly dress parades. If Bragg was paying attention to any Forrest-connected reports besides Wheeler's self-serving account of the Dover battle, he should have divined that the Tennessean was far more than an undisciplined irregular; he was in fact Bragg's best manager of that notoriously lax arm, the cavalry. Extant records for the period show that while the present-and-effective strength of the rest of Bragg's mounted force was 58 percent of its total number, Forrest's was 70 percent.[2]

Forrest soon received what he had vowed to get on that freezing night at Yellow Creek Tavern: a new commander. Bragg, outnumbered in Middle Tennessee by Rosecrans, had resisted sending more troops from his army to aid Vicksburg, particularly Forrest. As the winter wore on and every Union ploy in Mississippi appeared increasingly blocked, he beseeched western commander Joseph E. Johnston to return or at least replace some of the Army of Tennessee infantry units he had already sent. Instead, Johnston finally ordered Pemberton to dispatch to Middle Tennessee two-thirds of his Mississippi cavalry. It arrived under its checkered major general, Earl Van Dorn, who outranked Forrest militarily and socially.[3]

Although he graduated fifty-second in the fifty-six-member West Point class of 1842, Van Dorn was nevertheless a career soldier with a fat prewar resume. Thanks to his gallantry in the Mexican War and against the Comanches, he was a major in the US Army by January 31, 1861, when he resigned to join the Confederacy. But headstrong carelessness dogged his Confederate performance. Sloppy scouting cost his troops the battle of Pea Ridge in Arkansas in March 1862. Then, in April, his fixation on his own agenda delayed the arrival of his 15,000 troops east of the Mississippi, too late to aid Generals Albert Sidney Johnston and P. G. T. Beauregard at Shiloh. Bad reconnaissance helped defeat him at Corinth in October, after which Jefferson Davis demoted him from commander in Mississippi to chief of cavalry. But before coming north, Van Dorn had rehabilitated his reputation somewhat by wrecking Grant's Holly Springs supply base in December.[4]

Except in their Mississippi roots and fiery touchiness, Forrest and Van Dorn were opposites. Van Dorn was a plantation scion, conceited and highly polished. His family tree bristled with some of the South's more prominent people, especially such Tennesseans as Presidents Andrew Jackson and James K. Polk and the similarly prominent Donelson family. Van Dorn was a skilled painter, and his drawing room repartee sparkled with quotations from classic poets and philosophers. Brave and dashing, he paid marked attention to other men's spouses while markedly neglecting his own. His inattention to reconnaissance suggests questionable aptitude for fighting on the Civil War's mammoth scale. Forrest's achievements already outshone his new chief's. Van Dorn's careless dandyism and Forrest's rustic obsession with the job at hand hardly figured to bond them.[5]

Van Dorn reached Middle Tennessee in late February and set to work covering Bragg's left flank. Gathering his 6,300 effectives at Spring Hill, he headed north for Union-held Franklin on March 4—and ran into Federals with a hundred supply wagons approaching him on the Franklin Road. The Federals had heard about the Confederate camp at Spring Hill, and, wishing to verify enemy locations in front of his army, General Rosecrans in Nashville had ordered 2,800 infantry, artillery, and cavalry southward from Franklin. They were half of a two-pronged drive, the other being Union troops coming from Murfreesboro.[6]

North of Thompson's Station, a depot on the Tennessee & Alabama Railroad four miles above Spring Hill, the appearance of about 1,000 Confederate cavalry and two artillery pieces slowed the Franklin column. Federal Colonel John Coburn deployed his five regiments of infantry and five-gun battery and pushed forward. Artillery exchanges and skirmishing kept up during the afternoon. Concealing most of his force, Van Dorn withdrew behind the station and a nearby rock fence. Dusk fell. Overnight, scouts from each side probed the other's strength. Coburn's worried dispatches to Franklin got no reply. He concluded that his orders required him to advance or "show cowardice." Van Dorn, too, resolved to fight.[7]

Coburn pushed farther southward around 8 a.m. of March 5. The terrain, a succession of ridges, impeded vision more than half a mile in any direction except down the roadway. Coburn found Van Dorn's left-center, General W. H. "Red" Jackson's division, spread dismounted along hills astride the road. Colonel J. W. Whitfield's Texas Brigade held Jackson's left; Brigadier General Frank Armstrong's Arkansans and Mississippians held his right. Farther right, stretching nearly to a second north-south highway from Franklin to Lewisburg, Van Dorn had put Forrest's 2,000 troopers and Captain S. L. Freeman's battery.[8]

Forrest was still taking position when Federal artillery opened fire on Jackson. To counter the Union guns, Forrest sent Freeman forward a half mile onto a hill and moved up his dismounted cavalry for support. Freeman began firing. His guns chased the Twenty-second Wisconsin and the Nineteenth Michigan Infantry, along with some cavalry, from behind a stone wall to Forrest's left front. Freeman's fire also joined that of the Confederate Second Missouri Battery well to Forrest's left; together, the Confederate cannons drove two guns of the Eighteenth Ohio from along the road. The Ohioans hurried rearward with the wagon train, which Coburn by now had ordered to return to Franklin. Federal cavalry abandoned a cedar-covered hill to Forrest's front and joined the wagons and the Ohio guns in retreat.

Coburn's left had broken, but his center and right had charged. Hoping to turn Van Dorn's left, the Federals were nearly to the depot when Confederates rose from behind the rock fence and delivered a volley. The attackers took cover behind the railroad embankment. Van Dorn, seeing resistance melting in Forrest's front, sent the Tennessean hooking toward the Federal left rear.

Coburn saw Forrest moving. Now "convinced that we were in the neighborhood of an overwhelming force," he ordered a withdrawal from the depot. The rest of Coburn's support elements took that as an excuse to flee. His cavalry "disappeared," he reported. His staff tried to rally the artillery to cover a retreat, but a skedaddle on his left "took with it the One Hundred Twenty-fourth Ohio, the ambulance train, the ammunition train, and all hope of an orderly retreat or a continued successful resistance."[9]

Coburn's depot attackers fell back, chased by whooping Confederates. Abandoned by artillery, cavalry, and one regiment of infantry, the remaining Federals—men of the Thirty-third Indiana, Twenty-second Wisconsin, Nineteenth Michigan, and Eighty-fifth Indiana—held on for two more hours. They retreated to another cedar-crowned hill west of the road, where they repelled several Confederate assaults and a hail of artillery fire. They took prisoners, along with the battle flag of General Armstrong's brigade. But after five total hours of combat, with ammunition running out—and Mississippians gaining their right rear as Forrest charged from behind their left—Coburn became "convinced that a massacre" was in the offing. A climactic assault took Forrest's men within twenty feet of the Union line, at which point the ammunitionless Federals quit. Van Dorn described Forrest's charge as "deciding the fate of the day." Van Dorn reported 357 casualties but captured 1,200 Federals, including Coburn.[10]

Three weeks later, Forrest bagged the rest. He had learned that the remainder of Coburn's force had garrisoned fortifications and a bridge-guarding stockade at Brentwood, equidistant from Franklin and Nashville. With Van Dorn's approval, he set out for Brentwood on March 24. Commanding there was Lieutenant Colonel Edward Bloodgood of the Twenty-second Wisconsin, who had taken about half of the 378 members of the regiment with him in abandoning Coburn at Thompson's Station. With him now were also about 270 survivors of the Nineteenth Michigan and Thirty-third and Eighty-fifth Indiana, whose comrades' valiant stand atop the cedar-topped hill Forrest's charge had broken three weeks before.

General Rosecrans would characterize Bloodgood's resistance as "feeble"; it lasted half an hour. As Bloodgood remembered, Forrest sent in word that he "would cut us to pieces" unless the Federals surrendered. The Confederates had only to stop one escape attempt and ready a general charge before Bloodgood waved the white flag. With just one man killed and four wounded, Bloodgood surrendered the Brentwood works. A single cannon shot produced a similarly hasty capitulation at the bridge blockhouse two miles south. The total haul was some 750 men, a dozen or more wagons of supplies, several ambulances, weapons, and other military and medical goods. The railroad bridge and Bloodgood's camp were left in ashes.[11]

But Forrest did not escape this raid unscathed. Within an hour or so, he had moved his column a few miles back toward a Harpeth River crossing when some six hundred cavalry from Franklin under Brigadier General Clay Smith attacked his rear, which had been delayed while attending wounded. Major William DeMoss, leading the Confederate Tenth Tennessee Cavalry, reported that men from other commands in the rear came running through the column spreading panic. The Tenth broke, and the Federals recaptured some wagons. Smith reported chasing the Confederates for miles. Colonel James Starnes, who had been detached capturing a Union wood-gathering force, heard the firing. He came galloping back and attacked the Federal right flank. A core of officers led by Forrest meanwhile hurried toward the rear of the stampeding column. Forrest cursed his wild-eyed stragglers, gathering them up as he came. One said he waved a flag above his head, roaring, "Fall in, every damned one of you!" With this motley troop, he counterattacked, flanking and routing Federals from behind a stone fence and putting them to flight.[12]

It was an embarrassing end to a highly successful foray. Forrest lost and then recaptured some wagons of booty, which he had to burn because, in abandoning them, the Federals had cut the mule teams out of harness and run them off. His pursuit of the Union attackers took the Confederates back to where they could see the tents they had burned at Brentwood. Smith claimed to have killed, wounded, or captured four to five hundred Confederates, but Forrest reported total Confederate casualties of fifty-nine. He did acknowledge that, not knowing whether more Federals were approaching, he departed rapidly with his prisoners.[13]

The captures at Thompson's Station and Brentwood dramatically widened the natural gulf between Forrest and Van Dorn.

Van Dorn, widely perceived as greedy for glory, became angry over articles in the *Chattanooga Rebel* giving Forrest the laurels at Thompson's Station. In an encounter at Van Dorn's headquarters in late April, the Mississippi aristocrat accused Forrest of prompting his own staff members to write the articles. He also claimed Forrest had disobeyed orders by keeping booty that should have been forwarded to headquarters. Forrest denied both allegations and said he would saber whoever made them. He added that Van Dorn was too ready to credit criticism of him. Van Dorn called him a liar and said now was a good time to settle their differences. He grabbed his sword off the wall.[14]

Van Dorn's claim may have had a partial foundation, but obviously, as usual, he had not done his homework. Forrest, routinely given new and badly armed troops and no equipment, habitually allowed his men their pick of the arms and ammunition they captured. Forrest reported ordering wagons, ambulances, and animals turned in to the quartermaster at Columbia, but at Brentwood his unarmed men "got guns on the field." Those with inferior arms swapped them for better captured ones, "placing their old guns in the wagons." The implication was that Forrest expected the inferior arms to be turned in, although he had not personally seen to it.

Forrest staffers may have written articles about the Thompson's Station battle. He had journalists on his staff. Former *Memphis Avalanche* proprietor Matthew Gallaway was his assistant adjutant general, and the editor of the *Chattanooga Rebel*, Henry Watterson, was briefly a Forrest trooper also.[15]

Whatever the truth about the Thompson's Station articles, any man who called Forrest a liar risked his life. Van Dorn saw Forrest's face flame the dark crimson it took on in battle. Forrest seized his sword and half-drew the blade—then stopped and resheathed the weapon. It was the unpolished plebeian, not the refined aristocrat, who recognized the unpatriotic idiocy of what they were doing. A Van Dorn staff member said Forrest told Van Dorn that he did not fear him but would not fight him. The aide quoted Forrest as observing that it "would never do for two officers of our rank to set such an example to the troops."[16]

Van Dorn soon apologized. He told the staffer, Captain H. F. Starke, that he had gained a higher opinion of Forrest and that the two parted from this latest meeting—their last—on better terms. "Whatever else he is," Van Dorn said, "the man certainly is no coward." Van Dorn again had not done his homework. He should have known he was fortunate to still be breathing, a privilege he did not enjoy much longer. Two weeks later, a jealous husband shot him dead.[17]

Probably only hours following his narrowly averted duel with Van Dorn, Forrest got new orders. On April 23, Bragg directed him to rush his brigade south from Spring Hill to the Tennessee River in northern Alabama. There he should take command of the cavalry of Alabama colonel Philip Roddey, who was retreating before a combined force of nearly 10,000 Federal infantry, cavalry, and artillery heading east from Corinth under Brigadier General Grenville Dodge.[18]

Dodge was attempting an elaborate ruse: 8,000 of his men were to push Roddey, but the other 2,000 had a different agenda. Dodge's pursuit of Roddey was designed to mask the main threat: the launching of a drive by Colonel Abel Streight and 2,000 mounted infantry to cut Bragg's rail supply line in northern Georgia. Having fitted out his force in Nashville, Streight made his way to northern Alabama to embed, and thus hide, it in Dodge's column. Grant and Rosecrans were taking a leaf from Bragg's Forrest and Morgan playbook, authorizing quick thrusts deep into enemy territory to disrupt supply routes, divert attention, and weaken Confederates at Vicksburg and in Middle Tennessee. While Streight headed across northern Alabama to threaten Rome and military-industrial facilities in central and southern Georgia, Colonel Benjamin Grierson was riding south from Memphis through interior Mississippi to frighten the unprotected populace and slash Vicksburg's rail lines. Dodge, once he had launched Streight, would turn back toward his own base in northern Mississippi.[19]

The Streight mission was daring but ill conceived. Streight's idea, approved by Rosecrans, was to cross northern Alabama to Gadsden and

COLONEL ABEL STREIGHT

there, some forty miles from the Georgia line, split into two wings. One would strike Confederate installations at Rome, Georgia; the other would veer slightly south and, thirty-some miles east of Rome, destroy a critical trestle of the Atlantic & Western Railroad tracks to Atlanta. The plan was madness. Grierson, an adept horse soldier, could traverse Mississippi with scant resistance and continue south into Union territory at Baton Rouge, Louisiana. Streight, on the other hand, was an infantry rather than cavalry officer, and his mission called for penetrating northeastern Georgia, where major Confederate forces would be much closer; then he was expected to turn and fight his way out.[20]

The most problematic aspect of Streight's mission was its personnel. Instead of cavalry, which was in short supply, it drafted infantrymen for more than two hundred miles of hard riding. Union brigadier general David Stanley, a veteran cavalry leader, was appalled. He later termed it "the most senseless thing I saw done during the war to waste men and material." Stanley blamed the plan's approval on Brigadier General James Garfield, Rosecrans's chief of staff. Garfield, Stanley wrote, "had no military ability, nor could he learn." He added that Garfield and Streight had sold Rosecrans the scheme.[21]

Rosecrans knew the odds. He disingenuously told Streight to return via Alabama or Georgia. But if surrounded—as was all but certain—he should cost the enemy as much time and manpower as possible.[22]

Military snarls developed. Rosecrans supplied Streight's hazardous undertaking just as cavalierly as Streight himself had planned the operation. Rosecrans mounted the colonel's force on an insufficient number of horses and mules, some wild and unbroken, others sick and dying. Streight's superiors also expected him to take time to get the balance of the mounts he needed from the countryside through which he was to travel. And even some of those Streight had received were soon missing; a lax officer at Nashville allowed nearly four hundred to escape a corral, and only half were recovered. The junction with Dodge was delayed by a week by the corral stampede and the process of coordinating Streight's all-too-detectable river-borne move from Nashville to Eastport, Mississippi. To fade from certain Confederate notice, Streight had to join Dodge and blend into that general's ranks.

By the time Streight did join Dodge in late April, the latter's move from Corinth to Tuscumbia, Alabama, had naturally encountered Confederate opposition. Dodge's overwhelming numbers had pushed Roddey's 1,200 cavalrymen across Town Creek near Courtland, Alabama.[23]

There Dodge learned he had more than Roddey to contend with. A new commander faced him across Town Creek: Forrest, with artillery. In the thirty-six hours since he had received his orders from Bragg on April 23, Forrest had ridden ninety miles from Spring Hill to the Tennessee River's north bank at Browns Ferry, Alabama. When he arrived, he posted there George Dibrell's Eighth Tennessee Cavalry and a section of guns under Lieutenant John Morton. Morton had just become acting chief of artillery, following a numbing loss to Forrest.

Artillery captain S. L. Freeman had just died shockingly in a battlefield assassination. A Van Dorn advance against Franklin on April 19 had drawn a surprise attack from Federal cavalry, who had isolated and captured Freeman's battery. Confederate cavalry countercharged, and the fleeing Federals forced Freeman's thirty-some captured battery members to run in front of them in their retreat. Freeman, a prewar attorney, was unable to keep up and was shot point-blank in the face by a Federal cavalryman. On news of the artillerist's death, Forrest broke down and wept.[24]

Thus, at Browns Ferry Forrest assigned replacement artillery chief Lieutenant Morton to help Dibrell prevent Dodge's Federals from crossing the Tennessee, if that was what they were up to, or to harass their rear if they were headed farther east. Dibrell's men were to augment this harassment by spreading word in the community that Van Dorn's entire cavalry corps was on its way from Middle Tennessee.

Forrest meanwhile had taken the rest of his men to Town Creek to join Roddey in Dodge's front. There, leading 3,500 troops opposing Dodge's 9,000, he dueled Dodge's eighteen guns with some of his own eight for five hours. Then, with little alternative, he fell back, fighting, to Courtland, Alabama. Around nightfall on April 27, a Roddey scout rode in. The man said Dodge's column had separated. An estimated 2,000 Federals had peeled off southward and were now to the south and rear of Forrest's left flank. Forrest took no notice at first. He fell back farther toward Decatur, terminus of a rail line to Nashville, and awaited further developments.[25]

That night Dodge contacted Streight. The latter was at Mount Hope, Alabama, where he had arrived after splitting off from Dodge's troops earlier in the evening. He informed Dodge that he remained "all right" and was making for the Alabama hill country. If he got there, he would succeed in reaching Georgia, he and Dodge thought, because the rougher terrain, with its residents more in sympathy with the Union, would slow pursuers. But the two Union officers did not consider that the feared Forrest, facing Dodge's large force, would peel away to lead the pursuit of Streight.[26]

Forrest first ensured that his prey was cut off. He ordered Roddey and 2,000 men into the area between Dodge and Streight and directed Dibrell to harass Dodge's rear with cavalry and artillery.

Meanwhile, he kept his own troops between Dodge and Decatur and began preparing to pursue Streight's force as soon as Dodge had been stabilized. Since being ordered south from Spring Hill, Forrest's troopers had already ridden or fought for five days; now they spent the night of April 28 preparing to do both at once. Overseeing everything, Forrest had horses reshod, men and ammunition inspected, rations cooked, ten ears of corn issued per mount, and each trooper's gear checked. He took Morton's lightest guns along with a similiar battery from Roddey, hitching them to double teams of his best horses.[27]

On April 28, Dodge's ruse became more apparent. The Federal general, unable to get his artillery across rain-swollen Town Creek, had sent only his infantry and cavalry across, and on that day they turned around and recrossed; doubtless influenced by Dibrell's harassment and the phantom threat of Van Dorn, Dodge headed back toward the Mississippi border.[28]

For Forrest, psychology—inspiring fear and then capitalizing on it—was the essence of warfare. From his own raids at Murfreesboro and in West Tennessee, he knew the paranoia his foe would contend with far behind enemy lines. He therefore would follow his primary precept of combat— "Get 'em skeered, then keep the skeer on 'em"—and try to ratchet up the fear, making Streight and his men feel Fury itself on their heels and gaining ground.[29]

At daybreak on April 29, Forrest left Town Creek for Moulton, Alabama, twenty-five miles off. Streight had departed Moulton six hours earlier and was fifty miles ahead of Forrest. With him were the Fifty-first and Seventy-third Indiana, Third Ohio, Eightieth Illinois, and two companies of the so-called First Middle Tennessee Cavalry, comprising North Alabamans from the mountains who risked hanging for treason if captured.

Streight was hopeful about his prospects. Dodge had told him Forrest was at Town Creek, far to Streight's rear. Dodge's message on the night of April 27 said that he had "driven the enemy" and that Streight should proceed. Two days of road-miring rains had ceased, and Streight's men were welcomed by families of his "Middle Tennessee" cavalry and other predominantly unionist hill people. But when Streight bivouacked on April 29 at Day's Gap, thirty-five miles southeast of Moulton, his converted infantrymen already were saddle-sore and tiring.[30]

Next morning, the Federal commander received a shock. Only bands of Confederate guerrillas had opposed him so far, but early on April 30 he realized that had changed. He had gone no more than two miles from the previous night's campsite when enemies attacked his hindmost unit. As he learned about this, he later reported, "I heard the boom of artillery in the rear of the column." His blood must have frozen. Guerrillas did not carry artillery.[31]

Forrest had covered the distance between them in a day and a half. From the road Streight had taken out of Moulton—southeast toward Blountsville and Gadsden, rather than northeast toward Decatur—Forrest could surmise that all along the Federal goal had been more ambitious and sinister than Decatur: they were heading for Georgia, site of many of the South's military-industrial facilities as well as the vital Western & Atlantic Railroad that connected them to the battlefronts. Forrest pushed on with, if anything, more urgency. He had camped at midnight just four miles from Streight's bivouac and sent his brother Bill's scouts to reconnoiter the Federal position during the night. Soon after dawn, they were harassing the tail of the Union force.[32]

Streight had already planned a defense. He had learned that the road through Day's Gap crossed less-traveled routes winding north and south through smaller, flanking gaps. In his last message to superiors, he had said he hoped to have two or three days' head start, but if Confederates pursued him too hotly, "I will turn . . . and give them battle in the mountains." He did that now.[33]

The Union advance had reached the top of Sand Mountain, a rugged plateau extending northeast almost to Chattanooga. There, past the last of the flanking gap roads, Streight found thinly wooded sand ridges offering good defensive positions. While his rear held the attackers in check, he posted his two twelve-pounder howitzers to command the road and placed the balance of his force on each side of it. He put these infantrymen into prone positions behind the crest of the mountain while his rear fell back to draw the Confederates into his ambush.[34]

The Federal hind elements needed no urging to come running. Back there, surprised by Forrest's attack, a few of Streight's soldiers joined a stampede by hundreds of fugitive slaves who had attached themselves to the column. This disorganized horde scattered into surrounding hollows, leaving breakfasts on fires and abandoning fifty wagons. Despite these desertions, though, the ambush on the crest of the mountain worked. The organized remainder of the Union rear guard ran backward toward the crest, and the Confederates were in hot pursuit when Streight's hidden Federals rose and delivered a volley at short range. The heavy fire repulsed Forrest's vanguard. More Confederate troopers galloped up, dismounted, and counterattacked with small arms and artillery. Streight's men drove them off and countercharged, going for two cannons Forrest had pushed up close to the Union line. The Confederate gunners resisted stubbornly but briefly, then fled, leaving their guns. The Federals took forty prisoners. Captain Bill Forrest, his thigh shattered, was one of them.[35]

Bill's older brother was livid about the guns. Exponentially more powerful than small arms, the bigger pieces could spare the lives of troopers and magnify Forrest's ability to intimidate the foe. Morton being back at the Tennessee River with Dibrell, the artillery commander on Sand Mountain, Lieutenant A. Wills Gould, was a Morton friend and onetime schoolmate. Forrest cursed Gould for losing the precious cannons.

Forrest again showed his readiness to risk everything on psychology. He prepared for a dismounted charge to repel the Federals and reclaim the captured pieces. Barely 1,000 Confederates had reached the field, and Forrest would need every man—so this time, he left none to hold the horses. All his troopers were to tie their mounts to trees and bushes and join the assault. If they failed here, he grimly noted, they would need no horses.

The implication was simple: they had to stop the drive into Georgia at all costs, and they needed the guns to do it.

But Forrest's raging counterpunch struck nothing. About 11 a.m., after five hours of fighting, Streight had withdrawn again. He took the stolen guns with him.

F orrest's all-out, artillery-aided attack at Day's Gap did have an effect, though. Likely buttressed by creative tales from the captured Confederates, it had magnified Forrest's strength in Streight's mind. The latter reported learning at Sand Mountain that the Confederates were "fully three times our number, with twelve pieces of artillery under General Forrest in person." Worrying about his flanks and rear, he had opted to move on rather than risk a prolonged fight.[36]

Six miles from the Day's Gap battlefield, the Federals passed another crossroads. Up the route to his left, Streight discovered Confederates moving parallel to his path. Forrest had sent part of his troops north to cut off any attempt by Streight to give up his mission and turn back.

Four miles past the crossroads, Forrest again caught Streight's rear, this time at a stream called Crooked Creek. Streight arrayed for battle, now on Hog Mountain. Dusk gathered as Forrest assaulted the Federal right, then the left. The orders he issued were "Shoot at everything blue and keep up the skeer." The fighting kept up in bright moonlight until 10 p.m. It must have stung Forrest that the cannons captured from him a few hours earlier now aided the Federals in driving off his men.[37]

In the moonlit night, Streight moved off again. Short of horses and out of shells for the captured Confederate guns, he spiked and left them, burning the caissons. He had barely got moving, though, when he learned Forrest was again advancing behind him. Streight put men of the Seventy-third Indiana in a thicket twenty yards from the road, ordering them to fire into Forrest's flank as it passed. The ambush worked, stampeding the Confederates. The attacks tailed off.

Now amid forty miles of remote and barren country, Streight learned Forrest's men might be wearier than his own. Likely from captives, he heard that the Confederates had been on a forced march for two nights and a day before they attacked at Day's Gap. He thought that by exhausting the desolate area's meager supplies, he could force Forrest to halt for rest for at least a day. Just when he began to believe he had been right, however, Forrest assailed him again. Streight had to lay another ambush to drive him off.[38]

The bedraggled Federals reached Blountsville, Alabama, at 10 a.m. on May 1. Many mules in sorry condition at the start were ridden nearly to death and their riders now afoot. Streight found corn for his remaining usable mounts and issued rations and ammunition. The roads ahead were reported too rough for wagons, so he put his supplies on mules and burned his vehicles. After two hours of rest, he pushed on for Gadsden, thirty-five miles from Blountsville and nearly ninety from his target at Rome, Georgia.[39]

Forrest allowed Streight his two hours of Blountsville leisure because victory was now in sight. He gave his Confederates two hours' rest too. But before Streight's column left Blountsville, the Confederates were on the move again, driving in his pickets. Voracious, they had saved and gobbled food from the burning Federal wagons.

Streight kept laying ambushes with his rear guard, taking a Confederate toll. All of May 1 and into the following morning, Forrest slashed at Streight's rear. At 5 p.m. on May 1, the Federals had to form for battle again to gain time to cross the east branch of the Black Warrior River. From there Forrest allowed them to proceed toward Gadsden with only "small parties . . . harassing the rear of the column," Streight reported. Forrest was now sending his men to the chase in shifts, resting some by turns. The "skeer" was now so operative that lesser numbers could hound the Federals with impunity.[40]

It was a question of whose force would dissolve first. Forrest's, too, was straggling. Even men who didn't lag behind dozed in their saddles. The mood was tense, which showed when one of Bill Forrest's scouts came racing in. With Bill captured, the man had ranged off-route to reshoe his horse at a country blacksmith shop. There he heard that a large force of Union cavalry was four miles north moving parallel to the Confederates. "Did you see the Yankees?" Forrest countered. No, the man said; a citizen had galloped up to the blacksmith shop shouting that he had seen them.

Forrest grabbed the scout, yanked him off his horse, and started knocking
his head against a tree.

"Damn you," he said. "If you ever come to me again with a pack of lies
you won't get off so easy."

Forrest had a detachment of his own to the north, so he knew there
could be no enemy cavalry there. But such hearsay as the scout's might
unnerve some of the sleep-deprived, famished troopers.[41]

At a rocky ford of Black Warrior River, the Confederates found two
Federal pack mules that had drowned in another harried crossing. Some
of the weary pursuers cut soaked crates of once-hard bread from the backs
of the dead animals and wolfed the contents.[42]

Around 10 a.m. on May 2, a few miles from Gadsden, Forrest's vanguard chased a Federal horseman toward a burning bridge. On the
last rise overlooking wide Black Creek, the Federal saw the bridge in
flames. He reined in and gave up, surrendering to Forrest himself.

Then commenced one of the war's unlikeliest ascents to fame. To the
right of the bridge sat a dogtrot farmhouse. Three females, a mother and her
two daughters, stood in front of it. The youngest of the three, a tall, sixteen-
year-old girl, would later recall that the general rode up and told them he
and his men would protect them. Then he asked, "Where are the Yankees?"
Lined up just beyond the burning bridge, the woman replied. If the Confederates went farther, she warned, "they will kill the last one of you."

Arriving Confederates entered a field beside the farmhouse. They
started shooting across the creek at the line of Federals. As the fire increased, the females ran toward their house, the sixteen-year-old arriving
first. Forrest galloped up and interrupted her with a question. "Can you tell
me where I can get across that creek?"

There was an unsafe bridge two miles away, the girl said. But there was
also a fairly shallow place two hundred yards from the bridge. Nobody
knew about it, she added, but the family's cows sometimes waded across
there when the creek was low. If he would have a saddle put on her horse,
she would show it to him. There was no time for horse saddling. "Get up
here behind me," he commanded. He rode beside a bank flanking the road,
and she jumped from it onto the back of his horse.

Her mother, scandalized, ran up out of breath. "Emma, what do you mean?"

Forrest answered for the girl. "She's going to show me a ford where I can get my men over. Don't be uneasy. I'll bring her back safe."

He rode into a field, the girl holding on. She guided him into a thicketed ravine out of sight of the Federals. Near its mouth, she told him they needed to dismount, or they would be seen. They left the horse and snuck through bushes along the bank, the girl ahead. When they came out beside the creek, what looked to the girl like a battle was in full fire. She heard both cannon and small arms. Forrest stepped in front of her. "I'm glad to have you for a pilot," he said, "but I'm not going to make breastworks of you."

She pointed to where the cows had entered the stream and where they had exited on the far bank. Then she and Forrest crept back to the horse and rode to the house. On the way, he asked the girl her name. Emma Sansom, she said.

By the time they reached the house, cannon fire was heavy. Forrest told Emma, her older sister, and their mother to find shelter away from the house, which was an obvious target for Federal rifles. But the firing soon stopped, and the girl again met him on her way back to the house. He asked for a lock of her hair, a common token of remembrance then, and told her he had left her a note in the house. He also said one of his bravest troopers, Robert Turner, had been killed there and was in the house. He asked if she would see to Turner's burial in a nearby cemetery, then urged his horse toward the ford.[43]

The story of Emma Sansom and her ford spread fast. Forrest first mentioned it days later to a friend operating an Atlanta newspaper, the *Southern Confederacy*. Other papers across the South copied it. A Union account—a postwar reminiscence by a Streight aide—scoffed. The aide claimed it was a lie, that a captured Confederate soldier named Sansom had violated his parole by showing Forrest the ford. Emma Sansom did have a brother in the Confederate army, and he had been captured at Black Creek that morning. But the girl's help was no propagandistic fable.

Well after the war, Emma Sansom—whose last name by then would be Johnson—would provide proof that she, not her brother, had taken Forrest to the ford. Her proof indicated that Forrest had empathized with the poor farm girl. He too had grown up on out-of-the-way subsistence homesteads. His mother, like the girl's, had been widowed early, and he had had sisters— including his twin—who had died trying to pass to womanhood through the region's gauntlet of fevers. Or maybe he simply identified with the San- som girl's frank bravery, like that which he himself had cultivated in youth. Whatever it was, something about her obviously moved Forrest.[44]

Years later Emma Sansom Johnson would produce a few misspelled lines on a vertically lined sheet of account paper. No scrawl, the hand- writing looked incongruously neat and, except for the spelling and gram- mar, educated.

Hed Quaters in Sadle
May 2 1863

My highest Regardes to miss Ema Sansom for hir Gallant Conduct while my posse was skirmishing with the Federals a cross Black creek near Gadesden Allabama

> N.B Forrest
> Brig Genl
> Comding N. Ala-[45]

Less than a handful of unquestioned examples of Forrest's handwriting have surfaced, but those verifiably written to friends look indistinguish- able from the one inscribed to "Ema" Sansom. In the former, the letters all slant rightward at the same angle. They appear written by the same hand that inscribed the stained and aging note Mrs. Johnson presented in the 1890s to an enterprising Forrest biographer, who had taken the trouble to trace her to a small town in Texas.[46]

On the afternoon of May 2, after getting his men across the Black Creek ford, Forrest chased his prey through Gadsden. By now Streight had detected the two hundred troopers Forrest had previously sent to travel on a parallel line just to Streight's north. Fearing these Confederates were trying to get in front of him, Streight decided he would have to march his exhausted men all night. His progress was increasingly a ragtag affair. Some of his ammunition had got wet as his troops forded a creek before reaching the Black Creek bridge, and worn-out animals and men had fallen behind and into Confederate hands.

Even the dogged Streight was losing hope. His only chance now, he thought, was to cross the Oostanaula River at Rome and fire the bridge. That should delay Forrest a day or two and give Streight time to find new mounts and allow his men to sleep.[47]

While Streight agonized, Forrest's troopers kept up their continual skirmish with the Federal rear. About 4 p.m. on May 2, Streight stopped at a plantation fifteen miles beyond Gadsden. He knew that halting would force him to fight another battle, but he had decided that his shrinking column could not march another night without food and rest. A detail fed the animals while the rest of his men got into line to await Forrest. The rear guard—becoming Streight's front as his Federals turned to face Forrest—fell back, fighting, to the main line. The Confederates attacked the center, then the Union right. They were beaten back, but one of Streight's best officers, Colonel Gilbert Hathaway of the Seventy-third Indiana, was killed in the fray.

The Confederates withdrew to a ridge a half mile off, appearing to mass for an all-out charge. In gathering dusk, Streight ordered a resumption of the march and prepared another nocturnal ambush. He also sent two hundred of his best-mounted men ahead to take the bridge at Rome. Forrest's men circumvented the ambush, but Streight kept them from passing him by moving out again. Everything now depended on reaching Rome first. If Streight could cross, then torch, the Rome bridge, he could accomplish at least part of his mission.[48]

Most of the Federals were afoot now. Animals still walking were tender hoofed, sore backed, and used up. At the Chattooga River some ten miles from the Georgia border, Streight found no ferry; the men he had sent ahead to Rome had used the craft to cross an hour before, but then Confederates had found and removed it. Streight made for a bridge a few miles north. In the dark he got lost, and his men dissolved into small gangs in a maze of trails crossing a logging project. Day was dawning before he could assemble them again and cross the river. He burned that bridge and straggled on.[49]

At 9 a.m. on May 3, hunger and exhaustion finally forced Streight to halt. At a plantation belonging to a Mrs. Lawrence, twenty-some miles from Rome, he heard that a large Confederate detachment had gotten around him and was nearer Rome than he was.

Forrest soon drove in the Union pickets, and Streight had to fight again. Some of his 1,100 or so remaining Federals fell asleep under fire. Forrest's numbers on the field were fewer than six hundred now, but they were comparatively rested, thanks to two brief stops and their commander's innovative tactic of attacking in shifts. At the Lawrence plantation, though, he split his whole available force into three parts and set two to threatening Streight's flanks while personally leading a third to menace the center. Then he sent forward a flag of truce and demanded surrender.[50]

Streight conferred with his regimental commanders. By now they had learned that the men sent ahead to Rome had failed to take the Oostanaula Bridge. Confederate messengers had reached Rome first, carrying word that Streight was coming, and citizens had blockaded the bridges across both the Etowah and the Oostanaula Rivers with cotton bales. Hospitalized Confederate soldiers and all other able-bodied men and boys in the town had turned out to protect the bridges.[51]

Streight's subordinates wanted him to give up their foolhardy mission. Streight now considered it. While he did, he protested to Forrest that two Confederate artillery pieces that had just appeared were violating the truce by advancing. Forrest nodded to some of his officers, who in turn signaled the caisson drivers of the guns, the only two Confederate ones that had arrived on the field. The signal ordered the drivers to back away from the positions they had taken—but to keep moving in the background. Streight told Forrest he would surrender if shown that Forrest's numbers were larger than his own. While they talked, the drivers of the caissons began parading the two artillery pieces in and out of distant woods. Forrest, with his back to them, studied Streight.

"I seen him all the time we was talking looking over my shoulder and counting the guns," Forrest later told Confederate General Dabney H. Maury.

"Name of God!" he said Streight exclaimed after a few moments. "How many guns have you got? There's fifteen I've counted already."

Forrest recalled that he himself glanced backward. "I reckon that's all that has kept up," he casually replied.[52]

Minutes later, Streight surrendered. He handed the arms of more than 1,000 Federals to a few hundred Confederates before discovering the humiliating truth.[53]

23

MAY 1–18, 1863—
GRANT FROM PORT GIBSON
TO BIG BLACK RIVER

*"Men Who Know No Defeat and
Are Not Willing to Learn What It Is"*

The Confederate high command thought Grant had given up.

He had pushed most of his ironclads and transport boats past the Vicksburg cannons and had scant means of getting them back. To Major General Dabney H. Maury, commanding in Mobile, and fellow Confederates ranging from Pemberton in Vicksburg to Robert E. Lee in Virginia, the effort appeared harmless. They assumed his boats were headed down the Mississippi to join those based in New Orleans. His army, with radically weakened lines of supply and little means of returning to Memphis, would likely follow the boats down the west side of the river, his foes thought. No West Point mind could conceive of all but abandoning one's base to launch an offensive.[1]

With the threat to Vicksburg apparently subsiding, in early May the Confederacy seemed to get a second wind. Beauregard was holding off army-navy foes at Charleston; Confederate forces in Louisiana and Arkansas were holding their ground; Forrest had just destroyed Streight's drive into Georgia; and, most noticeably, at Chancellorsville, Virginia, Lee and Thomas Jonathan "Stonewall" Jackson were delivering a May 4 body blow to Federal general Fighting Joe Hooker's Army of the Potomac. The Lee-Jackson gambit, not Grant's, appeared to be the successful dare of long odds; mid-battle, Jackson pulled his whole army away from Lee's on an end run that smashed and whipped Hooker—but at awful cost: the life of Jackson himself, mortally wounded by friendly fire.

Unknowingly, the Confederates had discounted their most fearsome opponent. Grant's humble roots and manner, as well as his reputation as a sot, led even most of his associates to miss his capabilities as a soldier. A few, though, knew differently. Before another year passed, Grant's cousin by marriage, Confederate general James Longstreet, would say as much to Virginians looking down their noses at the Ohioan. "Do you *know* Grant? Well, I do. I was with him for three years at West Point, I was present at his wedding, I served in the same army with him in Mexico . . . that man will fight us every day and every hour until the end of this war."[2]

And now Grant was getting into the best position to battle them. If that position also entailed the worst risk, so be it. Since even before West Point, where his sole standout achievement was setting a horse-jumping record that stood for decades, he had relished making long vaults on faith. After graduation, he remained in top form. He showed it off during the overland late-April trek from Milliken's Bend to New Carthage—accompanied by a small mounted escort and his twelve-year-old son, Fred. Fred later recalled that when they came to a narrow bridge over a slough and everybody else awaited a turn on the structure, Fred's father turned his horse aside and "made one of his daring leaps" to the opposite bank. This leaper was no blithe youth assuming himself invincible. He was a man of forty hard years who remained uncowed.[3]

There was another reason the Confederates could not imagine Grant meant to attack from Vicksburg's south side. Never in history had anybody attempted an amphibious operation of such size.

But that was not all. Grant made it seem as if he were focused elsewhere. While he got all his men, ammunition, and other supplies down the road from New Carthage to Hard Times Landing on the Louisiana side, he created diversions. He had ordered Colonel Benjamin Grierson's cavalry south from Memphis to cut Vicksburg's eastward rail lines, and with Van Dorn gone north to Bragg, Grierson rampaged all but unopposed through the heart of Mississippi from April 17 to May 2. In addition, three shorter expeditions—under General William Sooy Smith and Colonels Edward Hatch and George Bryant—sowed confusion at various points near Grierson's path. All these raids helped keep Pemberton from concentrating his forces at Vicksburg.

Sherman mounted the longest decoy. On April 29, he took ten regiments on ten transport steamers along with an armada of mortar vessels and eight gunboats that remained north of Vicksburg—two ironclads, four tinclads, and two timberclads—and moved them back northward past Chickasaw Bluffs, scene of his December trouncing, to the farthest end of the Vicksburg defenses: Haynes Bluff, twelve miles northeast of the city. Grant had told Sherman that a demonstration there would be good, because it would pull major Confederate attention away from Grant's crossing of the Mississippi some thirty land miles downstream. But Grant said he hated to order Sherman even to feint an assault, lest the Northern public see it as another repulse.

Sherman improvised. On April 30, instead of attacking, he acted as though he had Grant's whole army with him and was preparing to. He had the gunboats and mortar craft bombard the bluffs as if softening them up preliminary to landing the infantrymen from the transports. The Confederates on the bluffs held their positions rather than move southward, but not because of Sherman so much as the suspicions of the Vicksburg ground commander, Major General Carter Stevenson; Stevenson feared that Grant's troops at Hard Times might be the diversion. On his way north on April 28, Sherman had seen Confederate scouts crossing from the bluff city to the Louisiana side of the Mississippi "to see what we are about." They would not discover much, he assured Grant, because they could not get where they needed to. The river had flooded their only road to Richmond, Louisiana, midway point of the roundabout wagon route on which elements of Grant's army were still moving to New Carthage.[4]

The Federals kept moving farther south, seeking the best landing site on the opposite bank. Those already at New Carthage slogged along the riverside levee to Hard Times Landing. On April 29, more than thirty miles downstream from Sherman's position at Chickasaw Bluffs, Admiral

Porter's seven ironclads launched a marathon bombardment at Grand Gulf, Mississippi, opposite Hard Times. They passed back and forth in front of that bluff-crowning town, slugging it out with the towering fortified Confederate artillery for six hours. Confederate brigadier general John S. Bowen, the West Point–trained Grand Gulf commander, saw a half dozen troop-crammed Union transports hovering on the Mississippi's far bank.[5]

But the transports did not attempt to cross, even when the Confederate artillery hushed. The ironclads had taken a licking. They lost eighteen sailors killed and fifty-seven wounded. Grant correctly suspected that the firing had not ceased because the Confederate guns had been destroyed. As he had learned all too well at Fort Donelson, gunboats forced to fire at a target well above them could not elevate their shots skillfully enough to ensure hitting it. He reported to Halleck that the boats had proved entirely unable to silence the enemy guns. He was right. The Confederates had only stopped firing because of a temporary shortage of shells. Their casualties were just three men killed and "12 or 15 wounded," Bowen reported.[6]

The Northern public would allow him just one assault, Grant figured, and this was not the place to make it. Crossing troops at Grand Gulf in the unarmed barges, even with gunboat escort, could be suicide. Numerically, the enemy was far inferior; Bowen had just 4,000 men at Grand Gulf. Yet 4,000, behind dug-in cannon, might drown Grant's amphibious assault before it made landfall.[7]

So Grant moved farther south that same day. In a tactic he would later use to bludgeon Robert E. Lee, he forced the Confederates to keep spreading their lines ever wider and thinner to protect their flanks. He ran past the Grand Gulf guns as he had those at Vicksburg and Warrenton. Disembarking his men and marching them farther down the Mississippi's west bank, he had the gunboats launch another attack after dark while his transports slipped past in the din. He intended to land them ten more miles downriver at Rodney, Mississippi—at first. But during the night of April 29, a Union cavalry patrol on the Louisiana side procured the aid of a slave who told them of a better landing spot. Halfway between Grand Gulf and Rodney, the man said, the village of Bruinsburg offered a good, shorter road leading toward Port Gibson and Grand Gulf.[8]

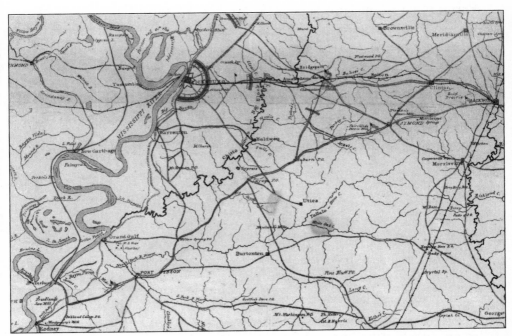

GRANT'S VICKSBURG CAMPAIGN: This 1863 map shows the area of Grant's five-battle run-up to the siege of Vicksburg. After crossing the Mississippi at Bruinsburg in the lower left, he took his army to Port Gibson, Raymond, and Jackson before turning back toward Vicksburg to fight at Champion Hill about halfway between Jackson and Vicksburg, then at Big Black River Bridge closer to Vicksburg.

By 8 a.m. on the last day of April, Grant was ready. He had assigned McClernand's corps to lead the amphibious attack, since it happened to be farthest in the advance when Grant made his downriver plan. Perhaps the position of honor also owed to Grant's continuing wariness of McClernand's Lincoln ties. Whatever the reason, McClernand's corps now filled barges, steamboats, and gunboats and cast off from Deshroon's Landing just south and opposite of Grand Gulf amid band music and reverberating cheers. They steamed some five miles downriver and hove to the east bank, where infantrymen of the Twenty-fourth and Forty-sixth Indiana splashed ashore first. They quickly arrested the only man they found on the Bruinsburg landing to prevent his spreading word of their coming. No uniformed Confederate was in sight.

Grant experienced a gladness he never forgot. Rather than send his troops against the ravaging Grand Gulf cannon, he had found them an open door with nobody waiting inside it. But the reality was even more euphoric than that: he was at last on the business side of the Mississippi. It gave him "a degree of relief scarcely equaled since," he wrote later. "All the campaigns, labors, and exposures from the month of December . . . to this time . . . were for the accomplishment of this one object." Now, at last, he could fight.[9]

W ith his men ashore, Grant's vanguard suddenly dawdled. Rather than dash on up to the high ground past Bruinsburg, 17,000 McClernand riflemen sat for four hours on their beachhead to allow distribution of rations. Somebody had forgotten to do it the evening before.[10]

This was just one of the myriad aggravations to which McClernand subjected his commander. Grant had ordered him to bend every effort toward a quick strike, but to little avail. Charles Dana, a former New York newspaperman who had recently become a special observer for the War Department, had reported to Stanton on April 25 that apparent confusion among McClernand's command and staff were delaying Grant's preparations to attack Grand Gulf. Although ordered to leave officers' horses and tents behind, McClernand "carries his bride along," Dana confided. Two days later, Dana wrote that the wait for a steamboat "carrying General McClernand's wife, with her servants and baggage," had delayed transportation of half a McClernand division.

The primary hindrance, though, was Mrs. McClernand's husband. Even the contingent of McClernand's corps that had arrived at New Carthage was not quickly put onto boats on April 26 because McClernand had not yet gathered the vessels. Instead, that afternoon he held a review of his Illinois troops for that state's visiting governor Richard Yates. The review included firing an artillery salute, violating Grant's repeated orders to conserve ammunition for use against the enemy, Dana wrote. Dana added that after finding the transport vessels had "at last" been assembled, Grant pocketed a "severe letter" he had written McClernand—apparently choosing to bide his time.[11]

Grant was not the only one seething at McClernand. Dana was cha-grined that McClernand had the front spot in the amphibious attack. The War Department emissary wrote Stanton that he had objected to entrust-ing such an important place to McClernand. Stanton, perhaps fearing other eyes—especially presidential ones—seeing his correspondence, sharply told Dana to quit offering advice on command assignments.[12]

But McClernand was hardly the only issue. Emancipation continued to roil Grant's Midwest-rooted army. The Union's decision to enlist and arm fugitive slaves also loomed forebodingly. Many white troops balked at the idea, as did some of their commanders. General Lorenzo Thomas had ar-rived at Milliken's Bend on April 11 to begin speaking to generals and regular soldiers about it, and Dana soon reported that officers who had told him three months earlier that they would never fight alongside black regiments now said they would obey orders.

Dana may not have talked with Grant division commander A. J. Smith. On the night of April 26, the day McClernand provided Illinois governor Yates with a troop review, Colonel H. C. Warmoth confided to his diary that General Smith, a Pennsylvania-born and West Point–schooled veteran, was so incensed at the prospect of fighting alongside blacks that he "will hang old Thomas if he comes into his camp making such a speech. Says . . . if Jesus Christ was to come down and ask him if he would be an abolitionist if he would take him to heaven, he answers that, 'I would say NO! Mr. Christ. . . . I would rather go to hell than be an abolitionist.'"[13]

T he enlistment of fugitive slaves presented a thorny problem, but on the eastern bank of the Mississippi, in the face of looming combat, its importance receded.

Grant launched a fast, hard-hitting campaign. He first had to cut off Vicksburg from rescue troops gathering in central Mississippi. Issuing three days' rations, he moved his men onto high ground toward Port Gibson, junction of a road to Grand Gulf and another circling east and then north to Vicksburg. He aimed to flank Grand Gulf, take it, then make it the base for a two-pronged move. He would send McClernand south to aid Major General Nathaniel Banks in destroying Port Hudson,

Louisiana, the only other formidable Confederate-held bastion on the Mississippi. Grant himself, meanwhile, would isolate Vicksburg and gather supplies for a campaign to capture it. Then he would recall Mc-Clernand's men, and Grant and Banks would combine forces against Vicksburg.[14]

Grant's advance units struck enemy skirmishers eight miles from Port Gibson. They had pushed the Southerners backward four miles by dusk, and the next morning, May 1, they advanced into a pitched battle. Bowen, the Confederate commander at Grand Gulf, had gathered just 7,000 men to march down and oppose Grant's 25,000, but he had selected a good site. The Bruinsburg Road forked into parallel routes into Port Gibson, and Bowen's men guarded both on ridges too narrow to allow more than fractions of Grant's strength to meet the Confederates at one time. Thickly overgrown hollows separated McClernand on the right from McPherson on the left. They could connect and aid each other only by re-treating to the fork.[15]

McClernand's Federals routed an Alabama brigade before noon, and Grant accompanied McClernand and Illinois governor Yates forward on the right-hand road to inspect the captured ground. Soldiers along the route cheered them, and McClernand and Yates could not resist making speeches. "A great day for the Northwest!" McClernand proclaimed to an aide. Grant sat through the impromptu stumping, then suggested that the rifle-toting prospective voters needed to get about pursuing Confederates.[16]

The enemy fought with tenacity, but Grant's strength prevailed. Under McPherson's command, Indianans and Illinoisans fought their way along and beside the left-hand road, pushing through a thicket of cane, trees, and underbrush in the ravine to the left of the roadway. They finally flanked a brigade of Alabamans as more of McPherson's men advanced from Bruinsburg and reinforced them. The Arkansans, Mississippians, and Missourians facing McClernand realized they could be flanked, cut off, and captured if their comrades on the other road broke, so they stole away from the battlefield at about 5 p.m. In ratio of loss to total Union numbers, it was an inexpensive victory; of his 25,000, Grant had lost 131 killed, 719 wounded, and 25 missing. For the Confederates, the battle was much more costly. They reported 60 killed, 340 wounded, and 387 miss-ing of their 7,000, and their figures were incomplete.[17]

Darkness prevented pursuit, and Grant told McClernand to advance at dawn of May 2. With daylight, the Union troops moved up cautiously until they saw scattered arms, equipment, dead horses, and Confederate corpses. The enemy was gone, and the pursuers marched unopposed into nearly deserted Port Gibson about 10 a.m. There Grant found a newspaper disclosing that Grierson's raid on rail lines in the Mississippi interior had been a smashing success.[18]

Confederates had burned bridges on the roads leading from Port Gibson to both Grand Gulf and Vicksburg, so the Federals laid pontoons. Grant was glad to see Lieutenant Colonel James Harrison Wilson of his staff enter the water and work alongside enlisted men, as Grant himself had done in the Mexican War. When they finished the makeshift bridge, the troops streamed over the pontoons, one wing heading directly toward Grand Gulf and the other skirmishing northeast toward Hankinson's Ferry on the Big Black River. Learning that the Confederates had abandoned Grand Gulf, Grant headed there with an escort of twenty cavalry.

He traveled light. He had left everything except the clothes on his back on the far side of the Mississippi with a five-hundred-wagon train winding from Milliken's Bend to Hard Times, so at Grand Gulf he borrowed an extra horse from a subordinate and clean underwear from a naval officer. Having had no tent and no food except such as he could filch from subordinates' headquarters, he got a bath and a meal on a gunboat. Then he wrote a May 3 letter to Halleck summarizing his effort so far and expressing pride in how Bowen's "bold . . . and well carried out" defense of Port Gibson had been vanquished by his Federals, "hardy men who know no defeat and are not willing to learn what it is." He also wrote orders to corps commanders as well as other subordinates left in charge farther up the Mississippi. Finishing a letter to Julia around midnight, he did not go to bed. Instead, remounting the borrowed horse, he rode on to Hankinson's Ferry, arriving before dawn.[19]

Grant now had to make some strategic changes on the fly. At Grand Gulf he learned Banks could not begin the anticipated McClernand-reinforced campaign against Port Hudson before May 10. Having come north from New Orleans, Banks—a militarily incompetent former governor of Massachusetts—was focused on Port Hudson, the first obstacle in his path, and said he could not join Grant until after its reduction. That would delay the Vicksburg attack by a month, and already the Vicksburg Confederates were gathering reinforcements. Grant could not wait. With some of his troops already well started toward the railroad connecting Vicksburg and Jackson, he forgot Banks, retained McClernand, and kept moving.[20]

Grant quickly instituted his new plan. He continued preparations to cram Grand Gulf with supplies floated across the Mississippi, but rather than wait for Banks, he would feint toward Vicksburg to confuse Pemberton, then head inland to the railroad linking the river fortress to Jackson. That would put him between Vicksburg and its potential rescuers and prevent a junction of the two.

This new scenario would stretch Grant's supply line paper-thin, beyond all bounds of West Point theory. Halleck would disapprove if he knew. But Grant saw no alternative. Like the run past the Vicksburg guns, moving eastward to cut off the city was the option that offered the best chance of success. He wrote Halleck a little of his developing scheme in the letter of May 3 from Grand Gulf, reporting that the countryside would supply forage and fresh beef. Halleck for months had urged his commanders to take advantage of such, so Grant knew that this part of his plan would go down well. Other supplies, Grant wrote, would have to come "a long and precarious route" from Milliken's Bend down to Hard Times Landing, then across the Mississippi to Grand Gulf. Knowing his message would take days to reach Washington, he headed away from the river, beyond Washington contact. There, out of Halleck's reach, he could revise his plan as resistance demanded.[21]

On Grant's order, Sherman now hurried his corps down from Chickasaw Bluffs to reinforce the two taking position east of Vicksburg. Grant wrote Sherman on May 3 that, on reaching Grand Gulf, he must draw three days' rations and make them last five, augmenting them with local fare and feeding his horses on indigenous supplies. Speed, Grant said, was crucial.[22]

Sherman protested, all but reciting the West Point principles Grant was flouting. He wrote Grant from Hankinson's Ferry on May 9, pleading with his chief to wait a little and organize. A wagon train large enough to supply an army moving into the interior, he advised, would jam roads, marooning itself and the rest of the column in some remote, dangerous place. Grant replied that he would employ no five-hundred-wagon train. Rather, he would make his army leaner and faster—and, if necessary, hungrier. Bringing full rations from Grand Gulf would require more roads than he had time to build, he told Sherman. Instead, Sherman must assemble a train a quarter the usual size, 120 wagons, and load it with bacon, bread, salt, and coffee, items unavailable in interior Mississippi in sufficient bulk to supply an army. Everything else would have to come from the territory through which they passed.[23]

From Bruinsburg on, Grant had troops scouring neighborhoods along the route for every wheeled conveyance that could haul ammunition. They assembled "a motley train," he later recalled, that included fine carriages loaded with cartridge boxes and drawn by mules in plough harness alongside ox-drawn cotton wagons.[24]

It must have looked more like a refugee procession than an army. In taking items from civilians, Grant ordered his men not even to fill out records until they had more time. His attitude toward nonmilitary secessionists was hardening. From Hankinson's Ferry he wrote General Hurlbut in Memphis on May 5 that only the homes, bodies, and most personal possessions of civilians would be off-limits to his soldiers from then on. Hurlbut should keep troops out of civilian houses, but everything outside them was fair game. They must feed themselves off the fields they passed and destroy every crop that could be useful to Confederates. They should take all the mules and horses they needed and destroy farm implements whenever doing so did not require too much time. In sum, he said, "cripple the rebellion in every way without insulting women and children or taking their clothing, jewelry &c." From now on, for opponents of his army, war would truly be hell—and not just on soldiers.[25]

Sherman's corps arrived and drew ammunition at Grand Gulf on May 6 and 7, and Grant launched a wide, fast sweep northeastward. Its purpose was to eliminate any risk of attacks from his rear when he turned back west to approach Vicksburg's land side. At Edwards Station, halfway out the Vicksburg-Jackson rail line, Pemberton was reportedly gathering significant forces. Grant would have to prevent them from connecting with reinforcements to the east and remove them from his own approach to Vicksburg.[26]

The three Federal corps advanced abreast south of the Vicksburg-Jackson rail line. That way, each had fresh fields to ravage for forage and food. McClernand led the left nearest the railroad, Sherman the center, and McPherson the right. From May 9 to 12, the Federals drove on parallel routes from Hankinson's Ferry, Rocky Springs, and Utica thirty miles toward Edwards Station, Bolton Depot just beyond it, and Raymond. Once Grant cleared the territory on the Jackson end of the railroad, he could safely turn west and assault Pemberton.

On May 11, Grant had ordered McPherson to Raymond. The urgency of finding food had increased. McPherson was to do his utmost to gather all available foodstuffs around Raymond. Needing to fight before their food gave out, they would have to make their rations last as long as possible. Grant reminded McPherson that on a previous occasion he had made two days' rations last seven, and he might have to do the same thing again.[27]

MAJOR GENERAL JAMES B. MCPHERSON

Grant was outrunning even his streamlined supply trains. This is likely why he recalled later, and historians have repeated, that he abandoned his base, cutting himself off from all sources of reinforcement and matériel. His letters and orders show he never meant to do that wholly. He had stockpiled supplies at Grand Gulf from wagon-borne cargoes that continued to clatter into Hard Times for ferrying across the Mississippi. He did, however, risk outdistancing his rations. McPherson reported that meat was plentiful, but bread less so, and his men also lacked horses, mules, and haul vehicles. McPherson said he barely had wagons enough to move camp equipment and ammunition; locally commandeered vehicles usually broke down. His troops were also badly in need of shoes. Nearly a third of his First Brigade had worn theirs out on the long march from Milliken's Bend. Many feet were bare and sore.[28]

On May 12, complying with a Grant order to enter and sack Raymond, McPherson had to fight his way in. Two miles south, 3,000 Confederates under Brigadier General John Gregg assailed his right. In this, his first full battle as on-site commander of a large unit, McPherson overestimated his opposition, guessing Confederate strength to be twice what it was. McPherson was no Grant, so his inflated figure gave him pause; 6,000 would have been more than half his own total of 10,000-plus—and roughly equal to the assailed part of his force. Gregg, for his part, had attacked because he did not know he was outnumbered. He thought he had in his front only a single Federal brigade "on a marauding excursion."[29]

The battle raged from noon to 4 p.m. By 2, the outcome was decided. Vicious enfilading of Confederates charging to the right and left of McPherson's center helped to turn the tide, as did a Federal counterattack and the deployment of 4,000 Union reinforcements under Brigadier General Marcellus Crocker. McPherson reported 66 killed, 339 wounded, and 37 missing. Partial Confederate totals were 73 killed, 252 wounded, and 190 missing. As at Port Gibson, the Union sum was small in relation to the number engaged; the Confederate one, daunting.[30]

After the Raymond fight, Grant again improvised. Gregg had retreated toward Jackson, where Confederates were reported massing, and Joe Johnston was expected there at any moment to take command. Grant knew he could not afford to leave such a prestigiously led force behind him when he about-faced to deal with Pemberton at Vicksburg.

He decided to attend to the Confederates at Jackson and, as he reported, "leave no enemy in my rear."[31]

Grant sent Sherman's and McPherson's corps hurrying to the Mississippi capital. McPherson followed the railroad, descending on the city from the northwest, while Sherman, accompanied by Grant, took a road from Raymond to strike Jackson from the southwest. The 24,000 Federals faced just 6,000 Confederates under Johnston, but the capital was fortified, and 7,000 more Confederates were racing toward it.[32]

Grant beat them to it. The Federals arrived in the mid-morning of May 14 in the mud of a four-hour rain. Sherman's artillery blasted aside a ragtag collection of Confederate mounted infantry, sharpshooters, and four cannons. Grant's McPherson-led northern pincer bayonet-charged a thin Confederate line and swept it into the Jackson earthworks. The Federals regrouped, advanced again by mid-afternoon, and found the trenches abandoned. Before 2 p.m., Gregg had pulled out and headed north toward Canton, Mississippi, bringing up the rear of Johnston's supply train. Gregg's men had fought hard, but he had learned at the last moment that McPherson was only half his foe. And Johnston had been no help, preemptively removing as many men and supplies as he could, rather than holding until reinforcements arrived. He had ordered a withdrawal at 3 a.m., hours before sighting the Union attackers. At Jackson, 42 Federals had died, 251 were wounded, and 7 were missing. Just one of the three Confederate brigades reported its casualties: 17 dead, 64 wounded, and 118 missing.[33]

Grant kept moving. He told Sherman to occupy the Jackson rifle pits and destroy rail and other facilities that might be useful to the Confederates. He himself took McClernand's and McPherson's corps and turned toward Vicksburg.

Grant now had even more reason to hurry. On the evening of May 13, just prior to the battle for Jackson, Joe Johnston had sent Pemberton a message by three different couriers. One, a Union spy, took the message to McPherson instead. The dispatch informed Pemberton that Union troops were at Clinton on the Jackson-Vicksburg rail line and ordered Pemberton to attack there immediately to prevent the fall of Jackson.[34]

If Pemberton was following Johnston's orders, then Grant might catch him outside the Vicksburg trenches. Assuming Johnston was now circling northward to try to beat him to the bluff fortress, Grant sent the two corps rushing to Bolton Station, halfway to Vicksburg. There, they could keep Johnston and Pemberton apart until Sherman had wrecked anything at Jackson that might help them if they returned there after he departed.[35]

Two days later, Grant fought the first of two battles with a conflicted Pemberton.

Pemberton and Johnston differed greatly from Grant. Both soldiered by the West Point book, and neither liked fighting. Instead of trying to join forces as each claimed to want to do, they moved farther apart, Johnston to the northeast from Jackson and Pemberton southeast from Edwards Station on the Vicksburg-Jackson rail line. Pemberton was a man in the middle—between Johnston, who wanted to unite outside the trap Vicksburg seemed to be turning into, and Jefferson Davis, who wanted Vicksburg defended to the death. Trying hesitantly to reconcile the two, Pemberton had come out of Vicksburg along the railroad but then decided that trying to get through Grant's army to join Johnston would be "extremely hazardous." Subordinates finally persuaded him to target a two-hundred-wagon Union supply train moving from Grand Gulf toward Raymond, but his heart obviously was not in it.[36]

Subordinates' animosity likely also influenced Pemberton. They showed less confidence in him than the questionable amount he showed in himself. A Philadelphia native, he had led only the obscure Department of South Carolina, Georgia, and Florida when promoted to major general in early 1862; he then rose to lieutenant general with his assignment to Vicksburg. Major General William Loring, a North Carolina–born career soldier who had lost an arm in the Mexican War, was openly contemptuous of him. And the prickly temperament of Brigadier General Lloyd Tilghman, who had faced Grant at Fort Henry, had chafed Pemberton for months. As they set out to nab Grant's wagons, an aide to Brigadier General Winfield S. Featherston overheard Loring, Tilghman, and Featherston laughing at Pemberton's orders.[37]

Confederate discord increased on May 14. Pemberton had argued against obeying Johnston's order to move farther from Vicksburg, and Loring urged grabbing Grant's Raymond-bound wagons instead. Pemberton reluctantly decided Loring's idea offered the only realistic chance

LIEUTENANT GENERAL JOHN C. PEMBERTON

to damage Grant. But, contrary to West Point dogma, Grant was not depending on his supply wagons to the usual extent. And Pemberton thought Grant was aiming to destroy Jackson, whereas Grant's actual goal was to destroy Pemberton.[38]

On May 15, Grant sent 32,000 of his Federals hurrying westward on three roads. Pemberton meanwhile plodded. A planning error delayed his 23,000 Confederates for five hours. No one had sent enough ammunition and rations to Edwards Station, the jumping-off point for the operation against Grant's wagon train. Then, despite headquartering two miles away, Pemberton failed to scout a bridge his troops needed to cross Baker's Creek. When they got there, flooding had washed it out, and a detour ate more hours. By day's end, Pemberton's men were exhausted. Some arrived in the target area—on the Raymond-Port Gibson Road and roughly halfway between those two towns—too late to sleep.[39]

At 5 a.m. on May 16, Grant got more Southern aid. Subordinates brought him two men who worked on the Vicksburg-Jackson rail line.

They said that they had passed through Pemberton's force a few hours earlier, and the Confederates were moving east 25,000 strong. Grant yet again revised his plan. He ordered Sherman to cut short his wrecking of Jackson and hurry a division west to Bolton with ammunition wagons. They were not to stop until they reached the rest of Grant's army.[40]

Soon after daylight, Pemberton heard firing. Scouts reported a strong Federal column approaching from the east. A courier also arrived with a re-iterated order from Johnston that Pemberton join him to the north. Only now did Pemberton learn that Jackson had fallen, rendering his previous orders from Johnston (which he had not obeyed) obsolete. Johnston now ordered him to rendezvous at Clinton, Mississippi, some ten miles west of Jackson. With his cavalry pickets already skirmishing and Federal artillery unlimbering on the head of his column, Pemberton forgot Grant's wagons and decided to return to Edwards Station and try to reach Johnston.

Pemberton soon found himself stymied in this effort too. At a hill on the farm of a family named Champion, the Confederates left under Major General Carter Stevenson met a Federal division of McClernand's corps under Brigadier General Alvin P. Hovey. Stevenson had no way of knowing that just behind Hovey, marching west from Bolton, was McPherson's whole corps: two divisions, led by generals "Black Jack" Logan and Marcellus Crocker. The Federal path southward led up Champion Hill and then down to a critical junction with the so-called Middle Road, another thoroughfare running from Edwards Station to Raymond. This was the middle of three routes on which Grant's forces were hastening west. It was also Pemberton's own intended route back to Edwards. Stevenson took position on Champion Hill to hold it open.

Confederate scouts then reported more Federals approaching on the Middle Road east of the junction, heading for Stevenson's right rear. This second Union column, a half mile south of Hovey and McPherson, comprised four brigades under McClernand division commanders Eugene Carr and Peter Osterhaus. And two miles south of them, on the main road from Raymond to Edwards Station, were four more brigades under Major Generals A. J. Smith of McClernand's corps and Frank Blair of Sherman's. Pemberton was in the crosshairs of ruin.[41]

Battle erupted at 7 a.m. with a cavalry clash on the lower Raymond road. Union artillery and Confederate sharpshooters joined in. Loring, facing Smith and Blair, suggested the Confederates form a battle line to fend off the imminent Union attack. Pemberton ordered him to block the lower Raymond road. But a Loring staff officer thought Pemberton looked as if he had made "no . . . plans for the coming battle."[42]

In mid-morning, McPherson joined the onslaught, attacking the Confederates' other wing. Pemberton, preoccupied with the lower Raymond road, ignored half of the Federal army for a couple of hours. Confederates under General Stevenson clung to Champion Hill and tried to fend off McPherson, but a Federal drive shoved them backward and overlapped their left. Grant's hard-fighting favorite, Major General "Black Jack" Logan, commanded this Federal flanking lunge. Logan did not even give his men the usual time to lay down their personal gear before leading them forward. "Damn them," he roared, "you can whip them with your knapsacks on!"[43]

Logan's punch had carried all the way to the Jackson Road, Pemberton's best route back to Vicksburg. Grant, at the Champion house with McPherson, sent an aide to Logan to tell him he was making history.[44]

McPherson's center fought from noon until 1:30 for the crest of Champion Hill. A bayonet charge took a battery of four Confederate guns, which then were lost to a withering counterattack. The Federals retreated, then with reinforcements mounted another charge, pushing back Confederates under brigade commanders Stephen Lee and Alfred Cumming. Confederates barely kept a grip on Jackson Road and the crossroads.[45]

Only at about 1 p.m. did Pemberton seek help for his embattled left. He summoned Loring and John Bowen from the lower Raymond road. Neither general obeyed immediately. Heavy Federal forces were in their front, they said. The aide who had delivered the first message finally returned to Bowen with a mandatory order: send at least a brigade to the left immediately. It was around 2:30 p.m. before 5,000 Missourians and Arkansans under Bowen hit the Federal line at the crossroads. Because of the hilly, much-forested terrain—one officer said it was impossible to see more than fifty to a hundred yards in any direction—Bowen's strike landed like a knockout sucker punch. His men ran the Federals off Champion Hill three-quarters of a mile, recapturing some of the cannons the Confederates had lost and getting close to Union ammunition wagons at the Champion house. Men in Bowen's First Brigade fired as many as ninety rounds apiece in this thrust—forty in their cartridge boxes, the rest scavenged from fallen friends and enemies. Federals rushing forward to help saw their comrades flee so brokenly that they threatened to panic the reinforcements.[46]

Grant did not panic, but he made a knee-jerk error. In sending more men to aid those on Champion Hill, he ordered a withdrawal of Logan's brigade, whose sweeping charge around the Confederate left had blocked Pemberton's Jackson Road retreat route. But Confederates farther out Jackson Road were too traumatized to react.[47]

Loring, meanwhile, was lost to Pemberton for an hour, having taken a little-used and longer road to reach the left. When he tardily neared the Jackson Road, the left of Stevenson's fought-out line had broken, and the delay had wasted Bowen's smashing charge as well as an accompanying countersurge by Stephen Lee to Bowen's left; Grant's men regained equilibrium. All Loring saw as he approached were fleeing Confederates, some without hats or weapons and looking, one staff officer thought, "as if they had just escaped from the Lunatic Asylum." But Loring and an indefatigable Lee were preparing another charge when Pemberton ordered them to retreat to Edwards Station.[48]

The Confederate disaster was immense. Pemberton lost at least 4,000 of his 23,000 troops at Champion Hill, 2,500 of them missing and captured. He also lost most of Loring's men, cut off from his army by the onrushing Federals. Union casualties were about 2,200.[49]

The Confederates marched or straggled back toward Vicksburg. Pemberton forgot about trying to reach Johnston, which was just as well. Pemberton had at least made an aborted attempt to get to his superior; Johnston made none to get to him. So Pemberton put his survivors back across Baker's Creek and ordered them to hold the crossing for Loring, who never arrived.[50]

Before dawn on May 17, the Confederates gave up on Loring. They fell back to an already fortified, mile-wide position straddling the railroad and guarding its bridge over Big Black River. Rearguard commander Bowen put 5,000 men into a formidable-seeming position on the river's east bank, their battle line stretching across the inside of a horseshoe bend in the Big Black. Around and south of the railroad, where Bowen expected the brunt of any Federal assault, bristled twenty cannons. On each wing, he placed his bloody, hard-fighting units from Missouri and Arkansas. Between, he put a Tennessee brigade under Brigadier General John C. Vaughn. Vaughn occupied rifle pits fronted by a parapet, a fifteen-foot-wide bayou, and knee-deep water filled with fallen trees. His men were "fresh . . . and not demoralized," Bowen thought.[51]

But demoralization was probably not an issue with these Tennesseans. Vaughn's troops were conscripts from the state's unionist eastern third. The Richmond government had thought marching them away from their people would make them better Confederates. It did not. They cared little for the Confederacy. And many of them—along with the Missourians and Arkansans and even their commander, John Bowen—wondered why Pemberton had ordered them there at all. All but Bowen likely forgot that Pemberton thought he must hold the bridge for the missing Loring, whose troops still might arrive. But doing so was dangerous. The deep Big Black and the sixty-foot bluffs on its west side seemed much better able to stop Grant—and they would dangerously impede the 5,000 Confederates left on the east bank. There were just two bridges over the river: one forming part of the railroad and, just south, a temporary one thrown across the deck of a steamboat. Both were narrow. They could accommodate 5,000 men only if their withdrawal was deliberate and orderly. Such was not to be.[52]

The Battle of Big Black River Bridge was brief and hot, an exclamation point following the Confederate disaster at Champion Hill. Grant had hedged his bet, sending more pontoons to cross the Big Black farther north and sidestep Pemberton if necessary. No sidestep was needed, though, thanks to Union troops under Brigadier General Michael Lawler. Commanding one of five advance Federal brigades facing three Confederate ones, the burly forty-seven-year-old native Irishman put his men in woods along the Big Black facing the northern end of the Confederate line. There an inward bulge caused by a swampy area interrupted the rifle pits. To the southeastern front of this gap, annual river overflow had carved a swale in a large field. Lawler's cavalry chief recognized a topographic gift. He told Lawler a brigade could cross part of the open field and then shelter in the swale. There they would be close enough that defenders could get off just one volley before a Federal charge overwhelmed them. Lawler began forming his troops into two heavy columns of fours.[53]

Grant sat watching the unit deployments near the road, which ran beside the railroad through the center of the Union and Confederate lines. A courier rode up and handed him a May 11 telegram from Halleck in Washington. It ordered Grant, "if possible," to join Banks in Louisiana and mount joint attacks on Port Hudson before trying Vicksburg. Grant read the wire, then put it in his pocket. Two days earlier, in a telegram that would not arrive in Washington until May 20, he had reported to Halleck that Banks had gone "off in Louisiana" and would be unavailable until May 10. Grant "could not lose the time" from his lightning campaign to drive off prospective rescuers to the east before assaulting or besieging Vicksburg, he concluded.[54]

Lawler lost no time now. At noon he threw his cheering troops across the field into the swale and onto the Confederate center. Seeing Federal strength building, the defenders got nervous about their bridges. They loosed a volley that ripped 199 casualties from Lawler's ranks. But then the bayonet-brandishing Midwesterners charged the Confederate center delivering a volley of their own. They leaped into the bayou ditch and splashed through logs and brush to the parapet.[55]

Most of the Tennesseans fled. The remainder raised white rags or puffs of cotton from the bales anchoring their parapet. Missourians and Arkansans on the flanks ran, too, and clogged the little bridges. Those arriving late tried to swim. Some drowned. Lawler's brigade took more prisoners than their own numbers. When most of their uncaptured comrades had crossed, the Confederates fired the turpentine-soaked bridges.[56]

The Federals counted coup. They had taken 1,751 more prisoners, 18 more cannon to add to 27 taken at Champion Hill, 1,525 artillery shells, 1,421 stands of small arms, and 6 battle flags. In seventeen days since leaving Bruinsburg, Grant's army had traveled two hundred miles and fought five battles. It had inflicted 7,000 casualties and lost half that. Pemberton returned to Vicksburg with just 9,000 of the 23,000 men he had taken out.

Employing or building crossings to the north and south, Grant quickly put Big Black River between himself and any force Johnston might gather behind him. Vicksburg was now surrounded. Unless Johnston did something quick and miraculous, it was doomed.[57]

The many letters Grant wrote over the next several days did not include one to Julia. On May 9 on the road to Raymond, he had written her that she should join him as soon as she heard Vicksburg had fallen, and he had not written her since. He thought, he later informed her, that Vicksburg would fall before another letter could reach her.

After Big Black River Bridge, he may also have wanted to buy time for the healing of a wound that would be best unreported to her. In a May 3 letter from Grand Gulf, he had told her that their twelve-year-old son, Fred, who had accompanied him on this remarkable trek, was "enjoying himself hugely." The boy had been close enough to combat to hear "balls whistle" and had not flinched, Grant reported. But at Big Black River Bridge, Fred had been too much of a chip off the old block. Excited by Lawler's charge, the boy spurred his horse, jumped the parapet with some support troops, and followed to the river to watch the swimming Confederates. There a bullet from the west bank grazed his leg. When Fred's father wrote Julia again on June 9, he was cryptic regarding their son.[58]

"Fred has enjoyed his campaign very much," the general wrote. "He has kept a journal which I have never read but suppose he will read to you."[59]

What Julia did not know could not hurt her.

24

MAY–JUNE 1863—FORREST IN MIDDLE TENNESSEE

"No Damned Man Will Kill Me and Live"

For a couple of May's first days, after his epic capture of Abel Streight, Forrest was the toast of Rome, Georgia. The entire Confederacy was buoyed, too, by Robert E. Lee's smashing victory over Fighting Joe Hooker at Chancellorsville in Virginia. But ominous events occurred alongside these. Grant had finally managed to cross the Mississippi below Vicksburg and was heading toward the Mississippi capital, and the wound Stonewall Jackson had suffered at Chancellorsville began to appear mortal.

Only momentarily could Forrest bask in the glory of his Streight capture. Rome citizens had planned a feast for May 6, but he and his men had to miss it. Word came that more Federals were headed south from Tuscumbia, Alabama, and late on May 5, Forrest rode off to intercept them. Learning at Gadsden that the report was false, he then headed his men back to their base at Columbia, Tennessee. At Huntsville, Alabama, however, he had to leave them and board a train to Shelbyville. Bragg had ordered Forrest to report to him. Forrest likely did not know then that on May 7 a jealous husband had assassinated Earl Van Dorn. Bragg needed a new west wing cavalry commander.[1]

Bragg greeted Forrest with surprising warmth. The Streight chase had obviously impressed the Army of Tennessee commander. That and the West Tennessee raid in December, despite the intervening Dover debacle, showed that Forrest, however unpolished, was a powerful asset. Bragg, in

MAJOR GENERAL EARL VAN DORN

much public disfavor since Stones River, needed to hoard every chit he could amass. On May 8, when a delegation from Mississippi visited Jefferson Davis asking for Forrest to help counter Grant's alarming depredations there, Bragg had rejected the idea. Forrest's force, he said, was "not in condition." Given Forrest's long hard ride on the heels of Streight, he doubtless spoke the truth.

Bragg would never admit erring in naming Wheeler his chief of cavalry, but he tried to smooth it over. Likely knowing Forrest had vowed at Dover never again to serve under Wheeler, he offered Forrest a promotion to Van Dorn's rank, major general.[2]

It was an empty gesture—Wheeler, who had already become a major general, would still outrank him—and Forrest refused it. Another officer would be better fitted, he said. Perhaps a sarcastic allusion to Wheeler's meteoric rise, the statement implies a determination not to agree to recognize his inferiority to the twenty-six-year-old. Also, Forrest seems to have grown, if anything, more uncomfortable in high company. Beauregard had had to press him to accept a brigadiership following Shiloh—and after consenting, he had seen some of the Confederacy's aristocratic officers and units, such as the First Louisiana Cavalry and its colonel, flatly refuse to serve under him. He may not have cared to invite more sneers.[3]

Such political maneuvering as Forrest engaged in made clear his feelings about this elite. Van Dorn had been a darling of the same upper crust that had rejected Forrest. Just prior to the Streight raid, Forrest had tried to escape his authority. Along with another Van Dorn subordinate, brigadier general and West Pointer W. H. "Red" Jackson, Forrest had urged politically powerful Brigadier General Gideon Pillow of Fort Donelson infamy to seek a cavalry command and take Forrest and Jackson with him. Now, with Van Dorn dead, Forrest suggested that Bragg give the proffered major general's rank to Pillow. Pillow had languished in minor commands, or none, since Fort Donelson; Jefferson Davis disliked Pillow and had deprived him of duty for six months after the battle. Now, Forrest's suggestion must have looked very like a rebuff to the Confederate command system and President Davis himself.[4]

Forrest's suggestion was of little avail. Bragg gave him Van Dorn's job without Van Dorn's rank. On May 16 he became Bragg's west wing cavalry chief. Under him were divisions led by Brigadiers Red Jackson and Frank Armstrong and brigades under Brigadiers George Cosby and Francis W. Whitfield and Colonel James Starnes.

Federal general Rosecrans at Nashville was readying a major move. Forrest soon noted some of the preparations from his Spring Hill headquarters in Middle Tennessee. He reported on June 1 that all Federal cavalry had gathered around Murfreesboro, and Nashville's streets were being lined with ditches and sandbags. The Federals, he said, "intend to move either forward or backward."[5]

Bragg paid attention but did little. The next day, June 2, he wrote Richmond that Rosecrans was about to do "something important"—possibly "attack or . . . reinforce Grant," who by then was besieging Vicksburg after twice unsuccessfully assaulting its trenches. Bragg asked for aid if the move turned out to be against Middle or East Tennessee and ordered a forward feint by his commanders on June 3 to develop the situation.[6]

While Forrest watched Rosecrans, Rosecrans eyed Forrest. Rosecrans had parried pleas from superiors to take one or the other course Bragg feared. On May 27, President Lincoln, fearing an attack on Grant's rear as he besieged Vicksburg, wired Rosecrans to "do your utmost, short of rashness," to see that Bragg did not leave Middle Tennessee. His foremost fear was obvious: "Where is Forrest's headquarters?" Messages flew between Washington and Tennessee concerning Forrest. Commanders feared he had gone to Mississippi. Intelligence soon indicated that much of his command, Jackson's division, had gone to Mississippi to aid Johnston.[7]

The object of all this concern set off from Spring Hill on a June 4 reconnaissance in force to Franklin. The operation yielded only the capture of a herd of beef cattle and a heavy skirmish with the Federal garrison at Franklin. The action soon became notable in another context, though.[8]

Artillery chief John Morton was absent on other duty, so on this mission, his friend Lieutenant A. Wills Gould commanded the cannons. Gould had incurred Forrest's rage a month earlier by losing two guns at Day's Gap during the Streight chase. At Franklin, Forrest scolded Gould again. Accusing him of timidity in carrying out orders to post his pieces atop a hill, he asked if the lieutenant was afraid. "No, General, I am only protecting my men from the sharpshooters," Gould replied. From all accounts, Gould was just being prudent. When Morton later inquired into the matter, he found that recoil had been pushing Gould's guns back down the hill; they had to be rolled forward after every shot. Morton apparently saw nothing timid about Gould; he several times commended his friend for bravery.[9]

Forrest, it seems, just did not like Gould. Perhaps he felt locked into antagonism by his own raging remarks to and about the lieutenant after the loss of the guns at Day's Gap. Morton wrote that the Day's Gap loss occurred because cavalrymen assigned to support Gould fell back under hot fire, and several of the horses had been shot and fallen, tangling their harnesses so that the guns could not be moved. It is also possible that Forrest had begun fancying contempt in the eyes of all educated officers who were not overtly admiring of him. Morton plainly idolized him, but Gould, Morton's schoolmate, was not so demonstrative. His manner tended to be quiet, and likely more so after Day's Gap. Friends described Gould as "slow and imperturbable" but also "supersensitive." How sensitive, Forrest would soon learn.

Forrest ordered Gould transferred, which Gould took as disparaging of his honor. Finding Forrest lunching at the home of a friend in Columbia, the lieutenant asked to talk. Forrest said they could meet that afternoon, June 14, in the Masonic hall where the command was headquartered. Morton heard about the appointment and doubtless feared its overtones. He tried to find Forrest; he did not know his chief was at the friend's home. Unable to locate him, Morton then rode to the artillery camp to find Gould—but Gould had already gone to see Forrest.[10]

Forrest had set the meeting at the quartermaster's office, where he had business. Gould arrived promptly, and Forrest suggested they talk outside the office, in a hallway. They began walking the hall, Gould wearing a linen duster over his uniform, Forrest toying with a half-opened pocketknife. Four young boys, having turned out to see the hero who had ridden down Streight, watched from outside on the building's front steps.[11]

Gould asked why he was being transferred. Forrest would say only that his mind was made up and Gould would no longer be in his command. Not "slow and imperturbable" now, Gould heatedly said that Forrest's order reflected on his honor. Forrest apparently made an accusation. An onlooker heard Gould say, "That's all false."

In that era, especially in the South, calling a man a liar was a provocation to fight. Forrest, pocketknife still in his hand, would have noted the outline of the pistol sagging the pocket of the lieutenant's duster.

Both men apparently sensed they had passed a point of no return. Forrest dodged to one side and raised a hand by reflex, trying to access his only weapon with the other. Bringing the half-open pocketknife to his mouth, he finished opening it with his teeth and lunged toward Gould. Gould fired his pistol through the duster pocket. The ball struck Forrest in the left side at the hip. Gould pulled the pistol from the duster pocket to fire again, and Forrest pushed it away with his free hand. With the other, he drove the knife forward, striking Gould between two ribs. The lieutenant, spurting blood, yanked free. He lurched past the four boys on the steps and reeled down the stairs and up the street.[12]

Forrest's quartermaster, Major C. S. Severson, ran out behind Gould. "Stop that man!" Severson shouted into the street. "He's shot General Forrest!"

Two civilian doctors supervising a Columbia hospital were walking together near the Masonic hall. They heard Severson's shout and saw a man
crossing the street with blood gushing onto his duster. "My God, it's Willis
[*sic*] Gould," exclaimed Luke Ridley of Murfreesboro. Ridley and the
other physician, James Wilkes of Columbia, hurried to Gould and helped
him into a tailor shop. They put him on a table to try to stop the bleeding, and Ridley hurried to the hospital for instruments. The four boys
from the Masonic building had followed Gould, and now a crowd gathered. They saw Wilkes roll Gould's shirt up to his armpit to reveal a stab
wound to the ribs. With every breath, "the blood would spurt out, often
spattering us boys," one recalled. The boys could not move because of the
press of the crowd. Wilkes tried to slow the bleeding with his hands until
Ridley could arrive with medical equipment.[13]

The doctor waited for his colleague in vain; his patient's violent encounter was not over. Forrest had hurried out of the Masonic hall into the
office of another physician, L. P. Yandell, who took a quick look and told
Forrest to get to the hospital. The wound was near the intestines, Yandell
said, and—with summer heat already setting in—could be fatal. Forrest
rebuckled his pants and headed for the street, vowing not to spend his
last energies in a bed while his assailant still breathed. "No damn man will
kill me and live," he raged leaving the doctor's office.[14]

Colonel Lee Bullock, the provost marshal, met Forrest on the street.
He told him there was no need to pursue; Gould's wound looked fatal.
Forrest ordered him out of the way: "I am mortally wounded and will kill
the man who shot me."[15]

This was the Forrest of the battlefield, unbridled and terrible. He grabbed
two pistols, one from a Confederate officer and one from a holster on a
horse at a hitching post in front of the doctor's office. He was heading
down an alley when he saw the crowd at the tailor shop. Entering its front
door with a pistol in each hand, he shouted, "Look out! Look out!" to get
the crowd out of his line of fire. The mob shied and Gould, all too aware
of the prospect of doom, lunged off the table, again bloodying the boys. He
dived out the back door as Forrest fired. The bullet hit a wall outside and
ricocheted into the leg of a soldier. But Gould's strength was spurting
away. He fell in a patch of high weeds behind the store. Forrest, furious,
had run back out the front door and now came down an alley beside the

shop. Arriving at the patch of weeds, he nudged a motionless Gould with his foot. "You have killed him, General!" onlookers said.[16]

"Damn him, he has killed *me*," Forrest said.[17]

He went back into the shop and told Wilkes to follow him. The doctor demurred, saying his first obligation was to his patient. Forrest cursed and let him know that, by God, he had another patient now. Going out the door, they met Ridley coming from the hospital, and Forrest ordered both of them into a buggy. He then got in under his own power. The vehicle picked up a third physician, a Dr. Sam Frierson, on the way to the home of a Confederate officer, Colonel William Galloway. The four young witnesses to the violence, unwilling to miss anything else, hung onto the back of the buggy. At the Galloway home, the doctors tried to help Forrest upstairs, but he pulled away and went up on his own, apparently infuriated that amid a war he could die so needlessly.[18]

Then he learned he would not die. The trio of doctors examined him and said the ball, having passed around the pelvic bone into what one of the boys—who later became a local historian—later delicately termed the "large muscles of the hip," had inflicted little more than a flesh wound. The projectile could be cut out, they said, and prepared to do it.

Forrest's manner changed mercurially. His selfish behavior—or perhaps his disclosure of his dread of death—now seemed to appall him. "It's just a little pistol ball; let it alone!" he roared. He ordered Ridley to hasten to his victim. If Gould was still alive, Ridley was to take him to the Nelson House Hotel and give him every comfort, at Forrest's expense. Ridley hurried to obey and found that one of Forrest's staff members had already taken Gould to the hotel. Wilkes and Frierson, meanwhile, treated Forrest.[19]

Gould lingered for a few days. One story has it that he asked to see Forrest and, when the general was helped to his bedside, requested forgiveness, saying he was thankful that if one of them had to die, it was him, so that Forrest would be "spared to the country." By this account, Forrest forgave Gould and said he regretted that his wound was mortal. Both men's declarations have been characterized as tearful.[20]

Another story says no such reconciliation occurred. Whatever happened, Forrest seems to have been ashamed and regretful of the incident. He afterward maintained that he "never wanted to kill anybody" except a wartime enemy of his country.[21]

The wound from Gould, Forrest's second of the war, kept him from the saddle for twelve days. Had he been mobile during that time, Bragg might have known more about a massive push that Rosecrans's Federals began against his army on June 24.[22]

Once again, the Federals appeared to fear Forrest more than Bragg valued him. In downpours of rain, a heavy Union column started south from Murfreesboro, threatening to separate Forrest at Spring Hill from the rest of Bragg's army. As they arrayed their troops, Federal commanders wired each other trying to ascertain his whereabouts.

The Murfreesboro move was a diversion. The primary Federal drive was southeast, around the Confederate right, to try to flank Bragg out of Middle Tennessee. The coordinated movements bewildered Bragg, headquartered at Shelbyville. He began falling back on June 26 in heavy rain, barely ahead of the enemy feinting southward from Murfreesboro.

Wheeler had only a small force with which to guard Bragg's long wagon train as it slipped and slid southeastward toward Tullahoma, so he ordered Forrest to join him on the Murfreesboro-Shelbyville highway. Forrest and his men had to breast driving rain and wade water and mud to get there. They arrived on the afternoon of June 27, by which time Federal cavalry under Major General David Stanley had chased Wheeler's outnumbered horsemen—Bragg's rear guard—past Forrest's front and across the Duck River into Shelbyville.[23]

Forrest sent Wheeler word to hold the Duck River Bridge, and Wheeler tried. He had just four hundred cavalrymen and two cannon, and Stanley's cavalry finally overran them. Wheeler and sixty troopers who had not fled or been captured jumped their horses twenty feet into the Duck and swam through hails of gunfire. Fewer than half made it. Meanwhile, assuming from the sound of the fighting that the bridge had fallen, Forrest took another route west and south of Shelbyville. He did not send word to Wheeler or know that Wheeler had defended the bridge for him so heroically.[24]

The Army of Tennessee had to resort to all but full flight to elude Rosecrans. Bragg headed for the Cumberland Mountains and Chattanooga beyond, his cavalry waging a running fight to keep his flanks free. Forrest's retreat, too, was almost headlong. At the railroad town of Cowan, from which Forrest's wife had hailed, he ran head-on into his growing legend. He was retreating at a gallop through town when a local woman denounced him.

"You great big coward, you, why don't you turn and fight instead of running like a cur?" she screamed. "If old Bedford Forrest was here, he'd make you fight!"[25]

The "coward" apparently loped on toward Chattanooga without replying.

25

MAY 19–JULY 3, 1863—
GRANT AT VICKSBURG

"The Enemy Are in Our Grasp"

Staggering after their humiliating stampede across the Big Black River, Major General John Pemberton's Confederate remnant limped back into Vicksburg on the night of May 17. Two days later, Grant ordered an assault. The effort was piecemeal, underequipped, and ill planned. Grant launched it because he and virtually all his subordinates believed the Confederates to be so demoralized that any offensive would drive them to quit.[1]

The Federals were wrong. Commanded so wretchedly in the crushing defeats at Champion Hill and Big Black River, Pemberton's troops were not so dependent on his nerve and sagacity once they were again behind Vicksburg's ramparts. Battle-hardened, they stiffened within their impregnable defenses that included trench-backed ramparts studded with nine mini-fortresses: multisided redoubts, spearhead-shaped redans, three-sided lunettes, and jutting salients. Boasting some 125 cannons, these fanned out to cover the seven major avenues of entry into the city: six roads as well as the Southern Railroad of Mississippi, the formal name of the tracks to Jackson.[2]

On May 19, Grant launched the assault he and his generals vainly hoped would induce the surrender of all this. His three corps semicircled a nine-mile Confederate front running from the Yazoo City Road along the Mississippi north of the city to the Warrenton Road along the Mississippi to

BATTLE OF VICKSBURG

its south. Only Sherman, who had possessed himself of the bluffs on the Federal right—which he had so disastrously attacked back in December—was close enough to the trenches to move in at the 2 p.m. starting time. Sherman so expected to see immediate white flags that his men did not even carry ladders to climb the enemy parapets.

Sherman's charge began with lusty cheers that soon died in a valley of cane, brush, fallen timber, and grass-hidden sinkholes. Fierce return fire sent his men diving for cover. Sherman had ordered his Second Brigade commander, Thomas Kilby Smith, to get his men up to the parapet and jump in when the Confederates yielded, but the Confederates did not yield. Hidden in trees, their sharpshooters picked off Union officers, and the parapets were too high to scale without ladders. Smith huddled below the parapets until dark, when the Confederates set houses afire to see how to throw explosives into the ditch protecting the Federals. A colonel realized the danger just in time and ordered a pullback from the ditch. By the time the Thirteenth US Infantry made it back to the Federal line, it had taken fifty-five bullets to its flag and lost 43 percent of its men.[3]

Around nightfall, Grant aborted the effort. He had suffered 942 casualties and gained only a few better positions from which to attack next time.[4]

The next Federal attempt came three days later. Grant was better prepared—and he quickly became even less satisfied with John McClernand than he had been before.

Like Grant, McClernand had to feel that the long Vicksburg campaign was nearing its climax. Unlike Grant, he had little reason for joy. Grant, Sherman, and McPherson had robbed him of leadership of the West's most momentous campaign. With that command went the political fruits of the looming victory. The final Vicksburg battle would likely be McClernand's last chance to share in the opening of the Mississippi, commercial lifeline of the Midwest. If he distinguished himself in the battle to come, his renown could induce fellow Illinois Democrats, who had won power in the legislature in 1862, to name him a senator, replacing incumbent William A. Richardson, in the upcoming 1864 elections. An Illinois governor's race was also in the offing, and glory at Vicksburg might put McClernand in a race against Governor Richard Yates. It would also reinforce his ties to Lincoln, who faced growing Democratic clamor for peace and would benefit from a bellicose Democratic running mate. A victorious general might even be able to win the Democratic Party's nomination to oppose Lincoln himself. Only battlefield fame could actualize such pipe dreams.

So McClernand remained a manic, recalcitrant pest. In Grant's zeal to press Pemberton while keeping Johnston off his rear, he sent a May 20 order to a McClernand subordinate, General Alvin Hovey, to hold Black River Bridge. McClernand, uninformed of Grant's order and seeking all available force for the attack on Vicksburg, ordered Hovey to join him in front of the city. Hovey obeyed but notified Grant to make sure the commander had okayed the McClernand directive. Hovey reminded Grant that the bridge was now unguarded.[5]

The usually cool Grant waxed hot. He had written Sherman on May 17 that he did not think Johnston would attempt a rescue of Vicksburg, but after his repulsed attack on May 19, he was no longer sure. Now his furious outburst over McClernand's abandonment of the Black River Bridge spawned a rumor that he had relieved the Illinois politician-general. He had not, obviously still respecting McClernand's Lincoln ties, but he was angry. McClernand, too fixated on his own advancement to heed Grant's ire, kept hyping his own deeds and denigrating others'. He informed Grant that he had "suffered considerable loss" getting his men into position on May 20 and heard "nothing" from McPherson and Sherman to his right. Concentration on a particular point would best assure success, he advised in one of five presumptuous dispatches he sent Grant on May 20 alone. The only other alternative, he said, was a siege.[6]

Grant quickly readied another attack, but with less ebullience than he had shown for that of May 19. In his order for the new assault, he justified this second try on the ground that it might be less costly than delaying further. Each passing day allowed Confederates to strengthen their defenses and increased the chance of aid from their comrades.[7]

G rant's second Vicksburg attack began early on May 22. It opened with a four-hour bombardment by more than two hundred land cannon plus others on Admiral David Porter's gunboats. At 10 a.m., the barrage decreased to pinpoint shelling, and the infantry surged forward behind detachments carrying scaling ladders.[8]

McClernand's men advanced along the Jackson railroad against three bastions in the Vicksburg defense line: the so-called Square Fort to the left, the Railroad Redoubt in the center, and, to the right, a crescent-shaped lunette manned by the Second Texas Infantry. Beyond the lunette, McPherson's men aimed for the so-called Great Redoubt on the Jackson Road. Still farther right, on Graveyard Road, Sherman confronted the Stockade Redan.[9]

These Confederate defenses were daunting. The Railroad Redoubt consisted of a fort surrounded by a ditch ten feet deep and six feet wide with walls twenty feet high, its front protected by enfilading musket and artillery fire from both flanks. Under already-murderous volleys, McClernand's Twenty-second Iowa formed atop a hill and advanced on the ditch fronting the redoubt. There the Iowans charged into both the enfilading and the head-on fire.[10]

McClernand's charge succeeded in penetrating the Railroad Redoubt. The deepest of minimal Union incursions, it was nevertheless superficial. Cannon fire had blown a hole where the redoubt jutted farthest toward the attackers, and twelve Iowans scaled the parapet and entered the breach. There, in a sort of foyer of the fort, they fought hand to hand with a small contingent of the Thirtieth Alabama, ejecting most of the Alabamans. Not all, though. A lieutenant and a dozen riflemen hid in a corner as the few survivors of the small group of Iowans planted their flag on the parapet and returned to the ditch. An hour later, after some fifteen more volunteers from the Thirtieth Alabama had tried and failed to drive the Federals from the ditch, some Iowans reentered the fort and captured the Alabama remnant. But that was as far as the Iowans would get.[11]

On the other end of the Union line, Sherman's men were even less successful. Under protective artillery fire, a 150-man volunteer scaling party went forward toward Stockade Redan in a northeastward bulge in the left of the Confederate battlements. The Thirtieth Ohio, behind the scaling detachment, ran forward in a hurrahing column of fours. A few of the ladder carriers got part way up the wall, and a private of the Federal Eighth Missouri planted there the headquarters flag of Sherman's brother-in-law and foster brother Brigadier General Hugh Boyle Ewing. Then two ranks of Confederate infantry drove them back, killing 19 and wounding 34 of the 150. The surviving ladder carriers and the infantry in their rear shot every Confederate who crawled out to capture the flag. But the Thirtieth Ohio was stopped, its path clotted with dead and wounded piling up from the hot Confederate small arms fire. The fire and carnage blocked the rest of Major General Frank Blair's three brigades to Sherman's immediate left. They sought a better route, but without success.[12]

Situated between Sherman and McClernand, McPherson's Seventeenth Corps was not as busy. Just one of the four brigades McPherson had on the field, that of Brigadier General John Stevenson, saw heavy action. Stevenson reported that his orders were to advance with fixed bayonets without firing a shot, so his Seventh Missouri and Eighty-first Illinois advanced silently to the right into "volley after volley." To the left, the Eighth Illinois and Thirty-second Ohio also advanced. Confederate fire forced their column farther leftward, but they pushed their way to the ditch fronting the Confederate fortifications.

Confederate fire tore great holes in the ranks to the left, and the Illinoisans and Ohioans dropped prone until it slacked. When it did, they charged. Five bearers of the green flag of the Missouri Irishmen went down, but the sixth jabbed its staff into the slope of the Confederate works. That was as far as they got. Beside them, two-thirds of the Eighty-first Illinois were killed or wounded. Still, they obeyed the order not to fire. "It seemed like madness," a member of the Thirty-second Ohio told his diary. By 10:30 a.m. Stevenson ordered the sufferers withdrawn. He had lost 272 men in half an hour.[13]

Grant watched from a hill. Within an hour after the infantry went forward at 10 a.m., the failure was obvious. Grant was about to ride to Sherman's headquarters to call it off when a courier arrived from Mc-Clernand. His message, penned at 11:15 a.m., said he was "hotly engaged" with enemy massing right and left and needed a strong assault by McPherson. McPherson had been minimally active up to then, but Grant had endured eighteen months of McClernand's attempts to command his army, and he was plainly fed up. At 11:50, Grant wrote back and told McClernand to use reserves as well as units shifted from inactive parts of his line. He did not know that all but one of McClernand's brigades were fighting for their lives.

Grant rode to meet Sherman, arriving as another courier found him. The note said McClernand's men were in enemy trenches "at several points, but are brought to a stand." Grant replied that Brigadier General John McArthur, marching from Warrenton since a day before, was to Mc-Clernand's left and should be used to best advantage. Grant obviously did not know McArthur was still three miles south of town.[14]

A third McClernand note came just past noon. It said McClernand had "*part* possession of two forts" and that the Stars and Stripes flew over them. He demanded a "vigorous push . . . all along the line." Grant's 2:30 p.m. reply repeated his unwittingly irrelevant instructions regarding McArthur. He added that he had ordered McPherson to send Brigadier General Isaac Quinby's division to McClernand's aid if Quinby could not pierce Confederate defenses where he was. But if

Quinby could make a successful charge on McClernand's right, Grant said, it would aid McClernand as much as reinforcements.[15]

Grant knew too well McClernand's tendency to self-promote. During the morning attack, from his hilltop, he had seen no indication that McClernand had broken through Vicksburg's defense line. But the hill from which Grant had been observing was a mile and a half from McClernand, and now, at Sherman's position, Grant was even farther off. There was no time to gallop over for a look. In deciding what to do, Grant doubtless considered what McClernand would tell Lincoln: that McClernand had the battle won until Grant refused help. At 2 p.m., Grant ordered Quinby sent to McClernand.[16]

McClernand's claims were disingenuous and incomplete. The brigade of the hard-fighting Irishman, Brigadier General Michael Lawler, did battle to the very mouth of the Railroad Redoubt and plant flags there, but hails of Confederate fire from both sides prevented him from getting more than a dozen or so men inside it. The brigades of Brigadier Generals William Benton and Stephen Burbridge did more damage on the Second Texas lunette, Burbridge's dragging up a cannon to fire into one of its gun windows and sow mayhem inside. At a critical moment, however, division commander Eugene Carr called away two of Burbridge's four regiments to shore up Benton in a move endorsed by McClernand. Time was of the essence for capitalizing on the toeholds at both the redoubt and the lunette, and the easiest unit to reinforce them with would have been that of William Spicely, one of McClernand's own. But McClernand did not order Spicely forward, and his unit did nothing in the fight.[17]

There followed an afternoon of bloody, uncoordinated lunges to comply with McClernand's demands for aid and stepped-up action by his fellow corps commanders. Sherman, hurrying to assist McClernand's effort as fast as he could get units ready, launched separate assaults at different points along his front at 2:15 p.m., 3 p.m., and 4 p.m. All failed. The intervals between each gave Confederates time to react in turn. Action was similar in front of McPherson and McClernand. McPherson's renewal of his minimal morning effort was even more lackluster.[18]

Perhaps the best chance for a real breakthrough was south of town. By mid-afternoon, McArthur—still roughly three miles from the Union lines—had his men forty yards from the so-called South Fort on the Warrenton Road. He claimed to be close enough to downtown Vicksburg to read building signs, and Admiral Porter's gunboats had the Confederates inside the fort so pinned down that they gave up trying to get artillery into position to resist a ground attack. McArthur had issued directions for an assault and was about to launch it when couriers arrived ordering him to go to McClernand. He did not arrive there until well after dark.[19]

McClernand's misleading messages had cost dearly. Hundreds more Federals had died and been wounded in the unnecessary afternoon actions. The day's Union total—compared to an estimated, never officially reported Confederate sum of 500—was 502 dead, 2,550 wounded, and 147 missing. Grant was angry. He had the grit to send men to die when their deaths seemed likely to reap gain, but this afternoon's carnage was sickening and hardly helpful to his own reputation. He considered cashiering McClernand on the spot.[20]

But he held off. Two of his favorite subordinates, Sherman and McPherson, had not distinguished themselves on this day, so he likely did not want to invite attention to their performances. He himself could have better coordinated some of the afternoon attacks, and he did not need to bring attention to that either. So he would suffer the politician-general a little longer, perhaps until Pemberton raised the white flag. Vicksburg's certain surrender, whenever it came, would bring cachet to counter McClernand's Lincoln connection.

G rant settled in to wait beneath the boiling Dixie sun. On May 23, in answer to a Porter letter informing him of McArthur's missed chance at South Fort, he praised Porter's efforts and said Vicksburg was doomed; the only question was when it would fall. Until it did, he intended to lose no more men in bloody charges.[21]

He waited until May 24 to write Halleck. When he did, he detailed the positions of his three corps and the completeness of their investment before mentioning the May 22 repulse. He said Vicksburg's defenses had been too strong—by nature and human improvement—to storm; his men had not been defeated, just stopped short of victory.

Then he got to McClernand. The Union loss had not been "very heavy" until McClernand called for aid and "misled me as to the real state of facts and caused much of the loss. He is entirely unfit for the position of Corps Commander both on the march and on the battlefield." Grant could be sure that Halleck shared this opinion. Ever since Halleck and he had collaborated in hijacking McClernand's army back in December, he knew for certain that Halleck disliked and distrusted McClernand as much as he himself did.

Still, Grant assured Halleck, the prospects at Vicksburg remained favorable, McClernand notwithstanding. "The enemy," Grant wrote, "are now undoubtedly in our grasp." There was, of course, the matter of the Confederates gathering in his rear, but he would be ready for them. He and Sherman had seen to it that the railroad to Jackson was now badly damaged, so the enemy would have to haul arms and supplies over the forty-five intervening miles by horse or mule. His own army, meanwhile, was "in the finest health and spirits."[22]

Well, not all of it. Refusing to signal any weakness of resolve to Pemberton or Washington, Grant did not request a truce to collect wounded and bury dead. The sun-blistered, stinking slaughter lay in front of the trenches until May 25. Finally, Pemberton requested the truce, and Grant agreed to a two-and-a-half-hour cease-fire. Most of the surviving wounded, who had groaned between the two lines for three days, were by then not long for the world.[23]

McClernand became, if anything, more confrontational after the botched May 22 attack. He wrote Illinois governor Yates on May 28 about rumors that he was being blamed for the attack's failure and for Sherman's and McPherson's casualties; his letter seemed to angle for a government inquiry. Then, on receiving a Grant order in early June, McClernand exploded. Grant aide James Harrison Wilson handed him the directive, and McClernand howled, "I'll be goddamned if I'll do it—I am tired of being dictated to—I won't stand it any longer; and you can go back and tell General Grant!" McClernand cursed Wilson, too, then backed off. "I am not cursing *you*," he said. "I was simply expressing my intense vehemence on the subject matter." The sentence became a recurring laugh line at Grant headquarters.[24]

On June 4, McClernand wrote to Grant to protest in person. The army's May 22 attack had failed, he said, despite "a determined effort, *at least on my part,*" to comply with Grant's order "to carry and hold the works." He demanded that Grant quell whispering about him within the army—rumors that, he said, amounted to a "systematic effort to destroy my usefulness and character as a commander." The last thing Grant cared to do was vouch for McClernand's military effectiveness. He did not reply.[25]

Two weeks later, though, McClernand overstepped again. This time, Grant pounced. On June 16, General Frank Blair saw in the Memphis *Evening Bulletin* a McClernand address congratulating his troops for their performance on May 22; in effect, McClernand was congratulating McClernand. The document also impugned Grant's leadership, asserting that "massing a strong force in time upon a weakened point would have probably insured success." Grant might well have coordinated the May 22 attack more efficiently, but McClernand would have done worse. He had divided up Quinby's division when it was sent to him, the reverse of what he said Grant should have done, and he had not used one of his own brigades, Spicely's, at all.

McPherson saw the same document in the St. Louis *Missouri Democrat* that Blair had seen in the *Evening Bulletin*. Blair took the paper to Sherman, who forwarded it to Grant. McPherson did the same, and Grant shot McClernand a curt note asking whether the published version was "a true copy" of the document. If it was not, he wanted one "as required by regulations and existing orders of the Department."

McClernand crawfished. He replied that the published version was indeed authentic but blamed his adjutant for not sending Grant a copy. He could not resist, though, issuing a direct challenge to his superior. He was ready, he said, "to maintain its statements."[26]

This time, McClernand had gone too far. With May 22 looking more and more like the climactic fight of the campaign, he was frantic to wring the last vote out of it. In so doing, he provided Grant with justification for finally casting this scheming, Lincoln-backed albatross from around his neck.

That Grant had functioned so well for so long while coping with McClernand reflected the commander's iron will and heady restraint— qualities by which he had disarmed or outlasted a string of others far above himself in pay grade and supposed quality. Henry Halleck, so frightened by Grant's aggressiveness early on that he had tried to replace him, by late 1862 had begun to perceive that the sometimes sloppy, nominal drunkard was not only competent but perhaps exceptional. Former general in chief George McClellan, grand on the drill field and wavering in battle, had been outraged at seeing Lieutenant Grant drunk on duty on the antebellum frontier—but McClellan was now sacked and retired. And Secretary of War Edwin Stanton, who had blown hot and cold about Grant, had been counterbalanced by Stanton's influential emissary, Charles Dana, an unequivocal Grant admirer. Grant's tenacity and willingness to flout military orthodoxy, so emphatically displayed in his bottling up of Vicksburg, had awed them all.

Halleck, McClellan, Stanton, and McClernand had epitomized the Federal high command's unconscious prejudice against the commoner. They also represented its shortcomings, typifying its bureaucratic fixation on self-preservation and advancement rather than on winning the war. But each had, in his own way, been neutralized—except McClernand. Now McClernand, too, had reached the brink. His pushy politics had backed an ultramilitary Halleck into Grant's corner; Halleck now staunchly supported Grant in conferences with McClernand's diffident sponsor, Lincoln. The last of Grant's major intra-army foes, McClernand—like Vicksburg on the Mississippi—was the final bastion of all-out anti-Grant antagonism in the West.

Now, Grant finally felt secure enough to do what he had long ached to do. Ignoring the statements in McClernand's published report, he focused on the fact that it had been published without permission. Dana wrote Stanton that this was only "the occasion" of Grant's action, "not its cause." Dana said the real cause was McClernand's repeated disobeying of orders, his continual spirit of insubordination, his incompetence, and, above all, his relations with peer commanders, which were so sour that he could not command the army if Grant were incapacitated.[27]

On the evening of June 18, John Rawlins issued an order he surely relished writing. McClernand, whom Rawlins had once termed a "damned, slinking, Judas bastard," was relieved of command. He was ordered home to Illinois and replaced by Major General Edward Ord.[28]

McClernand replied immediately. Noting that he had been appointed by Lincoln, he said he "might justly challenge" Grant's order but would not "at present." He raised the subject of, but did not quite call for, an investigation. Grant waited a week, perhaps for political fallout, then came as close to gloating as he ever did. In a letter to Adjutant General Lorenzo Thomas in Washington summarizing his action, he concluded that McClernand's removal "has given general satisfaction," McClernand's erstwhile corps "sharing, perhaps, equally in that feeling with the other Corps of the Army."[29]

McClernand was gone, but the job of starving out Vicksburg remained. Its Confederates were so tightly encircled that Joe Johnston could get messages inside only by entrusting coded versions to nocturnal swimmers whom he sent to ply the Mississippi. They had to hold onto logs and float down to a portion of the riverbank within the city's defenses. The process required days or weeks. Union shelling had run townspeople and soldiers into caves, where they ate pets and rats. Federals burrowed trenches ever nearer to the ramparts, threw primitive grenades inside, and took potshots at defenders—at all but point-blank range—when they peeked out.[30]

Despite the siege's successes, though, Grant had concerns. The vaunted Johnston lurked in the Mississippi interior with thin ranks swelled somewhat, apparently, by conscription. And early June had brought a Confederate attempt to destroy Grant's trans-Mississippi supply line. On June 7 and 8, at Pemberton's insistence, troops under Major General Richard Taylor attacked three Federal garrisons in Louisiana: Lake Providence, Young's Point, and Milliken's Bend. Two of these three were helping build the Union's new biracial—though segregated—army. The camp at Young's Point organized blacks into regiments, four of which formed most of the garrison at Milliken's Bend.[31]

The Louisiana attacks failed, but the overtones were enormous. Lincoln had first resisted the idea of black soldiery, but he relented as he considered the terror it could engender in Dixie. Southern-born and wedded into a slave-owning Kentucky family, he said the sight of large numbers of armed bondsmen would frighten Southerners into surrender. He was correct about the frightening, but he misjudged the result. Federal issuance of rifles to recent slaves risked sparking a race war within the war, and now

GENERAL JOSEPH E. JOHNSTON

the fuse had been lit in the western theater. Confederates now regarded Union victory as Armageddon. They and their forebears had always met mere hints of slave uprising with brutality, and they now redoubled it.[32]

When Taylor attacked the Louisiana garrisons, however, it was the black soldiers whose performance stood out. Confederate intelligence regarding Union numbers at the three Louisiana installations had been faulty, and the attackers were outnumbered at Lake Providence and Young's Point; the Federals chased them away with mere skirmishing. But at Milliken's Bend, 1,500 Texans under Brigadier General Henry McCulloch drove the 1,000-plus Federals backward into their camp. White Iowa infantrymen fled, and most white officers of the black units did too.

Not the black soldiers, though. Untrained but all too familiar with Dixie's age-old punishments for insurrection, the black troops at Milliken's Bend battled desperately. With minimal knowledge of their Austrian rifles, they got off just one volley at the charging Texans, yet most did not turn and run. They instead fought hand to hand with bayonets and musket butts, then retired to form a second line behind a levee. Huge artillery shells from a hundred-pounder Parrott cannon on the gunboat *Choctaw* kept the Confederates away from that second line. The Texans looted what they could from the part of the camp they had overrun, captured some Federals cut off from their comrades, and took cover. The approach of a second gunboat, the *Lexington*, was enough for McCulloch. He withdrew.[33]

Even the Confederate McCulloch indicated that the best Union soldiers at Milliken's Bend that morning were the black ones. The white Federals "ran like whipped curs," he reported, but the blacks "resisted . . . with considerable obstinacy."[34]

The white Federals may have thought they had more to fear at Milliken's Bend than their black counterparts. The Confederates had gone there to stop the arming of slaves—by committing selective, premeditated murder. They hawked this intent with a black flag emblazoned with a skull and crossbones. They shouted, "No quarter for the officers, kill the damned abolitionists, spare the niggers!" as they crossed the Federal barricades.[35]

These yells were politically correct in Dixie. General Beauregard had responded to the Emancipation Proclamation by calling for wholesale hanging of "abolition prisoners" beginning January 1, 1863, the day the proclamation took effect. A week earlier, Jefferson Davis had ordered all captured members of the new US Colored Troops to be delivered to state governments and tried for insurrection; the standard state penalty was death. But on May 1, 1863, undoubtedly at the behest of slaveholders, the Confederate Congress passed new legislation implicitly recognizing how important slaves were to the South's war effort. It mandated that black soldiers be returned to their masters.[36]

Such dubious mercy was unseen at Milliken's Bend. Despite the reported cry of the attackers, the blacks were not "spared." McCulloch lost 44 killed, 131 wounded, and 10 missing from his force of 1,500. By contrast, of their original 1,061, the inexperienced and outnumbered Federals lost more than half: 101 killed, 285 wounded, and 266 missing. The fates of the missing could only be surmised—at least, until a story from a Texan deserter came to Grant on June 22. The man said that, after retreating to Richmond, Louisiana, General Taylor had put his troops in formation to formally hang a white Federal captain and several black soldiers captured at Milliken's Bend.[37]

Grant wrote Taylor the day he heard the story. The behavior of African American troops at Milliken's Bend had changed his opinion of black soldiers. To the son of his old Mexican War hero, General Zachary Taylor, Grant noted that the attacked Federals had captured and spared the lives of six or eight prisoners despite the black flag they were flying. He threatened a response in kind if any other Confederate generals adopted a policy of executing prisoners taken in battle.

Writing back, Taylor lied. He confirmed that he had been at Richmond for several days following the battle. But he claimed he would have ordered "the punishment it deserved" had he heard of such an atrocity. He said the Confederate government had ordered that blacks captured in uniform be turned over to local authorities for punishment under state law.[38]

A deserter's story is questionable, but this one was not the only indication of Confederates killing officers and men of the US Colored Troops. Admiral Porter had gone ashore at Milliken's Bend on the day of the attack and seen dead black soldiers lining the ditch behind the first levee, "mostly shot on top of the head." Porter may have mistaken some hand-to-hand musket butt injuries for gunshot wounds, but whether all were inflicted in combat is open to doubt.

Beyond debate is the fact that at least some high Confederate officers ignored their Congress. They wanted all black or black-connected Union troops killed in or immediately after battles. In the few places where the policy was written down, no reason was mentioned, but—in addition to the obvious one of demanding the supreme penalty for insurrection—the practice eliminated the red tape, not to mention the required guard details, of returning blacks to masters, especially the significant numbers of US Colored Troops who had never been slaves. Brigadier General J. G. Walker reported that in breaking up Federal government-run cotton-raising operations between Milliken's Bend and Lake Providence, he had captured 2,000 African Americans "who have been restored to their masters, with the exception of those captured in arms. . . . I consider it an unfortunate circumstance that any armed negroes were captured." General Taylor's own official report, filed the day after the battle, said that a large number of blacks were killed and wounded and seemed to apologize for the fact that, "unfortunately, some 50, with 2 of their white officers," had been captured. A letter from Taylor's superior on June 13 was even clearer. Lieutenant General Edmund Kirby Smith wrote Taylor of his dissatisfaction at hearing that black troops had been taken alive: "I hope this may not be so, and that your subordinates who may have been in command of capturing parties may have recognized the propriety of giving no quarter to armed negroes and their white officers."[39]

To his discredit, Grant—possibly influenced by his admiration for Taylor's distinguished father—took Taylor's word. He wrote back that he could not believe the report, "although told so straight," and was "truly glad to have your denial." In his defense, he stood up for fairness to black troops at a time when precious few on either side would have. He said he did not know what the Federal policy would be if the execution report proved true, but "I cannot see the justice of permitting one treatment for them and another for the white soldiers." In other words, all uniformed captives should be treated as prisoners of war.[40]

Plainly, though, Grant shrank from further investigation of the looming, monstrous, and dreaded explosion of American racial hatred. He already had learned, when he had tried to send several hundred hungry and homeless fugitive slaves north from West Tennessee the previous autumn, that the overwhelming majority of Northern whites and politicians were unsympathetic. Their reaction to the killing of black soldiers after surrender was unlikely to be much different. Despite his wish that black and white soldiers be treated the same, Grant surely knew that backing for such a policy would be tepid at best. He kicked talk of the Milliken's Bend atrocities under the rug.

The prevailing racism of the time notwithstanding, there was almost certainly another reason Grant turned away from the subject so quickly. The day he wrote his second letter to Taylor, July 4, was a full one.

On July 3, Pemberton proposed a cease-fire. The Confederate commander wanted to name commissioners to arrange surrender terms, and he and Grant met under a flag of truce to discuss the matter. The two had served in the same unit in Mexico, and they now came together again on Vicksburg's bloody, sun-baked field. Grant later recalled that because of their prior association, he knew Pemberton well; nonetheless, this meeting was tense.

Pemberton had sent Grant a letter to propose the meeting. Grant had agreed to meet but said he could not agree to name commissioners to draft conditions for capitulation; his only terms were unconditional surrender. Now, as they met under a small oak tree, Grant greeted Pemberton as "an old acquaintance," but the atmosphere swiftly turned somber. Pemberton, apparently thinking Grant's letter to him had been a ploy, asked what terms he offered in return for Pemberton's surrender. The same as he had named in his letter, Grant replied. "The conference might as well end," Pemberton snapped, turning to leave.

"Very well," Grant said.[41]

The two parted but agreed to confer further by messenger. Pemberton warned Grant that, with no agreement, Grant would "bury more of your men before you enter Vicksburg." Grant made no reply except to give him a long look, not moving a muscle. The look said Pemberton would bury men too.[42]

That evening, subordinates asked Grant to bend a little. McPherson said paroling Pemberton's 30,000 men would cost the Union less than shipping them north for imprisonment. It also would prevent tying up steamboats needed elsewhere in the war. There was the danger that the Confederates would break their paroles and reenter the fight after being sent home, but the odds seemed against that happening generally. A number of the Confederates, especially Vicksburg's Tennessee and Georgia troops, were reportedly refusing to fight.

Grant thought many of them, paroled, would quit the war. He therefore took McPherson's suggestion. But he also loosed a psychological weapon to leverage Pemberton. As he sent his offer to the Confederate general, he ordered his commanders to tell their pickets to talk to their Confederate counterparts. The Federals were to confide that if the Confederates surrendered, the men could head directly home instead of to Virginia for the usual paroling process.[43]

At 10 a.m. the next morning, July 4, white flags appeared on Vicksburg's parapets. After hanging eight months in the balance, the Confederate Gibraltar was returning to the Union. Pemberton's 30,000 men—well fortified but starving—capitulated to Grant's 80,000. General John "Black

Jack" Logan's hard-fighting Illinois division marched into the city, unfurled the Stars and Stripes above the courthouse, and shared rations with the hungry Confederates. Aboard Porter's flagship, the admiral broke out celebratory wine. It was, as Sherman put it in a dispatch, "Glory Hallelujah the best fourth of July since 1776."[44]

The tenacious author of the Union victory indulged in one glass with Porter, then retired to plot further strategy. Joe Johnston and his army of 30,000 still lurked. Within hours, Grant had ordered Sherman to find Johnston and "inflict . . . all the punishment you can." Sherman left Vicksburg on July 5, pushed Johnston eastward from the Big Black River to Jackson, then put the Confederate capital under siege beginning July 10. Johnston evacuated Jackson six days later. He faded into the forests of the state's eastward interior, pursued for some ten miles by one Sherman division. The rest of Sherman's troops completed the damage they had done to Jackson and its railroads on their previous visit in May. With Johnston thus banished, Grant recalled Sherman to Vicksburg on July 25.[45]

Grant's mind may already have moved on to Johnston, but there was no overstating the importance of this July 4 and the Vicksburg surrender. The victory at Fort Donelson had been pivotal in Grant's rise because it threw open the gates of the western Confederacy to Union invasion. The skin-of-the-teeth win at Shiloh had throttled a western Confederate comeback and demonstrated that Grant's Donelson performance had been no fluke. But Vicksburg made the other two triumphs look Lilliputian. A showpiece of will, daring, and ingenuity, it solved one of military history's thornier problems and signified that the little man from an Ohio tanning shed, the shabby firewood hawker of the prewar St. Louis streets, had become one of the great captains of all time. His vanquishing of Vicksburg was more consequential than the half-consummated Union victory at Gettysburg the day before. There, Major General George G. Meade had let Lee's defeated troops escape to fight many more days. Grant, by contrast, had bagged a whole Confederate army—his second, doubling the numbers he disarmed at Fort Donelson. From Cairo, Illinois, and continual jeopardy of being replaced, in less than two years Grant had risen to unchallengeable command dominance in the west.

The Vicksburg capture won him a personal victory, but it was just as fateful for the Union. It fulfilled the so-called anaconda plan of old Winfield Scott, the war's first general in chief, who had prophesied this war would be won by capturing the South's rivers and coasts and strangling it to death. Vicksburg's fall and that of Port Hudson, Louisiana, three days later lopped off three whole states—Louisiana, Texas, and Arkansas—from the rest of the Confederacy. The opening of the Mississippi River would provide a powerful and speedy logistical highway for operations against the South's deep interior, the area to which its military industry had fled after Nashville fell. Perhaps most important, though, was the psychological symbolism. The Union had restored to itself the continent's supreme commercial and military artery, its Father of Waters, and had found an invincible general in the process.

The tenacity and ingenuity of Grant's campaign had won the faith of his fellow commoner in the White House. The rail-splitter president, who had endured even more sneers than Grant, seemed finally to see the front-rank potential in this member of their dogged class. Grant soon got an admiring letter, dated July 13, from this man who had dallied so long with his archenemy McClernand: "I write this now as a grateful acknowledgment for the almost inestimable service you have done the country," Lincoln's message read. To a White House confidant, the president made plain that the gratitude he had expressed was no passing fancy.

"Grant is my man and I am his," Lincoln said, "for the rest of the war."[46]

V

CHATTANOOGA

26

AUGUST–SEPTEMBER 1863—
FORREST AT CHICKAMAUGA

"Cross My Path Again at the Peril of Your Life"

From Richmond to deepest Dixie, loss of Vicksburg evoked shrieks for action. Somebody had to do something fast or the western Confederacy would be gone.

The majority of newspaper headlines focused on the war in the east, between the doorsteps of the executive mansions in Washington and Richmond, but much of the muscle, blood, and sinew of rebellion lay farther south and west. Since Confederate loss of the Middle Tennessee metal-forging region northwest of Nashville, most of the South's war-supporting industries had withdrawn far into the interior—to such towns as Selma, Alabama, and Rome and Macon, Georgia. Much food for sustenance of Confederate armies came from Mississippi, Alabama, and Georgia on railroads crucial for its transmission. With the trans-Mississippi now gone via the loss of Vicksburg and Port Hudson, beef and other products of Texas, Louisiana, and Arkansas were similarly cut off. Myriad shortages not already in effect were in prospect.

Two subordinate generals—James Longstreet in Virginia and Nathan Bedford Forrest in Tennessee—proposed solutions.

Longstreet, Robert E. Lee's senior subordinate, wanted out of the Army of Northern Virginia. He had seen Lee reject his counsel and order George Pickett's disastrous Gettysburg charge, and he thought he could better himself and the Confederacy on the other side of the Appalachians.

In the east Lee was supreme, but Braxton Bragg's inability in the west was obvious to all but Jefferson Davis and a few of his military and political supporters. Bragg had bungled his chance to destroy Don Carlos Buell's army in Kentucky in the fall of 1862 and had retreated from Stones River in early January 1863; now he was retreating to Chattanooga, vacating forage-rich central Tennessee and threatening also to cede the state's eastern third and its Virginia-to-Georgia rail line to a Union army moving south from Kentucky under Ambrose Burnside.

Lee reluctantly approved Longstreet's move. For too long he had essentially ignored all fronts but Virginia's; he now had to face reality. Federals were dismembering the lower South, threatening the very foundations of secession. So Lee agreed to send Longstreet to East Tennessee to counter the Kentucky-based threat. Once in the west, Longstreet hoped to succeed Bragg as commander of the Army of the Tennessee. If the Confederacy was to avoid defeat, somebody had to. "I hope that I may get west in time to save what there is left of us," Longstreet wrote a politician friend.[1]

Longstreet, in Virginia at the time, did not know the extent of the ruin. Forrest, in Tennessee, did. For fourteen months, he had had to serve under the vacillating, vengeful, and sickly Bragg, who was increasingly wracked by dyspepsia, neuralgia, and other pains of the stress of his position. Forrest wanted both to escape Bragg and to counter damage Grant had inflicted on the South at Vicksburg. In August, Forrest sent Richmond two copies of a letter—one through Bragg, the other straight to President Davis. He sent the second, he said, because he assumed Bragg would not forward the first.

Forrest's letter asked for a command behind enemy lines: all the forces he could organize between Vicksburg and Cairo, Illinois. In sixty days, he wrote, he could prevent Federal plying of the lower Mississippi and raise several thousand troops who had gone home and become unavailable to the Confederacy otherwise. All he needed, he wrote, was a nucleus of four hundred men armed with four hundred long-range Enfield rifles and four rifled cannons to blow Federal shipping out of the river. He noted that, having lived on the Mississippi for more than twenty years "buying and selling negroes," he knew both sides of it from Memphis to Vicksburg, as well as all the well-to-do slaveholders upriver and down. And the four hundred troops he wanted to accompany him included men who had rafted timber out of the delta and knew the region by heart.

Losing the territory in which he had labored for more than half his life had plainly shaken him. He seemed to lack faith that it could be retaken without desperate measures and a more original approach than Bragg appeared capable of. Forrest doubtless also wished to rid himself of Bragg's insults and injustice. But knowing Bragg was a Davis favorite, Forrest dissembled. He said he would leave his present post "with many regrets, as I am well pleased with the officers in command." Davis may have wondered why, if this was true, Forrest thought Bragg unlikely to forward the letter.[2]

Forrest's plan almost certainly was born, at least partly, of his sour relations with his commander, but likely without the overweening ego with which the chain of command was rife. Forrest claimed to be making his proposal "*entirely* for the good of the service." He added that he had never asked for advancement, which—unlike the claim that his proposition was advanced in complete selflessness—was true.[3]

Forrest's gambit, however, got nowhere. Jefferson Davis said the idea had value but sought Bragg's input. And despite Forrest's statement that he did not expect Bragg to forward the other copy of his letter, Bragg had done so—and effectively thwarted Forrest's ploy. Sending the note to Richmond five days after Forrest penned it, Bragg ambiguously wrote that he knew "no officer to whom I would sooner assign" the independent command Forrest requested. No task, he added, was more important than recovery of territory along the Mississippi. But removing Forrest from the Army of Tennessee would rob it "of one of its greatest elements of strength" at a time of ominous need.

Davis approved Bragg's recommendation of postponing Forrest's request for the time being. He added, though, that the plan might be approved when circumstances changed. Davis thus put off dealing substantively with his western problem.[4]

Circumstances in Tennessee were forbidding. In August, Major General Ambrose Burnside and 12,000 men of the Army of the Ohio neared Knoxville from Kentucky, liberating much of East Tennessee's long-suffering unionist majority.

The region's rage erupted. Mountaineers began taking revenge on secessionist sympathizers who had savaged them for two years. Confederate brigadier general A. E. Jackson reported from upper East Tennessee that many Confederate sympathizers were fleeing with their families and whatever they could carry, chased by unionist guerrillas who were committing "brutal murders." Federal cavalry had reached Knoxville and an abandoned Confederate base at Morristown, cutting Jackson off from East Tennessee commander Simon Buckner and preventing the two from coordinating their defense of the eastern section of the state.[5]

Buckner could not have helped Jackson anyway. On September 1, Bragg ordered Buckner and his 9,000 troops of the Department of East Tennessee to fall back to the Chattanooga area. Forrest at Kingston got the same directive. Two days later, Bragg named Forrest head of the cavalry gathering north of Chattanooga.

Forrest's new subordinates were unpromising. Division commander John Pegram, a thirty-one-year-old West Pointer from Richmond high society, tended toward indecision. He had been recommended for service in the west by Robert E. Lee—possibly, given Lee's lack of concern with the western theater, to get Pegram out of his department. Colonel John S. Scott of the aristocratic First Louisiana was the rich planter who had refused to serve under Forrest when General P. G. T. Beauregard first sent Forrest east from Mississippi. Scott resisted orders from men he deemed his social inferiors and even quarreled with Pegram, who was plainly not.

Forrest's previous associates, like his new subordinates, promised to give trouble. Cooperation between Forrest and Joe Wheeler, commanding the cavalry south of Chattanooga, was potentially problematic, given their Dover disagreement. Fellow Dover participant John Wharton, a brigadier who had been a Wheeler division commander but was for the moment under Forrest, was the Texas attorney with whom Forrest had had a flare-up during the Murfreesboro raid. Wharton's cheerful subordination to Forrest could hardly be taken for granted.[6]

Topping this list of potential recalcitrants was Bragg himself. His continual blunders had sapped his army psychologically. His top generals—Leonidas Polk, John C. Breckinridge, William Hardee, and the just-arriving Virginian Daniel Harvey Hill, brother-in-law of Stonewall Jackson—were (or in Hill's case, soon would be) in open revolt. Further down the chain of command, rampant dislike of Bragg engendered an atmosphere of incipient insubordination. The army's hard-fighting riflemen had seen their valor wasted by Bragg's vacillations in the face of the enemy and flouted by his petty vendettas against all who disagreed with him.

By appointing Forrest to head up one of his major cavalry contingents, Bragg had tossed him a bone—but a meatless one, and Forrest soon showed it had not mollified him. John Morgan had made an unauthorized cavalry raid across the Ohio River throughout most of July that resulted in the capture of Morgan and most of his troopers—and enraged Bragg. The commander had come to dislike Kentuckians as much as Tennesseans since his 1862 Bluegrass invasion, when, despite the promises of Morgan and others, Kentuckians had not flocked to his ranks. Cavalrymen took pride in being soldiers on horseback, but Bragg now directed that the remnant of Morgan's men who had survived the trans-Ohio raid be dismounted and redesignated infantry.

Bragg's September 3 directive naming Forrest commander of the cavalry north of Chattanooga placed the Kentuckians under him, and Forrest disobeyed the order to dismount them. In August, Kentuckian Adam Rankin Johnson, a onetime Forrest scout who had advanced to the rank of colonel under Morgan, had wangled permission from the War Department to reestablish Morgan's unit if he could find horses for it. Johnson worked with fellow Kentuckian Buckner, then still commander of the Department of East Tennessee, to acquire horses and gather several hundred Morgan troopers. Nonetheless, Johnson said, Bragg remained bent on dismounting them and "would have done so, had it not been for the resolute action of Forrest." One order affecting the Kentuckians may have been a general one Bragg issued on September 16 providing that all cavalrymen absent from their commands without authority be assigned to the infantry.

Forrest valued the bravery of the Morgan men, and if they remained mounted, they could be part of Forrest's command. He probably also felt some empathy for Morgan, his fellow cavalry leader. Morgan's background was more refined, but his prewar businesses had, like Forrest's, included slave trafficking, although on a smaller scale. The two were likely acquainted before the war, because Forrest's far-ranging slave buying and selling had taken him from Kentucky to Texas. As soldiers, he and Morgan showed much interest in each other's exploits. Forrest's empathy for his imprisoned fellow cavalryman likely strengthened as Morgan came under Bragg's wrath. According to Johnson, Forrest ran the risk of a court-martial by ignoring Bragg's order. Nonetheless, he did so, not only folding Morgan's troops into his own command but keeping them close to him during the next few days after Bragg's September 16 order.[7]

W hile Bragg busied himself trying to punish his soldiers and control his generals, Union commander William S. Rosecrans made an audacious move. During late August and early September, he sent Major General Thomas Crittenden's Twenty-first Corps to threaten Chattanooga from the north while the Fourteenth and Twentieth Corps of Major Generals George Thomas and Alexander McCook slipped south of the city, heading for Bragg's rear.

Chattanooga itself had a population of just 2,500, but its importance was vast. It was a strategic rail hub of the first rank, junction of the East Tennessee & Georgia Railroad to Virginia, the Western & Atlantic to the southeast coast, and the Memphis & Charleston to the west. Most important, it was the gateway to key military matériel-manufacturing facilities in Georgia and Alabama. Sitting in a wide bend of the Tennessee River at an altitude of 750 feet, ringed by mountains three times as high, it was hard to get into and out of. Even before Bragg's army began digging in after retreating there from Middle Tennessee in late summer of 1863, it was a fortress.

Bragg now paid dearly for having named Wheeler head of his cavalry so many months ago. The twenty-seven-year-old West Pointer guarded erratically, when at all. He left only troopers of the Third Confederate Cavalry to oversee fifty miles of mountain gaps and river crossings southwest of Chattanooga. The other two-thirds of his horsemen rested and refitted in Rome, Georgia, fifty miles away. He disregarded orders of August 30 and September 1 to keep an eye on passes through Lookout Mountain immediately southwest of the city and on a Federal concentration at nearby Bridgeport, Alabama. When Thomas and McCook were flanking Chattanooga from the southwest in late August, Bragg learned of these incursions from a civilian rather than Wheeler. He and his generals continued to believe Crittenden in the north was the main threat. Until September 2, thanks greatly to Wheeler's inactivity, they had no clue where the southern Federal stroke was aimed. They did not know for sure until September 5, when Bragg read a summary of Rosecrans's plan in a captured issue of the *Chicago Times*.[8]

Suddenly realizing that he was being flanked, Bragg ordered a pullout from Chattanooga southward on September 6. He directed his northern infantry, Buckner's, to hasten to bring up the rear of this move and ordered Forrest to screen Buckner with a brigade of cavalry. He meanwhile tried to rouse Wheeler and told him to run every risk to drive in all Federal pickets and locate the heaviest Federal concentrations. But he did not send this order until the afternoon of September 6. Even then, his southern cavalry commander seemed unwilling to understand the urgency of the situation.

Wheeler replied with a dispatch listing myriad reasons why he should not comply. His men were strung out across forty miles, the gaps between them blocked by felled trees; Bragg could get the desired information by "other means"; Wheeler's horses would be exhausted; following Bragg's order would expose Rome to the Federals. Wheeler's lethargy seemed accompanied by blithe witlessness as he added that he believed that "if General Rosecrans' army was commencing a vigorous campaign upon us, it was of the first importance that our cavalry be kept in as good a condition as possible, as it would be indispensable to protect our lines of communication." Knowing in what locality Rosecrans would commence this "vigorous campaign" appeared unimportant to him.[9]

Bragg limped through September 6 in the dark. His few working scouts provided mixed indications of where the enemy was, and he called off the withdrawal. The next day, September 7, Wheeler's minimal efforts and work by other scouts continued to produce conflicting reports. Bragg called his second council of generals in five days. The meeting showcased his poor performance under stress. He reached no decision in the council, then soon sent the generals another order to move south.[10]

Forrest could only have been frustrated by what followed. He was ordered south on September 8 to cover Rome, Georgia, and do the scouting Wheeler would not. On September 10 he got orders to return northward to find Crittenden's Federals again and discern where they were headed. Forrest now seemed to be covering his own assigned territory and Wheeler's—a circumstance that surely chafed him further.

That afternoon, Forrest found some of Crittenden's men in a foolhardy position. They had crossed to the south side of Chickamauga Creek at a bridge nine miles out of Chattanooga. The northward-running creek, actually more of a river, stretched south and then southwest from Chattanooga, and by crossing it the Crittenden unit had placed the stream between itself and help, if needed. Forrest sent couriers to Polk and Bragg, each six miles away, and readied his troopers to get to the Federals' rear and seize the bridge by which they had crossed the Chickamauga, trapping them.[11]

He heard nothing from Polk or Bragg. Around midnight he rode off to urge an attack, but found that Bragg and his army had pulled out southwestward toward LaFayette, Georgia. The opportunity was thus lost. The next day, September 11, Forrest conducted a fighting retreat. At Tunnel Hill, halfway between Ringgold and Dalton, he and Colonel Scott's nine hundred Louisianans were joined by Pegram and George Dibrell, a hard-fighting bootstrap Tennessee cavalryman like Forrest himself. To avail themselves of cover, their forces fought as infantry and stopped Crittenden's wary advance. In the process, Forrest sustained an unspecified wound serious enough for him to violate his teetotalism and take a drink of whisky. But he did not quit the field.[12]

Bragg had left Crittenden's vicinity to seek another vulnerable Union force. Major General James Negley's division of George Thomas's corps had advanced through a gap in Lookout Mountain into McLemore's Cove, twenty-some miles south of Chattanooga. There, across a branch of Chickamauga Creek, Negley's Federals were isolated. Bragg ordered ex–Arkansas congressman and now Major General Thomas Hindman to attack them on September 11. Both Bragg and Hindman waffled. Bragg sent Hindman a message telling him not to attack if unsure, then another telling him if he was going to do it, he should hurry. The day passed nearly to dusk before Hindman attacked—and struck nothing. Negley had retreated.[13]

Bragg turned back to Crittenden. By September 12, the Federal general was at Ringgold, still well north of Negley and Thomas and even farther north of McCook. Bragg ordered Polk to attack Crittenden at dawn on September 13. Polk ignored the order. Bragg then called an unproductive council of his generals. Instead of making an attack, Polk got his men into line and awaited one. It did not come. Crittenden had left Polk's front and gone to Lee & Gordon's Mill, nine miles south of Chattanooga and nearer—but still apart from—Thomas, McCook, and Rosecrans's other units.[14]

Bragg was like a man with no control over his legs and arms. His subordinates, cowed by his fierce irresolution and continual blaming of others when things went wrong, were as useless as he was. More depressed than usual, he temporarily abandoned attempts to exploit Rosecrans's rashness. Rosecrans meanwhile became more guarded, realizing the error in scattering his men across a fifty-mile front against an enemy not in retreat. Bragg's lassitude gave Rosecrans two days—September 14 and 15—to regather his army.[15]

F orrest's scouting of Rosecrans's left had been impaired by other wide-ranging duties. One was the fighting that resulted in his wound at Tunnel Hill.

Bragg had sent him on September 9 to headquarter at Dalton, junction of the Georgia & Tennessee Railroad to Knoxville and the Western & Atlantic to Chattanooga. From Dalton—where he retained only his sixty-man escort and, his report seems to stress in defiance of Bragg, "about 240 of General Morgan's cavalry"—he participated in the Tunnel Hill fight and supervised units guarding roads to his north, northwest, and west. But a week later, on the night of September 16, Bragg ordered him to seize two bridges and some fords on Chickamauga Creek; this was to be the Bragg army's first move to cross the Chickamauga and attack Rosecrans. Whether Forrest got this order, though, is questionable. His report does not mention it, and on September 17 he left Dalton. Soon after noon, he rode into Ringgold, where one of his units under Colonel John Scott was holding off an advance by elements of Crittenden's Federals.

Forrest's command numbered 3,500, but it was scattered. A brigade under Colonel George B. Hodge was up the Tennessee-Georgia tracks, watching for a Burnside advance from Athens, Tennessee, where the Union general had moved after capturing Knoxville. Colonel Scott's brigade was around Ringgold, protecting against Crittenden. Pegram was northwest of Dalton, screening Bragg's headquarters at Leet's Mill and Tanyard. Brigadier Frank Armstrong fronted Major General Frank Cheatham's infantry due west of Dalton and also west of LaFayette.[16]

Early next morning—Friday, September 18—Forrest received an out-of-the-blue order. He was to lead an attack by the right wing of Bragg's army. The plan was to turn the Federal left and cut Rosecrans's communications with Chattanooga and Nashville.[17]

Both Forrest and his commander on the right, Brigadier General Bushrod Johnson, were added to the mission as afterthoughts. Bragg had planned to advance across Chickamauga Creek at two points, Thedford's Ford and ten miles north at Alexander's Bridge. But late on the night of September 17, to be sure he overlapped the Union left flank, Bragg decided on a third crossing still farther north at Reed's Bridge. Johnson, who had a patchwork division eight miles east of the bridge at Ringgold, was in a prime location for the Reed's Bridge job—as was Forrest, who was also there. And Johnson's ranks were swelling with Longstreet's Virginians, whom Lee had finally agreed on September 5 to send to Chattanooga to aid Bragg.

But Longstreet was not as glad to be coming as he had expected to be. He had hoped to take Bragg's place, not to aid him. On September 18, as his men began to arrive from Virginia at the nearby Catoosa Railroad Station, Longstreet was chagrined.[18]

Bragg's order to begin the attack caught Johnson on the road. A previous order, written September 16, had directed Johnson from Ringgold west-southwest to Bragg's headquarters at Leet's Mill, and he was amid that march on the early morning of September 18 when a Bragg aide caught him. Turn around, the aide said. Go back to Ringgold and take the road due west to Reed's Bridge; Forrest's cavalry would screen his right and front. When they arrived at the bridge, Johnson should cross it and turn left. Then, joined by Simon Buckner's division from Thedford's Ford and W. H. T. Walker's from Alexander's Bridge, he was to strike Crittenden and drive him south.[19]

Forrest had received no such order, so Johnson started with just his own troops. With no cavalry to serve as his eyes, he moved slowly. He was halfway to Reed's Bridge when a single rifle shot—which hit nobody—

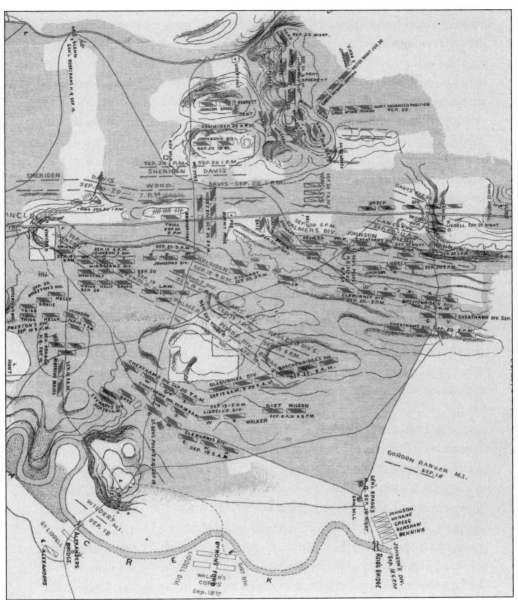

BATTLE OF CHICKAMAUGA: This Confederate-drawn map, with notable misspellings, shows Reed's Bridge where Forrest's men initiated the battle in the lower right quadrant; LaFayette Road running left to right and, at its right end, the "Cloud Yankee Hospital" captured by Forrest troopers on September 20, when they defended against Federal reinforcements under Gordon Granger. Snodgrass Hill, where George Thomas led the Federals' last stand, is at the top right center. Only infantry seems deemed worthy of mention here.

caused him to stop his entire advance. Warned by residents that a Federal force lurked at Peavine Ridge just west of a creek in his front, he put his four infantry brigades in line of battle and waited. A Bragg aide rode up with orders for him to "move forward immediately." About the same time, Forrest arrived with his escort and the couple of hundred Morgan troopers.[20]

Forrest did not scout the Federal position, perhaps because his arrival was almost simultaneous with that of Bragg's peremptory order to advance. The Morgan Kentuckians, reinforced by skirmishers from some Tennessee regiments in Johnson's ranks, moved forward into artillery fire supporting Federal cavalry. They worked their way across deep, muddy Peavine Creek, and their rifle fire killed the first man to die in the Battle of Chickamauga, a Federal private. His Union comrades withdrew in disorder, leaving a few horses and some gear and food. Over the next four hours, Johnson got several impatient orders from Bragg to press forward, informing Johnson that the rest of the army was waiting for him to attack, but to no avail.[21]

While Johnson dragged his feet, Forrest's men and the Twenty-fifth Tennessee struggled across Peavine Ridge. The uneven ground bristled with briary thickets, punishing the many barefooted infantrymen. Perhaps in rage at their discomfort or joy at its end, when they reached Reed's Bridge and saw it guarded by a strong Federal position, they spontaneously charged. The Tennesseans dispersed the guards before they could torch the structure, and at about 3 p.m., Johnson's men began crossing. Forrest's troopers led some across at an adjacent ford farther to the right.[22]

As they crossed, Johnson was relieved in more ways than one. Major General John Bell Hood of Longstreet's corps arrived at Catoosa Station, got his horse from a railroad car, and galloped to the front. Johnson reported to him, then faded back into division command. Hood took control a mile past Reed's Bridge. The vanguard of the column had veered to the left, as Bragg had ordered, and headed south on a road to Alexander's Bridge. Pegram's division had joined Forrest at Reed's Bridge, and their troopers spent the night of September 18 behind Hood's line of battle near Alexander's Bridge.[23]

At dawn, Bragg ordered Forrest to ride back toward Reed's Bridge to be sure the Confederate overlap of the Federal flank was complete. It was not. Rosecrans had detected the enemy buildup on his left and, during the night, sent George Thomas's corps there from his right. In woods just west of Reed's Bridge, Forrest and Pegram met a Thomas infantry brigade under Colonel John Croxton. Forrest saw that he was overmatched and sent an aide galloping to Polk asking for Armstrong's division of his cavalry for reinforcement. Forrest himself meanwhile hurried to find friendly infantry while Pegram tried to hold off Croxton. Back down the road toward Alexander's Bridge, he saw the Georgia brigade of Colonel Claudius Wilson, a Savannah lawyer, cooking breakfast after crossing the Chickamauga. Forrest asked for help. Wilson said he needed permission from his commander, touchy W. H. T. Walker. Walker then refused the permission without getting an okay from his own touchy commander, Bragg.[24]

Forrest went to Bragg. His report of significant Federal force well to the right of where it was supposed to be paralyzed the Army of Tennessee commander. Realizing his plans had been founded on out-of-date intelligence, he scrubbed his attack and vacillated. But he granted Forrest's request, and Forrest led Wilson back toward Pegram.[25]

Forrest also received additional cavalry, but not as much as he had requested. Polk sent only half of Armstrong's men: Colonel George Dibrell's brigade. It galloped to Pegram's right, dismounted, and stymied any possibility of further advance by Croxton, then moved around the Federals' left. There Dibrell ran into another advancing Federal brigade under Colonel Ferdinand Van Derveer. Dibrell fought Van Derveer in the woods for half an hour before pulling back around 9:30 a.m. Van Derveer's clash with Dibrell freed Croxton's left to again turn all its rifles on Pegram.

For much of the morning of September 19, Croxton and Pegram battled for a ridge west of a sawmill called Jay's. Nearly a third of Pegram's troopers fell. Although the only supporting Confederate battery was running out of ammunition and most of its horses had been shot, Forrest seemed unfazed. He moved up and down the line telling the men that infantry help was on its way. "Go to it, my little man," he told a mere boy frantically reloading and scanning the woods ahead. He patted the boy's shoulder, and the youth, seeing who had spoken to him, sprang forward to a large pine tree, aimed the newly loaded weapon, and fired.[26]

When Wilson's men arrived at the battlefield, they began driving Croxton back four hundred yards. Back and forth, the struggle ebbed, eddied, and flowed. With Dibrell now faltering on Reed's Bridge Road on the Confederate right, Forrest sought more help for the fight against Van Derveer. Forgetting General Walker, who plainly did not understand the urgency, he galloped toward Alexander's Bridge again and took matters into his own hands. Seeing Brigadier General Matthew Ector's brigade in a field a half mile away, he ordered it up to aid Dibrell. Accompanied by Forrest, Ector charged forward until Federals and an accompanying battery nearly surrounded him. Together, Forrest and Ector fell back fighting to their earlier position at Jay's Sawmill.

As morning wore into afternoon, the fighting sidled southward toward Alexander's Bridge. Forrest went with it. He saw Brigadier George Maney's brigade being pushed backward and sent a six-piece battery and Dibrell's dismounted cavalry to Maney's aid. The battery kept firing until the Federals were within fifty yards. Despite loss of horses, the cannoneers managed a retreat with all their pieces, thanks to help from Dibrell's men. But the greatest pressure on Maney was from his left. Under fire for just forty-five minutes, Maney's ranks were riddled; a colonel and two of four artillery officers died, and a lieutenant colonel and a major were badly wounded.[27]

Forrest did his last fighting of the day during their withdrawal. He gathered up Dibrell's men, fewer and scattering on Maney's right, and helped protect the retirement of the artillery. Toward dusk, Polk finally let Forrest have Frank Armstrong, a key Forrest subordinate. Armstrong gathered his division around Reed's Bridge for the night.[28]

Tension was beginning to take a physical toll on both Bragg and Rosecrans. By the evening of September 19, both armies' command chains had turned into dress parades of dysfunction.

Lieutenant General Longstreet had arrived in the afternoon. When he stepped off a railroad car at Catoosa Station, ten miles behind the Confederate right, the vaunted erstwhile second in command of the Army of Northern Virginia found no welcome. Bragg had not even sent an aide to conduct him to the battlefield. Longstreet and two subordinates waited two hours for their horses to chug in on a following train, then set out down Reed's Bridge Road, looking for headquarters. They had to navigate a rivulet of stragglers and wounded that turned into a bloody flood as they approached the front. Night befell them on the road. They blundered up to a Federal picket station and barely eluded capture. When they reached the headquarters camp at Thedford's Ford at 11 p.m., Bragg had bedded down in an ambulance.[29]

Turning in was the most helpful thing Bragg did that evening. A little earlier, he had reorganized his forces into two wings comprising disparate commands and then ordered an attack at dawn. Reorganization would have been perilous at anytime, let alone after the onset of a major battle. Then, with three lieutenant generals under him—Polk, Hill, and the arriving Longstreet—he snubbed one. Putting the army's right wing under Polk and its left under Longstreet, he left the flinty Hill virtually jobless as Polk's second in command. Next, he ordered Polk to initiate the next day's attack, although Polk argued against attacking without allotting more troops to the right. Bragg merely asked Polk if he understood his instructions and then dismissed him.

Bragg orally ordered Polk to assault at dawn, never writing out this critical directive; even an optimal subordinate needed a written copy to refer

LIEUTENANT GENERAL LEONIDAS POLK

to in the heat of battle, not to mention in his eventual reporting of it. Nor did Bragg inform Hill of his reduced status or the jumping-off time for the next day's assault. Hill came around at midnight looking for orders and could not find Bragg's headquarters. And Polk bivouacked apart from his command, so that Hill, apprised only secondhand of his reduced position, then could not find Polk either. Finally, Polk never told subordinates Hill and Breckinridge that Bragg expected a daybreak attack. So, the next morning Hill informed Polk that many of his men had not been fed in thirty hours; they could not attack until rations were issued and they had eaten, he said.[30]

All night, Confederates on the right had heard axes at work. This signaled construction of breastworks, meaning that the earlier the Confederates attacked, the better. Yet Polk only formed up to fight at 9:30 a.m. on September 20, three hours past Bragg's starting time. Polk commanded, and the far more experienced Hill was relegated to supervisor. During the night Hill had sent Breckinridge to the right to overlap the breastworks the Federals were heard throwing up, and Forrest got orders to extend Breckinridge's line farther right. He dismounted Dibrell's brigade and most of Armstrong's division to fight as infantry, placing Pegram's division in their right rear. Two Armstrong units—the First Tennessee and a 150-man battalion under Major Charles McDonald—were mounted.[31]

At 9:30, Polk's wing—the Confederate right, comprising 9,000 men under Patrick Cleburne and John Breckinridge, not including Forrest's—went forward. On the Confederate line's other end, Longstreet heard the action, and his men moved as soon as he could get them all into position. Hood, with two brigades, was Longstreet's spearhead on the Confederate left.

Forrest took his mounted detachment farther right to block the LaFayette Road. This road ran straight north to Chattanooga, its path slightly west of and roughly parallel to the snaking twists of Chickamauga Creek until it finally crossed the creek at Lee & Gordon's Mill, two-thirds of the way to Chattanooga. Less than five miles north of Forrest's position on this road on September 20, Federal Major General Gordon Granger headed a reserve corps on the Tennessee state line at Rossville, Georgia. Part of Forrest's task was to protect the Confederate flank by warning of, and trying to fend off, any Union force coming down

LaFayette Road from the north. That morning, he quickly blocked the road and captured a church beside it that had been converted into a 1,000-patient Union field hospital. Confederate cannons had targeted the bustling facility, and by the time two Armstrong units arrived there, all but about sixty nonambulatory patients had been moved to Chattanooga and the hospital abandoned. The cavalrymen rifled it of everything usable and mobile, including medical supplies and medicines precious in the blockaded Confederacy.[32]

The hospital captors comprised little more than a remnant. Forrest had dismounted most of Armstrong's men and sent them forward to attack with Breckinridge on Breckinridge's right, while keeping Pegram's division to his own right rear as a reserve overlooking LaFayette Road from the east. Three-quarters of a mile southward, to Forrest's left, blood now ran in rivers. Just west of LaFayette Road, the Federals had dug in on Horseshoe Ridge, a series of hills taking their name from the shape of the Federal line there. Before 1 p.m., Federal infantry under Major General George Thomas fought off two furious but ill-arranged charges by the Confederate right. To overlap the Federal left, Breckinridge had to assault in a single line against fortified Federals. Twice, his men—accompanied by Dibrell's and most of Armstrong's cavalry, dismounted—crossed LaFayette Road into Thomas's left rear, but their single line was too shallow. They ran out of steam and pulled back.[33]

Forrest split his time between his mounted men, covering LaFayette Road to the north, and those afoot with Breckinridge. He came back toward Breckinridge's main body as the fortified Federals threw it backward. Brigade commander Daniel W. Adams's Louisiana unit had charged to the right of the breastworks and reached the west side of LaFayette Road, in Thomas's rear, when they met a brigade of Negley's Federal division rushing up LaFayette Road from the south. Adams was captured, and his men were recoiling back up the road when Forrest rode up behind a battery of the Washington Artillery of New Orleans, which had gone forward with Breckinridge. He challenged its pride of manhood with his own. "Rally here, Louisianans," he shouted, "or I'll have to bring up my bobtail cavalry to show you how to fight." The cannoneers rallied and saved their guns.[34]

General Hill saw men fighting so well in front of him that he asked a nearby Forrest aide whose infantry they were. The men were Forrest's cavalry, Major J. P. Strange told him. Hill, Stonewall Jackson's brother-in-law, was taken aback. He had angered horse troops on the eastern front by saying he had never seen a dead cavalryman—meaning they never put themselves in harm's way—but the performance of Forrest's horsemen obviously made him rethink.[35]

Probably between noon and half past, Forrest galloped up to Hill. "That ever-watchful officer," as Hill's report described him, reported that Granger's heavy Federal reserve force was now approaching along the LaFayette Road from Rossville. Granger had heard the battle from Rossville and could tell by its direction that Rosecrans was in trouble. He now rushed toward the field. Hill turned the north end of Breckinridge's line to meet the new threat.

Overwhelming numbers bore down on Forrest's horsemen on the road, requiring more firepower. Two guns that the Confederate Fourth Kentucky had captured the day before had been added to Lieutenant John Morton's four, and Forrest also had another battery, Captain A. L. Huggins's. These were not enough. Forrest asked Breckinridge for more, and Breckinridge gave him a section of Kentuckians under Lieutenant Frank Gracey.

Forrest then pulled back from the hospital and arrayed Morton, Gracey, and Huggins on a ridge to the east paralleling LaFayette Road. They opened up on Granger's approaching Federals. Some of the shells struck the hospital. Forrest charged Granger's flank with both artillery and cavalry but was beaten back.[36]

Granger, too, had problems. For two of the five miles on his route to the field, Forrest's guns shelled him, killing and wounding a number of his troops. The Federals hurried off the road to their right as Forrest's cannon and musketry set fire to the woods sheltering them. But Granger would not be diverted. He sent Brigadier General James Steedman onward with 4,000 men carrying 95,000 rounds of ammunition. Steedman ordered up a brigade from Rossville under Colonel Dan McCook to deal with Forrest and kept heading south toward the embattled Federal line.[37]

Granger and Steedman probably saved Rosecrans's army. It was under mortal threat, having been struck hard at a charmed moment by the new arrival from Virginia: Longstreet. He had not even met his brigade commanders until he rode forward from Bragg's headquarters at dawn, but he had arranged them well. Instead of the single, two-mile-wide line Polk had to employ, he put his two divisions in a power punch five brigades deep across a quarter-mile front.[38]

All morning, Thomas at Horseshoe Ridge requested more and more men and ammunition to resist Breckinridge's assaults on the Federal left, and a nervous Rosecrans complied. Thomas's position was vital to Federal retreat routes northward via LaFayette Road, and Rosecrans steadily transferred men to him from the right. About 11 a.m., Rosecrans pulled the division of Major General Thomas J. Wood from the Federal line to double-quick leftward to support Thomas. Some of Wood's men were already skirmishing in his front, and enemy pressure was plainly building against the fortifications Wood had been told to abandon. Just ninety minutes earlier, however, a tired and shaky Rosecrans had given him a tongue-lashing for not promptly obeying an order. Angry, Wood obeyed now—leaving a quarter-mile gap in the breastworks.[39]

By coincidence, the Confederates chose that moment and that place to charge. Bushrod Johnson led Hood's vanguard of Longstreet's column through the gap Wood had left in the Federal front. Turning on Federals to his left and right, Johnson routed two Union divisions. The entire Federal line might have dissolved had it not been for the timely arrival of the 4,000 men and 95,000 rounds of ammunition Steedman had pushed past a far outnumbered Forrest. Thomas first hurried Steedman into line on the Federal left, then rushed him on rightward to a hill on the farm of a family named Snodgrass, where outnumbered Federals were trying to stem Bushrod Johnson's wholesale breach of their lines.

Forrest's men had done their best to stop Steedman. Lieutenant Colonel David Magee, marching his Eighty-sixth Illinois through the "smoking, burning sea of ruin" in a field west of LaFayette Road, said Forrest's cannons "played upon us with spherical case, shell, and almost every conceivable missile of death." Under the Forrest bombardment, Magee moved back into yet-unburned woods to his north and detailed men to extinguish the flames. The Federals unsuccessfully sent skirmishers to dislodge the Confederate guns. They could only lie down and wait out the continuing barrage. Yet Magee reported that he lost just one man killed and one wounded. An accompanying Ohio unit did not report its casualties, but its colonel reported that it remained under fire on a hill beyond the burning woods until nightfall. Perhaps the continued presence of pinned-down Union troops in his front encouraged Forrest to report wrongly that he had prevented most of Steedman's troops from reaching Thomas until nearly dark.[40]

Longstreet's breakthrough on the Confederate left eased Polk's task on the right, where Breckinridge's 10 a.m. assault had been repulsed in the late morning. Polk launched another charge all along his line in the late afternoon. In addition to weakened Union opposition, his men met Federals fleeing Longstreet up the LaFayette Road. Many surrendered and streamed through Breckinridge's lines and away from the combat. At dusk, masses of other Federals trying to get northwest of the woods beyond LaFayette Road became disoriented and ran to and fro. For Forrest's gunners, it appears to have been like shooting fish in a barrel. He reported that his guns fired at short range in open ground and killed "two colonels and many officers and privates." Federal Brigadier Absalom Baird, leading the leftmost division in Thomas's salient, reported total losses of 1,034 killed and 1,319 missing, most as his men tried to retreat in the gloom.[41]

At dusk on September 20, the right of the Army of Tennessee raised a howl of vengeful joy. The roar rolled all along Polk's line. But Thomas's remaining Federals hung on in a shrunken horseshoe. Only after dark did they slip off to Chattanooga.[42]

Thomas's holding out on embattled Horseshoe Ridge symbolized a broader trend that bloody day. The battle had been fought apart from its commanders. Much of its field was woods dotted with clearings, and both Bragg and Rosecrans had spent most of the day far behind the lines. In fact, by 3 p.m., Rosecrans had left the field to Thomas, thereafter forever known as the "Rock of Chickamauga." Like Rosecrans, Bragg had been in the dark to varying degrees all day. The next morning, the Confederate generals did not even know they had won. When Bragg found out, he seemed unconcerned with finishing the fleeing foe.[43]

The vast wreckage of equipment and men and commingling of regiments and divisions in the prolonged combat seemed to overwhelm his professional soldier's sense of order. "The army is so disorganized," he complained.[44]

Confederate casualties were ghastly. Complete figures, because of missing reports, are unknowable, but estimates run between 14,000 and 21,000, the latter approaching the combined losses of both sides at Shiloh. The Union total, more complete, was 16,000, bringing the combined loss of life and limb to at least 30,000, perhaps nearer 40,000. Shiloh's was 24,000. Chickamauga entered the list of America's bloodiest battles.

On the night of September 20, Forrest's men slept on the field. Nearby was the captured hospital, with a pile of amputated arms and legs a dozen feet high and twenty feet across.

Forrest seems to have been unfazed. Fighting meant killing, according to his credo, and he exhibited marked reluctance to stop doing it at a time such as this, when it had become easiest. As in his hounding of Abel Streight, his impulse today was to stay on the heels of the retiring Federals, despite Confederate weariness. The Federals were weary too—and their flight from the battlefield indicated that the "skeer" was on. His troopers had not eaten for two days, and they and their horses thirsted in the dry Georgia autumn. He had ordered during the battle that the horses get "a partial feed"; the men could rifle corpses and rob Union wounded for enough sustenance to get them by. Early on Monday, September 21, he pushed them toward Rossville, rounding up more gangs of prisoners, abandoned weapons, and wagons along LaFayette Road.[45]

At 7 a.m. on September 21, Forrest and General Armstrong, riding with an advance troop of four hundred, saw Federal cavalry ahead. The Confederates kicked their mounts into a gallop, and the Federals fired and withdrew. A bullet struck Forrest's horse in the neck. Seeing the animal's blood spurt, Forrest stuck a finger into the wound and continued the chase. At a ridge point above a gap through which LaFayette Road ran to Rossville and Chattanooga, the swift Confederate arrival trapped some Federals in a treetop lookout post. Forrest reined in and jumped off the wounded horse. It fell and died.

Forrest took the captured Federals' field glasses and climbed the lookout tree. He scanned the landscape ahead, then descended to dictate a message to Polk. He said he was a mile from Rossville on Missionary Ridge, the towering range that runs northeast along the eastern side of Chattanooga.

From there, he claimed to be able to see Chattanooga and its environs. Enemy wagon trains were going around the end of Lookout Mountain, he said, adding that he had captured Federals who said two pontoons had been laid across the Tennessee River to put it between Rosecrans and the Confederates. "I think they are evacuating as hard as they can go," Forrest's note finished. "They are cutting timber down to obstruct our passing. I think we ought to press forward as rapidly as possible."[46]

The postscript of Forrest's note asked Polk to forward the dispatch to Bragg. Polk might as well have forwarded it to Abraham Lincoln. Bragg had seen more than enough Federals for a while. Longstreet tried to get Bragg to move forward that morning—to no avail. Bragg himself said he dismissed Longstreet's suggestion out of hand. The Army of Tennessee could do nothing "for want of transportation," he reasoned. Almost half his army consisted of troops who had just arrived from Virginia on a train, bringing with them no wagons or artillery horses. And nearly a third of the artillery horses the army did have had been killed in the battle.

Forrest dictated another, similar message four hours later, near noon, saying he could hear axes ringing on the side of Lookout Mountain. The Federal rear guard was obviously throwing up obstructions to stop pursuit. Time was of the essence. Forrest brought up his artillery and dismounted his men. For several hours he tried to dislodge the Federals holding Rossville Gap and open a path for the Confederate infantry he assumed was on the way. But the Federal force was too large, and neither Polk nor Bragg replied to his notes. Bragg busied himself consolidating his troops, ordering them to pick up matériel left on the battlefield, and preparing recriminations for the tardy battlefield obedience of intra-army enemies. On September 22, while Forrest still waited, Bragg prepared to relieve Polk for disobeying his order to attack at daylight instead of 10 a.m. on September 20. Division commander Thomas Hindman would meet the same fate for not attacking in McLemore's Cove on September 10. Within two more weeks, the Polk firing would touch off an attempt by several other top generals—including Longstreet, Hill, and Buckner—to oust Bragg.[47]

In the meantime, on the evening of September 21, Forrest rode to Bragg's headquarters to ask why the army did not advance. Bragg, roused from sleep, parried with a question of his own. How could the army advance without supplies? "General Bragg," Forrest answered, "we can get all the supplies we need in Chattanooga." He left.

The next day, September 22, Forrest remained puzzled and furious. A member of Morton's artillery asked him if the army was going to advance. "No!" he stormed. Then he seemed to soliloquize on Bragg's folly. "I have given him information of the condition of the Federal army," he said, as if to himself. "What does he fight his battles for?"[48]

Forrest returned to his troops facing Rossville Gap. He formed a line of battle facing the gap and continued to wait. A single brigade under Major General Lafayette McLaws, finally sent by Bragg, arrived that afternoon. Forrest had moved up to the north end of Lookout Mountain, but his industry was of no use. McLaws's orders were to engage in little more than picket duty: to advance to two miles from Chattanooga. Forrest soon got orders to bivouac and refit. He likely gave vent to his eloquent profanity.[49]

Bragg hatched a comparatively puny alternative to pursuit. On September 23 he ordered Wheeler on a raid northwestward, to Rosecrans's rear; Wheeler's objective would be to cut the Federal supply line to Nashville. Five days after Chickamauga, Bragg ordered Forrest and his men farther north, but not to harm Rosecrans. They were to head northeast to drive off a force of Burnside's Knoxville-based army, which had reportedly advanced to Charleston, Tennessee. The Charleston foe turned out to be a brigade of mounted infantry, and Forrest shelled it into retreat. Learning that Federal cavalry was camped up the road near Athens, he thought it "necessary to follow" and chased the combined Union force through Athens past Sweetwater to Philadelphia, Tennessee. He stopped when the Federals crossed the Tennessee River at Loudon, eighty miles north of Chattanooga.[50]

This fighting dash up the Tennessee Valley on jaded horses netted only about 20 Federals killed or wounded and 120 captured. The pell-mell scamper seems to indicate Forrest's mounting post-Chickamauga frustration—a desire to do *something*—and his increasing resolve to escape Bragg.

Bragg remained more intent on disciplining subordinates than on pursuing the Federals. He proceeded with the suspensions of Polk and Hindman and prompted near rebellion within the officer corps. Dissatisfaction with him, which began after the Kentucky retreat a year earlier and increased following the Stones River withdrawal in January, verged on mutiny. Buckner, a stickler for every regulation, complained that Bragg had robbed him of his authority over the Department of East Tennessee. Hill branded Bragg's leadership inept, and Longstreet wrote letters to Richmond jockeying for his job. Frank Cheatham mulled asking for a transfer, and even Bragg's genial chief of staff, West Point classmate Brigadier William W. Mackall, wanted out. Mackall had known Bragg longer, and perhaps better, than anyone else in the army, and his judgment of his chief was damning. He wrote his wife that although Bragg gave himself totally to his work, he was "repulsive" in manner and loved flattery and deference. He was reluctant to give credence to bad news, and if it did prove true, he was not prepared to accept and act on it. And he demanded absolute obedience, which his continually changing orders made difficult to give.[51]

Forrest's East Tennessee chase infuriated Bragg. He soon told another subordinate that Forrest was "nothing more than a good raider" and that his "rampage" toward Knoxville epitomized his ignorance, especially of cooperation. And, Bragg raged, Forrest was all too typical. The Army of Tennessee, Bragg said, did not include "a single general officer of cavalry fit for command."[52]

Bragg apparently excluded Wheeler from his indictment. Although he quickly reorganized his army's mounted arm into a single unit again, he retained the erratic Georgian as its commander. As for Forrest, Bragg sent him new orders—twice. The first, on September 25, Forrest apparently ignored. Three days later, a Bragg aide wrote him to "without delay turn over the troops of your command previously ordered" to Wheeler.

Forrest fumed. According to his assistant adjutant general, Charles W. Anderson, Forrest exploded and dictated a wild letter resenting Bragg's treatment of him. Anderson said the letter accused Bragg of lying and informed him Forrest would soon visit headquarters to reaffirm his words in person. Anderson related that as a courier rode off with the letter, Forrest said, "Bragg never got such a letter as that before from a brigadier." The same day, Forrest wrote Wheeler that he was turning over the brigade of Armstrong and two under H. B. Davidson but keeping the ones under Dibrell and Pegram. He added that "neither men nor horses are in condition for an expedition" such as the raid Wheeler was embarking on into

Rosecrans's rear. Forrest was not exaggerating, Wheeler found. The running fight up the Tennessee Valley, following the days at and after Chickamauga, had utterly exhausted his troopers and horses.[53]

Forrest soon rode to Bragg's headquarters atop Missionary Ridge. His letter, or perhaps just his manner, led Bragg to tell him there that his cavalrymen were just on loan to Wheeler and would be returned after the raid. Bragg possibly added that Forrest would be arrested if he did not comply immediately with future orders; Forrest had flouted Bragg's order to dismount Morgan's men and turn them over to the infantry, and, according to a famous story, the subject would soon surface again.

Forrest took a breather after the meeting. Having vowed after the battle of Dover never to serve under Wheeler again, he now took a leave and let his men go on Wheeler's raid without him. But he had hardly arrived at LaGrange, Georgia, where Mary Ann Forrest was staying, when on October 5 he received another Bragg order. It said all his troops had been transferred to Wheeler. He was to report to the twenty-seven-year-old for instructions.[54]

This was the last straw. Forrest rode to headquarters again. This time an in-law, Forrest chief surgeon J. B. Cowan, accompanied him. Cowan later said he had no idea about the purpose of the ride. Forrest was unusually quiet. When they arrived at Bragg's tent, Forrest brushed past the sentry and found Bragg alone. Bragg rose to shake hands, but Forrest ignored the hand and jabbed his left index finger toward Bragg's face. He began spewing a litany of the slights Bragg had dealt him over seventeen months:

> You robbed me of my command in Kentucky and gave it to one of your favorites—men that I armed and equipped from the enemies of our country. . . . You drove me into West Tennessee in the winter of 1862 with a second brigade I had organized, with improper arms and without sufficient ammunition . . . and now this second brigade [*sic*], organized and equipped without thanks to you or the government, a brigade which has won a reputation for successful fighting second to none in the army . . . in order to humiliate me you have taken these brave men from me. . . .
>
> I have stood your meanness as long as I intend to. You have played the part of a damned scoundrel, and are a coward, and if you were any part

of a man I would slap your jaws and force you to resent it. You may as well not issue any more orders to me, for I will not obey them, and I will hold you personally responsible for any further indignities you endeavor to inflict upon me. You have threatened to arrest me for not obeying your orders promptly. I dare you to do it, and I say to you that if you ever again try to interfere with me or cross my path it will be at the peril of your life.[55]

This speech as reported by Cowan took insubordination to its ultimate extreme: an emphatic and contemptuous resignation, refusal to accept further orders, and a challenge to his superior to try to discipline him for it—not to mention the threat of murder if they ever met again.[56]

During the first week of October, apparently a few days after his raging encounter with Bragg, Forrest wrote his commander a letter of formal resignation from the Army of Tennessee. The letter arrived at headquarters at a lucky time. It turned out to constitute what would have been considered a minor addition to a major revolt.

On October 4, twelve generals in the Army of Tennessee signed and sent to Jefferson Davis a petition to sack Bragg. The signers included Lieutenant Generals Longstreet, Hill, and Polk, Major Generals Buckner and Cleburne, and seven others. Forrest's name was not among them.

At Bragg's urgent request, Davis hurried down from Richmond to resolve the dispute. Once he arrived, however, he displayed characteristic misjudgment of subordinates. He had not only predetermined to sustain Bragg but also resolved to find a place in Bragg's army for the now notorious General John Pemberton, loser of Vicksburg. Davis arrived on October 9 and stayed until October 14. If he thought he could talk Bragg's detractors out of their enmity or let them bluster themselves out of it, he was wrong. His obliviousness to their complaints only made things worse. After five days of raising the generals' hopes that their demand for Bragg's removal would be granted, he retained Bragg, let Bragg banish Hill, and transferred Polk to Joe Johnston in Mississippi. Longstreet sulkily headed his corps off toward Knoxville to battle Burnside.[57]

Forrest, a mere brigadier and comparatively unlettered, was likely not invited to sign the generals' petition. His name did figure, though, in Davis's talks with Bragg. Forrest's resignation was fresh, and Davis brought up Forrest's earlier request to operate independently along the Mississippi; that would keep the rough-hewn Tennessean in the war and placate some western constituents, who were increasingly alarmed as Federal armies ravaged their territory. Davis was as ignorant of Forrest's gifts as Bragg was impervious to them, but Davis knew the shrinking Confederacy needed all the help it could muster.

On October 13, Bragg sent a note to Davis's Richmond office releasing Forrest. The transfer of "that distinguished soldier . . . can now be granted without injury to the public interest in this quarter," Bragg disingenuously wrote.[58]

A week later, on October 20, Forrest remained unhappy. On that date, Bragg aide George Brent wrote in his diary, "Forrest is here and is much dissatisfied." Probably Bragg had objected to giving Forrest a modest detachment with which to form the nucleus of the army he planned to raise in Mississippi, Tennessee, and Kentucky. Forrest had requested his own 65-man escort, Morton's artillery, Major Charles McDonald's 160-man battalion, and the disputed 240 Kentuckians who had served with Morgan and whom Forrest had refused, in the face of a Bragg order, to dismount and convert to infantry.

Davis again mediated. Having extended his Georgia trip to rally war support, the Confederate president summoned Forrest to meet him in Montgomery, Alabama. The two then rode a train to Atlanta, and Davis wrote Bragg on October 29 suggesting that Bragg grant Forrest's request for the nucleus troops. Bragg complied with one exception: he kept the Kentuckians.[59]

Around November 1, Forrest left Bragg's neighborhood. He could never, however, escape Bragg's influence, because Bragg's long and disastrous stint with the Army of Tennessee was followed by service as Davis's principal military advisor in Richmond. Well after the war, Davis would tell a Tennessee governor that he himself never understood Forrest's worth before the contest was lost. By then, the deposed Confederate president seemed to recognize that this failure stemmed in considerable part from the shortsightedness of Bragg and commanders like him. But it never

would have occurred to Davis that the oversight was more generally attributable to the myopia and class consciousness of the Dixie elite.

"The trouble was that the generals commanding in the Southwest
never appreciated Forrest until it was too late," Davis said. "I was misled
by them."[60]

To the contrary, the trouble was the South's self-proclaimed "better class
of people." Forrest's hands were too callused by the axe and the hoe, his
nostrils too familiar with the stink of sweat, and his language too full of
the commonness of the cotton field for their gentility to countenance.
Davis and most of his generals were members of their circle. Forrest never
could be.

27

SEPTEMBER–OCTOBER 1863— GRANT HEADS TO CHATTANOOGA

"Hold at All Hazards . . . I Will Be There Soon"

Even before his troops entered Vicksburg, Grant itched to keep pushing forward. On July 10, less than a week after the surrender and the day before Union troops escorted the last Confederate parolees out of the city, he wrote General Nathaniel Banks in Louisiana that he had "little idea" as to the next task of the Union's western armies. But, he added, all his troops not needed to guard Vicksburg had started toward Jackson in pursuit of Joe Johnston the day Pemberton surrendered. William T. Sherman, commanding the pursuers, would "give Johnston no rest."[1]

Mopping up was the only job left in central Mississippi. Vicksburg's capitulation—and the resultant surrender of disheartened Confederates at Port Hudson, Louisiana, four days later—had eliminated the last major points at which Confederates west of the Mississippi might cross the river to reinforce or supply their eastern comrades. Minor trafficking was reported at Natchez, south of Vicksburg, but Grant put an end to it. He sent a Federal division to rustle 5,000 head of Texas cattle gathered there for Johnston, whom Sherman hoped to bottle up at Jackson. Grant was also collecting and sending to Memphis railroad stock that by early August he thought might total 100 locomotives and 1,500 cars. Grant had begun gathering these back in December for use in his Vicksburg drive, but now his aim was to keep them out of Confederate hands and to supply other Federal campaigns.

Sherman meanwhile began practicing the destructive tactics that would soon make him famous—or infamous—to Confederate adherents then and later. His men smashed rails, engines, cars, bridges, and machine shops for a hundred miles around, aiming for wreckage so thorough as to be irreparable as long as the war lasted. They also stripped the countryside of cattle, hogs, sheep, and poultry and appropriated corn in the fields to feed their transportation animals.

Sherman acknowledged the horror of his ravages but justified them as militarily necessary. "The wholesale destruction to which this country is now being subjected is terrible to contemplate," he wrote Grant on July 14, "but it is the scourge of war . . . destroying and weakening the resources of our enemy."[2]

The loss of Vicksburg had devastated Mississippi's spirit of rebellion. Sherman reported to Grant on July 21, and Grant repeated to Henry Halleck, that many of the most influential citizens of the state capital had approached Sherman about reorganizing the state's government under US authority so they would be spared further Federal destruction. "They admit themselves beaten . . . and charge their rulers and agitators with bringing ruin & misery on the state."[3]

While Sherman disemboweled south-central Mississippi, Grant focused on the horizon. Sherman had suggested that their next target should be Mobile, two hundred miles southeast of Vicksburg on the Gulf of Mexico. On July 18, Grant wrote Halleck to propose it. He added another Sherman suggestion: that the move should come from New Orleans, as a summer march from Vicksburg to Mobile would be too hot and dry. Sherman or Major General James McPherson should command, he wrote, because "the army does not afford an officer superior to either."[4]

Also seeking additional troops to garrison captured points and free up his army, Grant specifically asked that these new units be African American. He especially wanted an African American heavy-artillery unit to garrison Vicksburg. He wrote Union army adjutant general Lorenzo Thomas that he was "anxious to get as many of these" black regiments "as possible." Arms for them would be no problem. He mentioned that the

Vicksburg spoils included 50,000 stands of muskets and a large supply of cannon and shells.[5]

Grant even sided with new black troops in a controversy that infuriated many white ones. Before the Milliken's Bend battle, a white officer of a black unit had ordered a white soldier tied to a tree and whipped by black troops for "acts of wantonness" against the new enlistees and their families. Colonel Isaac Shepard of Massachusetts, the only officer in the area who had volunteered to lead a black unit without the common accompanying promotion to higher rank, ordered the whipping. He said he had seen many previous instances of white troops mistreating African Americans in his camp and in the neighboring village of the "contrabands"; he also claimed to have repeatedly protested to the whipped soldier's commander. A military court deliberated; Shepard's command of the First Mississippi African Descent was suspended pending a verdict. The Milliken's Bend fight occurred in the meantime, and Shepard fought in the ranks with his men.

The court's investigation found that two troopers of the Tenth Illinois Cavalry had entered Shepard's camp and, for no reason, beat and kicked a black private who was tied to a tree for disciplinary reasons. They also attacked two women and beat a fourteen-year-old boy. The Tenth's officers ignored these acts, so Shepard sent soldiers of the First Mississippi to get them. He took testimony from the private and the boy, then ordered a white trooper tied to a tree and whipped by black troops—with bushes, not a whip. He left the trooper tied to the tree for Illinois officers to retrieve.[6]

Its officers were called to other duty, so the court produced no final judgment. The troops themselves were bitterly divided over the episode; in their testimony, whites defended their comrades, and blacks defended theirs. Grant sided with the latter. He wrote Washington that the incident stemmed from "outrageous treatment of the Black troops by some of the white ones, and the failure of their officers to punish the perpetrators." He reinstated Shepard to command of his unit and endorsed Thomas's nomination of Shepard for promotion to brigadier general. But, to avoid further controversy, he refused Shepard's request that the court proceedings be published to counter bad publicity. An army officer should be satisfied with an investigation in which his superiors approved his conduct, regardless of a hostile press, Grant held. That was the only satisfaction Shepard got. The US Senate never confirmed the promotion of this officer who had let blacks whip a white man.[7]

Grant likely risked embracing such unpopular causes as black enlistment and Colonel Shepard's defense so stoutly because his own popularity was growing. After Vicksburg, Grant's public approval in and out of the army soared. When news of the surrender reached Washington, Halleck nominated him for major general in the regular army, rather than merely of volunteers, and he was swiftly confirmed. This made his rank and pay permanent, ensuring his family's security—provided the Union won the war. That Congress confirmed Gettysburg victor Major General George Meade as only a regular army brigadier reflects Grant's national standing after Vicksburg. Soon Sherman and McPherson, too, were made regular army brigadiers.[8]

Grant was emphatically rising, but his success did not beguile him into the pomposity or officiousness exhibited by most of his politicking superiors and peers. A letter he did not write illustrates the stark contrast between him and them: he sent no reply to the grateful note Lincoln wrote him on July 13 saying the Vicksburg campaign had proved Grant smarter than Lincoln himself. The president wrote again on August 9 to explain why the Mobile campaign Grant favored could not be undertaken just then. French activity in Mexico necessitated quick reestablishment of Federal power in West Texas. Lincoln also mentioned that he was "very glad" if, as War Department official Charles Dana had reported, Grant thought the Emancipation Proclamation was aiding war efforts.

Grant did reply to Lincoln's second letter. He thanked the president and said he saw the wisdom of the administration's wish to safeguard Texas. Emancipation, he added, was the heaviest blow yet struck against the Confederacy because, since its proclamation, the Confederates were getting reduced labor even out of those slaves who did not flee. He said he remained in favor of enlisting blacks to garrison points already taken and others likely to be seized soon.[9]

Grant probably had good reasons for not replying to Lincoln's first note. After the Vicksburg victory the president had begun to weigh the idea of bringing Grant to Virginia to lead the Army of the Potomac. Lincoln was deeply disappointed with General Meade's failure to pursue Robert E.

Lee after Gettysburg. Lee had been trapped in Maryland by the flooding Potomac for several days in mid-July; yet Meade waited a full week after the battle before going after him, and Lee had escaped to Virginia, where Meade now did little more than watch him. But Grant did not want to go east. He told Dana in a letter of August 5 that Dana and Halleck had correctly assumed a transfer eastward would bring him "sadness." In the west he knew all the commanders and their territories, he said; in the east he would have to start over. And importing a general into an army already full of them would engender dissatisfaction among the others.[10]

Grant's ambition was oblique at best. He sprang from a class accustomed to limited possibilities. His mother espoused religious humility, and if the religion did not stick so deeply in her son, the humility did. He also had a superstitious belief that grasping for advancement to a higher position invited bad luck once the position was gained. So Grant's ambition manifested itself as determination to do his best in every job, trusting that this would lead to promotion. But in the late summer of 1863, he did not want his hard work to lead him east. He had dealt with plenty of backstabbers where he was.[11]

On August 31, Grant wrote of an incident that boded ill for the Confederacy. To Halleck, he reported evidences of slave insurrection. Armed nonmilitary blacks had killed several white men north of Vicksburg, apparently because some of the local whites had tried to intimidate the blacks by whipping and even shooting them. Grant said the killings probably were cases of retaliation.

If Grant seemed untroubled by such reports of black retaliations against Southern whites, he also seemed too trusting about the fate of black soldiers who fell into Confederate hands. He continued to believe—or to want to believe—that General Richard Taylor, son of his old Mexican War role model, had told the truth after the Milliken's Bend battle, when he said the blacks captured there and elsewhere were being treated humanely. Grant wrote Halleck on August 29 that he had seen no evidence of ill treatment to any Federals "further than the determination to turn over to Governors of states all colored soldiers captured." About what even that might mean to the black captives, he did not speculate.[12]

The Army of the Tennessee was worn-out and increasingly ill with
malaria and the innumerable diseases of camp. Its two months of
battle and siege under the angry Mississippi sun demanded rest and
recuperation.

Its commander, though, was no good at resting. Idleness imperiled
Grant; his old thirst appeared to reassert itself when his job did not
demand his full attention. This danger mounted in late August, when he
accompanied Julia as far as Cairo as she took the Grant children to St.
Louis for a new school year. Julia's presence was the strongest bastion
against her husband's drinking; abstemious friend and aide John Rawlins
surely winced to see her go. Grant wrote a brother-in-law that he had
taken the Cairo trip for "a little recreation." Arriving back in Vicksburg
alone, he decided to go to New Orleans. He had orders from Halleck to
cooperate with General Banks in Louisiana, so he took the opportunity to
leave his department (and, perhaps not coincidentally, Rawlins) to visit
his colleague. In the New Orleans suburb of Carrollton, he accepted an in-
vitation to review Banks's army on September 4.[13]

He was given, or chose, a horse so unruly two men were required to
hold it as he mounted. Yet the review went well. Banks's men hurrahed the
resplendently uniformed Vicksburg hero.

Then came trouble. The holder of the West Point jump record loved a
hard gallop, but heading back toward his hotel in downtown New Orleans, he got more than even he could handle. The horse, spooked by the
blast of a whistle from a trolley, banged a shoulder against the vehicle and
became uncontrollable. The adept equestrian kept the saddle, but he might
have been better off had he not. The horse fell, and, going down, all but
crushed Grant's right leg beneath its body.[14]

Was he drunk? Almost certainly. Banks, Major General William B.
Franklin, and newspaper correspondent Sylvanus Cadwallader all suggested
as much. Even Grant's laconic account is ambiguous. It says the horse,
"shying at a locomotive in the street, fell, *probably* on me. I was rendered
insensible." His indication that he did not remember the horse falling on
him hints that he may already have been "insensible."[15]

He awoke at a hotel unable to move his right leg. Doctors said no bones
were broken, but he was feverish and in excruciating pain. His fever passed;
the agony did not. The injured leg had swollen from knee to thigh, and the

swelling continued up his body to the armpit, appearing ready to burst. For a week, pain prevented him from turning over in bed on his own. He ordered a steamboat to Carrollton to return him to Vicksburg, but ten days elapsed before he could board it. He finally did on a stretcher.[16]

He arrived back in Vicksburg on September 16. Rawlins wrote Halleck on September 17 that, although unable to walk, Grant was "able for duty." Hardly. He did not even write a letter until two days later, and that one he atypically dictated.[17]

Grant's injury hampered the Union war effort. Lincoln and Halleck, having long beseeched Rosecrans to move, now were frightened by his reckless dispersal of forces in northern Georgia and by Burnside's blithe slothfulness in linking up with him from East Tennessee. On September 13, a week before the massive Confederate offensive against Rosecrans at Chickamauga, Halleck wrote that he wanted Grant in command there. He lamented that Grant was unable to take the field.[18]

Grant's all-out efforts to help from afar suggest the difference he might have made at Chickamauga. Halleck ordered him to send Rosecrans as many men as he could spare, and Grant stripped his units to the minimum. He redirected two divisions that had already started toward Arkansas, added one of Sherman's and one of McPherson's, and put the whole under Sherman's command. He sent them by boat 220 miles to Memphis, where they were joined by a fifth division from General Stephen A. Hurlbut. The 20,000-man force then began to trek 240 miles overland to Chattanooga, to which Rosecrans had retreated from Chickamauga.[19]

For Sherman, it was an anguished time. Amid the frantic preparations, his healthy nine-year-old son fell ill with typhoid fever. At the Gayoso Hotel in Memphis, despite the ministrations of two physicians and the constant vigil of Ellen Sherman, the boy died in less than a week. The general's self-control, never formidable, all but dissolved. He wrote Grant, his commander and close friend, that this sole death among his progeny had robbed him of "the one I most prized." He said he could barely compose himself enough to work "but must and will do so at once."[20]

Tenuous Chattanooga-Washington and Washington-Vicksburg communications delayed word of Rosecrans's Chickamauga defeat on September 20; it was nearly October by the time Grant learned of the battle and its outcome. Almost as soon as he did, Halleck ordered him to

Nashville. From there, Grant was to supervise troops sent to aid Rosecrans's defense of Chattanooga. To reach the Tennessee capital, Grant had to travel by boat to Cairo, then roundabout by train to Indianapolis and Louisville. Secretary of War Edwin Stanton met him at Indianapolis to ride with him to Louisville. On the way, Stanton added Rosecrans's and Burnside's armies to Grant's list of responsibilities. The secretary also handed him two sets of orders, directing him to choose between them. One kept Rosecrans in command at Chattanooga; the other replaced him with George Thomas. Recalling Rosecrans's ungovernable behavior at Iuka and Corinth, Grant chose Thomas.[21]

Before they parted at Louisville, Stanton got a dispatch from Dana. It reported that the force in Chattanooga was outnumbered, encircled, and hungry, its animals starving to death by the thousands; Rosecrans, it said, was about to evacuate the city. Chattanooga was the rail hub of southeast Tennessee, key to any Confederate attempt to recapture the eastern half of the state. Losing the city, Grant knew, would deprive the Federals of not only a critical strategic point but also of Rosecrans's as yet uncaptured artillery—and perhaps even his whole army.[22]

The worried secretary of war would soon see that the Union now had the right man in charge. Grant hobbled on crutches to a table and wrote out an order taking charge of the Chattanooga region. He telegraphed that order to Rosecrans, along with the one from Washington putting Thomas in immediate command of the city. He then forbade retreat with a wire to Thomas: "Hold Chattanooga at all hazards. I will be there as soon as possible."[23]

The replacement of the shattered Rosecrans and the elevation of Grant and Thomas injected a new, resilient mood into the atmosphere at Chattanooga. Thomas's reply was proof of that. But its forcefulness also evinced a seeming edge, hinting that the "Rock of Chickamauga" had taken Grant's hold-at-all-hazards order as not only unnecessary but perhaps insulting. His answer was stark: "I will hold the town till we starve."[24]

G rant kept his vow to Thomas, heading for Chattanooga with all speed.

He had himself carried aboard a train to Nashville early on October 20, the morning after he wired Thomas. He had to lay over in the Tennessee capital because night travel was perilous, but the next morning he boarded another train to Bridgeport, Alabama. The Confederate siege had blocked all but the longest and most treacherous of the six routes into Chattanooga, so at Bridgeport he had to be lifted into the saddle by John Rawlins—"as if . . . a child," James Harrison Wilson remembered—to endure his first horseback ride since the Louisiana accident. The trek crossed fifty-plus miles in hard, cold rain on what Grant would remember as "the worst roads I ever saw." Aides lifted him off his horse and carried him over every slippery point they came to except one, which they noticed too late. The horse slid and fell, reinjuring Grant's leg.

The final stretch was hellish, and not just for Grant's teeth-grinding agony and the downpour. Stinking vistas of war's wreckage stretched in every direction. Smashed wagons and rotting bodies of mules and horses littered the road. The little party met fleeing unionist refugees. Wet and shivering mothers clutched babies they could shelter from the bone-chilling rain with only patches of the thinnest cloth. Rawlins had seen much of the human misery of war, "but never before in so distressing a form as this."[25]

No one in Chattanooga expected Grant to arrive so quickly. Just four days after leaving Nashville, on the evening of October 24, he was helped into the small house that was Union headquarters. He entered an atmosphere scarcely more welcoming than he had passed through. Thomas and his staff were cool and distant.

The "Rock of Chickamauga" was plainly unimpressed with the captor of Vicksburg. A Tidewater Virginian hailing from slaveholding stock, Thomas had preceded Grant at West Point by three years, graduated twelfth in his class, and spent a distinguished antebellum military life. His resolute stand had saved the Union army from utter ruin at Chickamauga and won him glory in the press. He likely thought he deserved Grant's job—which would already have been his if he had accepted the administration's offer to replace his superior, Major General Don Carlos Buell, the previous year. Not wanting to appear scheming, he had refused. For the same reason, he had been reluctant to take Rosecrans's place, only consenting to do so at the urging of Rosecrans himself on the ground that the army was face to face with the enemy and needed a leader. But Thomas's appearance of rudeness to Grant now was a mistake that Grant and his staff would appear to never forget.

Grant sat silent and dripping before the fireplace until James Harrison
Wilson protested. Could not Thomas's staff at least give the weary invalid
some dry clothes and a bite to eat? Thomas offered Grant a bedroom and
suggested he use it to change clothes. Grant declined. He wanted to get
to work—and perhaps to let Thomas and all others in the room know
who was in command. At Stevenson, Alabama, a couple of days before,
Grant had done just that with former eastern-front commander Major
General Fighting Joe Hooker. Hooker sent Grant a message that he was
not feeling well and inviting Grant by his headquarters to talk. Rawlins's
reply was steely: "General Grant himself is not very well and will not
leave his [train] car tonight. He expects General Hooker and all other
generals who have business with him to call at once, as he will start overland to Chattanooga early tomorrow morning." Grant himself then told
the messenger, "If General Hooker wishes to see me, he will find me on
this train."[26]

Now, after similar assertion of authority, Grant did take the light meal
Thomas's staff proffered. Quickly, though, he ordered a briefing.

MAJOR GENERAL JOSEPH HOOKER

The situation was even direr than advertised. Chattanooga was all but emptied of provisions; all supplies had to be entrained from Nashville to Bridgeport, then wagon-hauled to Chattanooga through sixty miles of mountains over the road on which Grant himself had arrived. The countryside was bare of forage. The soldiers were on fractions of rations, and the beef they got was skin and bones when it came in on the hoof. With colder weather coming, they needed shoes and coats. Most trees within the lines had been cut and burned, and there were no healthy horses or mules to haul others from outside. The only source of wood was standing timber on the Tennessee's opposite upstream bank. It had to be floated down, then carried on soldiers' shoulders to the camps.[27]

The Confederate siege was not complete, but nearly so. All but encircling Chattanooga, Bragg's 46,000 troops manned towering Missionary Ridge east of the city with infantry trenches at the bottom, then halfway up, and on top, with the crest crowned with cannon. They also occupied Lookout Mountain south of the city and overlooked the two most direct routes—railroad tracks and a good wagon road beside them—from Bridgeport. To the west, they had possession of Browns Ferry, by which the Tennessee River could be crossed to reach Chattanooga's back door. The only open road into even that rear entrance was the wretched one from the north that Grant had ridden. Its last leg was a pontoon bridge across the Tennessee into the city.[28]

Thomas reported all this to Grant, then introduced General William F. "Baldy" Smith. A flinty Vermonter, Smith had a risky plan. Other Thomas subordinates scoffed, but Rosecrans, before being relieved, had desperately approved, and Thomas had let Smith gather matériel to try. The idea was to seize the crossing of the Tennessee River at Browns Ferry, as well as the mountain overlooking it. That would permit construction of a pontoon bridge across which to push troops into so-called Lookout Valley before the Confederates did. These Union troops could link up with 15,000 more coming from Nashville under Hooker. The combined force would open the valley between Browns Ferry and Bridgeport, free up the river, cut the wagon haul to ten miles, and bring supplies flooding in on the water and overland.[29]

It was a high-risk, high-reward plan—just the kind Grant had adopted to get to Vicksburg. At Chattanooga, however, he was in an even tighter

spot. He wrote Julia on October 27 that Smith's proposal was "a desperate effort." Yet Smith's presentation had impressed him. The Vermonter
had masterfully explained everything, including the topography and the
two armies' positions within it.

Pallid with pain and weariness, Grant peppered the officers with ques-
tions. He especially wanted to know how much ammunition was on hand.
Hardly enough for a day's fight, he was told. But there was a stockpile at
Bridgeport, where Hooker's two corps were arriving. That settled it.

On the night of October 26, seventy-seven hours after Grant first
limped into Thomas's headquarters, Smith's plan went into motion. The
Federals floated pontoons and men down the Tennessee to Browns Ferry
under cover of darkness and overwhelmed the Confederate guards. Then
Grant ordered Hooker forward up Lookout Valley from Bridgeport.[30]

The Confederates reacted with the bungling that had become standard
under Bragg. Longstreet attacked Hooker's rear guard on October 29 at
Wauhatchie, halfway up the valley. But he did it at night, the best time for
confusion, and only with a fraction of the force Bragg proposed. The Federals prevailed and took control of Browns Ferry and a road across Raccoon
Mountain to another Tennessee River ferry, Kelly's. Kelly's was reachable
by steamboat from Bridgeport, opening the so-called Cracker Line, named
for the quarter-inch-thick crackers that were army-issue bread. Hooker's
15,000 men marched into Chattanooga unopposed. Sherman was on the
way from Memphis with 20,000 more.[31]

Grant was rapidly shoring up Rosecrans's erstwhile crumbling position
in Chattanooga. "If the rebels give us one week more time," he wired Halleck on October 28, "I think all danger of losing territory now held by us
will have passed away."

Then he could go on the offensive.[32]

NOVEMBER 1863–FEBRUARY 1864—FORREST ON THE MISSISSIPPI

"If Matters Are Not Arranged to My Satisfaction, I Shall Quit the Service"

The war was bleeding toward the end of a third year. Confederate losses at Vicksburg and Gettysburg and the wasted win at Chickamauga had produced crises of confidence. The attrition of Southern slave labor as a result of the Emancipation Proclamation, coupled with territorial shrinkage and the military shortfalls, had wrecked the Southern economy. Food and clothing prices leapt in Richmond and elsewhere. Bragg's loss of the East Tennessee rails to the Deep South and Grant's isolation of the trans-Mississippi had hardened the arteries of commerce. And Lincoln showed no inclination to compromise. He mounted a Gettysburg rostrum on November 19 to urge the North on to twofold triumph: the restoration of the old Union and the simultaneous making of it into a new, freer one.

Forrest, at last free of Bragg, was becoming a different man. His experience in the purgatory of the Army of Tennessee had shown its leaders to be hapless losers, and the prospect of their dooming the Confederacy—and with it, the fruits of his life's struggles—seemed to galvanize him. He was in no mood to brook additional aristocratic slights, and for a time it looked as if there might be no more. He had dressed down his hateful and hated ex-commander with impunity. The Confederacy's very president had all but begged him to stay in the army and help regain the indispensable southwest. And Forrest had found a more appreciative commander in thirty-year-old Major General Stephen Lee; Lee, having seen newspaper reports that Forrest had resigned from Bragg's army, wrote Bragg on November 6 requesting Forrest's assignment to occupied West Tennessee. Forrest's popularity there, Lee explained, "would enable him to raise at least 4,000 men otherwise lost to our service."[1]

The next day, to a note from Forrest, Lee responded in admiring terms. A brigade under Colonel R. V. Richardson was "nearly organized" and could form the nucleus of a large Forrest command, Lee wrote. And although he was a West Point–trained South Carolina gentleman, Lee all but pledged better conduct toward Forrest than Bragg had displayed. Lee assured Forrest that "we shall not disagree" and that he would be proud either to command or to cooperate with a cavalry officer of such established fame.[2]

Forrest must have already noticed that the trans-Appalachian South's common folk revered him while reviling most of his leaders. Perhaps because of this awareness of his own cachet, as well as disgust with the distracted way the elite seemed to fight this war, his relations with superiors soon became steelier.

In early November, Forrest headed west with his micro-army of fewer than three hundred men. He took them first to Rome, Georgia, where for two days they prepared for the ride across Alabama. They made the trek without their chief. He took a train to Selma, Alabama, to better outfit them from arms factories there, then went on to Meridian, Mississippi, to confer with the department commander, General Joe Johnston. On November 14, Johnston issued an order that must have surprised Union authorities. It named Forrest commander of Federal-held West Tennessee. His assignment would be part of the one he had requested during his final months under Bragg: to range through the captured area and rally—or conscript— as many of its citizens for Confederate service "as practicable."[3]

But appearances of Forrest's rising influence in the high command were illusory. He was promoted to major general in mid-December, but not for merit. The Federals were mounting a drive eastward from Vicksburg toward Meridian, and Johnston wanted West Pointer Stephen Lee to direct cavalry opposition in the state's southern half. Another major general of cavalry was meanwhile needed to supervise the northern half. Johnston asked Jefferson Davis not for Forrest but for Major General Wade Hampton, a South Carolina blue blood commanding cavalry in the Army of Northern Virginia. Davis replied that Virginia commander Robert E. Lee could not spare Hampton.

So Forrest was Johnston's second choice—if, in fact, Johnston chose him at all. Johnston wanted Hampton because Hampton owned vast Mississippi properties and thus presumably knew the territory; Johnston did not seem to care, if he even knew, that Forrest had lived and worked in the area since his early teens. Nor did Johnston have the excuse that Hampton was a West Pointer; he was not. So, because Robert E. Lee needed Hampton, Davis sent Johnston Forrest. And because Johnston said he needed another major general of cavalry, Davis promoted Forrest. Davis carefully pointed out, however, that Stephen Lee was already a major general and thus would remain the department's senior commander.[4]

Forrest's job was dangerous and would have to be done quickly. In addition to Sherman's looming advance on Meridian from Vicksburg in January, the Federals were also known to be preparing a thrust southward from Memphis. To guard against the latter, the Confederates needed in northern Mississippi both a major general and an appropriate number of troops for him to command. The only place to get them fast enough was Union-occupied West Tennessee.

Forrest set about recruiting an instant army—again, without sufficient tools. He asked for arms and equipment that he thought Davis had promised him in their meeting, but they did not materialize. He wrote Johnston on November 25 that it would be "rash" to take his now 450 men far behind Union lines without sufficient arms for themselves and the new units they expected to recruit, but a day or so later he went ahead anyway. With Stephen Lee ordering strikes against stations on the Memphis & Charleston Railroad to divert attention, Forrest left his Okolona headquarters 80 miles south of the Mississippi-Tennessee border and headed to Jackson, nearly 150 miles north.

He arrived on December 6. He either had men already working the area or had been mobbed by recruits on the road, because he wrote Johnston on November 6 that he was progressing spectacularly. He had gathered 5,000 troops and expected more as his presence at Jackson became better known.

He reported that, per day, fifty to one hundred men conscripted by the Federals in western Kentucky were deserting and joining his ranks. But he needed $100,000 to buy artillery horses, wagons, forage, and other matériel, as well as another $150,000 to pay troops returning to the army. In the interim, he had had to use $20,000 of his own.[5]

Two days later, he availed himself of a new potential source of aid: his personal acquaintance with Jefferson Davis. He sent a staff member to Richmond to inform Confederate authorities of his appeals to Johnston for the needed money and arms. In the accompanying letter, he told the government's highest representatives that if he received aid, he could regain for the Confederacy a great swath of Union territory, bringing along vast supplies not to be gotten in such cheap volume elsewhere.[6] If Stephen Lee could move up into West Tennessee and bring rifles for the recruits, he added, their forces could combine to destroy the Memphis & Charleston Railroad and drive south 4,000 to 6,000 head of cattle for Johnston's army. He sent a letter of similar appeal to Bragg, saying he believed he could send at least 5,000 members of the Army of Tennessee back to Bragg if he got the desired arms and money.

None of this was to be. An early-December shake-up was continuing to paralyze the western chain of command. On November 29, Bragg resigned, to be replaced by Joe Johnston. But formal resignations and news of them traveled slowly, especially behind Federal lines, and Forrest did not know these things for a while.[7]

Forrest first learned only that he had to scale back his hopes. On December 13, he sent his first regiment of new troops southward—unarmed and dodging opposition as they went. Five days later, he appealed to Johnston to advance two Mississippi cavalry brigades north to help him. Nearly 15,000 Federals were gathering against him, and he had 1,000 weapons for his remaining 3,500 troops. No response arrived from Johnston or Lee. Minus arms and supplies, his mobs of recruits were all but worthless. Without additional money or reinforcements, just escaping with his new units and on-the-hoof beef and pork he had gathered for his new levies would be a feat.[8]

He left Jackson on Christmas Eve. Most commanders in such straits might have abandoned the two hundred cattle and three hundred hogs already rounded up, but Forrest continued to drive the animals with his wagon train. To get the outnumbered and poorly armed column safely south, he divided his troopers and played tricks. To create a diversion while Colonel Tyree Bell led a detachment over the Hatchie River, he waited until nightfall, then attacked six hundred Federals with just his escort. His sixty widely spaced, loudly shouting men crashed through a cornfield's withered, rattling stalks, bawling instructions over their shoulders to a phantom brigade and causing the Federals to retreat ten miles. At an Estenaula River crossing the same night, he jumped waist deep into the icy water to cut out of harness a mule thrown in by a capsizing ferryboat.[9]

On Christmas, he gave his troops the present of another triumphant bluff. Lining up his weaponless men alongside his few armed ones, he routed a Federal detachment.

He used the same stratagem two days later to frighten off Federal troops guarding a bridge across Wolf River. On that evening, he eluded still more Federals at Collierville by feinting toward Memphis and then, early the next morning, cutting back southward to cross the Coldwater River. On December 29 he reported to his department commander that, had he received the requested aid, he could have nearly doubled his recruits. Instead, he had had to leave behind 3,000 men not yet gathered into units.[10]

By now, he had learned that the department commander was no longer Joe Johnston. Johnston had gone to Georgia to lead Bragg's erstwhile Army of Tennessee. Lackluster Leonidas Polk had taken Johnston's place in Mississippi, and Forrest quickly negotiated more formal autonomy for a behind-the-lines command that was already autonomous in actuality. On January 13, he met with Polk and Stephen Lee, then issued a general order announcing his increased independence. The order outlined a territorial subdivision in northern Mississippi and West Tennessee to be called Forrest's Cavalry Command. Its southern boundary ran west from Aberdeen to just north of Cleveland, Mississippi.[11]

Not all of his new subordinates were overjoyed. Among the displeased was Brigadier General James R. Chalmers, who had commanded the

Confederate cavalry in northern Mississippi until Forrest arrived. The two had known each other, more or less, for many years—and not very congenially. By early March, Chalmers would complain to the high command that Forrest had taken his tent and given it to one of his brothers, and Forrest would try unsuccessfully to transfer Chalmers to another command—basically, for being a major annoyance. But the high command sided with Chalmers. Leonidas Polk kicked the issue to Richmond, and Richmond stayed Forrest's hand, saying he had insufficient authority to make such a transfer.[12]

Chalmers was a member of the plantation elite in the region where Forrest had spent his latter teens. A South Carolina–educated Holly Springs lawyer, Chalmers had commanded Forrest at Shiloh in the ravine on the Confederate right on the evening of April 6. So small in stature that his enlisted men referred to him as "Little 'Un," Chalmers admired Bragg and was one of his favorites, which would have commended neither Chalmers to Forrest nor vice versa. The two had antebellum history too. Chalmers's father, a senator who owned a number of slaves, had officially approved Forrest's appointment as DeSoto County constable in the 1840s. Both Chalmerses, father and son, had practiced law in adjoining Marshall County, where a teenaged Forrest had worked his family's leased hill farm. Chalmers, a decade younger than Forrest, had been a gentleman; Forrest, a hired gun of the area gentry.[13]

Forrest had not been long in northern Mississippi before he was reminded that in the Confederate army, despite his new major general's rank, he was still the social inferior he had been in his youth. On February 1, Johnston wrote Polk asking for aid in returning to the Army of Tennessee 2,869 absentee infantrymen serving in Forrest's cavalry; obviously, they included some of the soldiers Forrest had found and rerecruited behind Federal lines. Polk replied that he had sent Johnston's letter on to Forrest but suggested that Johnston defer to a later date his attempt to repossess them. Forrest's department was under threat of attack, Polk wrote, and an attempt to take the men after Forrest had just coaxed them back into the army would "stampede" them back out of the service.[14]

No record of Forrest's reaction to Johnston's letter has surfaced, but it can be imagined. The high command had sent him behind Federal lines to recover these men with the understanding that they would be his to command. Now that he had done it, he was ordered to give them up. He had repeatedly endured this kind of treatment under Bragg, and on February 5 he fired off a curt note to Polk implying he had had enough: "Have telegraphed General Lee to come up. Desire greatly that you meet him here. If matters are not arranged to my satisfaction I shall quit the service."[15]

Johnston apparently desisted, and Forrest turned to bigger business. He reorganized his units and, on February 12 at Oxford, Mississippi, instilled discipline in his new recruits and conscripts by condemning nearly twenty deserters to death by firing squad, then reprieving them at the last moment as they stood in front of coffins, freshly dug graves, and brandished rifles.

In announcing his new fiefdom, Forrest had ordered all cavalry commanders to report their units' strength and condition. The vigor and thoroughness of his recruiting and reorganization seems to have galvanized Polk and Lee into aiding him, for in proclaiming his new command, he added that he brought to it a "full supply of arms, ammunition, and accouterments.

"There are men enough in the department, if properly organized, to drive the enemy from our soil," he asserted. "Let us then be . . . ready for the spring campaign."[16]

They were ready before spring—and had to be. The latter half of February brought an expected Union move southward from Memphis. In an attempt to link up with a Federal drive of destruction from Vicksburg to Meridian, a cavalry force of 7,000 men under Brigadier General William Sooy Smith headed from West Tennessee toward the Mobile & Ohio tracks south of Corinth, striking them around Okolona and destroying them and their surroundings as it proceeded.[17]

Forrest caught this Federal force at West Point, Mississippi. Racing to join a skirmish already begun by the brigade of his brother Jeffrey, he encountered a hatless, fleeing recruit. Chalmers, who was present, said Forrest leaped off his horse, dragged the recruit to the side of the road, and began beating him with a clutch of brush. Finishing, he turned his hapless victim back toward the fighting with a bracing warning: "Now, goddamn you, go back there and fight. You might as well get killed there as here, for if you ever run away again you'll not get off so easy."[18]

Forrest's force, half the size of Smith's, tried to trap the Federals at West Point, fifteen miles northwest of Columbus. When Smith refused to take the bait and began retreating, Forrest gave chase. He hounded the Federal column nearly fifty miles, from West Point to Pontotoc. In the forefront of the Confederate attack at Okolona, Colonel Jeffrey Forrest, the youngest Forrest sibling, took a minié ball in the throat and died in his eldest brother's arms. Forrest spoke Jeffrey's name several times in tears, then put the young man's hat over his face and ordered another charge. Adjutant J. P. Strange later said he feared his chief had become suicidal. Forrest charged the Federal position and drove it backward until five hundred Federals formed a battle line around a wrecked artillery piece. He then charged this position with just his sixty-man escort and a few members of Jeffrey Forrest's brigade. He and this small group were all but surrounded, fighting hand to hand in the road, when another of his brigade commanders, Colonel Bob McCulloch, brought up his unit and, waving a bloody, bandaged hand over his head, spurred forward. "My God, men," McCulloch shouted, "will you see them kill your general?" McCulloch's men followed him, and the Federals retreated. By the time they did, Forrest himself had killed or wounded three of them in the road.[19]

This campaign's final flourish occurred ten miles southeast of Pontotoc. There Forrest had three horses shot under him, two of them killed, and he and three hundred troopers, fighting dismounted, had to repel what he reported as "the grandest cavalry charge I ever witnessed" by the Union rear guard.[20]

But Smith returned to Memphis on February 26. Northwest Mississippi had been saved.

29

NOVEMBER 1863–FEBRUARY 1864—GRANT AT, AND AFTER, CHATTANOOGA

"The Responsibility of Guarding All Devolves upon Me"

Grant waited anxiously for Sherman in Chattanooga. The daring Federal strike across the Tennessee River had opened up a reliable supply line to Bridgeport, Alabama, and thence to Nashville. A week and a half later, though, the Confederates were menacing Federal gains to the north. On November 5, Bragg sent Longstreet's 15,000 men marching past Grant to attack Burnside in Knoxville. The recent Federal conquest of East Tennessee, a longtime Lincoln priority because of the area's predominant unionism and strategic importance, was in jeopardy. Halleck, Secretary Stanton, and President Lincoln all beseeched Grant to rescue Burnside and move on Bragg.[1]

Grant's impatience for Sherman's arrival was both military and personal. He plainly missed his loyal friend, a feeling the chill at Thomas's headquarters would only have heightened. Grant soon found a place of his own, a secessionist mansion that he opened to nightly gatherings of his generals and their staffs. There they relieved the pressure of the siege by swapping laughs and tales from the old army. Thomas and Grant participated, although less animatedly than the others.

But the military pressure on Grant was incessant and mounting. Washington wires rife with anxiety for Burnside kept coming. On November 5,

Halleck telegraphed that the insular East Tennessee geography made Burnside's position—and even Grant's at Chattanooga—tenuous, the opened Cracker Line notwithstanding; it forbade sending more Federal troops to either place, "lest they perish for want of supplies." So Grant and Burnside would have to rely on each other. On November 3, Burnside himself had wired Grant that holding East Tennessee would be "hard" if the Federals in Bragg's front did not keep the Confederates "constantly occupied." Grant said that salvation lay in the arrival of Sherman; if he got to Chattanooga before the Confederates beset Burnside, Grant expected to drive Bragg back to "a respectful distance." He thought Sherman would get to Bridgeport on November 9.[2]

But Grant had run out of time. Now, on November 5, Longstreet was reported headed for Knoxville and Burnside. Burnside had been asking for at least a demonstration in Bragg's front to try to force Longstreet back to Chattanooga. Grant sent out scouts to verify the Longstreet move, then accepted some advice from General Baldy Smith, author of the successful plan to open the Bridgeport supply line. Smith suggested the kind of demonstration Burnside had called for. Since the Federal lines at Chattanooga were very near the Confederate trenches, and since the crowding mountains afforded no room for maneuver, Smith said Thomas's Army of the Cumberland should just bluff a sudden rush at the Confederate right. That, Smith thought, might prompt Bragg to recall Longstreet to Chattanooga, and there could be no downside if it did not.[3]

Smith, though, did not know that Chattanooga's new commander rarely took half measures when a fuller one might work. On November 7 Grant issued Thomas an order that sounded as if Grant felt the frosty Virginian had been foot-dragging. Thomas was to prepare not a demonstration but a full-scale assault for "not . . . one moment later than to-morrow morning," November 8. Rather than the Confederate right, where Grant wanted to send Sherman, Thomas's assault was to hit the center. And if it broke Bragg's line, Thomas was to pursue him into northern Georgia.

Thomas and Smith were dismayed. They knew that their soldiers, whose supplies were just finally starting to come in from Bridgeport, had yet to recover from weeks of near starvation. Their long-famished horses and mules were too feeble to pull cannons and wagons, let alone sustain a pursuit if Bragg retreated. Seemingly oblivious to these obstacles, Grant said they could make the plan work by dismounting officers and taking horses and mules from ambulance teams.[4]

Thomas begged Smith to get the order changed. If it was not, Thomas said, he would "lose my army." Smith suggested that he and Thomas find an alternative to the attack Grant had ordered. They rode toward Grant's left and discovered potential for cutting off communication between the Knoxville-bound Longstreet and Bragg's right—as well as the railroad toward Atlanta that both Bragg and Longstreet needed for supplies and possible retreat. But Thomas could not make the assault on Bragg's right without dangerously thinning the center of his own line. To avoid that risk, they should wait for Sherman and let him make the attack. Meanwhile, Thomas's men and animals could get a few days stronger.

Smith and Thomas returned to headquarters, where Smith exploited his cachet with Grant. He told Grant that they should indeed attack, as Grant wanted. But instead of an assault on the center by Thomas, the more promising ploy was a lunge from their left against the north end of Missionary Ridge. The prize there was a hill beneath which tunneled the Chattanooga & Cleveland Railroad. Capturing that would turn Bragg's right flank and cut his retreat route. Smith then used a magic word in suggesting who should command the leftward lunge: Sherman.

Thomas, perhaps loath to be seen accepting another's plan rather than advancing his own, now suddenly second-guessed Smith. He said the attack should come from the Union right at Lookout Mountain. He added, to Grant's visible irritation, that his animals were in such condition that he could not move one cannon. Thomas's nay-saying, along with Smith's championing of Sherman and the agreement of War Department representative Charles Dana, probably ensured Grant's approval of Smith's plan. He specified, though, that Sherman too must also endorse it.[5]

But disappointment loomed. Grant would be dealing with subordinates of schizophrenic mind-set and ambiguous motivation. Thomas's skepticism and the glory-greed of Joe Hooker were challenges still to be reckoned with as well. Most problematic of all, however, would be the dazed distraction of Sherman himself.

G rant's demeanor brightened when Sherman arrived by steamboat from Bridgeport, Alabama, ahead of his army on November 14. The closeness between Grant and the redheaded general, one of Thomas's best friends at West Point, surely gave Thomas pause. Grant relinquished both his chair and his shell of reserve as Sherman entered the parlor of Grant's headquarters. Grant handed him a cigar and, in playful parody of courtesy, his seat.

"Take the chair of honor, Sherman."

"The chair of honor? Oh, no! That belongs to you, general."

"I don't forget, Sherman, to give proper respect to age."

Sherman laughed. "Well, then, if you put it on that ground, I accept."[6]

Grant and Sherman's rapport, even their appearance, differed sharply from those of other West Pointers at headquarters. Their dress was careless, their talk informal and direct. In contrast to the buttoned-up image consciousness of Thomas and his staff, they were western: rougher-mannered and straighter-talking men whose victories were pushing them upward in the Union army.[7]

They got down to work. It was obvious that Grant had given Sherman every detail of the plan, and Sherman had digested each. Grant turned to Thomas only for simple information about the advantages and drawbacks of the area; Sherman, by contrast, was a fount of opinions that Grant appeared to value. This all likely irked Thomas, not least because his knowledge of Sherman was probably more extensive than any other general's in the army. They had roomed together at West Point, and in 1861 Thomas had been second in command during Sherman's nervous breakdown, or whatever it was, in Kentucky.[8]

The deference Grant showed Sherman in this three-way tête-à-tête likely confirmed suspicions of their closeness that Thomas would have had for at least a week—especially after Grant had said Sherman must agree with Smith's attack plan.

The joviality that marked Sherman's demeanor on arrival would be short-lived. As in Kentucky in the fall of 1861, when he had imagined himself surrounded by phantom Confederate hosts, the redheaded general was seeing apparitions. This time they were not Confederate. His dead son haunted him. He blamed himself for the nine-year-old's death. He had, after all, directed that the family rendezvous with him in Mississippi, where the boy had contracted the typhoid fever that killed him.

"Everywhere I see poor little Willie," he wrote Ellen Sherman.[9]

Grant, by contrast, was waxing confident in dispatches to superiors and subordinates in early November. Privately, he was less sanguine. A letter he wrote Julia on November 14 indicates that Thomas's attitude had cast a pall over Grant at Chattanooga, even after the opening of the Cracker Line. It was the day Sherman arrived, and even that happy event did not seem to raise Grant's spirits. His language in the letter is un-characteristically self-doubting and almost a little self-pitying: the enemy was "threatening Memphis, Corinth, East Tennessee & Chattanooga: and the responsibility of guarding all, to a great extent, devolves upon me," he wrote. Nonetheless, he was optimistic that "if not failed by any officer in immediate command" at vital Chattanooga, within three weeks the national military situation would be better than at any time since the onset of war. If not, "no fault shall rest upon me."[10]

Ultimately, and understandably, Grant would feel he had little control. Much of this would be attributable to his favorite subordinate. Sherman's performance would show that, for all his brilliance, he could be a very or-dinary general when Grant's example and leadership were not paramount in his consciousness.

S herman's actions varied from trademark bursts of wild energy to episodes of seeming sleepwalking. Missing a steamboat after leaving his Chattanooga conference with Grant, he commandeered a big canoe and helped enlisted men paddle it all night to return to Bridgeport, where the rest of his force awaited. From then on, though, he tended more to-ward somnambulism and fright. On the march from Bridgeport up the valley beside Lookout Mountain to Browns Ferry and then across the Tennessee River into Chattanooga, he slowed the progress of his troops by not detaching his long wagon train and hurrying his combat forces on ahead of it. Some of his deliberate pace was justified. After marching across Tennessee, his troops were ragged and walking barefoot on frosty ground. Expected on November 9 at Bridgeport (where not nearly enough shoes and fresh uniforms awaited), his initial division did not arrive for another week. They would not reach the pontoons bridging the Tennessee River for nine more days.

The road up Lookout Valley was wretched and pelted by rain and sleet. The wagons churned it into cold goo. Grant became so dissatisfied with the pace of the march that he likely would have criticized Sherman, had they not been such friends. Instead, Grant "says the blunder is his," War Department official Dana reported to Secretary Stanton. Grant, Dana wrote, maintained that he should have ordered Sherman to leave behind the wagons. But, Dana added, "no one was so much astonished as Grant on learning that they had not been left, even without such orders." Sherman, on the other hand, blamed himself.[11]

The delays forced Grant to postpone an attack scheduled for November 21. Sherman's column was still strung out between Bridgeport and Browns Ferry, but Grant felt he had no choice but to wait for them. Part of Grant's old Vicksburg force, Sherman's were the only ones in whom Grant now had faith. In a letter to Halleck on the evening of November 21, Grant described the woeful condition of Thomas's starved troops and support animals. The letter perhaps also hints that Grant was becoming bitterly resigned to the weakness of Thomas's army and its commander's balking cooperation. He said he had ordered an attack two weeks before—the aborted one of November 8—but the horses and mules that had not already perished could barely move themselves. The Army of the Cumberland, the Ohio-rooted force that Don Carlos Buell had commanded before being replaced by Rosecrans and now Thomas, had barely survived Chickamauga. Its condition was "fixed and immovable," Grant grumbled.[12]

Grant's tone with Sherman finally became tinged with restrained exasperation. On November 20 he wrote that he saw that the attack intended for November 21 could not happen, but could Sherman not be in position on November 22? Time, Grant said, was "of vast importance." But more time passed. On November 22, with ammunition issued to his other troops and rations already cooked, Grant informed Sherman that his absence had required a delay of "yet another day." He was to hurry on even if it meant leaving behind some of his units.[13]

Longstreet now reportedly had Burnside besieged at Knoxville. Desperate, Grant turned to temporary stopgaps. On November 23, worrying that

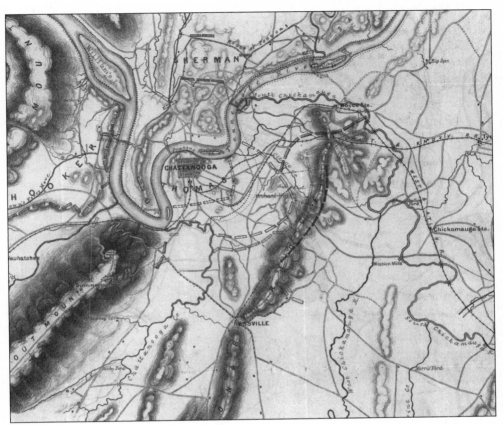

BATTLES FOR CHATTANOOGA: This map, drawn soon afterward, shows Grant's and Bragg's respective lines through the three days of conflict: it illustrates the original positions of Thomas in Grant's center, Sherman on his left, and Hooker on his right. Orchard Knob, or Hill, is in map's center; Tunnel Hill, where the Chattanooga & Knoxville Railroad passes through Missionary Ridge, is in the upper right quadrant; Lookout Mountain is in the bottom left quadrant; and Bragg's troops are spread from Lookout Mountain up Missionary Ridge from Rossville nearly to Tunnel Hill.

Bragg might march north to Knoxville to join Longstreet and overwhelm Burnside, Grant directed Thomas to drive Confederate pickets from his front at the base of Missionary Ridge to see if Bragg was retiring. Thomas complied. He ordered Brigadier General Thomas J. Wood to make a reconnaissance in force in front of the Confederate right-center on Missionary Ridge. There, enemy rifle pits crowned hundred-foot-high Orchard Knob.[14]

Word in the Federal camps had it that Grant regarded the Army of the Cumberland as spineless. To prove otherwise, Wood's 8,000 infantrymen exceeded orders. Flanked by two more divisions, Phil Sheridan's on the right and Sam Beatty's on the left, they formed the center of a line stretching nearly two miles. Confederates gawked from Missionary Ridge, thinking it a huge review in Grant's honor, until Wood and Sheridan advanced double-quick at 1:30 p.m. Six hundred pickets of the Twenty-fourth and Twenty-eighth Alabama on Orchard Knob got off only a single volley before 14,000 Federals swamped them.[15]

Wood signaled Thomas from the top of Orchard Knob. What should he do now? He was well ahead of the rest of the Union line, and Thomas and Grant hesitated. Rawlins interjected an opinion. Like Grant, he thought first and foremost like a rifleman. It would be bad, Rawlins said, to withdraw Wood's men and then make them retake the knob later. Grant agreed. "Intrench them and send up support," he told Thomas.[16]

Whereas forward elements of the Confederate right-center had been so easily pushed backward, the enemy's left looked impregnable. On the southern side of Chattanooga, the Confederates sat atop Lookout Mountain, crowned by vertical bluffs thirty feet high near its top. These natural defenses were so formidable that some commanders on both sides thought a comparative handful of troops could probably hold the mountain, and after Wood took Orchard Knob, Bragg ordered the shifting of all but a brigade away from Lookout. Thomas, though, thought it might be taken, and his view had merit. A demonstration against Lookout might keep significant Confederate strength near that end of the line, away from the Federal target to the north on Bragg's right. And if a Federal foray to Lookout broke through, it could reach Rossville and flank Bragg off Missionary Ridge.

On November 23 the rain-swollen Tennessee River damaged the pontoon bridge at Browns Ferry and prevented Sherman's fourth division from reaching the attack site. Grant, under continually increasing pressure to do something to aid Burnside in Knoxville, acquiesced to Thomas's plan. He ordered the Sherman division cut off by the broken pontoon, Brigadier General Peter Osterhaus's, to join Hooker in a jab against Lookout. If circumstances permitted, Grant said, Hooker could expand the jab into a knockout punch.[17]

Fighting Joe was jubilant. On November 21 he had implored Thomas to give him a part in the impending battle, and with Grant's approval, just after midnight on November 24, Thomas ordered him to make a demonstration. With fame in prospect, demonstration be damned. The ever-ambitious Hooker told his men they were to take—not just feint at—Lookout Mountain.[18]

By evening of November 23, Sherman's three remaining divisions had crossed Lookout Valley and camped northwest of the Tennessee River. Their march up the valley had been in Confederate view until they vanished behind wooded hills. Grant hoped this would mask the destination of Sherman's men, so that Bragg could not tell whether they were heading for Knoxville to aid Burnside or beyond the north end of his line at Tunnel Hill, the crucial promontory through which ran the Chattanooga & Knoxville Railroad. A mile and a half east of the hill, the Chattanooga-Knoxville track joined the Western & Atlantic Railroad to Atlanta, Bragg's lifeline.

At midnight, a Sherman brigade boarded more than a hundred boats hidden in North Chickamauga Creek, well beyond the north end of Missionary Ridge. To aid secrecy, muskets remained unloaded until the last minute, preventing accidental firing. This brigade, Brigadier General Giles Smith's, floated in silence down the Tennessee and landed two regiments just above Chickamauga Creek's southern branch. They captured all but one of the Confederate pickets there while their comrades drifted past the creek mouth to occupy and fortify a low hill on the Tennessee's east bank. The boats then began ferrying Sherman's main body across the river.[19]

Sherman had the advantage of surprise, but he moved with maddening caution. His lead elements fortified the first hill, then moved up five hundred yards to a higher one. No Confederate was in sight, but Sherman ordered entrenching on that hill too. He would not advance without all three of his divisions—those belonging to Brigadier Generals Morgan Smith, John E. Smith, and Hugh Ewing. The rear one, Ewing's, fell behind schedule crossing the Tennessee. It took well into the afternoon of November 24 to get all three up. While his men were digging trenches where they were, Sherman got a friendly 11:20 a.m. note from Grant that showed rising concern about a question Sherman should have

answered for himself hours earlier: "Does there seem to be a force prepared to receive you east of the ridge?"[20]

Sherman had not reconnoitered during the protracted ferrying operation. Perhaps he thought that would attract Confederate attention, from
which he seemed to shrink during this advance. He did not get all three of
his divisions moving forward out of their hastily made breastworks before
1:30 p.m. He then inched his way forward, fearing an attack on his right
by Confederates on Missionary Ridge. Because of the lack of reconnaissance, he did not know that no Confederates were near enough to make
such an attack; the closest were two miles south. James Harrison Wilson,
watching from one of the boats, concluded that "Sherman, with all his bril-
liancy, was not the man for such bold . . . operations."[21]

Had Sherman sent a lead element charging forward, he would have
found his assigned target, Tunnel Hill, undefended. Adequate scouting
also would have disclosed information even more critical. The ridge his
men were advancing toward was not Tunnel Hill at all.[22]

Sherman's target was actually the next hill beyond the one he thought
it was, and a deep vale intervened. Realization of his error sapped his remaining confidence. He was unquestionably frightened. While he had
marched slowly onto the wrong hill, Confederates had rushed onto the
right one. They now opened up with four artillery pieces.[23]

The Federal crossing of the Tennessee had caught Bragg by surprise.
He thought Grant's attack might come from the Confederate right, but
not this far right. He could not decide whether Sherman's move was a
massive diversion, so to counter the advance, he sent only a brigade of
Tennesseans and Arkansans from the division of Major General Patrick
R. Cleburne. Bragg kept the rest of Cleburne's division in reserve. Lieutenant General William Hardee, commanding the entire Confederate
right, did nothing until the massed Federals advanced out of their
makeshift breastworks on the two minor ridges. Shortly afterward, at
2 p.m., Hardee sent a message to Cleburne to bring the rest of his division toward Tunnel Hill.[24]

When Sherman's skirmishers met Cleburne's advance and its hasty cannon fire, the Federal general recoiled. He saw only three regiments on
Tunnel Hill, but three were enough for the grief-addled general this time.

Sherman started digging entrenchments again at around 4 p.m. Light would soon fade from another cold, late-autumn day that Sherman had squandered.[25]

O n the Federal right, Hooker used that day, November 24, to more advantage than Sherman had on the left. He was bent on making a bold showing at Lookout Mountain, and his troops shared the sentiment. His men—from New York, New Jersey, and Pennsylvania—were as proud as their commander. When Sherman's tattered, shoeless Westerners had arrived from Memphis and marched past them in Lookout Valley a few days before, some Hooker men derided them as "Grant's Vicksburg gophers." The latter responded in kind. Passing the Thirty-third New Jersey—which was decked out in the exotic Zouave uniform of white leggings, red baggy pants, blue sash, short red cape, and blue tasseled red fez—one hooted in derision, "What elegant corpses they'll make!"[26]

Hooker did not get an early start up. He did not know until that morning that Osterhaus would be temporarily added to his force, swelling it to three divisions. And continual rain had swollen Lookout Creek, which his attackers had to cross. But by 9:45 a.m. they had done so and entered the fog and evergreens veiling the west side of the mountain. Bragg's all but denuding of Lookout had yet to be completed. By 10:30 the Federals were fighting two pitifully stretched and overextended Confederate brigades, under Brigadiers Edward Walthall and John C. Moore, that constituted the lower defense of Lookout Mountain, fronting three more brigades on the crest. At 1:25 p.m., Hooker sent Thomas a self-glorifying report saying his troops were on the east side of Lookout following a brilliant performance with minimal loss and a harvest of 2,000 Confederate captives.[27]

Hooker's message was premature and inaccurate. The prisoner estimate was inflated, and Hooker's men had yet to climb Lookout's summit; they were merely in the process of ascending its steep eastern slope. And just after Hooker wrote Thomas, his men's upward trek hit its toughest stretch. The narrow trails would not allow two men to proceed abreast, and Hooker feared enemy reinforcements would stop his fogbound Federals, whose visibility was negligible. He ordered his subordinate on the mountainside,

Brigadier John Geary, to call a halt. But Geary was too far in their rear to control his men or know their situation. At 2:45 p.m., Hooker sent Thomas a far different note than that of an hour and a half earlier: "Can hold the line I am now on; can't advance. Some of my troops out of ammunition; can't replenish."[28]

For the first of several times in the battle for Chattanooga, Federal riflemen saved their generals. Because the bullet-shy Geary stayed well to the rear of his force, his men got no word to halt. They kept going. The brigade commanders had never even asked for ammunition or other aid; Geary beseeched Hooker for that on his own, prompting Hooker's plea to headquarters. After his initial concern, however, his men's progress reassured Hooker. By 4 p.m., he ordered them to dig in. As dusk fell, his men's fires blazed on Lookout's slope, elating the Federals facing Missionary Ridge to their left.

Hooker ordered Geary to prepare to advance into Chattanooga Valley next morning. He predicted Bragg's all but isolated left wing would flee Lookout by dawn.[29]

The next morning, November 25, the Confederates were indeed gone. They had hurried northeast to join the rest of Bragg's army on Missionary Ridge across the Chattanooga Creek valley from Lookout. Hooker sent the Eighth Kentucky to the crest of Lookout Mountain to plant the Stars and Stripes, whose fluttering folds wrought cheers from the six-mile Union line to their left. Thomas ordered Hooker to leave two regiments on Lookout and move the rest of his troops down the eastern slope and toward Missionary Ridge. But the Confederates had burned the bridge over Chattanooga Creek. Stymied, Hooker had to put engineers to rigging a dry crossing.[30]

Six miles north, at the other end of the Union line, Sherman remained in his personal fog. He had more than three divisions, some 16,000 men, while his opponent on Tunnel Hill, Pat Cleburne, could muster just 4,000. But Sherman's men were worn-out. All night long most had been kept at their picks and shovels or pushing cannon up their muddy hill, fortifying their position on orders from their insecure commander. Perhaps Sherman's mind was flashing back to the Confederate horde that burst yipping out of the morning mist onto his astonished camps at Shiloh. Whatever the case, he had used up much of his troops' energy. He also ignored a midnight Grant order to attack at dawn. He did not direct his men to lay down their shovels until 8 a.m. on November 25. The sun by that point was two hours high.[31]

Then his belated assault resembled a feint. With nine brigades at his disposal, Sherman used just two to make the attack, holding the others in reserve. Loyalty to Sherman caused Grant—very uncharacteristically—to make the same mistake, letting his favorite subordinate squander the main chance while neglecting his other officers. Such use as he made of Hooker was an afterthought, a concession to Thomas born of desperation with Sherman's languor. And he held back Thomas altogether. The Virginian was not itching to fight anyway. He wanted to wait until Bragg's flanks were turned before facing his daunting task: assaulting head-on up a five-hundred-foot-high ridge gashed with rifle pits.

Grant was thoroughly thwarted. All depended on Sherman, whose performance was pathetic. Sherman's verbal attack order on November 25— issued to his brother-in-law and foster brother, Brigadier General Hugh Ewing—amounted to a shrug. "I guess, Ewing, if you're ready, you might as well go ahead," he said. "Keep up the formation till you get to the foot of the hill." What then? Ewing asked. "Oh," said Sherman, "you may go up the hill if you like—if you can." He added that Ewing should not call for aid until he really needed it.[32]

This diffidence communicated none of the urgency of Grant's attack order, and Ewing can hardly be blamed for reacting the way he did. The 1,100 men he and Sherman sent directly against Tunnel Hill mounted an unsynchronized two-pronged assault. Split into two detachments under two separate commanders, Brigadier General John Corse and Colonel John Loomis, they tried to capture the hill separately. Loomis's four regiments of Illinoisans and Indianans to Corse's west did little more than watch as their comrades struggled up the hill. Loomis took his position under heavy cannon fire from both flanks as well as from the hill. Having been told by Ewing to "under no circumstances . . . bring on a general engagement," he obeyed.[33]

Around 10 a.m., Sherman's manner swung from cavalier to frantic. Colonel Theodore Jones of the Thirtieth Ohio, who had initiated the morning's combat by taking the rifle pits on the ridge in front of Tunnel Hill, was sent to inform Sherman of the stiffened opposition. By then Sherman had learned Grant was unhappy with his lack of progress. Sherman's tone became all but contemptuous as he ordered Jones to return to his battered command and charge. "Time," Sherman declared, "is everything."[34]

But Sherman's time had passed. The Confederates had robbed him of it. Two Southern brigades that had evacuated Lookout Mountain, together with the so-called Orphan Brigade of Kentuckians from Bragg's center, rushed into line on and around Tunnel Hill. Cannoneers pushed guns up amid the infantrymen. The Confederate position was now too strong for Sherman's piecemeal approach. The few troops he had assigned to take the hill could only continue to try and bloodily fail.

Grant's order of the night before had said Thomas would join in after Sherman attacked the left, and Sherman wondered about the promised aid. At 12:45 p.m., he sent a message by signal to inquire about it: "Where is Thomas?" Fifteen minutes later, Thomas himself replied from Orchard Knob. "Am here," he signaled back. "My right is closing in from Lookout Mountain, toward Mission Ridge." But Thomas's message was misleading. Reluctant to launch his assault until the Confederates had been damaged elsewhere, he was waiting for Hooker, commanding on his right, to attack Bragg's left. And Hooker was not yet "closing in"; he was still bridging Chattanooga Creek.[35]

Grant began to worry about Sherman's safety. He and others had seen Confederates rushing along the crest of Missionary Ridge toward Bragg's right, Sherman's vicinity. Grant and Thomas were both on Orchard Knob with their staffs, but the two generals and their retinues avoided each other. Grant's men focused on Sherman, Thomas's on Hooker. Around 2:30, Grant walked over to his West Point roommate, Kentucky native Thomas J. Wood, with whom he felt more comfortable than with Thomas. A brigadier in Thomas's Army of the Cumberland, Wood had been the man who obeyed Rosecrans's erring order to pull his division out of line at Chickamauga, opening the fatal gap that had nearly destroyed the Federal army. But that was the only major mistake in Wood's career. Now, Grant said Sherman appeared to be struggling. Wood agreed.[36]

"It seems as if we ought to help him," Grant added, almost to himself. Again Wood agreed, adding that he and his men would try to do whatever Grant ordered. That seemed to be the nudge Grant needed. "If you and Sheridan advance your divisions to the foot of the ridge and there halt, I think it will menace Bragg's forces and relieve Sherman," Grant said. Wood replied that he thought such an advance could capture the first Confederate trench line, which fronted the base of Missionary Ridge.[37]

Grant now took the idea to Thomas. The Army of the Cumberland commander stared through field glasses at Hooker's bridging effort on Chattanooga Creek, on the Federal right. Grant asked if it might be a good idea for Thomas to advance on the lower line of Confederate rifle pits to divert attention from Sherman. Thomas did not lower the field glasses. Only Grant heard his reply, but it was plainly negative. Thomas was without one of his divisions, Absalom Baird's, which Grant had sent off to aid Sherman around noon. That left Thomas with 19,000 men, which seemed thin for a frontal assault up a ridge bristling with enemy

MAJOR GENERAL GEORGE H. THOMAS

trenches. And it had been more than an hour since Hooker last reported his progress bridging Chattanooga Creek.[38]

Grant said nothing further and walked away. His forbearance enraged John Rawlins. Thomas subordinate Gordon Granger infuriated him all the more. Throughout the Grant-Thomas exchange, Granger had indulged in a habit of his, loudly sighting cannons for nearby artillerymen. Rawlins plainly thought Granger and Thomas should show more concern for Sherman and deference to Grant. The inactivity of Thomas and his staff went on for another half hour. Grant staffer James Harrison Wilson begged Rawlins to do something. Finally, Rawlins approached Grant. In low tones, he appeared to upbraid his chief for letting the tragicomedy play out as if no one were in charge. His words hit home. Grant took command.

"General Thomas," Grant said, "order Granger to turn that battery over to its proper commander and take command of his own corps. And now order your troops to advance and take the enemy's first line of rifle pits."[39]

Thomas did not reply. He just called Granger over and talked with him for a moment. Granger ambled off. Time kept passing. War Department official Charles Dana, who was there on Orchard Knob, thought an hour passed. Rawlins told Grant he did not believe Thomas's troops had been ordered forward. Grant, embarrassed, said he thought they had. He asked Wood, who had originally encouraged the idea of an assault, why his troops remained in place. Wood said they had received no order to move. "General Thomas," Grant said, turning to him, "why are not these troops advancing?" Thomas said he did not know, that Granger had been told to move them up. It did not look like it. Granger, again amusing himself among the cannons, acted as if he had been ordered to continue delaying while Hooker finished his bridge.

"General Granger, why are your men waiting?" Grant asked with increasing edge.

"I have no orders to advance," Granger said.

Grant had taken enough mocking. He now let both Thomas and Granger know their ploy was played out. "If you will leave that battery to its captain and take command of your corps," Grant told Granger in iron tones, "it will be better for all of us."[40]

Granger hurried from the cannons. He told Wood that Wood and Sheridan were to move their divisions up at the firing of six of the cannons

Granger had been fooling with. They were to take the first line of trenches and halt there. Orders also went to Richard W. Johnson's division on Sheridan's right and to Baird's just-returning division on Wood's left. These orders originated with Grant; Thomas appears to have given none. Having been reluctant to attack since Grant first took command at Chattanooga, he now seemed to fear destruction of his understrength army in what he likely viewed as a reckless bid to pull Sherman out of trouble. Having saved the Army of the Cumberland from Rosecrans's blunders, Thomas seemed to feel he must also save it from Grant's.

But Grant, unlike Rosecrans at Chickamauga, did not leave the field to Thomas. Because Granger had dawdled in the face of the first order, Grant repeated it directly to the division commanders, bypassing Thomas. The advance on the face of Missionary Ridge was finally about to move.[41]

G rant's order appalled its rifle-carrying recipients. They would have to advance under fire across a mile of flat ground. If they managed to take the first line of trenches at the foot of Missionary Ridge, they would still be under fire from more trench lines above them, on the side of a five-hundred-foot slope whose angle of ascent was forty-five degrees. Yet, according to the orders some received, they would not even be allowed to advance up the ridge to try to silence the fire from above. Their orders were to stop at the first trench line and wait amid the fusillade.[42]

This order, which Grant had first given Thomas on Orchard Knob, was obviously unsound. It likely was born of desperation to aid Sherman as well as exhausted patience with, and rising rancor toward, Thomas and the exasperating Granger. Grant later claimed he included within his order the authority to "re-form . . . and carry the ridge" after Thomas's troops overran the initial trench, but few others remembered such a provision. James Harrison Wilson did tell General Absalom Baird that the charge into the first Confederate line was to be "preparatory to a general assault on the mountain," but that appears to have been Wilson's own amendment to the Grant order.[43]

Some officers never understood that they were to stop at the foot of the ridge. One division commander, Phil Sheridan, could not believe the goal was just the first trench line because, once gained, he said, it would be "untenable." He sent a staff officer to Orchard Knob for clarification, but before the officer could return, the order came to charge. At least one recipient seemed fatalistically untroubled by the confusion. When bellicose brigadier August Willich of Wood's division told his officers their assignment, a major asked where they were to stop.

"I don't know," Willich replied. "At Hell, I expect."[44]

But the Federals were not as close to hell's gates as they thought. The Confederate position had shortcomings not evident from a mile across the plain. Bragg and Major General John C. Breckinridge, who commanded the middle of the line, were fixated on their flanks. They assumed the ridge's steepness made it madness to attack the center—until they saw the Federals massing there in the afternoon. Even then, they erred. Their one-behind-the-other mountainside trench scheme had thinned their resistance, spreading it across the face of Missionary Ridge from base to crest, and they now further weakened it. They issued orders for a brigade in the center of their forward line, Major A. W. Reynolds's of Patton Anderson's division, to fire a volley and retire up the mountain if the enemy closed to within two hundred yards. They told only officers, apparently concerned for the effect such an order might have on morale.[45]

It was nearly 4 p.m. when the Army of the Cumberland started forward. Sherman had ceased his fragmentary, bloody efforts to take Tunnel Hill, and Hooker still had not crossed Chattanooga Creek. Federals watching from Orchard Knob, having seen the passage of Pat Cleburne's and Alfred Cumming's Confederates and the Orphan Brigade of Kentuckians from Lookout Mountain, believed—erroneously, it would prove—that much of Bragg's army had shifted to the Confederate right to stop Sherman. The bulk of Bragg's troops, however, remained in front of the Army of the Cumberland as well as somewhat to its left as it headed for the first line of Confederate trenches.[46]

The Union divisions filed into long, full lines. Parallel to Missionary Ridge, they made Confederate riflemen on the ridge as apprehensive as the attackers. For much of the way across the plain, the Federals were protected by an oak forest from which autumn had stripped the leaves. But the final quarter to half mile was open, the oaks having been cut for firewood or visibility. Before the Union line had even reached the denuded woods that would cover most of their approach, the Confederate

BATTLE OF MISSIONARY RIDGE

cannons roared, their thunder multiplied by echoes in the surrounding mountains. This din contrasted with the silence of the oncoming Federals, who had been ordered not to fire until they reached the rifle pits. The cannons, having to be repeatedly depressed as the Federals came on, did little damage.[47]

The attackers burst from the bare trees and broke, yelling, into a run. They hoped to cross the rest of the plain before the cannons could find them. Hardly had they begun the sprint when Confederates in the center of the trenches fired a volley and fell back. Seeing them turn to run transformed the Federals' trepidation into elation. Willich's skirmishers of the Sixth Ohio reached the trenches first. They had run nearly a mile carrying full battle gear, but the storm of fire from above spurred them into and past the trench line. Those who still had sufficient breath kept running, straight for log huts the Confederates had built on a low plateau between the rifle pits and the foot of the ridge. These little buildings offered at least some protection from the Confederate rifles above and were well past where the cannons could be depressed to aim.[48]

Other panicking Confederates, following those abandoning the lower trench line, scrambled up the slope, blocking the firing lanes of their comrades in the lines behind and above them. When they reached those rearward lines, the retreating troops threw them, too, into disarray as they stumbled through. Those Confederate riflemen who could fire at all fired high.

The Federals were just as confused as their foes. Some officers who had gotten Grant's order to halt at the lower trench line tried first to stop their troops, then gave up and joined them in ragged surges upward. Wood, who had encouraged Grant to make the attack, never tried. When his first line surged out of the captured pits ahead of him and his second line begged, over the cannon roar, to follow, he waved them on. Willich and others never tried to halt at all. The men had recognized the reality as fast as, or faster than, their officers.[49]

"To have stopped . . . would have been annihilation," reported Major Samuel Gray of the Forty-ninth Ohio at the attack's front and center. "Our only hope was to charge the hill."[50]

On Orchard Knob, well behind the stampede up Missionary Ridge, the Federal charge looked exactly like the chaos it was. Grant saw clots of men from Wood's and Sheridan's divisions pass the first trench line and begin disconnected attempts to scale the ridge beyond. He could not believe it. If the enemy counterattacked, a Bragg trademark, they could sweep the Federals off the mountainside, keep coming, and knock out the center of Grant's army. It would mean defeat and disaster: loss of East Tennessee and perhaps the war. Seething over his inability to get anybody in the Army of the Cumberland to obey his orders, Grant abandoned military courtesy and shouted, "Thomas, who ordered those men up the ridge?"

"I don't know. I did not."

"Did you order them up, Granger?"

"No, they started without orders," Granger said. "When those fellows get started, all hell can't stop them."

"Well," Grant growled, "somebody will suffer if they don't stay there."[51]

But they did more than stay. Raggedly, they swept up the ridge's long, steep face. The First Ohio found a spot where a jut protected an area under its lip, just three yards beneath the crest. Here several hundred men gathered, out of the cannon and rifle fire. When they had assembled a sizable force, the Ohioans shouted and surged forward. They poured onto the ridge top into the midst of terrified Confederates, many of whom surrendered. As the Forty-ninth Ohio reached the crest, it was enfiladed by Confederate cannons turned to fire down the trench line. The Federals leveled their rifles at the flanked cannoneers, who got off a volley that targeted their own rifle pits as well as the attackers. Then they fled to join the wildly withdrawing infantrymen. The Ohioans pursued for a quarter mile, grabbing many prisoners and helping capture several pieces of artillery. Their comrades in the Fifteenth Ohio, cresting the ridge where a road headed east and down the opposite slope, found Confederates frantically trying to get cannons and caissons down that road. The Ohioans pursued, shooting horses and capturing guns and cannoneers in the gathering dusk.[52]

It was not yet 5:30 p.m. From the tardy obedience to Grant's order to charge to the victorious conquest of the crest, the entire assault had spanned less than ninety minutes. Charles Dana wrote the next morning that it constituted "one of the greatest miracles in military history."

It was a miracle that no general, only riflemen, could take credit for. "Neither Grant nor Thomas intended it," Dana went on. "Their orders were to carry the rifle-pits along the base of the ridge and capture their occupants, but when this was accomplished the . . . spirit of the troops bore them bodily up those impracticable steeps, over the bristling rifle-pits on the crest and thirty cannon enfilading every gully."[53]

But at 8 p.m. on November 25, with the wondrous feat not three hours old, Dana began recording a sidelight worth noting. The Federals, he wrote to Secretary Stanton, were "frantic with joy and enthusiasm" and "received Grant, as he rode along the lines after the victory, with tumultuous shouts. Good."[54]

Dana's one-word approval rings. He appeared to realize that, despite Grant's order prohibiting the troops' climb to victory, his relentless spirit had put them in position to make it. In so many respects, as he rode amid their cheers, the unkempt general mirrored the men hurrahing him. Figuratively, they applauded themselves.

The overjoyed Federals' pursuit of Bragg was late and minimal. The rush up Missionary Ridge was so astounding that, in the hours immediately after, Grant seemed rocked back on his heels, torn between his chase-and-destroy instinct and the urgency of preventing the hapless Burnside from surrendering to Longstreet at Knoxville. Longstreet had cut telegraph wires into the city, and Lincoln's and Halleck's dispatches on Burnside's behalf were continual. Only Grant could help. On November 26, the day after the battle at Missionary Ridge, he ordered Granger to take 20,000 men to Knoxville.[55]

Having sent aid to Burnside, Grant ordered a two-pronged move on Bragg. He sent Sherman east toward the railroad at Chickamauga Station to interpose his army between Bragg and Longstreet. He gave Thomas a more southerly route, toward Rossville, to try to catch Bragg in flight. Thomas again acted like the rock he had been proclaimed—but not as admirably this time. He did not send Hooker forward toward Rossville until the afternoon of November 26, and even then Hooker had to ask to go. Hooker marched his men hard, but the Confederates had burned bridges across two creeks to discourage pursuit. Hooker surmounted these obstacles as fast as he could and drove on toward Ringgold, pushing his men into evening, then night. They marched by moonlight along roads littered with Confederate wagons, caissons, tents, and blankets.[56]

But his persistence was to no avail. Approaching Ringgold Gap, Hooker's 15,000 troops ran into as fine an infantry commander as served Bragg's army and perhaps the whole of Dixie. Major General Pat Cleburne guarded Bragg's rear with just his single division of 4,100 men. On him, Bragg had stressed, depended the life of the Army of Tennessee. It proved to be in good hands. That day, November 27, Cleburne's men blocked the gap and killed or wounded five hundred Federals, losing less than half that many Confederates. By mid-afternoon, having saved the motley train of matériel that Bragg had salvaged from Missionary Ridge, Cleburne pulled out eastward. Hooker let him go.[57]

Burnside's relief would be even tardier. Granger did not leave for Knoxville until the afternoon after Cleburne mauled Hooker. Grant had had enough of the cannon sighter. Making other arrangements, he called off the pursuit of Bragg—because, he reported, he was drafting Sherman, who was part of the pursuit, to instead lead the Knoxville expedition in place of Granger, and it was "already getting late" to reach Knoxville before Burnside's ten days' worth of supplies ran out. He wrote Sherman that he had "lost all faith" in Granger's "energy and capacity."[58]

Sherman blanched. Knoxville's surrounding countryside, wooded mountains, and deep gorges—all of which offered perfect cover for hordes of stealthy enemies—reminded him of his Kentucky paranoia of 1861. "Recollect," he wrote Grant, "that East Tennessee is my horror."[59]

But at least he was no longer the Sherman of Tunnel Hill, paralyzed by his son's death. His men remained ill clothed and badly shod, but, having received Grant's order on November 30, he immediately began driving them hard toward Knoxville. A day out, Burnside dispatched that Sherman was no longer needed—which Sherman soon saw for himself. He and Granger rode on into the city on December 6 to find that, three days after Burnside's supplies were expected to be gone, they were nowhere near depleted. Hearing of the Confederate disaster at Chattanooga, Longstreet had assaulted Burnside, been repulsed, and faded off into upper East Tennessee. And all along, Burnside's troops at Knoxville had been better off than Sherman's and Granger's at Chattanooga. At Knoxville the two visiting generals found pens full of fat cattle and a garrison largely free from enemy threat. Burnside himself was ensconced in a mansion, eating like a lord on fare supplied by local loyalists.[60]

For Confederates, the Chattanooga-Knoxville campaign was a psychological, martial, and geographical disaster. At Chattanooga, they reported losing 40 cannon and 6,600 casualties, two-thirds of whom were captives. Grant reported taking 7,000 stands of small arms and 6,100 prisoners, 2,000 more than Confederates claimed they had lost. Desertion from Bragg's army had been so high that Confederate officers possibly believed many of their missing had simply gone home. The Federal losses had not been much less; Grant tallied Union casualties for the Chattanooga battles at 757 killed, 4,529 wounded, and 330 missing. The totals at Knoxville were more favorable. The Confederates had lost 1,296 in killed, wounded, and captured; the Federals, 681.[61]

But the Confederate losses, large as they were, comprised but a small fraction of what Grant and his troops had gained for the Union at Chattanooga. Immediately, in the East Tennessee & Georgia Railroad they had captured Richmond's most direct rail route to the Deep South, and in lifting the threat to Burnside at Knoxville, they had liberated the heart of the most profoundly unionist region in the Confederacy. Even that was nowhere near half the plunder. More important, they had captured the rail gateway to the Deep South, transforming East Tennessee from a Confederate staging area for such northern offensives as Bragg's alarming Kentucky campaign of 1862 into a Union one for a thoroughgoing invasion of Georgia. They had laid open such vital Southern industrial centers as Rome, Etowah, Augusta, and Macon and made it possible for Sherman soon to take pivotal Atlanta. His fiery March to the Sea would follow, burning the last sustenance and spirit out of Southern secession.

In two and a half hard and dogged years, the Ohio tanner's son had kicked Dixie's door down at Fort Donelson and captured one of its armies. He then took another in the masterful Vicksburg campaign that had opened the Mississippi River and cut the Confederate States of America in two. Now at Chattanooga he had set the stage for the final phase: the destruction of every remaining railroad track, industry, and agricultural field that kept the South in the war.

Victory's writing was finally on the wall, and it was signed "US Grant, Major General Commanding."

The extent of the achievement of Grant and his army at Chattanooga dawned quickly on the North. Lincoln's first message had been cryptic: "Well done. Many thanks to all. Remember Burnside." But on December 7, having learned that both Knoxville and Chattanooga were safely again part of the Union, the president sent Grant and the army his "profoundest gratitude for the skill, courage and perseverance with which you and they, over so great difficulties," had rescued East Tennessee. Two weeks later, Congress passed a joint resolution thanking Grant and his troops. It ordered a gold medal struck in Grant's likeness for presentation to him.

Lincoln himself promoted the project. On December 24, a New York lithographer wrote Congressman Elihu Washburne proposing that the medal put images of Lincoln and George Washington alongside Grant's.[62]

The reference to the Father of the Country was apt. Grant began to find himself rising toward Washington's lofty pinnacle in the public mind. On December 7, Washburne, the primary pusher for recognition of Grant's achievements, introduced a bill in Congress to revive the rank of lieutenant general. Its only previous holder had been Washington (Winfield Scott had also held it, but only by brevet), and while Washburne's bill did not name Grant, its beneficiary was obvious. On the day Washburne introduced it, a leader of the Ohio Democratic Party's war-supporting wing—as opposed to the other, peace-promoting faction—wrote Grant asking permission to nominate him for president at a convention in Cincinnati on January 8, 1864. Grant's response was polite, immediate, and emphatic:

> The question astonishes me. I do not know of anything I have ever done or said which would indicate that I could be a candidate for any office whatever. . . . I shall continue to do my duty, to the best of my ability, supporting whatever Administration may be in power, in their endeavor to suppress the rebellion and maintain national unity, and never desert it because my vote, if I had one, might have been cast for different candidates. . . . Your letter I take to be private. Mine is also.[63]

Grant had written similarly to Washburne, and Lincoln was gratified to hear from the congressman that Grant appeared immune to the presidential bug. The commander in chief could continue to elevate his new favorite general without endangering his own reelection. Not satisfied with the performance of Major General George G. Meade, Gettysburg's methodical victor, the president and Secretary Stanton began to press Grant further to come east to the Army of the Potomac. Grant responded with unfeigned reluctance. Parrying, he suggested Sherman, who knew something of national politics, or General Baldy Smith, who had been such an indispensable advisor at Chattanooga. Perhaps because he hoped to keep Sherman alongside him in the west, his firmest recommendation was for Smith.[64]

Looking back, something he rarely cared to do, the tanner's son would have seen that he had come a seemingly impossible distance. In less than three years since leaving his father's employ, he had risen from second choice for command of the Twenty-first Illinois to a none-too-eager candidate for the Federal top command. In addition to myriad Confederates, he had roundly overcome the poverty that nearly swamped his family in the late 1850s. Yet he was essentially unchanged. A visitor who had seen Grant hardly more than a week before the battle of Chattanooga—Pittsburgh resident William Wrenshall Smith, a cousin of Julia's—informed his diary on November 13 that he had arrived at headquarters on that day and been greeted "cordially" by the general. Smith, who likely did not know of the iciness between Thomas and Grant, noted that his host seemed happy to have a friend to talk to. Grant gave his guest the run of his headquarters and horses, engaged him in extensive conversation, and regaled him with information about the Grant children.

He also talked about his finances. Since coming back into the army, he had invested $5,000 in federal bonds, bought some of the property of Julia's father in Missouri, and now was trying to arrange collateral to purchase $5,000 worth of stock in a Chicago interurban railway. He had been as honestly aggressive about building a brighter future for his family as he had been about salvaging that of his country. He had, Smith wrote, been "saving all the money he could for the future, not knowing when his fortunes might change and he be thrown out of his office." Now that he was a regular army major general, of course, he would be harder to oust. The rank was for life.[65]

Yet this toast of the Union remained essentially the same man he had always been—and an all too human one.

As always, Grant's closest associates had to worry about his inner demons. The day after Julia's cousin arrived at Chattanooga, a member of Grant's staff hosted—in the cousin's words—"quite a disgraceful party." Smith gives no indication that Grant participated in the drinking, adding that Grant himself broke up the event at 4 a.m. and was "much offended at" the staffer responsible, Colonel Clark Lagow. Another long-term visitor to Grant at Chattanooga, Federal General David Hunter, said he saw

Grant virtually every hour for three weeks, during the entirety of which Grant took two drinks. Dana described the headquarters party organizer, Lagow, as "a worthless, whiskey-drinking, useless fellow." Smith expected Grant to fire him, and he soon did.

That was not good enough for John Rawlins, though. Rawlins wrote his fiancée on November 17 that the party had forced him to change plans to visit her. His continued presence was absolutely required, Rawlins explained, "by the free use of intoxicating liquors at Head Quarters which . . . had reached to the general commanding. I am the only one here (his wife not being with him) who can . . . prevent evil consequences. . . . I had hoped, but it appears vainly, his New Orleans experience would prevent him ever again indulging with this, his worst enemy."[66]

The same day, Rawlins put in writing the kind of blistering message Grant would tolerate only from him or, presumably, Julia. It warned his revered boss and friend that his behavior risked "the bitterest imprecations of an outraged and deceived people struggling in blood to preserve their liberties and their nationality." In a comment perhaps reflecting his former life as a Galena lawyer, Rawlins added, "Indulgence in intoxicating liquors . . . becomes criminal . . . where it unfits one for the discharge of the obligations he owes his country, family, and friends."[67]

Rawlins's concern is admirable, but his anguish at that moment was groundless. A major battle loomed. His friend had consumed, if any, no more than two drinks in the carousal. For the rest of his life, one presumes, Ulysses Grant would now and then binge and disappoint loved ones. Never, though, when given a chance to fight.[68]

EPILOGUE

HARD ROADS ONWARD

FORREST: 1864–1877

Nathan Bedford Forrest would serve out the balance of America's Civil War on the conflict's western margins. His physical and mental cunning would earn him the sobriquet "Wizard of the Saddle" throughout the South. Increasingly, however, his war would concern race.

In April 1864, at Fort Pillow in West Tennessee, Forrest became a headlined "butcher" by incompletely following the Confederacy's authorized, yet unacknowledged, policy of executing captured black troops and any whites fighting alongside them. His 1,500 troopers overran 580 Federals, white and black, killing one-third of the former and two-thirds of the latter. Large numbers of both had surrendered only to die afterward, many heinously. African American units would soon get on their knees in Memphis, swearing to "remember Fort Pillow," and they would make good the pledge. Taking a Confederate cue, they became less and less likely to take prisoners.

Over the next year, the backcountry western war played itself out bloodily. After Robert E. Lee capitulated in Virginia and Joseph Johnston followed suit in North Carolina, Forrest disdained politicians' calls to fight on. Branding as a lunatic anyone who still wanted to fight, he said, "You may all do as you damn please, but I'm a-going home."

Home, however, was scarcely recognizable. The barbarous social system that had made and sustained Southern riches for 240 years had vanished, along with Forrest's fortune. As for the people whom he had made much of his money buying and selling, they were now free—and resentful. Tennessee's postwar government would disenfranchise ex-Confederates, and Forrest soon followed former comrades into the budding Ku Klux Klan, which strove to win back the vote and white supremacy. Reputedly electing him its first chief, the Klan would spearhead vicious intimidation of blacks and moderate whites to earn reenfranchisement of ex-Confederate Tennesseans in 1869. The terror campaign would return to similar intimidation that had helped snatch the state from the Union in 1861, as well as to long-standing antebellum punishments for incipient abolitionism.[1]

Forrest's efforts to recoup financially would all fail. But trying to succeed in the New South in business—insurance and railroading—or some less obvious motivation, began to change him. He would make speeches welcoming Northern investors to the former Confederacy. He seemed to grow conciliatory in other respects as well. He would never admit to membership in the Klan (he could hang if he did) and soon publicly repudiated its proliferating violence. Finally, in 1875, as he began to bow ominously to chronic dysentery and other war-related illnesses, the *Memphis Appeal* reported that he had made a short speech to an African American political rally for the Democratic Party. He told his audience he came despite "the jeers of some white people, who think that I am doing wrong." He had disregarded the scoffing, he said, because he believed he could "exert some influence . . . in strengthening fraternal relations." He added something Abraham Lincoln himself had never said: he would "do all in my power to elevate every man—to depress none. I want to elevate you to take positions in law offices, in stores, on farms, and wherever you are capable of going."[2]

Was this egalitarian rhetoric sincere or just more wily wizardry? Likely the former. Forrest had always been deferential to religion and now, in advancing age, seemed to exhibit fear of the hereafter. He had encouraged ministers in his wartime ranks to hold their services in his camps, but unlike many comrades high and low, he had been unwilling to make pious promises that he suspected circumstances forbade keeping. Now, with the Reaper approaching, the inner conflagration that had ruled him would burn out. Tearfully pronouncing himself the man who had, in Christ's parable, built his house on sand, he would join the Cumberland Presbyterian Church of his wife and his mother. A wartime intimate would be astonished to observe that his old commander had become "as gentle as a woman."[3]

Death finally freed Forrest from infirmity at age fifty-six. Thousands would trail the hearse. They would include that leading exemplar of Dixie's elite, Jefferson Davis, as well as hundreds of African Americans, many doubtless there to see him gone.

For fourscore subsequent years, many white Southerners would celebrate his birthday. At least until the 1950s, they likely did so not because the bulk of his frantic life had embodied their near-ubiquitous belief in white supremacy. More probably, they did it to pay tribute to a fellow commoner they were convinced was smarter, more valiant, and more victorious than the elite who had led them to ruin.

GRANT: 1864–1885

Ulysses Simpson Grant did as asked and went east. For more than another year, he and Robert E. Lee battered each other. Grant was statistically no more—or less—a butcher than Lee, yet he attained that reputation by throwing Union lives into hails of Confederate iron and lead. But his grim determination to win despite the costs, combined with the damage he had done in the west, proved fatal to the Confederacy. With the South's supply lines severed and Lee's allies in other theaters all but vanquished, the quintessential Southern gentleman surrendered to the tanner's son.

Six years after his final day of clerking in Galena, Illinois, Grant had become his era's most popular American. Grateful countrymen named him president in 1868. But reuniting the shattered, debt-ridden nation he had saved proved possible in name only—for more than a century. According to many in the North and South (Grant's own mother among them), America was forever changed, its two halves divided by the rule of Lincoln's Republican Party. No wonder they would think so. With Dixie under martial law or, in many of its areas, none, bestial furies on both sides gratified their hates.

The most enduring legacy of the country's deep divisions would grow out of the racial sadism of antebellum Dixie: the masked, night-riding

Klansmen whom Forrest purportedly once led. Grant would fight them with far less success than he had battled the South's more formal armies, but he would try.

Yet it was Grant's trusting nature, not the bitter legacy of war, that nearly did him in. Friends corrupted his administration. Perhaps the most celebrated case was that of Secretary of War William W. Belknap, whom a congressional investigation caught taking kickbacks from the military trading post at Fort Sill in Oklahoma. Then, around 1880, Ulysses S. Grant Jr. and a partner enlisted heavy Grant investment and partnership in their Wall Street firm; five years later, it failed and bankrupted him. He was able to free his family from the resurrected specter of want only by writing a memoir that, while occasionally self-serving, remains a military and literary masterpiece. In the most heroic victory of his embattled life, he completed it just days prior to succumbing to throat cancer. The millions of cigars admirers had sent him ever since Fort Donelson killed him.

Lying on the couch that soon became his deathbed, able to communicate only by handwritten note, Grant left a most fitting epitaph for himself with one of his final visitors. With a humility that confirmed him as one of the commonest of American history's common men, he wrote that a man's destiny is forever a mystery and that he had embarked toward his with no thought of the possibility of attaining high military rank or preeminence in politics. Had anyone suggested early on that he might become an author, he wrote, he would not have been "sure whether they were making sport of me or not." Yet, he would note, he had now managed to finish "a book which is in the hands of the manufacturers.

"I ask you to keep these notes very private," the terminal patient would add, "lest I become an authority on the treatment of diseases. I have already too many trades to be proficient at any."[4]

ACKNOWLEDGMENTS

A large number of generous people have been crucial in making this book possible.

Preeminent on the list have to be adept literary agent Deborah Grosvenor, who expertly guided the crafting of its initial plan and proposal, and first readers Gordon Berg and Timothy B. Smith. Gordon—past president of the Washington, DC, Civil War Roundtable and omnivorous journalistic chronicler of Civil War history and new developments in its continuing evolution—consented to read the first draft and made many salient points that helped form, refine, and push its narrative path. A good friend at the outset, he has become an indispensable one.

Dr. Smith's full-time job is teaching history at the University of Tennessee, Martin, but he obviously has another full-time vocation: writing and editing Civil War books, of which he already—at a still stunningly early age—had produced seven when he agreed to look over my manuscript. He has probably published a couple more by now. Despite his small children and his wife's broken arm, he wielded his time and pencil with great generosity, saving me from many small errors that would have added up to a large embarrassment.

My sister, retired English teacher Carol Carlson of Maryland and North Carolina, also lent her eyes, proofreading skills, and encouragement to the project and thereby also aided in getting the manuscript in shape to be submitted to Basic Books.

There, Vice President Lara Heimert judiciously directed the conceiving of a title and the cutting down and streamlining of a bulky and wandering initial manuscript by more than 25 percent, and Associate Editor Alex Littlefield completed the streamlining process by giving wholehearted attention to every line—rearranging some, calling for the addition of others, and generally doing much hard work to clarify and liberate the narrative. Editorial assistant Katy O'Donnell was an eleventh-hour godsend in acquiring pictures and maps, and Kay Mariea, editorial services director for Perseus Books, brought the project home. Copyeditor Jennifer Kelland Fagan, unfailingly pleasurable to deal with, made many fine-tuning improvements by suggesting perfect words and bringing ideas into sharper focus.

All these people were unfailingly kind and considerate to a writer who, after a long history in journalism, still has much to learn about publishing. They all deserve special thanks. Only one, my sister, had an idea what she was getting into when taking on the job. She knew better, but did it anyway.

Others, too, are due significant credit. Dr. William Bernet, professor of psychiatry at Vanderbilt University School of Medicine, very kindly took the time to render his extremely helpful informed opinion on how being the twin of a sister who did not live to adulthood, along with other privation, might have influenced the personality of Nathan Bedford Forrest. I thank Dr. Bernet and also my friend John Howser, vice chancellor for news and communications at Vanderbilt University Medical Center, for connecting me with him.

Chris Howland of the Weider History Group went to much trouble to get me Civil War author Frank Cooling's 1963 article on the Battle of Dover and to introduce me online to Bill Breidenstein, also of Weider, regarding a map that, along with Mr. Cooling's article, aided my understanding of the battle. This was after Mr. Cooling told me how to locate it. I thank all of them for their kindnesses.

The staffs of the Tennessee State Library and Archives as well as the libraries of Vanderbilt University, Tennessee Technological University, and Middle Tennessee State University and the Justin Potter Library in Smithville, Tennessee, were all very helpful. Dr. Alan D. Boehm at Middle Tennessee State was particularly helpful in getting me two books that I might not have gotten access to otherwise. Jimmy Manning at the Oaklands Historic House Museum in Murfreesboro, the residence in which Nathan Bedford Forrest accepted the surrender of Murfreesboro in July

1862, shared from his files several important pieces of information on Forrest's raid. There are, I'm sure, other givers of aid whose names have fallen through the cracks of my memory, for which I sincerely apologize.

I would also like to thank inaugural president Ed Copeland, present president Kent Dollar, Vice President Sharyl Hansen, Secretary Karen Goluszka, and all members of the Upper Cumberland Civil War Roundtable in Cookeville, Tennessee—as well as readers of the blog Civil War & Civil Rights (http://civwrandcivrts1.wordpress.com)—for their interest in the Civil War and for encouraging my attempts to keep it in the public consciousness.

Finally, I have to thank my beloved and long-suffering wife, Donna, who has the misfortune to be married to a man who spends far too much time upstairs in the 1860s.

NOTES

INTRODUCTION

1. Robert S. Henry, *"First with the Most" Forrest* (New York: Bobbs-Merrill, 1944), 193.

2. *The War of the Rebellion: Official Records of the Union and Confederate Armies* (Washington, DC: GPO, 1880) (1), vol. 10, pt. 1, 464; hereafter cited as O. R. (1).

3. John Allan Wyeth, *Life of General Nathan Bedford Forrest* (Dayton, OH: Morningside [reissue], 1975), 265–266.

4. Ulysses S. Grant, *Personal Memoirs* (Penguin [one-volume reissue], 1999), 320–321; Jean Edward Smith, *Grant* (New York: Simon & Schuster, 2001), 262.

5. John Y. Simon, ed., *The Papers of U. S. Grant* (Carbondale: Southern Illinois University Press, 1982), 9:302; Smith, *Grant*, 265–268.

6. Smith, *Grant*, 277–280.

7. Ibid., 283.

8. For the South's generals and lieutenant generals, see Ezra Warner, *Generals in Gray* (Baton Rouge: Louisiana State University Press, 1959), xxi.

9. Kenneth M. Stampp, *The Peculiar Institution: Slavery in the Antebellum South* (New York: Alfred A. Knopf, 1956), 31–32.

10. William C. Davis, *Jefferson Davis: The Man and His Hour* (New York: Harper Collins, 1991), 130; James M. McPherson, *Battle Cry of Freedom: The Civil War Era* (New York: Oxford University Press, 1988), 196; James H. Hammond, *Selections from the Letters and Speeches of the Hon. James H. Hammond, of South Carolina* (New York: J. F. Trow & Co., 1866); James M. McPherson, *Drawn with the Sword: Reflections on the American Civil War* (New York: Oxford University Press, 1996), 19.

11. McPherson, *Drawn with the Sword*, 19.

12. Smith, *Grant*, 91–92; *Memphis Daily Appeal*, April 7, 1858, 3.

CHAPTER 1

1. For Kountz charges, see Simon, *Papers of U. S. Grant*, 4:111–113n.

2. O. R. (1), vol. 7, 679–684; Simon, *Papers of U. S. Grant*, 4:320.

3. Grant, *Personal Memoirs*, 170.

4. For charges, see Simon, *Papers of U. S. Grant*, 4:111–113n.

5. Ibid., 298n; John Brinton, *Personal Memoirs* (New York: Neale Publishing Company, 1914), 143; Grant, *Personal Memoirs*, 171–173.

6. The overwhelming bulk of the above summarizes information in the author's previous volume on Grant and Forrest, *Men of Fire* (New York: Basic Books, 2007); the information on Buell and the Duck River Bridge is found in Larry Daniel, *Shiloh: The Battle That Changed the War* (New York: Simon & Schuster, 1997), 114, and Smith, *Grant*, 182–183; the quotations from Grant's letters to Julia Grant are from Simon, *Papers of U. S. Grant*, 5:7. Grant was intended merely to be a caretaker of the army at Pittsburg Landing until Halleck could get there and take command of the planned drive on Corinth. That Halleck was coming is announced in O. R. (1), vol. 10, pt. 2, 24–25.

7. O. R. (1), vol. 10, pt. 1, 90–91.

8. Ibid., 89; Grant, *Personal Memoirs*, 179–180.

CHAPTER 2

1. Regarding the "million and a half of dollars," the 1860 census, in which he is mislabeled "W. B. Forrest," says he owned $171,000 in Memphis real estate and $90,000 in "personal property." That probably wasn't all. By October he had at least 3,345 acres in Coahoma County, Mississippi, having just swapped a 1,346-acre plantation in Phillips County, Arkansas, for 1,445 more acres in Coahoma County valued at $100,000; these figures come from Shelby County, Tennessee, register's records, Book 41-1, 96, and Coahoma County, Mississippi, chancery clerk's records, Book BB, 519.

2. This chapter vastly compresses information scattered throughout *Men of Fire* as well as the author's *Nathan Bedford Forrest: A Biography* (New York: Alfred A. Knopf, 1993). The figures on planter slaveholdings are from Stampp, *The Peculiar Institution*, 30–31.

CHAPTER 3

1. Robert S. Henry, *As They Saw Forrest: Some Recollections and Comments from Contemporaries* (Jackson, TN: McCowat-Mercer Press, 1956), 56–57; Alfred

Roman, *The Military Operations of General Beauregard* (New York: DaCapo Press [reissue], 1994), 1:269.

2. Roman, *The Military Operations of General Beauregard*, 1:269–270.

3. O. R. (1), vol. 10, pt. 2, 379; Henry, *As They Saw Forrest*, 57; Wyeth, *Life of General Nathan Bedford Forrest*, 35.

4. Thomas Jordan and J. P. Pryor, *The Campaigns of Lieutenant General Forrest and Forrest's Cavalry* (Dayton, OH: Morningside Press [reissue], 1977), 113; Basil W. Duke, *The Civil War Reminiscences of General Basil W. Duke, C. S. A.* (New York: Cooper Square Press [reissue], 2001), 345; O. R. (1), vol. 7, 64–66, 329.

5. O. R. (1), vol. 10, pt. 1, 393–394; Daniel, *Shiloh*, 96, 118–120.

6. O. R. (1), vol. 10, pt. 2, 54; ibid., pt. 1, 385; O. Edward Cunningham, Gary D. Joiner, and Timothy B. Smith, eds., *Shiloh and the Western Campaign of 1862* (New York: Savas Beatie, 2007), 140.

7. O. R. (1), vol. 10, pt. 1, 93.

8. Daniel, *Shiloh*, 125.

9. O. R. (1), vol. 10, pt. 1, 567.

10. Daniel, *Shiloh*, 128.

11. O. R. (1), vol. 10, pt. 2, 389.

12. William Preston Johnston, *The Life of General Albert Sidney Johnston* (New York, 1879), 585.

13. O. R. (1), vol. 10, pt. 1, 454.

14. Daniel, *Shiloh*, 131, 322.

CHAPTER 4

1. O. R. (1), vol. 10, pt. 2, 87, 88, 89, 92, 93.

2. Daniel, *Shiloh*, 132.

3. Ibid., 105, 139–140; for the extent of the flooding, see Halleck to Stanton, O. R. (1), vol. 8, 634.

4. Grant, *Personal Memoirs*, 178.

5. Daniel, *Shiloh*, 136–137; John F. Marszalek, *Sherman: A Soldier's Passion for Order* (New York: Free Press, 1993), 176–177.

6. Daniel, *Shiloh*, 137–138, 141, 145–147; O. R. (1), vol. 10, pt. 1, 280.

7. O. R. (1), vol. 10, pt. 1, 280.

8. Ibid., 249; Daniel, *Shiloh*, 157–159.

9. Daniel, *Shiloh*, 157–159.

10. Marszalek, *Sherman*, 35, 53–75.

11. Ibid., 126, 135–137.

12. O. R. (1), vol. 10, pt. 1, 252; Lloyd Lewis, *Sherman: Fighting Prophet* (New York: Harcourt, Brace, 1932), 197–201.

13. O. R. (1), vol. 10, pt. 1, 281.

14. Daniel, *Shiloh*, 111.

15. Ibid., 174; O. R. (1), vol. 10, pt. 1, 184; Ezra Warner, *Generals in Blue* (Baton Rouge: Louisiana State University Press, 1964), 293, 536.

16. O. R. (1), vol. 10, pt. 1, 184; Daniel, *Shiloh*, 174, 355n; Cunningham, Joiner, and Smith, *Shiloh and the Western Campaign of 1862*, 156, 156n.

17. Smith, *Grant*, 190.

18. Ibid., 190–191; O. R. (1), vol. 10, pt. 1, 185.

19. Daniel, *Shiloh*, 175; O. R. (1), vol. 10, pt. 1, 185.

20. Smith, *Grant*, 189, 191.

21. Ibid., 191–192; Timothy B. Smith, *The Untold Story of Shiloh: The Battle and the Battlefield* (Knoxville: University of Tennessee Press, 2006), 33–34; Cunningham, Joiner, and Smith, *Shiloh and the Western Campaign of 1862*, 240–241.

22. Smith, *Grant*, 191, Daniel, *Shiloh*, 175–176.

23. Smith, *Grant*, 192, 193; O. R. (1), vol. 10, pt. 1, 278.

24. Lewis, *Sherman*, 222.

CHAPTER 5

1. For Willie Forrest and his companions, see Henry, *"First with the Most" Forrest*, 78–79.

2. For Confederate weariness and hunger, see, for example, O. R. (1), vol. 10, pt. 1, 545, 553; Daniel, *Shiloh*, 173; and Cunningham, Joiner, and Smith, *Shiloh and the Western Campaign of 1862*, 141.

3. O. R. (1), vol. 10, pt. 1, 454; Henry, *"First with the Most" Forrest*, 77.

4. O. R. (1), vol. 10, pt. 1, 612.

5. Robert U. Johnson and Clarence C. Buel, *Battles and Leaders of the Civil War* (New York, 1988), 1:604–605; Daniel, *Shiloh*, 196.

6. Gilbert V. Rambaut, "Forrest at Shiloh," in Henry, *As They Saw Forrest*, 59. Jordan and Pryor, *The Campaigns of Lieutenant General Forrest*, 127; O. R. (1), vol. 10, pt. 1, 454; Warner, *Generals in Gray*, 210.

7. Rambaut in Henry, *As They Saw Forrest*, 60.

8. Ibid., 61; Daniel, *Shiloh*, 221.

9. Charles P. Roland, *Albert Sidney Johnston: Soldier of Three Republics* (Austin: University of Texas Press, 1964), 336–338.

10. Rambaut in Henry, *As They Saw Forrest*, 61; Daniel, *Shiloh*, 169.

11. Cunningham, Joiner, and Smith, *Shiloh and the Western Campaign of 1862*, 259n.

12. Daniel, *Shiloh*, 229–237; O. R. (1), vol. 10, pt. 1, 409–410. For W. H. L. Wallace's fatal wounding, see Steven E. Woodworth, *Nothing but Victory: The Army of the Tennessee* (New York: Random House, 2005), 201.

13. Rambaut in Henry, *As They Saw Forrest*, 61.

14. O. R. (1), vol. 10, pt. 1, 554, 559, 409.

15. Ibid., 554, 559; Rambaut in Henry, *As They Saw Forrest*, 62. The officer Polk assigned to "take command of all cavalry at hand," O. R. (1), vol. 10, pt. 1, 410, Colonel A. J. Lindsay, reported sending his own regiment after the fleeing Federals and then, finding he "could get no other cavalry," O. R. (1), vol. 10, pt. 1, 459, indicating that Forrest's and perhaps other units had galloped headlong eastward as soon as word arrived that Polk wanted cavalry for pursuit.

16. Rambaut in Henry, *As They Saw Forrest*, 62; Jordan and Pryor, *The Campaigns of Lieutenant General Forrest*, 134.

17. Daniel, *Shiloh*, 253; Cunningham, Joiner, and Smith, *Shiloh and the Western Campaign of 1862*, 307–309; O. R. (1), vol. 10, pt. 1, 534–535, 550–552.

18. O. R. (1), vol. 10, pt. 1, 550–552, 534.

19. Jordan and Pryor, *The Campaigns of Lieutenant General Forrest*, 135.

CHAPTER 6

1. Daniel, *Shiloh*, 186–191, 175, 186.

2. Johnson and Buel, *Battles and Leaders*, 1:492.

3. Daniel, *Shiloh*, 243.

4. Johnson and Buel, *Battles and Leaders*, 1:493, 493n; Cunningham, Joiner, and Smith, *Shiloh and the Western Campaign of 1862*, 318, 318n.

5. Johnson and Buel, *Battles and Leaders*, 1, 493, 493n; Cunningham, Joiner, and Smith, *Shiloh and the Western Campaign of 1862*, 315–317; Daniel, *Shiloh*, 242–243.

6. O. R. (1), vol. 10, pt. 1, 328, 323; Grant, *Personal Memoirs*, 185.

7. Daniel, *Shiloh*, 256–261; Cunningham, Joiner, and Smith, *Shiloh and the Western Campaign of 1862*, 338–339.

8. Daniel, *Shiloh*, 188.

9. Ibid., 224, 246, 223, 245, 225.

10. Cunningham, Joiner, and Smith, *Shiloh and the Western Campaign of 1862*, 319, 319n; Daniel, *Shiloh*, 246, 248.

11. Daniel, *Shiloh*, 247, 249.

12. Daniel, *Shiloh*, 250; William T. Sherman, *Memoirs of General William T. Sherman* (Westport, CT: Greenwood Press [reissue], 1972), 246.

13. Grant, *Personal Memoirs*, 185, 184.

14. Johnson and Buel, *Battles and Leaders*, 1:482.

CHAPTER 7

1. Henry, *"First with the Most" Forrest*, 78–79; Jordan and Pryor, *The Campaigns of Lieutenant General Forrest*, 135n.

2. Jordan and Pryor, *The Campaigns of Lieutenant General Forrest*, 22; Warren County, Mississippi, register's records, Books AA and BB; Frederic Bancroft, *Slave Trading in the Old South* (Baltimore: J. H. Furst Company, 1931), 311; Henry, *"First with the Most" Forrest*, 31.

3. Information on twin psychology is from Dr. William Bernet, professor, Department of Psychiatry, Vanderbilt University School of Medicine, personal communication, May 20, 2009; for Forrest's antilynching committee posts, see *Memphis Daily Appeal*, May 20 and June 25–28, 1857.

4. F. O. Matthiessen, *Theodore Dreiser* (New York: Greenwood Press [reissue], 1976), 131.

5. Wyeth, *Life of General Nathan Bedford Forrest*, 630; Henry, *"First with the Most" Forrest*, 474n; Shelby County, Tennessee, register's records, Book 16, 468; Bancroft, *Slave Trading in the Old South*, 250, 265; *W. H. Rainey & Co.'s Memphis City Directory and General Business Advertiser for 1855–56*, 251; and *Memphis Daily Appeal*, January 14, 1860, 3.

6. See, for example, Wyeth, *Life of General Nathan Bedford Forrest*, 630–631.

7. Jordan and Pryor, *The Campaigns of Lieutenant General Forrest*, 136–137.

8. Roman, *The Military Operations of General Beauregard*, 1:305.

9. Daniel, *Shiloh*, 262; for Gilmer and Fort Henry, see General Tilghman, O. R. (1), vol. 7, 723, and Gilmer, O. R. (1), vol. 7, 735; for Gilmer and Nashville, see O. R. (1), vol. 7, 741.

10. Roman, The Military Operations of General Beauregard, 1:306n; Grady McWhiney, *Braxton Bragg and Confederate Defeat* (Tuscaloosa: University of Alabama Press, 1969), 244; Jordan and Pryor, *The Campaigns of Lieutenant General Forrest*, 135; Johnson and Buel, *Battles and Leaders*, 1:602.

11. Henry, *"First with the Most" Forrest*, 79; for Chalmers, see *Southern Historical Society Papers*, 52 vols. (Richmond: Johns & Goolsby Printers, 1876–1959), 7:458.

12. Daniel, *Shiloh*, 264; Roman, *The Military Operations of General Beauregard*, 1:305; Thomas Jordan in Johnson and Buel, *Battles and Leaders*, 1:602; Jordan

and Pryor, *The Campaigns of Lieutenant General Forrest*, 136–137. The distance is estimated from Roman's account of where Hardee was in relation to Beauregard and maps in Daniel, *Shiloh*, 107, 165.

13. O. R. (1), vol. 10, pt. 1, 617. Again, Trabue's approximate location and its relation to Beauregard's is estimated from maps in Daniel, *Shiloh*, 107, 165.

14. Daniel, *Shiloh*, 264; Jordan and Pryor, *The Campaigns of Lieutenant General Forrest*, 137.

15. *Southern Historical Society Papers*, 7:458.

CHAPTER 8

1. Daniel, *Shiloh*, 249; Augustus Chetlain, *Recollections of Seventy Years* (Galena, IL: Gazette Publishing Company, 1899), 89; *Chicago Tribune*, November 21, 1880.

2. Grant, *Personal Memoirs*, 187; Johnson and Buel, "Shiloh Reviewed," in *Battles and Leaders*, 1:519; as for Wallace, his report indicates no attempt to find Grant that night, O. R. (1), vol. 10, pt. 1, 170; Woodworth, *Nothing but Victory*, 193.

3. Grant, *Personal Memoirs*, 188; Daniel, *Shiloh*, 266.

4. Smith, *Grant*, 200.

5. Grant, *Personal Memoirs*, 187.

CHAPTER 9

1. Daniel, *Shiloh*, 269; Jordan and Pryor, *The Campaigns of Lieutenant General Forrest*, 139.

2. Cunningham, Joiner, and Smith, *Shiloh and the Western Campaign of 1862*, 334, 341–342; Daniel, *Shiloh*, 278, 262–264; Sam Davis Elliott, *Soldier of Tennessee: General Alexander P. Stewart and the Civil War in the West* (Baton Rouge: Louisiana State University Press, 2004), 43, 45; Roman, *The Military Operations of General Beauregard*, 1:309n; Craig L. Symonds, *Stonewall of the West: Patrick Cleburne and the Civil War* (Lawrence: University Press of Kansas, 1998), 72–73.

3. Roman, *The Military Operations of General Beauregard*, 1:311; Jordan and Pryor, *The Campaigns of Lieutenant General Forrest*, 139.

4. Roman, *The Military Operations of General Beauregard*, 1:342.

5. Daniel, *Shiloh*, 289–291; Cunningham, Joiner, and Smith, *Shiloh and the Western Campaign of 1862*, 367–368.

6. Lewis, *Sherman*, 229 (emphasis added).

CHAPTER 10

1. Grant, *Personal Memoirs*, 188.

2. Daniel, *Shiloh*, 249; Cunningham, Joiner, and Smith, *Shiloh and the Western Campaign of 1862*, 343; McPherson, *Battle Cry of Freedom*, 413.

3. Daniel, *Shiloh*, 289–291.

4. Grant, *Personal Memoirs*, 191; O. R. (1), vol. 10, pt. 2, 94.

5. McPherson, *Battle Cry of Freedom*, 413; O. R. (1), vol. 10, pt. 2, 97.

6. Marszalek, *Sherman*, 23; Lewis, *Sherman*, 97; O. R. (1), vol. 7, 595; Smith, *Grant*, 152; Simon, *Papers of U. S. Grant*, 4:215n, 216n; Grant, *Personal Memoirs*, 169.

7. Marszalek, *Sherman*, 6–10, 23, 113–114.

8. Ibid., 6, 15–16, 7, 402, 114–116.

9. Ibid., 160–169, 171, 173. Richard L. Kiper, *Major General John Alexander McClernand: Politician in Uniform* (Kent, OH: Kent State University Press, 1999), 56, 60, 29–30; Smith, *Grant*, 83; Bruce Catton, *Grant Moves South, 1861–1863* (Boston: Little, Brown, 1960), 87–89; Simon, *Papers of U. S. Grant*, 3:324, 360n, 361; ibid., 4:22–23, 114, 166.

CHAPTER 11

1. Daniel, *Shiloh*, 296.

2. Ibid., 295–296; O. R. (1), vol. 10, pt. 1, 620, 640; ibid., pt. 2, 399.

3. Daniel, *Shiloh*, 296; O. R. (1), vol. 10, pt. 1, 640.

4. O. R. (1), vol. 10, pt. 1, 640; Daniel, *Shiloh*, 296–297; O. R. (1), vol. 10, pt. 1, 263, 640; Wyeth, *Life of General Nathan Bedford Forrest*, 78; Henry, *"First with the Most" Forrest*, 80–81; Jordan and Pryor, *The Campaigns of Lieutenant General Forrest*, 146–148. The official reports are O. R. (1), vol. 10, pt. 1, 262–264, 639–641, 923–924.

5. Harvey Mathes, *General Forrest* (New York: D. Appleton and Company, 1902), 60; Jordan and Pryor, *The Campaigns of Lieutenant General Forrest*, 146–148; Wyeth, *Life of General Nathan Bedford Forrest*, 78–81; Henry, *"First with the Most" Forrest*, 80–81.

6. For Terry's Texas Rangers, see Patricia Faust, ed., *Historical Times Illustrated Encyclopedia of the Civil War* (New York: Harper & Row, 1986), 750.

7. O. R. (1), vol. 10, pt. 1, 627, 923–924.

8. For Wharton's and Harrison's backgrounds, see Warner, *Generals in Gray*, 331–332, 127.

9. For example, at the battle of Dover, Tennessee, with Wharton and Major General Joseph Wheeler in February 1863 and with Major General Stephen Lee at Tupelo in July 1864.

10. Duke, *The Civil War Reminiscences of General Basil W. Duke, C. S. A.*, 348–349; Wyeth, *Life of General Nathan Bedford Forrest*, 9–10.

11. Andrew Lytle, *Bedford Forrest and His Critter Company* (New York: McDowell, Obolensky, 1931), 14–15; Wyeth, *Life of General Nathan Bedford Forrest*, 35.

12. Albert T. Goodloe, *Confederate Echoes* (Nashville: Methodist Publishing House, 1907), 179.

CHAPTER 12

1. Daniel, *Shiloh*, 304.

2. Ibid., 304–305.

3. Simon, *Papers of U. S. Grant*, 4:47, 102; Brooks D. Simpson, *Ulysses S. Grant: Triumph over Adversity, 1822–1865* (New York: Houghton-Mifflin Company, 2000), 44.

4. Simon, *Papers of U. S. Grant*, 4:119, 73, 102, 78.

5. O. R. (1), vol. 10, pt. 1, 292; Smith, *The Untold Story of Shiloh*, 27–28.

6. O. R. (1), vol. 10, pt. 1, 113–114.

7. Simon, *Papers of U. S. Grant*, 3:324, 325–328, etc.; Daniel, *Shiloh*, 304–306; Simon, *Papers of U. S. Grant*, 5:51n; Daniel, *Shiloh*, 306.

8. John Marszalek, *Commander of All Lincoln's Armies: A Life of General Henry Halleck* (Cambridge, MA: Harvard University Press, 2004), 122–123.

9. Simon, *Papers of U. S. Grant*, 5:48–49n.

10. Ibid., 72, 102.

11. Daniel, *Shiloh*, 306–308; *Official Records of the Union and Confederate Navies in the War of the Rebellion,*(Washington, DC: GPO, 1894), vol. 22, 280–281; Simon, *Papers of U. S. Grant*, 4:115–116n.

12. William S. McFeely, *Grant: A Biography* (New York: W. W. Norton, 1981), 116.

CHAPTER 13

1. Simon, *Papers of U. S. Grant*, 5:105–106n.

2. Ibid., 114, 115n. For the Grant-Halleck exchanges in the wake of Fort Donelson, see Grant, *Personal Memoirs*, 174–176; Smith, *Grant*, 177, 178; Simon, *Papers of U. S. Grant*, 4:344n, 318, 320, 327, 331, 331n, 344n, 353, 354n, 355.

3. Simon, *Papers of U. S. Grant*, 5:116, 120.

4. Ibid., 110; Grant, *Personal Memoirs*, 203–204; Smith, *Grant*, 659n.

5. Simon, *Papers of U. S. Grant*, 5:118; Grant, *Personal Memoirs*, 204; O. R. (1), vol. 10, pt. 2, 223, 225, 228.

6. Marszalek, *Commander of All Lincoln's Armies*, 123–124.

7. Lew Wallace, *An Autobiography* (New York: Harper & Brothers, 1906), 1:575–576.

8. Simon, *Papers of U. S. Grant*, 5:117, 127, 130, 135, 103, 124; Smith, *Grant*, 94.

9. Lewis, *Sherman*, 235.

10. Simon, *Papers of U. S. Grant*, 5:130, 103.

11. Ibid., 5:140, 141n.

12. Benson Bobrick, *Master of War: The Life of General George H. Thomas* (New York: Simon & Schuster, 2009), 114–115, 95, 36–37, 275.

13. Ibid., 4, 14, 15, 28–38, 42.

14. Ibid., 115. Bobrick views Thomas's act as a self-sacrifice done out of "regard for Grant." Jean Edward Smith, in his biography of Grant, *Personal Memoirs*, 266, pictures the two men more than a year later as stoic, kindred spirits who understood each other intuitively and were "bonding." Both characterizations seem strained. But other sources indicate that there was a mutual Grant-Thomas coolness and that it dated from Thomas's brief command of Grant's army.

15. Simon, *Papers of U. S. Grant*, 5:142–143.

CHAPTER 14

1. O. R. (1), vol. 16, pt. 1, 692–714.

2. Roman, *The Military Operations of General Beauregard*, 1:402; Jordan and Pryor, *The Campaigns of Lieutenant General Forrest*, 159, 159n. For John Scott, see David A. Powell, *Failure in the Saddle: Nathan Bedford Forrest, Joseph Wheeler, and the Confederate Cavalry in the Chickamauga Campaign* (New York: Savas Beatie, 2010), xxxv.

3. Jordan and Pryor, *The Campaigns of Lieutenant General Forrest*, 159.

4. T. Harry Williams, *P. G. T. Beauregard: Napoleon in Gray* (Baton Rouge: Louisiana State University Press, 1955), 156–157; Roman, *The Military Operations of General Beauregard*, 1:401–402; Jordan and Pryor, *The Campaigns of Lieutenant General Forrest*, 144, 146–147; Wyeth, *Life of General Nathan Bedford Forrest*, 627; Duke, *The Civil War Reminiscences of General Basil W. Duke, C. S. A.*, 346.

5. Mathes, *General Forrest*, 63.

6. Kate Cumming, *A Journal of Hospital Life in the Confederate Army of Tennessee from the Battle of Shiloh to the End of the War* (Louisville, KY, 1866), 12–19.

7. Roman, *The Military Operations of General Beauregard*, 1:402.

8. Ibid.; Jordan and Pryor, *The Campaigns of Lieutenant General Forrest*, 159–161; Henry, *"First with the Most" Forrest*, 83, 85.

9. O. R. (1), vol. 16, pt. 2, 722–723.

10. Ibid., 102.

11. Ibid., pt. 1, 711.

12. Ibid., 775.

13. Jordan and Pryor, *The Campaigns of Lieutenant General Forrest*, 173n.

14. John C. Spence, *Annals of Rutherford County* (Nashville: Williams Printing Co., 1991), 2:170.

15. Spence, *Annals*, 2:167; Henry Down Jamison and Marguerite McTigue, *Letters and Recollections of a Confederate Soldier, 1860–1865* (Nashville, 1964), 17; John C. Spence, *A Diary of the Civil War* (Nashville: Williams Printing Co., 1993), 40, 41; Spence, *Annals*, 2:167; Spence, *Diary*, 35.

16. Charles W. Bennett, "Historical Sketches of the Ninth Michigan Infantry," quoted in a July 1937 newspaper clipping on file at Oaklands Museum, Murfreesboro, Tennessee; O. R. (1), vol. 16, pt. 1, 794, 808, 801.

17. Spence, *Diary*, 38–39; Wyeth, *Life of General Nathan Bedford Forrest*, 90–91; Henry, *"First with the Most" Forrest*, 482n.

18. O. R. (1), vol. 16, pt. 2, 83, 93.

19. Ibid., pt. 1, 35.

20. Ibid., 794–795.

21. Ibid., 810.

22. Ibid.; Jordan and Pryor, *The Campaigns of Lieutenant General Forrest*, 162–163; Lytle, *Bedford Forrest and His Critter Company*, 91.

23. "Forrest's Birthday Party," a 1937 newspaper clipping on file at Oaklands Museum, Murfreesboro, Tennessee.

24. O. R. (1), vol. 16, pt. 1, 801; Mathes, *General Forrest*, 65; O. R (1), vol. 16, pt. 1, 810; H. W. Graber, *The Life Record of H. W. Graber, a Terry Texas Ranger, 1861–1865* (H. W. Graber, 1916), 66.

25. Jordan and Pryor, *The Campaigns of Lieutenant General Forrest*, 164; O. R. (1), vol. 16, pt. 1, 810.

26. O. R. (1), vol. 16, pt. 1, 798.

27. "Forrest's Birthday Party," a 1937 newspaper clipping on file at Oaklands Museum, Murfreesboro, Tennessee; O. R. (1), vol. 16, pt. 1, 798.

28. "Forrest's Birthday Party" clipping; O. R. (1), vol. 16, pt. 1, 802.

29. O. R. (1), vol. 16, pt. 1, 804, 802, 795, 805; Spence, *Diary*, 44; Graber, *Life Record*, 66; Jordan and Pryor, *The Campaigns of Lieutenant General Forrest*, 165n; John Randolph Poole, *Cracker Cavaliers: The Second Georgia Cavalry Under Wheeler and Forrest* (Macon, GA: Mercer University Press, 2000), 22.

30. Graber, *Life Record*, 66–67.

31. Jordan and Pryor, *The Campaigns of Lieutenant General Forrest*, 166; Graber, *Life Record*, 67.

32. Wyeth, *Life of General Nathan Bedford Forrest*, 90.

33. O. R. (1), vol. 16, pt. 1, 799; Graber, *Life Record*, 68.

34. Graber, *Life Record*, 67.

35. O. R. (1), vol. 16, pt. 1, 810. The Georgians were with the Second Georgia.

36. Spence, *Diary*, 44; O. R. (1), vol. 16, pt. 1, 796. These Georgians apparently were from both the First and Second Georgia regiments. The Texans were a detachment accompanying the Georgians on the first assault on the square.

37. O. R. (1), vol. 16, pt. 1, 805; Spence, *Diary*, 45.

38. O. R. (1), vol. 16, pt. 1, 810; Jordan and Pryor, *The Campaigns of Lieutenant General Forrest*, 168; Spence, *Diary*, 45. Here Forrest's official report apparently misidentifies Morrison as being with the Second Georgia.

39. Spence, *Diary*, 45; O. R. (1), vol. 16, pt. 1, 801, 796.

40. Wyeth, *Life of General Nathan Bedford Forrest*, 91.

41. Jordan and Pryor, *The Campaigns of Lieutenant General Forrest*, 169.

42. O. R. (1), vol. 16, pt. 1, 799.

43. Ibid., 810, 799; Jordan and Pryor, *The Campaigns of Lieutenant General Forrest*, 169; Lytle, *Bedford Forrest and His Critter Company*, 96.

44. O. R. (1), vol. 16, pt. 1, 800; Jordan and Pryor, *The Campaigns of Lieutenant General Forrest*, 170; O. R. (1), vol. 16, pt. 1, 810.

45. O. R. (1), vol. 16, pt. 1, 805.

46. Ibid., 807.

47. Jordan and Pryor, *The Campaigns of Lieutenant General Forrest*, 171; for remembering Donelson and Shiloh, see Lytle, *Bedford Forrest and His Critter Company*, 97.

48. Graber, *Life Record*, 68–69; O. R. (1), vol. 16, pt. 1, 802.

49. O. R. (1), vol. 16, pt. 1, 805.

50. Ibid., 806.

51. Ibid., 805, 806; "Forrest's Birthday Party," a 1937 newspaper clipping on file at Oaklands Museum, Murfreesboro, Tennessee.

52. Jordan and Pryor, *The Campaigns of Lieutenant General Forrest*, 171; Graber, *Life Record*, 69.

53. O. R. (1), vol. 16, pt. 1, 805–806.

54. Ibid., 799, 808, 807.

55. Ibid., 799. Forrest's report says only that he summoned both camps to surrender.

56. Lytle, *Bedford Forrest and His Critter Company*, 98; O. R. (1), vol. 16, pt. 1, 811, 808, 802.

57. O. R. (1), vol. 16, pt. 1, 807–808, 792, 799–800.

58. Ibid., 808, 809, 811.

59. "Forrest's Birthday Party," a 1937 newspaper clipping on file at Oaklands

Museum, Murfreesboro, Tennessee; Jordan and Pryor, *The Campaigns of Lieutenant General Forrest*, 175; O. R. (1), vol. 16, pt. 1, 806–807.

60. Jordan and Pryor, *The Campaigns of Lieutenant General Forrest*, 170; Graber, *Life Record*, 70. Wyeth, *Life of General Nathan Bedford Forrest*, 92; Brian Steel Wills, *A Battle from the Start: The Life of Nathan Bedford Forrest* (New York: Harper-Collins, 1992), 77.

CHAPTER 15

1. Simon, *Papers of U. S. Grant*, 5:204, 207n.

2. O. R. (1), vol. 16, pt. 1, 793.

3. Smith, *Grant*, 213–214; Grant, *Personal Memoirs*, 211–212.

4. Simon, *Papers of U. S. Grant*, 5:182n, 190n, 192n.

5. Ibid., 225; Grant, *Personal Memoirs*, 207.

6. Simon, *Papers of U. S. Grant*, 5:226n.

7. Ibid., 218, 264.

8. Ibid., 311.

9. Ibid.

10. Kiper, *Major General John Alexander McClernand*, 129–131.

11. Simon, *Papers of U. S. Grant*, 5:168n, 168, 169, 169n.

12. Ibid., 227, 250, 251n, 278.

13. Ibid., 338, 340.

14. Ibid., 51.

15. Ibid., 340.

16. Ibid., 250; O. R. (1), vol. 16, pt. 2, 783.

17. Simon, *Papers of U. S. Grant*, 5:169, 169n.

18. O. R. (1), vol. 17, pt. 1, 52–55.

19. Ibid., 60–65.

20. Ibid., 61–62.

21. Ibid., 65.

22. Ibid., 65–66; ibid., pt. 2, 222.

23. Ibid., pt. 1, 65, 118, 66.

24. Ibid., 66–67, 118–119.

25. Ibid., 123, 119.

26. Ibid., 90, 94; *The Official Military Atlas of the Civil War* (New York: Crown, 1978), plate 25, no. 2; O. R. (1), vol. 17, pt. 1, 99, 97, 91, 107, 108, 95–96, 88, 92, 104, 109–110.

27. O. R. (1), vol. 17, pt. 1, 67.

28. Ibid., 68.

29. Ibid., 79.

30. Ibid., 107.

31. O. R. (1), vol. 17, pt. 1, 352–353, 344, 251, 168, 252–253, 386, 254–257, 205, 227, 168–169.

32. Ibid., 157–158; Simon, *Papers of U. S. Grant*, 6:106.

33. Simon, *Papers of U. S. Grant*, 6; O. R. (1), vol. 17, pt. 1, 158, 160.

34. O. R. (1), vol. 17, pt. 1, 169, 257, 259–260, 227.

35. Ibid., 201, 281, 228; Smith, *Grant*, 219.

36. O. R. (1), vol. 17, pt. 1, 173–176, 382–384, 158.

37. Ibid., 267.

CHAPTER 16

1. Jordan and Pryor, *The Campaigns of Lieutenant General Forrest*, 175–176; Henry, *"First with the Most" Forrest*, 91; O. R. (1), vol. 16, pt. 2, 363.

2. O. R. (1), vol. 16, pt. 2, 157, 162, 146, 169.

3. Ibid., pt. 1, 818, 852; Jordan and Pryor, *The Campaigns of Lieutenant General Forrest*, 176–177.

4. O. R. (1), vol. 16, pt.1, 818–819.

5. Ibid., 816; ibid., pt. 2, 266, 234.

6. McWhiney, *Braxton Bragg*, 3, 2; Jordan and Pryor, *The Campaigns of Lieutenant General Forrest*, 18–19.

7. McWhiney, *Braxton Bragg*, 1, 2, 4.

8. Ibid., 19.

9. Ibid., 16, 17; for the old-army anecdote, see Grant, *Personal Memoirs*, 362.

10. Roman, *The Military Operations of General Beauregard*, 1:594.

11. The face-to-face meeting appears to have occurred sometime around August 10. Jordan and Pryor, *The Campaigns of Lieutenant General Forrest*, 178; O. R. (1), vol. 16, pt. 2, 749, 757, 761; Henry, *"First with the Most" Forrest*, 96.

12. O. R. (1), vol. 16, pt. 2, 749.

13. Ibid., 748.

14. Ibid., 761.

15. Ibid., 368, 364.

16. Ibid., 770.

17. Ibid., 452.

18. Henry, *"First with the Most" Forrest*, 96–97; Jordan and Pryor, *The Campaigns of Lieutenant General Forrest*, 180–181.

19. O. R. (1), vol. 16, pt. 2, 453.

20. Ibid., 761; Faust, *Historical Times Illustrated Encyclopedia of the Civil War*, 818; O. R. (1), vol. 16, pt. 1, 893.

21. O. R. (1), vol. 16, pt. 2, 462–463.

22. Craig L. Symonds, *Joseph E. Johnston: A Civil War Biography* (New York: W. W. Norton, 1992), 271.

23. Jamison and McTigue, *Letters and Recollections of a Confederate Soldier*, 19, 18, 20.

24. Jordan and Pryor, *The Campaigns of Lieutenant General Forrest*, 182.

25. O. R. (1), vol. 16, pt. 2, 483; Jordan and Pryor, *The Campaigns of Lieutenant General Forrest*, 181–183.

26. O. R. (1), vol. 16, pt. 1, 893, 894.

27. Ibid.; Jordan and Pryor, *The Campaigns of Lieutenant General Forrest*, 184. The latter says Forrest arrived in Glasgow "about September 8," but the actual date must have been September 12 or 13.

28. John P. Dyer, *Fightin' Joe Wheeler* (Baton Rouge: Louisiana State University Press, 1941), 3–4, 9–11.

29. Ibid., 17–18, 9, 11n.

30. Ibid., 23–25, 27.

31. Ibid., 39, 15, 14; Joseph Wheeler, *Campaigns of Wheeler and His Cavalry* (Atlanta: Hodgins Publishing Company, 1899), 8.

32. O. R. (1), vol. 16, pt. 2, 824, 828, 832, 827.

33. *Southern Historical Society Papers*, 7: 455; US census records for 1850, 368; Warner, *Generals in Gray*, 7.

34. Johnson and Buel, *Battles and Leaders*, 3:10.

35. O. R. (1), vol. 16, pt. 2, 830, 856, 861, 856, 858.

36. Stephen W. Sears, *Landscape Turned Red: The Battle of Antietam* (New York: Ticknor & Fields, 1983), 296; O. R. (1), vol. 16, pt. 2, 846, 852, 889.

37. O. R. (1), vol. 16, pt. 2, 837–838.

38. Jordan and Pryor, *The Campaigns of Lieutenant General Forrest*, 185n. For lore on Forrest's Bragg grousing, see Lytle, *Bedford Forrest and His Critter Company*, 110.

39. O. R. (1), vol. 16, pt. 2, 856, 863.

40. Ibid., 865–866, 868.

41. Ibid., 876–877, 868.

42. Jordan and Pryor, *The Campaigns of Lieutenant General Forrest*, 186.

43. Henry, *"First with the Most" Forrest*, 102, 104.

44. Jordan and Pryor, *The Campaigns of Lieutenant General Forrest*, 189.

45. O. R. (1), vol. 16, pt. 2, 918, 929, 931, 952, 972.

46. Henry, *"First with the Most" Forrest*, 106.

47. O. R. (1), vol. 17, pt. 1, 420; Jordan and Pryor, *The Campaigns of Lieutenant General Forrest*, 192.

48. John Watson Morton, *The Artillery of Nathan Bedford Forrest's Cavalry* (Nashville: Publishing House of the Methodist Episcopal Church South, 1909), 33, 45, 46–47.

49. O. R. (1), vol. 20, pt. 2, 435.

CHAPTER 17

1. Simon, *Papers of U. S. Grant*, 6:131n, 132n; Grant, *Personal Memoirs*, 226.

2. Simon, *Papers of U. S. Grant*, 7:130, 131, 131n, 132n.

3. Ibid., 134.

4. Warner, *Generals in Blue*, 410–411.

5. Simon, *Papers of U. S. Grant*, 6:131–132n.

6. Brinton, *Personal Memoirs*, 115.

7. Simon, *Papers of U. S. Grant*, 6:164, 164n.

8. Ibid., 166–167n.

9. Ibid., 161; O. R. (1), vol. 17, pt. 2, 286–287.

10. O. R. (1), vol. 16, pt. 2, 640–642.

11. Simon, *Papers of U. S. Grant*, 6:243, 243n.

12. Samuel Carter , *The Final Fortress: The Campaign for Vicksburg, 1862–1863* (New York: St. Martin's, 1980), 18; Grant, *Personal Memoirs*, 315.

13. For some of Grant's communications related to the Confederate evacuation of Holly Springs, see Simon, *Papers of U. S. Grant* 6:255n, 262, 263, 264n, 268, 270n, etc. For Pemberton's reversal of the Confederate decision to evacuate Holly Springs, see O. R. (1), vol. 17, pt. 1, 468.

14. Simon, *Papers of U. S. Grant*, 6:285; O. R. (1), vol. 17, pt. 1, 486–487.

15. Simon, *Papers of U. S. Grant*, 6:285–286.

16. Ibid., 252.

17. Ibid., 252, 180, 315.

18. Grant, *Personal Memoirs*, 230; Simon, *Papers of U. S. Grant*, 6:315, 315–317n.

19. Simon, *Papers of U. S. Grant*, 6:317n.

20. Ibid., 283.

21. Simon, *Papers of U. S. Grant*, 7:50.

22. Smith, *Grant*, 226; Arndt M. Stickles, *Simon Bolivar Buckner: Borderland Knight* (Chapel Hill: University of North Carolina Press, 1940) 39.

23. Smith, *Grant*, 225; Simon, *Papers of U. S. Grant*, 6:273–275.

24. Simon, *Papers of U. S. Grant*, 7:8, 45, 53n.

25. Ibid., 53–55n.

26. Ibid., 53n.

27. Ibid., 6:290–291, 296–297, 306n; ibid., 7:6.

28. O. R. (1), vol. 17, pt. 2, 348; ibid., pt. 1, 467, 471.

29. O. R. (1), vol. 17, pt. 1, 470.

30. Ibid.

31. Kiper, *Major General John Alexander McClernand*, 143; O. R. (1), vol. 17, pt. 1, pt. 2, 282.

32. Simon, *Papers of U. S. Grant*, 6:310, 180n. For Grant-Curtis unfriendliness, see, for example, ibid., 375, 376–377n.

33. O. R. (1), vol. 17, pt. 1, 469.

34. Grant, *Personal Memoirs*, 231; Simon, *Papers of U. S. Grant*, 6:362.

35. Simon, *Papers of U. S. Grant*, 6:371, 372, 372n.

36. Ibid., 406–407, 404.

37. Ibid., 408–409.

38. O. R. (1), vol. 17, pt. 1, 474.

CHAPTER 18

1. O. R. (1), vol. 17, pt. 2, 788–790.

2. Ibid., 780, 781; Davis, *Jefferson Davis*, 482–483.

3. O. R. (1), vol. 17, pt. 2, 781.

4. Ibid., 755; ibid., vol. 20, pt. 2, 422; Jordan and Pryor, *The Campaigns of Lieutenant General Forrest*, 193–194.

5. O. R. (1), vol. 20, pt. 1, 63–64; ibid., vol. 17, pt. 2, 781.

6. Ibid., vol. 17, pt. 1, 592; Jordan and Pryor, *The Campaigns of Lieutenant General Forrest*, 192, 193–194; Henry, *"First with the Most" Forrest*, 108; O. R. (1), vol. 20, pt. 2, 422.

7. James A. Ramage, *Rebel Raider: The Life of General John Hunt Morgan* (Lexington: University Press of Kentucky, 1986), 82–83, 127–128; McWhiney, *Braxton Bragg*, 217, 185; Wheeler, *Campaigns*, 25, 26.

8. Morton, *The Artillery of Nathan Bedford Forrest's Cavalry*, 45–47.

9. Henry, *"First with the Most" Forrest*, 350, 520n.

10. *Memphis Daily Appeal*, July 21, 1858, 2; Shelby County, Tennessee, register's records, Book 18, 105.

11. Jordan and Pryor, *The Campaigns of Lieutenant General Forrest*, 41–42, 194; Wyeth, *Life of General Nathan Bedford Forrest*, 92.

12. Jordan and Pryor, *The Campaigns of Lieutenant General Forrest*, 194; Wyeth, *Life of General Nathan Bedford Forrest*, 107–108; Morton, *The Artillery of Nathan Bedford Forrest's Cavalry*, 48; Henry, *"First with the Most" Forrest*, 109.

13. O. R. (1), vol. 17, pt. 1, 593.

14. Jordan and Pryor, *The Campaigns of Lieutenant General Forrest*, 194, 195.

15. Ibid.; Henry, *"First with the Most" Forrest*, 108.

16. O. R. (1), vol. 17, pt. 2, 400, 405, 415, 423.

17. Ibid., 426, 427, 428, 431.

18. Ibid.

19. Ibid., pt. 1, 553–554.

20. Morton, *The Artillery of Nathan Bedford Forrest's Cavalry*, 47–48, 51.

21. Jordan and Pryor, *The Campaigns of Lieutenant General Forrest*, 195; O. R. (1), vol. 17, pt. 1, 554.

22. Jordan and Pryor, *The Campaigns of Lieutenant General Forrest*, 195; O. R. (1), vol. 17, pt. 1, 554.

23. O. R. (1), vol. 17, pt. 1, 554, 593; Jordan and Pryor, *The Campaigns of Lieutenant General Forrest*, 195–196.

24. O. R. (1), vol. 17, pt. 1, 598, 300–301.

25. Ibid., 482, 555–556.

26. Ibid., 598, 593.

27. Ibid., 551, 568.

28. Ibid.

29. Ibid., 594, 564; Morton, *The Artillery of Nathan Bedford Forrest's Cavalry*, 57; Jordan and Pryor, *The Campaigns of Lieutenant General Forrest*, 199.

30. O. R. (1), vol. 17, pt. 1, 560–561, 566; Jordan and Pryor, *The Campaigns of Lieutenant General Forrest*, 200–201.

31. O. R. (1), vol. 17, pt. 1, 561–562; Jordan and Pryor, *The Campaigns of Lieutenant General Forrest*, 200–201.

32. Morton, *The Artillery of Nathan Bedford Forrest's Cavalry*, 57–58; Jordan and Pryor, *The Campaigns of Lieutenant General Forrest*, 201. The authorized biography says that Forrest delivered the "subjugation" quote "in effect."

33. O. R. (1), vol. 17, pt. 1, 593; Jordan and Pryor, *The Campaigns of Lieutenant General Forrest*, 202; Jac Weller, "The Logistics of Nathan Bedford Forrest," in *Military Analysis of the Civil War* (Millwood, NY: Krauss-Thompson Organization, Ltd., 1977), 176–177, notes that Forrest's deprivation in youth focused him on the worth of everything.

34. Henry, *"First with the Most" Forrest*, 111; O. R. (1), vol. 17, pt. 1, 550.

35. Wyeth, *Life of General Nathan Bedford Forrest*, 108–109; Henry, *"First with the Most" Forrest*, 110–111.

36. O. R. (1), vol. 17, pt. 1, 594; Jordan and Pryor, *The Campaigns of Lieutenant General Forrest*, 202–203.

37. Henry, *"First with the Most" Forrest*, 113. As Henry notes, Mathes, aided by Forrest's son Willie, as well as some of Forrest's staff attest to Forrest's usual

practice of drawing his sword with his right hand, as opposed to Wyeth's mistaken report.

38. Ibid., 248; O. R. (1), vol. 17, pt. 1, 594.

39. O. R. (1), vol. 17, pt. 1, 548–549.

40. Ibid., 594; Jordan and Pryor, *The Campaigns of Lieutenant General Forrest*, 205.

41. O. R. (1), vol. 17, pt. 1, 594, 567–568.

42. Ibid., 595; Henry, *"First with the Most" Forrest*, 116; Morton, *The Artillery of Nathan Bedford Forrest's Cavalry*, 62. For Forrest's prowess with an axe, see Jordan and Pryor, *The Campaigns of Lieutenant General Forrest*, 22, and Henry, *"First with the Most" Forrest*, 24.

43. O. R. (1), vol. 17, pt. 2, 428; ibid., pt. 1, 550; Wyeth, *Life of General Nathan Bedford Forrest*, 121.

44. O. R. (1), vol. 17, pt. 1, 572–573.

45. Ibid., 594; Jordan and Pryor, *The Campaigns of Lieutenant General Forrest*, 208.

46. O. R. (1), vol. 17, pt. 1, 580; Jordan and Pryor, *The Campaigns of Lieutenant General Forrest*, 209. For a description of the Forty Thieves, see Wyeth, *Life of General Nathan Bedford Forrest*, 124n.

47. Jordan and Pryor, *The Campaigns of Lieutenant General Forrest*, 209n; Morton, *The Artillery of Nathan Bedford Forrest's Cavalry*, 64.

48. O. R. (1), vol. 17, pt. 1, 580.

49. Jordan and Pryor, *The Campaigns of Lieutenant General Forrest*, 209–211, 217; O. R. (1), vol. 17, pt. 1, 580–581, 595.

50. Wyeth, *Life of General Nathan Bedford Forrest*, 125.

51. Ibid., 125–126; Jordan and Pryor, *The Campaigns of Lieutenant General Forrest*, 210–211; O. R. (1), vol. 17, pt. 1, 580–581; Edwin C. Bearss, *The Vicksburg Campaign* (Dayton, OH: Morningside Press, 1985), 1:260–261.

52. O. R. (1), vol. 17, pt. 1, 581; Jordan and Pryor, *The Campaigns of Lieutenant General Forrest*, 210–211.

53. Jordan and Pryor, *The Campaigns of Lieutenant General Forrest*, 211; O. R. (1), vol. 17, pt. 1, 597; Morton, *The Artillery of Nathan Bedford Forrest's Cavalry*, 64.

54. O. R. (1), vol. 17, pt. 1, 580–581; Jordan and Pryor, *The Campaigns of Lieutenant General Forrest*, 212.

55. O. R. (1), vol. 17, pt. 1, 582; Jordan and Pryor, *The Campaigns of Lieutenant General Forrest*, 212–213.

56. O. R. (1), vol. 17, pt. 1, 581; Jordan and Pryor, *The Campaigns of Lieutenant General Forrest*, 213; Wyeth, *Life of General Nathan Bedford Forrest*, 127–128; Bearss, *The Vicksburg Campaign*, 1:262.

57. O. R. (1), vol. 17, pt. 1, 589; Wyeth, *Life of General Nathan Bedford Forrest*, 127; Bearss, *The Vicksburg Campaign*, 1:262.

58. O. R. (1), vol. 17, pt. 1, 596, 583; Wyeth, *Life of General Nathan Bedford Forrest*, 129; Jordan and Pryor, *The Campaigns of Lieutenant General Forrest*, 213.

59. O. R. (1), vol. 17, pt. 1, 596, 569, 578, 576; Mathes, *General Forrest*, 92; Wyeth, *Life of General Nathan Bedford Forrest*, 128.

60. O. R. (1), vol. 17, pt. 1, 578, 579, 573, 570, 553. Pages 578 and 589 are two of the Federal references giving the time of the Union surprise attack; page 570 gives the formation for the attack, and 553 shows that the Fuller guns were, like Dunham's, part of the Seventh Wisconsin.

61. Jordan and Pryor, *The Campaigns of Lieutenant General Forrest*, 218; O. R. (1), vol. 17, pt. 1, 596; Bearss, *The Vicksburg Campaign*, 1:267; Wyeth, *Life of General Nathan Bedford Forrest*, 134.

62. Jordan and Pryor, *The Campaigns of Lieutenant General Forrest*, 217–218; Bearss, *The Vicksburg Campaign*, 1:266.

63. Jordan and Pryor, *The Campaigns of Lieutenant General Forrest*, 214–215, and Wyeth, *Life of General Nathan Bedford Forrest*, 134–135, describe Forrest's charge to save his guns.

64. Wyeth, *Life of General Nathan Bedford Forrest*, 135; O. R. (1), vol. 17, pt. 1, 570, 578, 573.

65. Morton, *The Artillery of Nathan Bedford Forrest's Cavalry*, 66, 67–68. Forrest's misapprehension of McLemore's action is in his report, O. R. (1), vol. 17, pt. 1, 597. He later learned the facts of the case.

66. O. R. (1), vol. 17, pt. 1, 553, 510, 571; Jordan and Pryor, *The Campaigns of Lieutenant General Forrest*, 215.

67. Bearss, *The Vicksburg Campaign*, 1:268; O. R. (1), vol. 17, pt. 1, 578.

68. Jordan and Pryor, *The Campaigns of Lieutenant General Forrest*, 218, 219; Bearss, *The Vicksburg Campaign*, 1:268, 269–270; O. R. (1), vol. 17, pt. 1, 597.

69. O. R. (1), vol. 17, pt. 1, 552, 597; Henry, *"First with the Most" Forrest*, 488n; Bearss, *The Vicksburg Campaign*, 1:272.

70. O. R. (1), vol. 17, pt. 1, 548–549; Bearss, *The Vicksburg Campaign*, 1:346; Grant, *Personal Memoirs*, 235.

CHAPTER 19

1. O. R. (1), vol. 17, pt. 2, 424; ibid., pt. 1, 607.

2. Kiper, *Major General John Alexander McClernand*, 29–30.

3. Lewis, *Sherman*, 258; Bearss, *The Vicksburg Campaign*, 1:128, 194.

4. Bearss, *The Vicksburg Campaign*, 1:128; O. R. (1), vol. 17, pt. 1, 605, 604, 616.

5. O. R. (1), vol. 17, pt. 1, 605–606.

6. Ibid., 606, 638; Johnson and Buel, *Battles and Leaders*, 3:463.

7. O. R. (1), vol. 17, pt. 1, 607.

8. Marszalek, *Sherman*, 206, sources the report by the black man.

9. O. R. (1), vol. 17, pt. 1, 637, 606–607, 631.

10. Ibid., 607–608.

11. Ibid., 638, 647; Johnson and Buel, *Battles and Leaders*, 3:466; Bearss, *The Vicksburg Campaign*, 1:194–195.

12. Johnson and Buel, *Battles and Leaders*, 3:467.

13. Ibid.; Bearss, *The Vicksburg Campaign*, 1:188–189, 192; O. R. (1), vol. 17, pt. 1, 635; ibid., 634, describes the path up the bank.

14. Johnson and Buel, *Battles and Leaders*, 3:467.

15. O. R. (1), vol. 17, pt. 1, 649–650.

16. Ibid., 628, 634, 608.

17. Ibid., 625, 638.

18. Ibid., 673, 625, 671.

19. Ibid., 609–610.

20. Simon, *Papers of U. S. Grant*, 7:61–62, 62n.

21. Ibid., 34n; Kiper, *Major General John Alexander McClernand*, 154–155.

22. O. R. (1), vol. 17, pt. 2, 528.

23. Kiper, *Major General John Alexander McClernand*, 153.

24. O. R. (1), vol. 17, pt. 2, 528; Marszalek, *Commander of All of Lincoln's Armies*, 162.

25. Simon, *Papers of U. S. Grant*, 7:31–32.

26. Woodworth, *Nothing but Victory*, 285.

27. O. R. (1), vol. 17, pt. 2, 529.

28. Simon, *Papers of U. S. Grant*, 7:186, 193.

29. Ibid.

30. Ibid., 186, 186–187n.

31. O. R. (1), vol. 17, pt. 1, 700, 701, 612.

32. Ibid., 701, 570–571; Grant, *Personal Memoirs*, 238.

33. O. R. (1), vol. 17, pt. 2, 553–554.

34. Ibid., 559; Johnson and Buel, *Battles and Leaders*, 3:452–453; Kiper, *Major General John Alexander McClernand*, 175, 166; Sherman, *Memoirs*, 301; Marszalek, *Sherman*, 212–213.

35. O. R. (1), vol. 17, pt. 2, 555.

36. Ibid., 566–567.

37. Kiper, *Major General John Alexander McClernand*, 184, names three notable Union non–West Pointers—Generals Clinton Fisk and Thomas Kilby Smith and

Admiral David Dixon Porter—who did not like McClernand. Fisk's siding with Grant indicates either that Grant's alcohol consumption was not as egregious as some have contended or that Fisk found McClernand's personality worse than Grant's drinking; Fisk was such a strong teetotaler that he ran for president on a prohibition ticket two decades later.

38. Kiper, *Major General John Alexander McClernand*, 182.

39. Simon, *Papers of U. S. Grant*, 7:220, 80n, 226–227; Brinton, *Personal Memoirs*, 131; Simon, *Papers of U. S. Grant*, 4:222n, 223n.

40. Simon, *Papers of U. S. Grant*, 7:226, 234.

41. Simon, *Papers of U. S. Grant*, 7:253, 257–258, 265n.

42. Ibid., 264.

43. Ibid., 267n.

44. Ibid., 274.

CHAPTER 20

1. Bragg authority McWhiney discusses in detail Bragg's bad planning at Stones River and the public and private criticism, as well as his loss of nerve at and after Stones River, in *Braxton Bragg*, 347–352, 363–366, 372–374; for a succinct explanation of Bragg's battle plan, see Peter Cozzens, *No Better Place to Die: The Battle of Stones River* (Urbana: University of Illinois Press, 1990), 76; for Hanson's comment, see Davis, *Jefferson Davis*, 491.

2. Davis, *Jefferson Davis*, 490–491.

3. O. R. (1), vol. 17, pt. 1, 592; Ramage, *Rebel Raider*, 135–136.

4. Jordan and Pryor, *The Campaigns of Lieutenant General Forrest*, 223–224.

5. Jordan and Pryor, *The Campaigns of Lieutenant General Forrest*, 224–225. The authorized biography also says here that Bragg told him that an expedition had been directed for the capture of Fort Donelson. This does not seem to have been the case, because Wheeler in his report, O. R. (1), vol. 23, pt. 1, 39, says he had gone to the area to interdict Federal river traffic. The Forrest authorized biography is thus mistaken, unless Wheeler and Bragg discussed the possibility of also attacking Fort Donelson if an opportunity arose, which may have been the case.

6. Warner, *Generals in Gray*, 333; Dyer, *Fightin' Joe Wheeler*, 90. For Wheeler's feat on the eve of Stones River, see McWhiney, *Braxton Bragg*, 348–349.

7. O. R. (1), vol. 23, pt. 1, 39, 40.

8. Ibid., 40, 41.

9. Ibid., 40.

10. Forrest aide Charles Anderson's recollection of Forrest's disclosure of his opposition to the attack to Anderson and Dr. Ben Woods, a Kentucky surgeon

then on the staff, is in Wyeth, *Life of General Nathan Bedford Forrest*, 147. See Warner, *Generals in Gray*, 332, for how Wharton died. Forrest's report of the Murfreesboro raid, O. R. (1), vol. 16, pt. 1, 810, does not hint at Forrest's anger at Wharton's withdrawal and in fact seems, with glowing descriptions of Wharton's valor, to try to atone for it.

11. Benjamin Franklin Cooling , "The Attack on Dover, Tenn.," *Civil War Times Illustrated* (August 1963): 11; O. R. (1), vol. 23, pt. 1, 35.

12. O. R. (1), vol. 23, pt. 1, 35, 39.

13. Ibid., 36, 39; Cooling, "The Attack on Dover, Tenn."

14. O. R. (1), vol. 23, pt. 1, 40; *Official Military Atlas of the Civil War*, plates 11–5, 114–5.

15. O. R. (1), vol. 23, pt. 1, 40, 36.

16. Ibid., 37.

17. Ibid., 40, 38.

18. Ibid., 37.

19. Ibid., 40, 38.

20. Ibid., 40.

21. Ibid., 40–41; Cooling, "The Attack on Dover, Tenn," 11.

22. O. R. (1), vol. 23, pt. 1, 38.

23. Wyeth, *Life of General Nathan Bedford Forrest*, 151.

24. O. R. (1), vol. 23, pt. 1, 41, 33, 38; Jordan and Pryor, *The Campaigns of Lieutenant General Forrest*, 229.

25. Wyeth, *Life of General Nathan Bedford Forrest*, 151.

26. Mathes, *General Forrest*, 99. The language in Anderson's version of the story is flowerier. Woods's version sounds more like Forrest.

27. *Southern Historical Society Papers*, 7:462.

28. Wyeth, *Life of General Nathan Bedford Forrest*, 151.

CHAPTER 21

1. Simon, *Papers of U. S. Grant*, 7:270–273.

2. Ibid., 301.

3. Ibid., 302–303n; O. R. (1), vol. 17, pt. 2, 575.

4. Simon, *Papers of U. S. Grant*, 7:301; Warner, *Generals in Blue*, 513, 278–279, 102, 116, 389–390, 476, 189–190.

5. Simon, *Papers of U. S. Grant*, 7:301.

6. Ibid., 326, 285n.

7. Ibid., 270, 276.

8. Ibid., 288–289, 281.

9. Ibid., 281–282; for Lincoln's interest, see Smith, *Grant,* 229.

10. Simon, *Papers of U. S. Grant,* 7:287n.

11. Ibid., 282n.

12. Ibid., 286, 288.

13. Ibid., 284–285.

14. Ibid., 311, 312–313, 313n.

15. Ibid., 316.

16. Ibid., 317–318.

17. Ibid., 325.

18. Ibid., 339, 343, 344n, 381, 381n.

19. Ibid., 368, 378–379n, 380–381n, 370, 371–372n, 385–387n; see Smith, *Grant,* 410, for the Halleck-Lincoln-Burnside situation.

20. Simon, *Papers of U. S. Grant,* 7:275n.

21. Ibid., 307–308n.

22. Ibid., 347; Warner, *Generals in Blue,* 178–179.

23. Simon, *Papers of U. S. Grant,* 7:452, 467–468, 469n.

24. Ibid., 275n. Grant would show considerable deference to McClernand over the next weeks not only by naming McClernand to command his move to get troops south of Vicksburg but also by being markedly polite in many of his communications with the general.

25. Lewis, *Sherman,* 269.

26. Simon, *Papers of U. S. Grant,* 7:446, 455–456, 478; Bearss, *The Vicksburg Campaign,* 1:550–557; O. R. (1), vol. 24, pt. 3, 168.

27. Kiper, *Major General John Alexander McClernand,* 203.

28. Bearss, *The Vicksburg Campaign,* 1:734.

29. Simon, *Papers of U. S. Grant,* 7:455–456, 231, 464, 486; ibid., 8, 3–4. That the Mississippi was falling on March 29 is noted in the diary of a Louisiana Confederate captain at Vicksburg, quoted in Bearss, *The Vicksburg Campaign,* 2:xv.

30. Simon, *Papers of U. S. Grant,* 7:471n, 474n, 479n, 486n. Under cover of darkness, the Union had sent other boats past the guns more or less successfully. See, for example, the runs of the *Queen of the West,* February 1, on 263 and 263n, and the *Indianola,* February 12, on 346n.

31. O. R. (1), vol. 24, pt. 3, 179–180.

32. Marszalek, *Sherman,* 217–218; Lewis, *Sherman,* 270.

33. For McClernand's support of the plan, see Lewis, *Sherman,* 270, and Kiper, *Major General John Alexander McClernand,* 207–208.

34. Simon, *Papers of U. S. Grant,* 8:63–64n; O. R. (1), vol. 24, pt. 1, 46.

35. Bearss, *The Vicksburg Campaign,* 2:71, 66.

36. Ibid., 67–71.

37. Ibid., 58, 64, 65, 59. In addition to the Union withdrawal from Yazoo Pass, Grant had ordered boats of General Alfred Ellet's marine brigade north to the Tennessee River to deal with Confederate operations there; Bearss, *The Vicksburg Campaign*, 2:131–132 and O. R. (1), vol. 24, pt. 3, 520.

38. Bearss, *The Vicksburg Campaign*, 2:73; Simon, *Papers of U. S. Grant*, 8:82–83n.

39. Bearss, *The Vicksburg Campaign*, 2:74–79.

40. O. R. (1), vol. 24, pt. 1, 49; Bearss, *The Vicksburg Campaign*, 2:253; O. R. (1), vol. 24, pt. 2, 214; Bearss, *The Vicksburg Campaign*, 2:131.

41. Simon, *Papers of U. S. Grant*, 8:132–133.

42. Lewis, *Sherman*, 271. For the lowest levels of the road above the surrounding swamp, see Simon, *Papers of U. S. Grant*, 8:53.

CHAPTER 22

1. Jordan and Pryor, *The Campaigns of Lieutenant General Forrest*, 230–231.

2. Ibid., 232; O. R. (1), vol. 23, pt. 2, 638; Henry, *"First with the Most" Forrest*, 127–128.

3. See, for example, O. R. (1), vol. 17, pt. 2, 811, 813, 835, etc.

4. Warner, *Generals in Gray*, 314–315; Robert G. Hartje, *Van Dorn: The Life and Times of a Confederate General* (Nashville: Vanderbilt University Press, 1967), 157, 136–161; Cunningham, Joiner, and Smith, *Shiloh and the Western Campaign of 1862*, 95; O. R. (1), vol. 17, pt. 1, 414–459.

5. Hartje, *Van Dorn*, 324–325. The information on his pedigree comes from Hartje and from a letter written by a sister of Van Dorn to another sister, Emily Van Dorn Miller, from Belvoir, Maryland, on February 5, 1863, obtained through an Internet link to "Emily Van Dorn Miller," http://milleralbum.com/tmm/?article =OctaviaVanDorn.

6. O. R. (1), vol. 23, pt. 2, 718; ibid., pt. 1, 73, 80, 86.

7. Ibid., pt. 1, 86, 116, 98, 123.

8. Ibid., 86–87, 116.

9. Ibid., 107, 114, 105, 81, 103, 99, 88, 89.

10. Ibid., 89, 120, 117, 119, 90.

11. Ibid., 187, 193, 84, 177, 179, 192, 184, 186, 188.

12. Ibid., 188, 194; *Confederate Veteran*, vol. 27, 416; Henry, *"First with the Most" Forrest*, 135.

13. O. R. (1), vol. 23, pt. 1, 192, 180–181.

14. Henry, *"First with the Most" Forrest*, 143; Wyeth, *Life of General Nathan Bedford Forrest*, 176–177.

15. O. R. (1), vol. 23, pt. 1, 188–189; Thomas Harrison Baker, *The Memphis Commercial Appeal: The History of a Southern Newspaper* (Baton Rouge: Louisiana

State University Press, 1971), 95; Joseph Frazier Wall, *Henry Watterson: Reconstructed Rebel* (New York: Oxford University Press, 1956), 36–38.

16. Henry, *"First with the Most" Forrest*, 142–143; *A Soldier's Honor, by His Comrades* (New York, 1902) 276–279; Wyeth, *Life of General Nathan Bedford Forrest*, 176–177. Three versions of this story appear in *A Soldier's Honor*, which was compiled by a sister of Van Dorn, although she did not put her name on it; Wyeth gives another version. The account here uses details from all.

17. Henry, *"First with the Most" Forrest*, 143; *A Soldier's Honor*, 279; Warner, *Generals in Gray*, 315.

18. O. R. (1), vol. 23, pt. 1, 294, 245, 247.

19. Ibid., 243.

20. Ibid., 247, 282.

21. Stephen Z. Starr, *The Union Cavalry in the Civil War* (Baton Rouge: Louisiana State University Press, 1985), 3:221.

22. O. R. (1), vol. 23, pt. 1, 248, 282. (A good idea of where the Etowah River Bridge was and the distances to it from Rome, and so forth, is provided by comparing plate 49 of *The Official Military Atlas of the Civil War* with a modern Georgia road map.)

23. Ibid., 286, 248; Henry, *"First with the Most" Forrest*, 142.

24. O. R. (1), vol. 23, pt. 1, 227; Jordan and Pryor, *The Campaigns of Lieutenant General Forrest*, 246–247.

25. Jordan and Pryor, *The Campaigns of Lieutenant General Forrest*, 253; Bearss, *The Vicksburg Campaign*, 2:153; O. R. (1), vol. 23, pt. 1, 294. For Freeman's death, see O. R. (1), vol. 23, pt. 2, 277; Jordan and Pryor, *The Campaigns of Lieutenant General Forrest*, 246–247, 247n; Wyeth, *Life of General Nathan Bedford Forrest*, 182–184.

26. O. R. (1), vol. 23, pt. 1, 248, 246.

27. Jordan and Pryor, *The Campaigns of Lieutenant General Forrest*, 254–255.

28. Bearss, *The Vicksburg Campaign*, 2:154–155.

29. Wyeth, *Life of General Nathan Bedford Forrest*, 644; Morton, *The Artillery of Nathan Bedford Forrest's Cavalry*, 181.

30. Jordan and Pryor, *The Campaigns of Lieutenant General Forrest*, 255; O. R. (1), vol. 23, pt. 1, 285, 287–288.

31. O. R. (1), vol. 23, pt. 1, 288.

32. Bearss, *The Vicksburg Campaign*, 2:159; O. R. (1), vol. 23, pt. 1, 288.

33. O. R. (1), vol. 23, pt. 1, 283.

34. Ibid., 288.

35. Jordan and Pryor, *The Campaigns of Lieutenant General Forrest*, 257, 257n; O. R. (1), vol. 23, pt. 1, 288–289.

36. Henry, *"First with the Most" Forrest*, 147; O. R. (1), vol. 23, pt. 1, 289.

37. Jordan and Pryor, *The Campaigns of Lieutenant General Forrest*, 256–257; Henry, *"First with the Most" Forrest*, 148; O. R. (1), vol. 23, pt. 1, 289.

38. O. R. (1), vol. 23, pt. 1, 289–290.

39. Ibid., 290.

40. Ibid.; Henry, *"First with the Most" Forrest*, 149.

41. Wyeth, *Life of General Nathan Bedford Forrest*, 206. Wyeth quotes the final word of this sentence as "easily," but Forrest likely was not fussy about adverbs.

42. Jordan and Pryor, *The Campaigns of Lieutenant General Forrest*, 265; Wyeth, *Life of General Nathan Bedford Forrest*, 207.

43. Wyeth, *Life of General Nathan Bedford Forrest*, 210–212.

44. Atlanta *Southern Confederacy*, May 8, 1863, 1; Henry, *"First with the Most" Forrest*, 151.

45. Wyeth, *Life of General Nathan Bedford Forrest*, 18A.

46. Ibid., 18A, 211–212; Henry, *As They Saw Forrest*, 289, 290, 293.

47. O. R. (1), vol. 23, pt. 1, 290.

48. Ibid., 291.

49. Ibid., 291–292.

50. Henry, *"First with the Most" Forrest*, 155–156; Starr, *The Union Cavalry in the Civil War*, 3:220.

51. O. R. (1), vol. 23, pt. 1, 292; Henry, *"First with the Most" Forrest*, 153–155.

52. Dabney H. Maury, *Recollections of a Virginian in the Mexican, Indian, and Civil Wars* (New York: Charles Scribner's Sons, 1894), 209; Henry, *"First with the Most" Forrest*, 157.

53. Maury, *Recollections*, 209.

CHAPTER 23

1. O. R. (1), vol. 23, pt. 2, 795; Smith, *Grant*, 237.

2. Smith, *Grant*, 301.

3. Bearss, *The Vicksburg Campaign*, 2:269–270.

4. Ibid., 183; Marszalek, *Sherman*, 220; O. R. N, vol. 24, 591; O. R. (1), vol. 24, pt. 1, 576–577; Lewis, *Sherman*, 272.

5. O. R. (1), vol. 24, pt. 1, 575, 593.

6. Bearss, *The Vicksburg Campaign*, 2:314–315; O. R. (1), vol. 24, pt. 1, 575.

7. O. R. (1), vol. 24, pt. 1, 574; Bearss, *The Vicksburg Campaign*, 2:305–306; Warner, *Generals in Gray*, 29.

8. O. R. (1), vol. 24, pt. 1, 32, 48; Grant, *Personal Memoirs*, 261.

9. Grant, *Personal Memoirs*, 262.

10. Bearss, *The Vicksburg Campaign*, 2:318–319.

11. O. R. (1), vol. 24, pt. 1, 80–81.

12. Ibid., 74–75.

13. Bearss, *The Vicksburg Campaign*, 2:78, 293–294.

14. O. R. (1), vol. 24, pt. 1, 49.

15. Ibid., 48.

16. Bearss, *The Vicksburg Campaign*, 2:385–386.

17. Ibid., 353–372, 373–398, 367, 405, 407.

18. Ibid., 409; Grant, *Personal Memoirs*, 266–267. Grierson, coming down through the middle of Mississippi, tore up the Southern Railroad around Newton, midway between Meridian and Jackson, and then continued south to Hazlehurst, Mississippi, to ravage the New Orleans, Jackson, and Great Northern Railroad.

19. Grant, *Personal Memoirs*, 267–268; Simon, *Papers of U. S. Grant*, 8:147, 155.

20. O. R. (1), vol. 24, pt. 1, 49–50.

21. Grant, *Personal Memoirs*, 268; Simon, *Papers of U. S. Grant*, 8:147.

22. Simon, *Papers of U. S. Grant*, 8:151.

23. Ibid., 153, 162, 164, 168, 172, etc.; ibid., 178–179n, 183.

24. Grant, *Personal Memoirs*, 266.

25. Ibid.; Simon, *Papers of U. S. Grant*, 8:160.

26. O. R. (1), vol. 24, pt. 3, 282; Bearss, *The Vicksburg Campaign*, 2:461–462.

27. Simon, *Papers of U. S. Grant*, 8:200.

28. Ibid., 201n; O. R. (1), vol. 24, pt. 1, 707. Bearss, *The Vicksburg Campaign*, 2:480–481, emphasizes a fine distinction obvious in Grant's contemporary letters and the official records but missed by many historians and inaccurately described by Grant in his memoirs: while he did separate himself from his Mississippi supply bases and the Union river armada, he never severed his supply line. He did markedly thin it and then almost outran it.

29. Bearss, *The Vicksburg Campaign*, 2:512, 515, 517; O. R. (1), vol. 24, pt. 1, 737.

30. Bearss, *The Vicksburg Campaign*, 2:502, 506, 517, 515.

31. O. R. (1), vol. 24, pt. 1, 50.

32. Bearss, *The Vicksburg Campaign*, 2:554.

33. Ibid., 537–538, 543–544, 545, 531, 556, 557.

34. O. R. (1), vol. 24, pt. 3, 877; Bearss, *The Vicksburg Campaign*, 2:530, 547.

35. O. R. (1), vol. 24, pt. 3, 310.

36. Ibid., pt. 1, 261.

37. Warner, *Generals in Gray*, 193–194, 232–233; Bearss, *The Vicksburg Campaign*, 2:620, 620n.

38. O. R. (1), vol. 24, pt. 1, 261.

39. Ibid., 262; Bearss, *The Vicksburg Campaign*, 2:573, 577.

40. Grant, *Personal Memoirs*, 279.

41. O. R. (1), vol. 24, pt. 1, 263; ibid., pt. 2, 101; for a map, see Bearss, *The Vicksburg Campaign*, 2:588.

42. O. R. (1), vol. 24, pt. 2, 87, 75; Bearss, *The Vicksburg Campaign*, 2:581–583.

43. Bearss, *The Vicksburg Campaign*, 2:596.

44. Ibid., 605.

45. O. R. (1), vol. 24, pt. 2, 55–56, 102.

46. Bearss, *The Vicksburg Campaign*, 2:607, 609, 614; O. R. (1), vol. 24, pt. 2, 111.

47. O. R. (1), vol. 24, pt. 1, 718; Bearss, *The Vicksburg Campaign*, 2:615–616.

48. O. R. (1), vol. 24, pt. 1, 265; Bearss, *The Vicksburg Campaign*, 2:624.

49. O. R. (1), vol. 24, pt. 2, 32; Bearss, *The Vicksburg Campaign*, 2:640, 645, 651. Bearss's exact rendering of casualties is as follows: Confederate—381 killed, 1,018 wounded, and 2,441 missing; Union—396 killed, 1,838 wounded, and 187 missing.

50. Bearss, *The Vicksburg Campaign*, 2:658–659, 635–637.

51. Ibid., 656–657; Larry Gordon, *The Last Confederate General: John C. Vaughn and His East Tennessee Cavalry* (Minneapolis: Zenith Press, 2009), 58–62; O. R. (1), vol. 24, pt. 1, 267.

52. Gordon, *The Last Confederate General*, 48–49; O. R. (1), vol. 24, pt. 3, 322; Bearss, *The Vicksburg Campaign*, 2:667–670; O. R. (1), vol. 24, pt. 1, 266.

53. O. R. (1), vol. 24, pt. 1, 152; Bearss, *The Vicksburg Campaign*, 2:670–671, and map, 664.

54. Simon, *Papers of U. S. Grant*, 8:220, 221n.

55. O. R. (1), vol. 24, pt. 2, 137–138.

56. Ibid., pt. 1, 267–268.

57. Ibid., 618; Bearss, *The Vicksburg Campaign*, 3:752.

58. Simon, *Papers of U. S. Grant*, 8:189, 155; Bearss, *The Vicksburg Campaign*, 2:677.

59. Simon, *Papers of U. S. Grant*, 8:332.

CHAPTER 24

1. Jordan and Pryor, *The Campaigns of Lieutenant General Forrest*, 280–281; Henry, *"First with the Most" Forrest*, 160.

2. Jordan and Pryor, *The Campaigns of Lieutenant General Forrest*, 280–281.

3. Ibid., 281.

4. Henry, *"First with the Most" Forrest*, 160.

5. O. R. (1), vol. 23, pt. 2, 856.

6. Ibid., 857.

7. Ibid., 365, 369, 370–373.

8. Jordan and Pryor, *The Campaigns of Lieutenant General Forrest*, 286.

9. Henry, *"First with the Most" Forrest*, 494n.

10. Morton, *The Artillery of Nathan Bedford Forrest's Cavalry*, 101–102.

11. Ibid.; Wyeth, *Life of General Nathan Bedford Forrest*, 224.

12. Frank H. Smith, account in Tennessee State Library and Archives, first printed in *The Nashville Banner* on April 29, 1911. Smith, one of the boys watching from the steps of the Masonic hall, later became a prominent teacher and preserver of Maury County history.

13. Ibid.

14. Morton, *The Artillery of Nathan Bedford Forrest's Cavalry*, 103; Wyeth, *Life of General Nathan Bedford Forrest*, 225. The original quote in Morton is "No d——d man shall kill me and live!" This writer doubts that under the stress of the moment, if ever, Forrest would have used the word "shall"; nor would he have dressed up "damn." Lytle, *Bedford Forrest and His Critter Company*, 181, probably has it closer to the truth in his "No damn man can kill me and live."

15. Frank Smith.

16. Ibid.; Morton, *The Artillery of Nathan Bedford Forrest's Cavalry*, 103.

17. Wyeth's full quote is longer and, for the most part, unnaturally formal. Presented here are its very natural-sounding guts.

18. Frank Smith; Morton, *The Artillery of Nathan Bedford Forrest's Cavalry*, 103.

19. Frank Smith.

20. This version appears in *Wyeth, Life of General Nathan Bedford Forrest*, 225–226, and Morton, *The Artillery of Nathan Bedford Forrest's Cavalry*, 104, both purporting to come from the same unnamed eyewitness.

21. Wills, *A Battle from the Start*, 127; Mathes, *General Forrest*, 132. The story that Andrew Wills Gould's family said no reconciliation occurred emanates from the biography by historian Wills, who cites no specific source.

22. O. R. (1), vol. 23, pt. 1, 10.

23. Ibid., pt. 2, 460, 461; Jordan and Pryor, *The Campaigns of Lieutenant General Forrest*, 290–291; Wyeth, *Life of General Nathan Bedford Forrest*, 231.

24. Wyeth, *Life of General Nathan Bedford Forrest*, 231–232.

25. Morton, *The Artillery of Nathan Bedford Forrest's Cavalry*, 110.

CHAPTER 25

1. Simon, *Papers of U. S. Grant*, 8:232–233.

2. Bearss, *The Vicksburg Campaign*, 3:760, 780–785.

3. Ibid., 772, 761, 763, 765; O. R. (1), vol. 24, pt. 2, 268–269.

4. O. R. (1), vol. 24, pt. 1, 273–274; Bearss, *The Vicksburg Campaign*, 3:773, 772.

5. O. R. (1), vol. 24, pt. 3, 331–332.

6. Ibid., 332. Bearss, *The Vicksburg Campaign*, 3:813–814, himself a distinguished combat veteran, has, as a park historian for the government, all but lived on the ground over which Grant had to attack. He says the broken and obstacle-clogged nature of that ground offered only one area—in front of Sherman—where troops might possibly be massed in sufficient strength to do what McClernand advised and that Sherman tried to exploit that area. Bearss adds that in McClernand's own troop arrangements, the general did not follow his own advice.

7. O. R. (1), vol. 24, pt. 3, 334.

8. Bearss, *The Vicksburg Campaign*, 3:814, 828, 823–824.

9. See map in Bearss, *The Vicksburg Campaign*, 3:838.

10. O. R. (1), vol. 24, pt. 2, 244, 242.

11. Bearss, *The Vicksburg Campaign*, 3:825–827; O. R. (1), vol. 24, pt. 2, 243, 140.

12. O. R. (1), vol. 24, pt. 2, 257; Bearss, *The Vicksburg Campaign*, 3:816, 816n, 817, 817n; O. R. (1), vol. 24, pt. 2, 282, 257–258.

13. O. R. (1), vol. 24, pt. 1, 719; Bearss, *The Vicksburg Campaign*, 3:821–822, 822n.

14. O. R. (1), vol. 24, pt. 1, 172–173. For the location of McArthur's troops, see ibid. pt. 2, 302.

15. Ibid., 173.

16. Ibid., 56.

17. Bearss, *The Vicksburg Campaign*, 3:824–833.

18. Ibid., 837–844, 845–846; O. R. (1), vol. 24, pt. 1, 710.

19. Bearss, *The Vicksburg Campaign*, 3:856–857.

20. Ibid., 858; O. R. (1), vol. 24, pt. 1, 87.

21. Simon, *Papers of U. S. Grant*, 8:257, 258n.

22. Ibid., 261–262.

23. O. R. (1), vol. 24, pt. 1, 276–277; Bearss, *The Vicksburg Campaign*, 3:860–861, 861n.

24. Quoted in Kiper, *Major General John Alexander McClernand*, 270; Simon, *Papers of U. S. Grant*, 8:307; Bearss, *The Vicksburg Campaign*, 3:880n; Kiper, *Major General John Alexander McClernand*, 270.

25. O. R. (1), vol. 24, pt. 1, 165–166.

26. Ibid., 159–164, 161; Bearss, *The Vicksburg Campaign*, 3:876–879.

27. O. R. (1), vol. 24, pt. 1, 103.

28. Ibid., 103.

29. Simon, *Papers of U. S. Grant*, 8:428–429.

30. For the delivery of messages into Vicksburg, see Symonds, *Joseph E. Johnston*, 211–212.

31. Bearss, *The Vicksburg Campaign*, 3:1174–1175.

32. For Lincoln's initial and later views regarding arming slaves, see McPherson, *Battle Cry of Freedom*, 565.

33. Bearss, *The Vicksburg Campaign*, 3:1174; O. R. (1), vol. 24, pt. 2, 448–449, 447–448.

34. O. R. (1), vol. 24, pt. 2, 448, 467.

35. Ibid., pt. 1, 102; Bearss, *The Vicksburg Campaign*, 3:1180.

36. Joseph Glatthaar, *Forged in Battle: The Civil War Alliance of Black Soldiers and White Officers* (New York: Free Press, 1990), 201; McPherson, *Battle Cry of Freedom*, 565–566.

37. Bearss, *The Vicksburg Campaign*, 3:1183; O. R. (1), vol. 24, pt. 3, 425–426.

38. O. R. (1), vol. 24, pt. 2, 446; ibid., pt. 3, 425–426, 443–444.

39. Simon, *Papers of U. S. Grant*, 8:327n; O. R. (1), vol. 24, pt. 2, 466, 459; Glatthaar, *Forged in Battle*, 325n; David Williams, *A People's History of the Civil War: Struggles for the Meaning of Freedom* (New York: The New Press, 2005), 366.

40. Simon, *Papers of U. S. Grant*, 8:468.

41. Grant, *Personal Memoirs*, 307.

42. Bearss, *The Vicksburg Campaign*, 3:1286–1287.

43. O. R. (1), vol. 24, pt. 1, 115; Grant, *Personal Memoirs*, 309; Bearss, *The Vicksburg Campaign*, 3:1289.

44. O. R. (1), vol. 24, pt. 3, 1000; David D. Porter, *Incidents and Anecdotes of the Civil War* (New York: D. Appleton and Company, 1885), 201, quoted in Smith, *Grant*, 256; Simon, *Papers of U. S. Grant*, 8:464, 461n.

45. Porter, *Incidents and Anecdotes*; Simon, *Papers of U. S. Grant*, 8:479; Faust, *Historical Times Illustrated Encyclopedia of the Civil War*, 392–393.

46. Smith, *Grant*, 257; T. Harry Williams, *Lincoln and His Generals* (New York: Alfred A. Knopf, 1952), 272, quoted in Smith, *Grant*, 259.

CHAPTER 26

1. Jeffry D. Wert, *General James Longstreet: The Confederacy's Most Controversial Soldier* (New York: Simon & Schuster, 1993), 300, quoting Longstreet to Confederate senator Louis T. Wigfall of Texas, August 18, 1863.

2. O. R. (1), vol. 30, pt. 4, 508–509.

3. Ibid., 509; Jordan and Pryor, *The Campaigns of Lieutenant General Forrest*, 281.

4. O. R. (1), vol. 30, pt. 4, 508–510.

5. Ibid., 589.

6. Powell, *Failure in the Saddle*, xxv–xxvii, xxix, xxxv–xxxvii.

7. Adam R. Johnson, *The Partisan Rangers of the Confederate States Army* (Austin, TX: State House Press [reissue], 1995), 150–160. It is unknown whether Johnson is referring to a more general order that Bragg issued around this time. On September 16, 1863, the Army of Tennessee commander directed that all cavalry found to have been absent from their commands without authority be dismounted and sent to headquarters for assignment to the infantry, O. R. (1), vol. 30, pt. 4, 656. This seems particularly wrongheaded because it punishes men returning from unauthorized trips home to see and aid their families, while encouraging those who *have* returned to leave again—for good. For Morgan's slave trafficking and card playing, see Ramage, *Rebel Raider*, 33–38.

8. Peter Cozzens, *This Terrible Sound: The Battle of Chickamauga* (Urbana: University of Illinois Press, 1996), 48–49, 37, 55; Powell, *Failure in the Saddle*, 40–41.

9. Powell, *Failure in the Saddle*, 68–69.

10. O. R. (1), vol. 30, pt. 4, 610–611; Cozzens, *This Terrible Sound*, 56–57.

11. Powell, *Failure in the Saddle*, 69–70; Jordan and Pryor, *The Campaigns of Lieutenant General Forrest*, 306–308, 308n.

12. Jordan and Pryor, *The Campaigns of Lieutenant General Forrest*, 307, 308; Wyeth, *Life of General Nathan Bedford Forrest*, 240.

13. Cozzens, *This Terrible Sound*, 65–74.

14. Ibid., 81–85.

15. Ibid., 85–87.

16. Cozzens, *This Terrible Sound*, 90; O. R. (1), vol. 30, pt. 2, 524.

17. Cozzens, *This Terrible Sound*, 102.

18. Ibid., 59–60, 90.

19. Ibid., 102.

20. O. R. (1), vol. 30, pt. 2, 451–452.

21. Ibid., 31.

22. Ibid., pt. 2, 488, 472, 452.

23. Ibid., 524. Powell, *Failure in the Saddle* (see, for example, 124, 120, 104) notes that this, bivouacking in the rear of the infantry, is one of several instances during the Chickamauga campaign in which Forrest neglected the cavalry responsibility to provide reconnaissance for the infantry; instead, he frequently dismounted his men and joined the foot troops. This illustrates a downside of a Forrest trait that also had its upsides: he never considered himself "just cavalry"; he was a fighter first and a cavalryman second.

24. Cozzens, *This Terrible Sound*, 128.

25. O. R. (1), vol. 30, pt. 2, 524, 248; Cozzens, *This Terrible Sound*, 128.

26. Cozzens, *This Terrible Sound*, 129–131.

27. O. R. (1), vol. 30, pt. 2, 524, 95, 525.

28. O. R. (1), vol. 30, pt. 2, 95, 525; Cozzens, *This Terrible Sound*, 186.

29. Cozzens, *This Terrible Sound*, 299, 301.

30. Ibid., 299–300; O. R. (1), vol. 30, pt. 2, 141, 47.

31. Ibid., 141, 198, 525.

32. Ibid., pt. 1, 261.

33. Ibid., pt. 2, 141–142, 241, 246.

34. Glenn Tucker, *Chickamauga: Bloody Battle in the West* (New York: Bobbs-Merrill, 1961), 237, quoting *Confederate Veteran*, September 1895, 279.

35. Wyeth, *Life of General Nathan Bedford Forrest*, 252; Henry, 183.

36. O. R. (1), vol. 30, pt. 2, 144, 210, 241, 200; ibid. pt. 1, 862.

37. O. R. (1), vol. 30, pt. 1, 860, 862, 877; Cozzens, *This Terrible Sound*, 453.

38. O. R. (1), vol. 30, pt. 1, 288; Cozzens, *This Terrible Sound*, 316.

39. Cozzens, *This Terrible Sound*, 311–313, 326–327, 362–363.

40. Ibid., 369, 389, 451, 453; O. R. (1), vol. 30, pt. 1, 876, 874; ibid. pt. 2, 576.

41. O. R. (1), vol. 30, pt. 2, 525; pt. 1, 280.

42. For more on the howl, see Cozzens, *This Terrible Sound*, 501.

43. Cozzens, *This Terrible Sound*, 470, 517.

44. Tucker, *Chickamauga*, 378.

45. O. R. (1), vol. 30, pt. 2, 525.

46. Wyeth, *Life of General Nathan Bedford Forrest*, 259; O. R. (1), vol. 30, pt. 4, 681. Powell, *Failure in the Saddle*, 178–179, says this dispatch was misleading because Forrest, if he could indeed see all he said he saw, did not mention a strong Federal line drawn up west of Missionary Ridge to hold off Confederate pursuit. But the Federal line seems to have been a fluid, stopgap measure. The wagon trains rounding Lookout Mountain and the "pontoons" that the deserters said had been thrown across the Tennessee indicated exactly what Forrest said he thought: "They are evacuating as hard as they can go." Thomas had held his part of Rosecrans's army together, but even that part was low on ammunition, O. R. (1), vol. 30, pt. 1, 145, and the rest were spooked and scattered, as indicated by the dispatches of the fleeing Rosecrans and the War Department's Dana in Chattanooga, Cozzens, *This Terrible Sound*, 470, 479. Longstreet would claim after the war that Forrest's initial dispatch from the Union lookout post caused Bragg to dawdle. If the Federals were "evacuating as hard as they can go," why detain them? That may have been how Bragg took it, but it was not how Forrest meant it. He urged pursuit "as rapidly as possible." And he was correct about the Fed-

eral evacuation. At that time, Rosecrans considered abandoning Chattanooga—as indicated by the pontoons mentioned by Forrest's Federal captive.

47. O. R. (1), vol. 30, pt. 2, 525; Cozzens, *This Terrible Sound*, 519, 517–518, 528–532.

48. Wyeth, *Life of General Nathan Bedford Forrest*, 267. Forrest's instinct—as well as the military precepts he had never studied—dictated giving all-out pursuit to a fleeing foe. He plainly believed that the "skeer," as he often called it, was on, and a significant fraction of Bragg's army could have been pushed forward to keep Rosecrans running beyond Chattanooga while its trains could be brought along by the balance of the force. Powell, *Failure in the Saddle*, 179, argues that because Forrest was unable to get past the Federal blockage, he should have assumed that a large infantry force also could not; for Forrest's soliloquy, see Henry, *"First With the Most" Forrest*, 193, quoting the manuscript, found in the Tennessee State Library and Archives, of a lecture by Tully Brown, a lieutenant in Morton's artillery and later adjutant general of Tennessee.

49. O. R. (1), vol. 30, pt. 2, 526; Morton, *The Artillery of Nathan Bedford Forrest's Cavalry*, 128. Either man, Forrest two years after the war or McLaws decades later, may be correct in claiming to have been the most bellicose on this day, but by the time they met, it hardly mattered. As Powell, *Failure in the Saddle*, 195, notes, Forrest by this point had himself tried several times to penetrate the rear guard; he also notes McLaws said Forrest, in arguing against an attack, cited the Confederate army's location seven miles behind them. Forrest no doubt decried the fact that no more of the army had been sent forward. By now, he may well have thought the opportunity lost.

50. O. R. (1), vol. 30, pt. 2, 526. For Wheeler's raid, see ibid., 722–728.

51. Judith Lee Hallock, *Braxton Bragg and Confederate Defeat, Volume II* (Tuscaloosa: University of Alabama Press, 1991), 89–105.

52. Hallock, *Braxton Bragg*, 100.

53. Wyeth, *Life of General Nathan Bedford Forrest*, 264; O. R. (1), vol. 30, pt. 2, 723.

54. Jordan and Pryor, *The Campaigns of Lieutenant General Forrest*, 357.

55. Wyeth, *Life of General Nathan Bedford Forrest*, 265–266.

56. Hallock, *Braxton Bragg*, 101; Wyeth, *Life of General Nathan Bedford Forrest*, 266. No historian has been able to date the confrontation. That fact, together with a Bragg aide's seemingly nonchalant diary entry noting no more than that Forrest was "much dissatisfied" around this time, has led a few historians to conclude that an elderly Cowan concocted the incident. Cowan's version is obviously polished, but at least two of its expressions—"slap your jaws" and "stood your meanness as long as I intend to"—sound authentic. That Bragg's aides appear to have been ignorant of the incident fits both the circumstances and Bragg's own personality. He was a brave soldier when acting on orders from higher up, but when he

had to decide what action to take, he vacillated. And it seems likely he would have done so now, with an infuriated Forrest standing in his face; after all, when Forrest confronted Bragg about his reassignment of Forrest's troops to Wheeler, Bragg seems to have hemmed and hawed. Now, if he had again vacillated, he would have been unlikely to humiliate himself by disclosing he did nothing.

57. Cozzens, *This Terrible Sound*, 532; Davis, *Jefferson Davis*, 518–522.

58. O. R. (1), vol. 31, pt. 3, 604.

59. Hallock, *Braxton Bragg*, 101; Davis, *Jefferson Davis*, 522; Jordan and Pryor, *The Campaigns of Lieutenant General Forrest*, 358; O. R. (1), vol. 31, pt. 3, 645–646.

60. Wyeth, *Life of General Nathan Bedford Forrest*, 634.

CHAPTER 27

1. Simon, *Papers of U. S. Grant*, 9:18.

2. Ibid., 45–46n. For the capture of the herd of cattle, see ibid., 70. For the railroad rolling stock, see ibid., 164, 165n.

3. Simon, *Papers of U. S. Grant*, 9:90n, 156n.

4. Ibid., 36n, 63n, 70, 109.

5. Ibid., 23, 24.

6. National Archives, Record Group 393, Department of the Tennessee. I am greatly indebted to Washington-area scholar/researcher Gordon Berg for personally inspecting the Shepard records and providing their essentials.

7. Simon, *Papers of U. S. Grant*, 9:23–24, 26–27n.

8. Ibid., 69, 69n, 97–98, 99n.

9. Ibid., 196–197, 197n.

10. Ibid., 146.

11. For more on superstition, see Grant, *Memoirs*, 248–249.

12. Ibid., 220, 210.

13. Simon, *Papers of U. S. Grant*, 9:200, 222n. Carrollton, Louisiana, no longer appears on maps, having become part of the city of New Orleans proper. It does, however, appear on some maps of the time, including plate 90-1 of *The Official Military Atlas of the Civil War*.

14. Ibid., 222n.

15. Grant, *Memoirs*, 320–321.

16. Simon, *Papers of U. S. Grant*, 9:223n; Grant, *Memoirs*, 321.

17. Simon, *Papers of U. S. Grant*, 9:223n, 221–222.

18. For Halleck's wish to put Grant in command of Rosecrans's force on September 13, see O. R. (1), vol. 30, pt. 1, 37.

19. Simon, *Papers of U. S. Grant*, 9:229.

20. Ibid., 274n; Marszalek, *Sherman*, 237–238.

21. Simon, *Papers of U. S. Grant*, 9, 297–298n.

22. Grant, *Memoirs*, 326.

23. Simon, *Papers of U. S. Grant*, 9:302.

24. Ibid., 303n.

25. Grant, *Memoirs*, 329–330; Peter Cozzens, *The Shipwreck of Their Hopes: The Battles for Chattanooga* (Urbana: University of Illinois Press, 1994), 45, quoting Rawlins to Mary E. Hurlbut, November 23, 1863.

26. Cozzens, *Shipwreck*, 44.

27. Grant, *Memoirs*, 326–328.

28. Cozzens, *Shipwreck*, 32, 54–55.

29. Ibid., 47, 42.

30. Simon, *Papers of U. S. Grant*, 9:334, 330, 335; Cozzens, *Shipwreck*, 50, 51.

31. Cozzens, *Shipwreck*, 80–99.

32. Simon, *Papers of U. S. Grant*, 9:335.

CHAPTER 28

1. O. R. (1), vol. 31, pt. 3, 641.

2. Ibid., 646.

3. Henry, *"First with the Most" Forrest*, 201–202; O. R. (1), vol. 31, pt. 3, 618–619, 694.

4. O. R. (1), vol. 31, pt. 3, 817, 829.

5. Ibid., 789.

6. Jordan and Pryor, *The Campaigns of Lieutenant General Forrest*, 364; O. R. (1), vol. 31, pt. 3, 797.

7. Ibid., 789, 797–798; Cozzens, *Shipwreck*, 397.

8. O. R. (1), vol. 31, pt. 3, 817, 844; Henry, *"First with the Most" Forrest*, 206.

9. Henry, *"First with the Most" Forrest*, 207–208; Jordan and Pryor, *The Campaigns of Lieutenant General Forrest*, 366–369; Wyeth, *Life of General Nathan Bedford Forrest*, 283–284.

10. O. R. (1), vol. 31, pt. 1, 614–618, 620–621; Jordan and Pryor, *The Campaigns of Lieutenant General Forrest*, 375–376.

11. O. R. (1), vol. 32, pt. 2, 617.

12. Ibid., pt. 3, 609, 610, 622, 644, 648.

13. Andrew Ward, *River Run Red: The Fort Pillow Massacre in the American Civil War* (New York: Viking, 2005), 148.

14. O. R. (1), vol. 32, pt. 2, 616, 662–663.

15. Ibid., 673.

16. Ibid., 617.

17. Ibid., pt. 1, 181.

18. Wyeth, *Life of General Nathan Bedford Forrest*, 302–303.

19. O. R. (1), vol. 32, pt. 1, 257, 353; Morton, *The Artillery of Nathan Bedford Forrest's Cavalry*, 152–153; Wyeth, *Life of General Nathan Bedford Forrest*, 314–317.

20. O. R. (1), vol. 32, pt. 1, 354.

CHAPTER 29

1. Cozzens, *Shipwreck*, 103; Grant, *Memoirs*, 340–341.

2. Simon, *Papers of U. S. Grant*, 9:364n, 344n, 349, 359.

3. Cozzens, *Shipwreck*, 106, 111.

4. Ibid., 107; O. R. (1), vol. 31, pt. 3, 73.

5. Cozzens, *Shipwreck*, 108.

6. Cozzens, *Shipwreck*, 105, 107, 111, 113; Marszalek, *Sherman*, 242, quoting Oliver Otis Howard, *The Autobiography of Oliver Otis Howard* (New York, 1907), 473–474.

7. Marszalek, *Sherman*, 242.

8. Bobrick, *Master of War*, 15, 88.

9. Lewis, *Sherman*, 310.

10. Simon, *Papers of U. S. Grant*, 9:396–397.

11. Cozzens, *Shipwreck*, 121–122; Lewis, *Sherman*, 318.

12. Simon, *Papers of U. S. Grant*, 9:428. This communication is often cited as evidence of Grant's enmity toward Thomas. Their tension was overt, but to this writer, this letter attributes the immobility of Thomas's army much more to his starved animals than to Thomas himself. The letter's defense of Sherman seems more obvious than an attempt to denigrate Thomas.

13. Simon, *Papers of U. S. Grant*, 9:421, 430–431. For distribution of ammunition and three days' rations, see Cozzens, *Shipwreck*, 128.

14. Simon, *Papers of U. S. Grant*, 9:427n; Cozzens, *Shipwreck*, 127–128.

15. O. R. (1), vol. 31, pt. 2, 77.

16. Cozzens, *Shipwreck*, 128–133; O. R. vol. 31, (1), pt. 2, 95.

17. Grant, *Memoirs*, 342, 343, 346; Johnson and Buel, *Battles and Leaders*, 3:721.

18. Johnson and Buel, *Battles and Leaders* 3:722; Cozzens, *Shipwreck*, 144.

19. Cozzens, *Shipwreck*, 145–146; O. R. (1), vol. 31, pt. 2, 94; Johnson and Buel, *Battles and Leaders*, 3:712.

20. Cozzens, *Shipwreck*, 150.

21. Ibid., 148, 150.

22. Ibid., 148–149, 151.

23. O. R. (1), vol. 31, pt. 2, 573.

24. Cozzens, *Shipwreck*, 151.

25. Ibid., 154.

26. Ibid., 123.

27. Ibid., 165, 168, 163–164, 190.

28. Ibid., 190, 191. Johnson and Buel, *Battles and Leaders*, 3:723.

29. Cozzens, *Shipwreck*, 191.

30. Simon, *Papers of U. S. Grant*, 9:443n; Johnson and Buel, *Battles and Leaders*, 3:723.

31. Cozzens, *Shipwreck*, 204–205; Simon, *Papers of U. S. Grant*, 9:443.

32. Lewis, *Sherman*, 320.

33. Cozzens, *Shipwreck*, 206; O. R. (1), vol. 31, pt. 2, 633.

34. Cozzens, *Shipwreck*, 210.

35. Ibid., 211; Simon, *Papers of U. S. Grant*, 9:446n.

36. Cozzens, *Shipwreck*, 246–247.

37. Cozzens, *Shipwreck*, 247, quoting Thomas J. Wood, "The Battle of Missionary Ridge," in *Sketches of War History, 1861–1865*, vol. 4 of *Papers Prepared for the Ohio Commander of the Loyal Legion of the United States, 1890–1896*, 22–51 (Cincinnati: Robert Clarke, 1896), 34, and "A Thrilling War Chapter. The Battle of Missionary Ridge. Recollections of Gen. Thomas J. Wood," *New York Times*, July 16, 1876, and William F. Smith, "An Historical Sketch of the Military Operations Around Chattanooga, Tennessee, September 22 to November 27, 1863," in *The Mississippi Valley, Tennessee, Georgia, Alabama, 1861–1864*, vol. 3 of *Papers of the Military Historical Society of Massachusetts*, 149–247 (Boston: Military Historical Society of Massachusetts, 1910), 216.

38. Cozzens, *Shipwreck*, quoting Francis F. McKinney, *Education in Violence: The Life of George H. Thomas and the History of the Army of the Cumberland* (Detroit, MI: Wayne State University Press, 1961), 294, and Smith, "An Historical Sketch," 221.

39. O. R. (1), vol. 31, pt. 2, 68; Cozzens, *Shipwreck*, quoting McKinney, *Education in Violence*, 294; "Correspondence Relating to Chickamauga and Chattanooga," in *The Mississippi, Tennessee, Georgia, Alabama, 1861–1864*, vol. 8 of *Papers of the Military Historical Society of Massachusetts*, 247–272 (Boston: Military Historical Society of Massachusetts, 1910), 249; and James Harrison Wilson, *Under the Old Flag: Recollections of Military Operations in the War for the Union, the Spanish War, the Boxer Rebellion, etc.* (New York: D. Appleton, 1912), 1:297–298.

40. Cozzens, *Shipwreck*, 246–248; O. R. (1), vol. 31, pt. 2, 68.

41. Cozzens, *Shipwreck*, 246–248; Johnson and Buel, *Battles and Leaders*, 3:724; Simon, *Papers of U. S. Grant*, 9:447n; O. R. (1), vol. 31, pt. 2, 68.

42. Cozzens, *Shipwreck*, 259. The 45 percent angle of ascent comes from War Department official Charles Dana, O. R. (1), vol. 31, pt. 2, 68.

43. Grant, *Memoirs*, 358n; Cozzens, *Shipwreck*, 260.

44. Cozzens, *Shipwreck*, 261.

45. Ibid., 249–255.

46. Ibid., 262, 392; Johnson and Buel, *Battles and Leaders*, 3:723; Grant, *Memoirs*, 357.

47. Cozzens, *Shipwreck*, 258, 265; O. R. (1), vol. 31, pt. 2, 276.

48. Cozzens, *Shipwreck*, 273.

49. Ibid., 272–276.

50. O. R. (1), vol. 31, pt. 2, 278.

51. Cozzens, *Shipwreck*, 286, 282.

52. O. R. (1), vol. 31, pt. 2, 282, 275–276, 278.

53. Ibid., 69.

54. Ibid.

55. Simon, *Papers of U. S. Grant*, 9:440, 454n, 449.

56. O. R. (1), vol. 31, pt. 2, 45; Cozzens, *Shipwreck*, 353, 364, 365.

57. Cozzens, *Shipwreck*, 369–384.

58. O. R. (1), vol. 31, pt. 2, 49; Simon, *Papers of U. S. Grant*, 9:564.

59. Simon, *Papers of U. S. Grant*, 9:474n; O. R. (1), vol. 31, pt. 3, 297.

60. Cozzens, *Shipwreck*, 387.

61. Cozzens, *Shipwreck*, 389; O. R. (1), vol. 31, pt. 2, 36; Faust, *Historical Times Illustrated Encyclopedia of the Civil War*, 421.

62. Simon, *Papers of U. S. Grant*, 9:503–504n.

63. Simon, *Papers of U. S. Grant*, 9:522n, 541.

64. Ibid., 502n.

65. Ibid., 397–398n.

66. Ibid., 475n, 476n.

67. Ibid.

68. Ibid., 476n. Major General David Hunter, who also visited Grant at this time, reported to Halleck on December 14 that he "saw [Grant] almost every moment, except when sleeping, of the three weeks I spent in Chattanooga. I mention these, to you otherwise very unimportant facts, to show you that I had a first-rate opportunity of judging of the man. He is a hard worker, writes his own dispatches and orders, and does his own thinking. He is modest, quiet, never swears, and seldom drinks, as he only took two drinks during the three weeks I was with him. He listens quietly to the opinions of others and then judges promptly for himself; and he is very prompt in the field to avail himself of all the errors of the enemy. He is certainly a good judge of men." Lagow submitted his resignation on November 18.

EPILOGUE

1. See Dan T. Carter, *When the War Was Over* (Baton Rouge: Louisiana State University Press, 1985), 9, for Forrest's reaction to the appeal to continue fighting. For the Klan tactics' similarity to prewar intimidation in Tennessee, see Derek Frisby, "The Vortex of Secession: West Tennesseans and the Rush to War," in *Sister States, Enemy States: The Civil War in Kentucky and Tennessee*, edited by Kent Dollar, Larry Whiteaker, and W. Calvin Dickinson (Lexington: University Press of Kentucky, 2009), 46–71; and James B. Jones Jr., *"The Reign of Terror of the Safety Committee Has Passed Away Forever": A History of the Committees of Safety and Vigilance in West and Middle Tennessee* (Nashville: Tennessee Historical Commission, 2010).

2. *Memphis Daily Appeal*, July 6, 1875, 1.

3. Wyeth, *Life of General Nathan Bedford Forrest*, 621.

4. Smith, *Grant*, 627–628; Edmund Wilson, *Patriotic Gore: Studies in the Literature of the Civil War* (New York: Farrar, Straus & Giroux, 1962), 138–139.

BIBLIOGRAPHY

NEWSPAPERS CONSULTED

Atlanta Southern Confederacy
Chicago Tribune
Memphis Daily Appeal
Memphis Eagle & Enquirer
Montgomery Daily Mail

BOOKS AND ARTICLES

Baker, Thomas Harrison. *The* Memphis Commercial Appeal: *The History of a Southern Newspaper*. Baton Rouge: Louisiana State University Press, 1971.

Bancroft, Frederic. *Slave Trading in the Old South*. Baltimore: J. H. Furst Company, 1931.

Bearss, Edwin C. *The Vicksburg Campaign*. 3 vols. Dayton, OH: Morningside Press, 1985.

Blanton, Deanne, and Lauren M. Cook. *They Fought like Demons: Women Soldiers in the Civil War*. New York: Vintage Press, 2002.

Bobrick, Benson. *Master of War: The Life of General George H. Thomas*. New York: Simon & Schuster, 2009.

Brinton, John. *Personal Memoirs*. New York: Neale Publishing Company, 1914.

Carter, Dan T. *When the War Was Over: The Failure of Self-Reconstruction in the South, 1865–1867*. Baton Rouge: Louisiana State University Press, 1985.

Carter, Samuel. *The Final Fortress: The Campaign for Vicksburg, 1862–1863*. New York: St. Martin's, 1980.

Catton, Bruce. *Grant Moves South, 1861–1863*. Boston: Little, Brown, 1960.

Chetlain, Augustus. *Recollections of Seventy Years.* Galena, IL: Gazette Publishing Company, 1899.

Cooling, Benjamin Franklin. "The Attack on Dover, Tenn." *Civil War Times Illustrated* (August 1963).

"Correspondence Relating to Chickamauga and Chattanooga." In *The Mississippi, Tennessee, Georgia, Alabama, 1861–1864*, vol. 8 of *Papers of the Military Historical Society of Massachusetts*, 247–272. Boston: Military Historical Society of Massachusetts, 1910.

Cozzens, Peter. *No Better Place to Die: The Battle of Stones River.* Urbana: University of Illinois Press, 1990.

———. *The Shipwreck of Their Hopes: The Battles for Chattanooga.* Urbana: University of Illinois Press, 1994.

———. *This Terrible Sound: The Battle of Chickamauga.* Urbana: University of Illinois Press, 1996.

Cumming, Kate. *A Journal of Hospital Life in the Confederate Army of Tennessee from the Battle of Shiloh to the End of the War.* Louisville, KY, 1866.

Cummings, Charles M. *Yankee Quaker, Confederate General: The Curious Career of Bushrod Rust Johnson.* Rutherford, NJ: Associated University Presses, 1971.

Cunningham, O. Edward, Gary D. Joiner, and Timothy B. Smith, eds. *Shiloh and the Western Campaign of 1862.* New York: Savas Beatie, 2007.

Daniel, Larry. *Shiloh: The Battle That Changed the War.* New York: Simon & Schuster, 1997.

Davis, William C. *Jefferson Davis: The Man and His Hour.* New York: Harper Collins, 1991.

Duke, Basil W. *The Civil War Reminiscences of General Basil W. Duke, C. S. A.* New York: Cooper Square Press (reissue), 2001.

Dyer, John P. *Fightin' Joe Wheeler.* Baton Rouge: Louisiana State University Press, 1941.

Elliott, Sam Davis. *Soldier of Tennessee: General Alexander P. Stewart and the Civil War in the West.* Baton Rouge: Louisiana State University Press, 2004.

Faust, Patricia. *Historical Times Illustrated Encyclopedia of the Civil War.* New York: Harper & Row, 1986.

Feis, William B. *Grant's Secret Service.* Lincoln: University of Nebraska Press, 2002.

Frisby, Derek. "The Vortex of Secession: West Tennesseans and the Rush to War." In *Sister States, Enemy States: The Civil War in Kentucky and Tennessee*, edited by Kent T. Dollar, Larry Whiteaker, and W. Calvin Dickinson, 46–71. Lexington: University Press of Kentucky, 2009.

Glatthaar, Joseph. *Forged in Battle: The Civil War Alliance of Black Soldiers and White Officers.* New York: Free Press, 1990.

Goodloe, Albert T. *Confederate Echoes.* Nashville: Methodist Publishing House, 1907.

Gordon, Larry. *The Last Confederate General: John C. Vaughn and His East Tennessee Cavalry*. Minneapolis: Zenith Press, 2009.

Graber, H. W. *The Life Record of H. W. Graber, a Terry Texas Ranger, 1861–1865*. H. W. Graber, 1916.

Grant, Ulysses S. *Personal Memoirs*. New York: Penguin (one-volume reissue), 1999.

Hallock, Judith Lee. *Braxton Bragg and Confederate Defeat, Volume II*. Tuscaloosa: University of Alabama Press, 1991.

Hammond, James H. *Selections from the Letters and Speeches of the Hon. James H. Hammond, of South Carolina*. New York: J. F. Trow & Co., 1866.

Hartje, Robert G. *Van Dorn: The Life and Times of a Confederate General*. Nashville: Vanderbilt University Press, 1967.

Henry, Robert S., ed. *As They Saw Forrest: Some Recollections and Comments from Contemporaries*. Jackson, TN: McCowat-Mercer Press, 1956.

———. *"First with the Most" Forrest*. New York: Bobbs-Merrill, 1944.

Horn, Stanley F. *Invisible Empire: The Story of the Ku Klux Klan, 1866–1871*. Boston: Houghton Mifflin Co., 1939.

Howard, Oliver Otis. *The Autobiography of Oliver Otis Howard*. New York, 1907.

Hurst, Jack. *Men of Fire: Grant, Forrest, and the Campaign That Decided the Civil War*. New York: Basic Books, 2007.

———. *Nathan Bedford Forrest: A Biography*. New York: Alfred A. Knopf, 1993.

Jamison, Henry Down, and Marguerite McTigue. *Letters and Recollections of a Confederate Soldier, 1860–1865*. Nashville, 1964 (copy at Jean and Alexander Heard Library, Vanderbilt University).

Johnson, Adam R. *The Partisan Rangers of the Confederate States Army*. Austin, TX: State House Press (reissue), 1995.

Johnson, Robert U., and Clarence C. Buel. *Battles and Leaders of the Civil War*. 4 vols. Secaucus, NJ: Castle, 1988.

Johnston, William Preston. *The Life of General Albert Sidney Johnston*. New York, 1879.

Jones, James B., Jr. *"The Reign of Terror of the Safety Committee Has Passed Away Forever": A History of the Committees of Safety and Vigilance in West and Middle Tennessee*. Tennessee Historical Commission, 2010.

Jordan, Thomas M., and J. P. Pryor. *The Campaigns of Lieutenant General Forrest and Forrest's Cavalry*. Dayton, OH: Morningside Press (reissue), 1977.

Kiper, Richard L. *Major General John Alexander McClernand: Politician in Uniform*. Kent, OH: Kent State University Press, 1999.

Lewis, Lloyd. *Sherman: Fighting Prophet*. New York: Harcourt, Brace, 1932.

Lytle, Andrew. *Bedford Forrest and His Critter Company*. New York: McDowell, Obolensky, 1931.

Marszalek, John F. *Commander of All Lincoln's Armies: A Life of General Henry Halleck*. Cambridge, MA: Harvard University Press, 2004.

———. *Sherman: A Soldier's Passion for Order*. New York: Free Press, 1993.

Mathes, Harvey. *General Forrest*. New York: D. Appleton and Company, 1902.

Matthiessen, F. O. *Theodore Dreiser*. New York: Greenwood Press (reissue), 1976.

Maury, Dabney H. *Reflections of a Virginian in the Mexican, Indian, and Civil Wars*. New York: Charles Scribner's Sons, 1894.

McFeely, William S. *Grant: A Biography*. New York: W. W. Norton, 1981.

McKinney, Francis F. *Education in Violence: The Life of George H. Thomas and the History of the Army of the Cumberland*. Detroit, MI: Wayne State University Press, 1961.

McPherson, James M. *Battle Cry of Freedom: The Civil War Era*. New York: Oxford University Press, 1988.

———. *Drawn with the Sword: Reflections on the American Civil War*. New York: Oxford University Press, 1996.

McWhiney, Grady. *Braxton Bragg and Confederate Defeat*. Tuscaloosa: University of Alabama Press, 1969.

Morton, John W. *The Artillery of Nathan Bedford Forrest's Cavalry*. Nashville: Publishing House of the Methodist Episcopal Church South, 1909.

Official Military Atlas of the Civil War, The. New York: Crown, 1978.

Official Records of the Union and Confederate Names in the War of the Rebellion. Washington, DC, 1984.

Poole, John Randolph. *Cracker Cavaliers: The Second Georgia Cavalry Under Wheeler and Forrest*. Macon, GA: Mercer University Press, 2000.

Porter, David D. *Incidents and Anecdotes of the Civil War*. New York: D. Appleton and Company, 1885.

Powell, David A. *Failure in the Saddle: Nathan Bedford Forrest, Joseph Wheeler, and the Confederate Cavalry in the Chickamauga Campaign*. New York: Savas Beatie, 2010.

Ramage, James A. *Rebel Raider: The Life of General John Hunt Morgan*. Lexington: University Press of Kentucky, 1986.

Roland, Charles P. *Albert Sidney Johnston: Soldier of Three Republics*. Austin: University of Texas Press, 1964.

Roman, Alfred. *The Military Operations of General Beauregard*. New York: Da Capo Press (reissue), 1994.

Sears, Stephen. *Landscape Turned Red: The Battle of Antietam*. New York: Ticknor & Fields, 1983.

Sherman, William T. *Memoirs of General William T. Sherman*. Westport, CT: Greenwood Press (reissue), 1972.

Simon, John Y., ed. *The Papers of Ulysses S. Grant*. 31 vols. Carbondale: Southern Illinois University Press, 1964–2008.

Simpson, Brooks D. *Ulysses S. Grant: Triumph over Adversity, 1822–1865.* New York: Houghton-Mifflin Company, 2000.

Smith, Jean Edward. *Grant.* New York: Simon & Schuster, 2001.

Smith, Timothy B. *The Untold Story of Shiloh: The Battle and the Battlefield.* Knoxville: University of Tennessee Press, 2006.

Smith, William F. "An Historical Sketch of the Military Operations Around Chattanooga, Tennessee, September 22 to November 27, 1863." In *The Mississippi Valley, Tennessee, Georgia, Alabama, 1861–1864.* Vol. 3 of *Papers of the Military Historical Society of Massachusetts*, 149–247. Boston: Military Historical Society of Massachusetts, 1910.

A Soldier's Honor, with Reminiscences of Major General Earl Van Dorn, by His Comrades. New York: Abbey Press, 1902.

Southern Historical Society Papers. 52 vols. Richmond: Johns & Goolsby Printers, 1876–1959.

Spence, John C. *A Diary of the Civil War.* Nashville: Williams Printing Company, 1993.

———. *Annals of Rutherford County.* Nashville: Williams Printing Company, 1991.

Stampp, Kenneth M. *The Peculiar Institution: Slavery in the Antebellum South.* New York: Alfred A. Knopf, 1956.

Starr, Stephen Z. *The Union Cavalry in the Civil War.* Baton Rouge: Louisiana State University Press, 1985.

———. *The War in the West, 1861–1865.* Vol. 3 of *The Union Cavalry in the Civil War.* Baton Rouge: Louisiana State University Press, 1985.

Stickles, Arndt M. *Simon Bolivar Buckner: Borderland Knight.* Chapel Hill: University of North Carolina Press, 1940.

Symonds, Craig L. *Joseph E. Johnston: A Civil War Biography.* New York: W. W. Norton, 1992.

———. *Stonewall of the West: Patrick Cleburne and the Civil War.* Lawrence: University Press of Kansas, 1998.

Taylor, Richard. *Destruction and Reconstruction.* New York: D. Appleton and Company, 1879.

Todd, Helen. *A Man Named Grant.* Boston: Houghton-Mifflin Company, 1940.

Tucker, Glenn. *Chickamauga: Bloody Battle in the West.* New York: Bobbs-Merrill, 1961.

Wall, Joseph Frazier. *Henry Watterson: Reconstructed Rebel.* New York: Oxford University Press, 1956.

Wallace, Lew. *An Autobiography.* New York: Harper & Brothers, 1906.

War of the Rebellion: The Official Records of the Union and Confederate Armies. Washington, DC: US Government Printing Office, 1880–1902.

Ward, Andrew. *River Run Red: The Fort Pillow Massacre in the American Civil War.* New York: Viking, 2005.

Warner, Ezra J. *Generals in Blue*. Baton Rouge: Louisiana State University Press, 1964.

———. *Generals in Gray*. Baton Rouge: Louisiana State University Press, 1959.

Weller, Jac. "The Logistics of Nathan Bedford Forrest." In *Military Analysis of the Civil War*. Millwood, NY: Krauss-Thompson Organization, Ltd., 1977.

Wert, Jeffry D. *General James Longstreet: The Confederacy's Most Controversial Soldier*. New York: Simon & Schuster, 1993.

Wheeler, Joseph. *Campaigns of Wheeler and His Cavalry*. Atlanta: Hodgins Publishing Company, 1899.

Williams, David. *A People's History of the Civil War: Struggles for the Meaning of Freedom*. New York: The New Press, 2005.

Williams, T. Harry. *Lincoln and His Generals*. New York: Alfred A. Knopf, 1952.

———. *P. G. T. Beauregard: Napoleon in Gray*. Baton Rouge: Louisiana State University Press, 1955.

Wills, Brian Steel. *A Battle from the Start: The Life of Nathan Bedford Forrest*. New York: Harper-Collins, 1992.

Wilson, Edmund. *Patriotic Gore: Studies in the Literature of the American Civil War*. New York: Farrar, Straus & Giroux, 1962.

Wilson, James Harrison. *Under the Old Flag: Recollections of Military Operations in the War for the Union, the Spanish War, the Boxer Rebellion, etc.* New York: D. Appleton, 1912.

Wood, Thomas J. "A Thrilling War Chapter. The Battle of Missionary Ridge. Recollections of Gen. Thomas J. Wood," *New York Times*, July 16, 1876.

———. "The Battle of Missionary Ridge." In *Sketches of War History, 1861–1865*. Vol. 4 of *Papers Prepared for the Ohio Commander of the Loyal Legion of the United States, 1890–1896*, 22–51. Cincinnati: Robert Clarke, 1896.

Woodworth, Steven E. *Nothing but Victory: The Army of the Tennessee 1861–1865*. New York: Random House, 2005.

Wyeth, John Allan. *Life of General Nathan Bedford Forrest*. Dayton, OH: Morningside (reissue), 1975.

Young, J. P. *The Seventh Tennessee Cavalry*. Dayton, OH: Morningside (reissue), 1976.

INDEX